Alexander Del Mar

History of Monetary Systems

Alexander Del Mar

History of Monetary Systems

ISBN/EAN: 9783337338695

Printed in Europe, USA, Canada, Australia, Japan

Cover: Foto ©ninafisch / pixelio.de

More available books at **www.hansebooks.com**

HISTORY

OF

MONETARY SYSTEMS

A RECORD OF ACTUAL EXPERIMENTS IN MONEY MADE BY VARIOUS STATES OF THE ANCIENT AND MODERN WORLD, AS DRAWN FROM THEIR STATUTES, CUSTOMS, TREATIES, MINING REGULATIONS, JURISPRUDENCE, HISTORY, ARCHÆOLOGY, COINS, NUMMULARY SYSTEMS, AND OTHER SOURCES OF INFORMATION.

BY

ALEXANDER DEL MAR,

AUTHOR OF "*History of the Precious Metals*," "*Money and Civilization*," "*Ancient States*," "*Money and Civilization*," "*The Science of Money*," ETC.

CHICAGO:
CHARLES H. KERR & COMPANY,
175 MONROE STREET,
1895.

Copyright 1895
BY ALEXANDER DEL MAR

PUBLISHERS' ADVERTISEMENT.

The present work, in substantially this form, was published in England in the spring of this year. Its great importance and timeliness, and the prompt welcome it received from English critics, make no excuse necessary for an American edition at a price within the reach of every student of money and finance.

To bring the work within the necessary compass, certain portions, which are chiefly of interest to antiquarians, have been omitted, while other portions have been elaborated for the benefit of American readers. The work of revision has been performed entirely by the author himself, who is an American citizen and controls the copyright of the work.

For the benefit of the younger generation in the United States, a brief sketch of Mr. Del Mar's public services may not be out of place.

Alexander Del Mar was born in the city of New York, August 9, 1836. After graduating at the Polytechnic, he was educated as a Civil and Mining Engineer. In 1857 he formed the design of writing a history of the precious metals. This led to his study of money. In 1862 he published "Gold Money and Paper Money," and in 1865 "Essays on the Treasury." In this year he was appointed Director of the Bureau of Statistics, at that time a Board of Trade, with executive functions, among others of the supervision of the Commissioners of Mines, Immigration, etc. In 1872

(Greeley's campaign) he was nominated by Mr. Greeley's friends for Secretary of the Treasury. In the same year he represented the United States at the International Statistical Congress in St. Petersburg, Russia.

In 1876 he was appointed Mining Commissioner to the United States Monetary Commission; 1878, Clerk to the Committee on Naval Expenditures, House of Representatives; 1879, he published his "History of the Precious Metals," the labor of twenty-two years; 1881, he published "A History of Money in Ancient States;" 1885 "Money and Civilization, or a History of Money in Modern States;" 1889 "The Science of Money;" and 1895 his crowning work, "A History of Monetary Systems in Various States." All of these are voluminous works. Mr. Del Mar is likewise the author of more than a hundred pamphlets and other minor works chiefly on monetary and other politico-economical topics.

For the past fifteen years, Mr. Del Mar has given practically his whole time to original research in the great libraries and coin collections of Europe on the subject of the history of money and finance. The present volume embodies the result of his labors.

PREFACE.

The author concluded a former work on Money in these words:—"That which has engaged the attention without harmonizing the convictions of such master minds as Aristotle, Plato, Tycho Brahe, Copernicus, Locke, Newton, Smith, Bastiat, and Mill, is surely a study which none can afford to approach with rashness, nor to leave with complacency. Money is perhaps the mightiest engine to which man can lend an intelligent guidance. Unheard, unfelt, unseen, it has the power to so distribute the burdens, gratifications, and opportunities of life that each individual shall enjoy that share of them to which his merits or good fortune may fairly entitle him, or, contrariwise, to dispense them with so partial a hand as to violate every principle of justice, and perpetuate a succession of social slaveries to the end of time." I begin the present work in the same spirit with which I closed the former one, that is to say, without bias concerning any system of money, and only anxious to examine and profit by the experience of the past.

The scope of the work includes a recension of my former chapters on Rome, a continuation of the Roman history from the monetary system of Augustus to the downfall of the Empire, and an examination of the Merovingian and Carlovingian systems, the Moslem systems, the systems of Britain from the earliest times to the reign of Edward III., and the systems of Saxony, Scandinavia, the Netherlands, Germany, and the Argentine Republic.

As the monetary conflicts of to-day turn mostly upon questions concerning the relative value of gold and silver, the origin, nature, tendency, and influences of this Ratio and its amenability to legal control, I have taken especial pains to trace its historical development in all ages of which any coinage or other numismatic remains exist. In carrying out this design a mass of information has been brought together which can scarcely fail to be of service in future monetary discussions.

The origin and progress of Private Coinage has also been an object of attention. Private coinage, or, as it is now euphemized, "free" coinage, namely, the license granted to private individuals to coin the precious metals without limit, or to compel the State to make coins for them and to confer upon such coins the legal functions of money, coupled with license to export and melt down the coins, was unknown to the ancient world. In the great states of antiquity money was a pillar of the constitution. In the republics of Greece and Rome it was a social instrument, designed, limited, stamped, issued, and made current by the State,—in short, invented, owned, and regulated by the State. It is now generally admitted that the so-called gentes coins of Rome were not of private fabrication, but issued by the State, and stamped with the gens mark of the State moneyers. There appears to have been no private coinage in Europe before the issuance of Mahomet's Koran and its scornful repudiation of the Roman religion and political system. The baronial and ecclesiastical mints of the middle ages, when not authorized by the German Empire, or by the princes of the Western States, were baronial or ecclesiastical only in name; they were really "robbers' dens," and were so termed in the official proclamations of the time. Their trade of private coinage was both surreptitious and unlawful, and was often expiated with the lives of the proprietors. The Plantagenet kings broke up some thousands of them.

After the fall of the Roman Empire in 1204 the prerogative of the coinage was exercised for a brief period by the emperors of Germany, but soon afterward fell to the various independent states that rose upon the ruins of the old Empire. In a process commenced by the procureur-général under Philip IV., against the Comte de Nevers, for melting down the coins of the realm, it was held that this was a royal prerogative which belonged to the king alone, and which in case of necessity he might employ, not indeed for his private advantage, but in defense of the State. The prerogative was, however, much more fully and completely laid down by Sir Matthew Hale in the celebrated case of the Mixed Moneys. Its unwilling surrender by the Crown took place under the Stuarts. Events have demonstrated that the Act is wholly inconsistent with the safety of the State, and that it demands revision.

If in view of the existing monetary conflict, the reader should be led to inquire whether this is a "monometallic" or "bimetallic" work, the answer is, It is neither. These terms, and many others employed in the monetary literature of to-day, the author regards as misleading. They involve doctrines which are fallacious, and defeat a correct comprehension of this difficult subject, by promoting the discussion of false issues, or the adoption of make-shift or mischievous measures. Monometallism and bimetallism both imply that money consists of a metal or metals, and that this is what measures value. The implication is erroneous; the theory is physically impossible. Value is not a thing, nor an attribute of things; it is a relation, a numerical relation, which appears in exchange.* Such a relation cannot be accurately measured without the use of numbers, limited by law, and embodied in a set of concrete sym-

*Bastiat, "Harmonies of Polit. Econ."

bols, suitable for transference from hand to hand. It is this set of symbols which, by metonym, is called money. In the Greek and Roman republics it was called (with a far more correct apprehension of its character) nomisma and nummus, because the law (nomos) was alone competent to create it. The number of the symbols may be limited, but rudely; the limit may even—though equitably it should not—be left to the chances of conquest or mining discoveries, still, repeated experiments prove that it is the number of the symbols that definitively measures value, not the quantity or quality or merit of the materials of which they may be composed. A ready proof that it is the numbers and not material of money which measures value is this: If the sum or integer of the symbols is altered, so will be the expression of value (the price) of all things; whereas the material may be altered, *c. g.* from gold to silver, or from both to inconvertible paper, without at all affecting the expression of value —provided that the combined denominations or sum and legal function of the symbols remain unchanged.

These principles of money—namely, that Money is a Measure, and must be of necessity an Institute of Law, that the Unit of money is All Money within a given legal jurisdiction, that the practical Essence of money is Limitation, and that coins and notes alike are Symbols of money—are fully discussed and illustrated in my "Science of Money." It is true that at the present time their operation is greatly obscured by the license and abuse of Private Coinage, but even through this bewildering medium they can still be discerned. It is out of the confusion created by this practice, it is from the fallacy of mistaking metal (which, apart from numbers, cannot measure value any more accurately than barter can) for money (which, apart from metal, can and does accurately measure value) that all contentions on the subject have arisen; nay, more, this confusion is to-day imperiling the peace of the world. The wheels of Industry are at this moment clogged, and what clogs them chiefly is that gross, that sensual, that materialistic conception which mistakes a piece of metal for the measure of an ideal relation, a measure that resides not at all in the metal, but in the numerical relation of the piece to the set of pieces to which it is legally related, whether of metal, or paper, or both combined. In short, it is this misconception which is responsible for the Demonetization of Silver in the Western world, and the consequences traceable to that event.

While such are the views of the author, he must do himself the justice to say that he has not laid his historical works under contribution to support them, nor has he any currency scheme to propose. To entertain, rightly or wrongly, a distinct conception of money, and the manner in which its function is mechanically fulfilled, is one thing; to apply such conception to a given condition of affairs is another. This may only be done by the statesman, who is not satisfied to inquire what is correct, but must also know what is practicable and what is prudent. The political circumstances of each state have usually molded, and must continue to mold, its monetary system; and rash are those teachers who have sought or who yet seek to change it for any other reason or upon any other grounds.

These views indicate in another way the scope of the present work; it is not confined to gold money, nor silver money, nor paper money; it embraces all money, and it seeks, by analyzing the various experiments that have been made with this subtle instrument, to derive from them whatever light they may be able to throw upon the questions that vex us to-day.

CONTENTS.

	PAGE
PREFACE	5
BIBLIOGRAPY	11
I. ROME.	17
II. THE SACRED CHARACTER OF GOLD	66
III. POUNDS, SHILLINGS AND PENCE	94
IV. GOTHIC MONEYS	113
V. MOSLEM MONEYS	125
VI. EARLY ENGLISH MONEYS	149
VII. MONEYS OF THE HEPTARCHY	165
VIII. ANGLO-NORMAN MONEYS	187
IX. EARLY PLANTAGENET MONEYS	198
X. LATER PLANTAGENET MONEYS	223
XI. EVOLUTION OF THE COINAGE PREROGATIVE	245
XII. SAXONY AND SCANDINAVIA	254
XIII. THE NETHERLANDS	307
XIV. GERMANY	341
XV. PRIVATE COINAGE	386
XVI. STATISTICS OF THE RATIO	393
XVII. BANK SUSPENSIONS SINCE THE ERA OF PRIVATE COINAGE	402
XVIII. EXISTING MONETARY SYSTEMS	412
INDEX	431

BIBLIOGRAPHY.

The following list of books is to be read in connection with the lists published in the author's previous works on the Precious Metals and Money.

AL-MAKKARI (Ahmed, ibn Mohammed): Selections from his History of the Mohametan dynasties. Translated from Arabic to English by Pascual de Gayangos. London, 1840-43. 2 vols., 4to.
ANDERSON (James): History of Commerce. London, 1787. 4 vols., 4to.
ARRIAN (Flavius): The Anabasis of Alexander, literally translated by E. J. Chinnock. London, 1884. 8vo.
——— Voyage round the Euxine Sea. Translated by W. Falconer. Oxford, 1805. 4to.
——— Voyage of Nearchus and Perplius of the Erythrean Sea. Greek and English, translated by W. Vincent. Oxford, 1809. 4to.
AVILA (Gil Gonsalez de): Spanish Numismatic Work.
BABELON (Ernest): Description historique et chronologique des monnaies de la République Romaine, vulgairement appelées monnaies consulaires. Paris, 1885. 2 tom. 8vo.
BAILLY (M. A.): Histoire Financière de la France, depuis l'origine de la Monarchie jusq'à la fin de 1786, par M. A. Bailly, Inspecteur générale des Finances. Paris, 1830. 8vo.
——— Les Finances de France, par M. A. Bailly. Paris. 8vo. Written on the plan of Sinclair's History of the British Revenue, and possibly its model.
BERGMANN (Dr. E. von): Die Nominate der Munzreform des chalifen Abdulmelik. Ak. der Wissenschaften v. Wien, May, 1870. Sitzungs berichte. Philosoph. histor. classe.
BIÆUS (Jacobus): La France Metallique. Paris, 1636. Fol.
——— Numismata Imperatorum Romanorum.
BIE (Jacques de): *See* BIÆUS.
BIRCHEROD (Thomas Broderus): Specimen Antiquæ Rei Monetariæ Danarum, etc. Hafniæ, 1701. 4to.
BLACAS (Louis C. P. Casimir, duc de): Histoire de la Monnaie Romaine par Th. Mommsen, traduic. Paris, 1865. 8vo.
BLANCIUS (Franciscus): *See* LE BLANC.
BOISARD (Jean): Traité des Monnoyes. Paris, 1714. 2 vols., 12mo. A useful and excellent work with a good index.
BRANDIS (Johanus): Das Munz Mass und Gewichtswesen in Vorderasien bis auf Alexander den grossen. Berlin, 1866. 8vo.
BREREWOOD (Edward): De Ponderibus et Pretiis Veterum Nummorum. London, 1614. 4to. A useful little tract, with a chapter on the Ratio.
BRUGSCH (Heinrich): On the relative value of gold and silver in ancient times; an article in the Deutsche Rundschau, a periodical published at Berlin, 1874, etc. 8vo.
BURSIAN (Conrad): Jahresbericht uber die Fortschritte de classischen Alterthumswissenschaft. Berlin. 8vo *In Progress.*
BYEL (M. Gabriellis): De Monetis. The author was a licentiate of Spires, who died in 1495.

CAMBRIDGE ESSAYS: pp. 267—269.
    CAMDEN (William): Remains. Art. "Money," p. 241.
———- Britannia. Original edition in Latin, London, 1586. 8vo. English translation by P. Holland. London, 1610.
CARDAN: Trattato di numeri e misure. 1555 to 1560.
CARLI: Treatise on money. 1760. (*See* ITALIANA SCRITTORI.)
CARTAILHAC (Emile): (*See* REVUE D'ANTHROPOLOGIE.)
CARTE: History of England. Fol.
CASTRO Y CAVALLERO: Spanish Numismatic Work. (*See* GARCIA.)
CAVALLERO: (*See* GARCIA.)
COCHETAUX: The Connection of Monetary Systems. Pamphlet. Brussels, 1884. 8vo.
COHEN (Henri): Description historique des Monnaies frappées sous l'empire Romaine. Paris, 1880. 8 vols., 8vo.
COIGNARD: Essai sur les Monnois, ou Réflexions sur le Rapport entre l'argent et le denrees. Paris, 1746.
COLQUHOUN (Patrick): Roman Law. 4 vols, 8vo. London, 1849-60.
COMINES, or COMMINES (Philip de): Mémoires. (On the leathern coins of John, *see* vol. i., p. 507.)
COPERNICUS: Treatise on Money. Translated by Wolowski Paris, brochure, 1868.
CUSTODI (P.): (*See* ITALIANI SCRITTORI.)
D'AVANT (Poey): Monnaie Feodale. Paris, 1875. 4to.
DE VIENNE: Origines de la livre d'Argent, by Colonel Maurice de Vienne. Paris, 1887. 8vo. Brochure.
DAVIES (C. M.): History of Holland. London, 1842. 3 vols., 8vo. (For pasteboard dalers of Leyden.)
DE LUZAC (Jean): La Richesse de la Hollande. London, 1778. 2 vols., 8vo.
DUERR (Julius): Die Reisen des Kaisers Hadrian. See Abhand. des Archaeol. der Univer. Wien, 1883.
DU HALDE (Father Jean Baptiste, Jesuit): History of China. Trans. into Eng. London, 1736. 4 vols., 8 vo.
DUREAU DE LA MALLE (A. J. C. A.): Economie politique des Romaines. Paris, 1840. 2 tom., 8vo.
DUTOT: Finances and Commerce of France. 1739. 8vo. Eng. Trans.
EGYPTE: La Reforme Monetaire en Egypte. Le Caire, 1885. 4to. A collection of interesting financial essays.
ENGLAND, Present State of. (Mentions 2d. and 3d. sterlings.)
FAUCHER (Leon): Precious Metals. Trans. by Thomas Hankey, jun., Governor of the Bank. Eng. London, 1852. 8vo.
FICHTE (J. G.): The Science of Rights. Trans. by A. E. Kroeger, of St. Louis. Phila. (Lippincott), 1869. 8vo, pp. 504.
FILMER (Sir Robert): Discourse on Usury. London, 1678. 12mo.
FINLAY (George, LL.D.): Roman and Byzantine Money, in his Hist. of Greece, etc. London, 1877. 7 vols., 8vo.
FINLAY (George, LL.D.): Greece under the Romans. Edinburgh, 2nd edit., 1857. 8vo.
FLEETWOOD (Bishop William); Chronicon Preciosum. London, 1707, 8vo.
FREHERI (Marquardi): De Re Monetaria Veterum Romanorum. Lubduni, 1605, 4to.
——— De Constantini Imperatoris Byzantini Numismate, etc. Paris, 1604. 4to. A reply to Scaliger.
GARCIA (Jose Cavallero): Breve cotejo y valance de las Pesas y Medidas de varios naciones, comparadas y reducidas á las que corren en estos reynos de Castilla. Madrid, 1731. 4to.

GENT.'S MAGAZINE, 1756, p. 465, and 1812, p. 331. Dr. Samuel Pegge on the Iaku, or Iacchus.
GIBBON (Edward): Decline and Fall of the Rom. Emp. London, 1781. 2nd ed., 6 vols., 4to.
―――― Miscellaneous Works. London, 1815. 3 vols., 4to.
GIBBS (Henry H.): A Colloquy on Currency. London, 2nd edition, 1895. 8vo.
GODEFROY (Denis): Monnoyes de France, par Denis Godefroy, procureur du roy en la cour des monnoyes (17th century).
GRÆCARUM Thesaurus Antiquitatum. Lugduni Batavorum, 1699. 12 vols., fol.
GREAT BRITAIN: An Account of the Constitution and Present State of Great Britain. London, 1760. 8vo.
GRONOVIUS: De Numismate Antiquis; included in Græcarum Thesaurus (*which see*).
GROTIUS (Hugo): De Jure Belli et Pacis. Cambridge, 1853. 3 vols., 8vo. Lib. II., cap. xii., Michael Ephesius says, and after him Grotius repeats that, "whatever is adopted as the measure of value ought to be itself the least subject to change."
GUERARD: Polyptique de l'Abbé Irminon. Edited and annotated by Benj. E. C. Guérard. Paris, 1884. 4to. This work is one of the Collection des documents inedits sur l'Histoire de France. Its full title is "Polyptique de l'Abbé Irminon, ou Denombrement des Manses, des Serfs, et des Revenues de l'Abbaye de Saint Germain des Pres, sous le regne de Charlemagne." The annotations or "Eclaircissements" of M. Guérard occupy pp. 907-975.
GUIRANUS (Gaillardus): Explicatio duorum Vetustorum Numismatum, etc. Rabanum, 1655. 4to.
HALE (Sir Matthew): Essay on Population. London, 1782. 4to. 436, d, 24.
―――― Inrolling and Registring of Land Conveyances. London, 1664. 4to.
―――― Pleas of the Crown. London, 1716. 8vo.
―――― Treatise on Sheriff's accounts and Money. London, 1683. 8vo.
HALHED (Nathaniel Brassey): Code of Gentoo Laws. Eng. Trans. London, 1776. 4to.
HAWKINS (Edward): Silver Coins of England. 3rd ed., with alterations and additions by R. L. Kenyon. London, 1887. 8vo.
HEISS (Alois): Description generale des Monnais Antiques de l'Espagne, Paris, 1870. 4to.
―――― Descripcion general de las Monedas Hispano-Cristianos. Madrid, 1865-9. 3 vols., 4to. (The best work on the subject of Spanish moneys yet met with.)
―――― Monnois des rois Visigoths d'Espagne. Paris, 1872. 4to.
HEMINBURGH: (*See* WALTERUS).
HEMINFORD: (*See* WALTERUS).
HOTMAN (François). Sometimes Hotimani and Hottoman: De re numaria. Paris, 1585. 2 parts, 8vo.
HULTSCH (Frederick): Griechische und Romische Metrologie. Berlin, 1862. 8vo.
HUSSEY (Robert): Essay on Ancient Weights, Money and Measures. Oxford, 1836. 8vo.
IRMINON: (*See* GUERARD).
ITALIANI SCRITTORI CLASSICI. Florence, 1751. 8vo., series.
JUSTIN (N. de): De Moneta. Jena, 1757. For writing this treatise on money, De Justin was imprisoned by the king of Prussia.
KEARY (C. F.): Catalogue of English coins. London, 1887. 8vo.

—— A Guide to the Study of English Coins, by the late William Henfrey. New and revised edition by C. F. Keary. London, 1885. 8vo. This patriotic work proves that the kings of England neither debased, degraded, nor altered the value of their coins!

KELLY (P.): The Universal Cambist and Commercial Instructor. London, 1821. 4to.

LAVOIX (Henri): Catalogue des Monnais Musulmanes de la Bibliothèque Nationale. Paris, 1891. 3 vols., 4to.

LEAKE (Stephen Martin): Historical Account of English Money. London, 1726. 8vo.

LE BLANC (François): Traité des Monnayes de France. Amsterdam, 1692. 4to.

LE CLERC (Jean): (For Union of Utrecht and its coinage regulations).

LENORMANT (Fr.): Monnaies et Médailles. Paris, 1879. 8vo.

LENORMANT (Fr.): La Monnaie dans l'Antiquité. Paris, 1879. 3 vols., 8vo.

LONGPERIER (Adrienne de): Œuvres. Paris. 7 vols., 8vo.

LOWNDES (William): A report containing an Essay for the Amendment of the Silver Coins. London, 1695. 8vo.

MAKRISI (Ahmad Ibn Ali Ibn Abd-al-Kadir Al-Makrizi): Traité des Monnoies Musulmanes, trad. par. A. I. Sylvestre de Sacy. Paris, an. V. (1797). 8vo.

MANU, Ordinances of, or the Damathat. London, 1884. 8vo.

MEDIOBARBUS BIRAGUS (Franciscus): *See* MEZZABARBA.

MEZZABARBA BIRAGO (Francisco): Imperatorum Romanorum Numismata, ab A Occo (of Augsburg) olim congesta nunc. aucta studio et cura F. Mediobarbi Biragi. Mediolano, 1730. Fol.

MIGNE (Jacques Paul, l'Abbé): Patrologiæ Cursus Completus. Paris, 1857. 4to.

—— Advantages of dealing at the Ateliers Catholiques and of investing in the Abbé Migné's Loan. Paris, 1863. 4to.

MOMMSEN (Theodor): Ueber den Verfall des Römischen Münzwesens in der Kaiserzeit. Dresden, 1857. 8vo.

—— History of Rome. Eng. Trans. by Rev. William P. Dickson, D.D. London, 1862-75. 4 vols., 8vo.

—— De l'organisation financière chez les Romains, traduit par Albert Vigié. Paris, 1888. 8vo. brochure.

—— Corpus Inscriptionum Latinarum. Berlin, 1873. Fol., 15 vols. In vol. iii., part 2, are the "Res Gestae Divi Augusti," including the Monumentum Ancyranum (p. 788).

MOMMSEN: (*See* BLACAS.)

MULENIUS (Joannes): Numismata Danorum Hafniae, 1670. 8vo.

MURATORI (Lodovico Antonio): Ant. Italiæ. 1738-42. 6 tom, fol.

—— A Relation of the Missions of Paraguay. Eng. trans. from the French. London, 1759. 8vo.

MYRI (Wernerus Christophorus): De Re Nummaria. V. et N. T. in J. Harduinum (Jean Hardouin). Helmstadii, 1711. 4to.

NERI: Osservazioni sopra el prezzo legale delle Monete (Observations on the Legal Value of Money), by Pompeo Neri. Florence, 1751. A new ed., 1803, 8vo.

—— Documenti annessi alle osservazioni sopra il prezzo legale delle monete. An appendix to the former work.

—— Delle Monete commercio. See also ITALIANI SCRITTORI.

NIKIOU (Bishop of): (*See* JOHN of Nikiou, Nikios, or Nikieus).

NISARD (M.): Collection des Auteurs Latins, avec la traduction en Français publiée sous la direction de M. Nisard. Paris, 1851. Large 8vo. 28 volumes.

NUMISMATIC CHRONICLE for 1884: Poole on Mahometan Coins. London. 8vo. Third series.
NUMISMATIC CHRONICLE for 1884: Third series, vol. iv, p. 122, Coins Struck by Hannibal in Italy.
OCCO (A., of Augsburg, Numismatist): (*See* MEZZABARBA).
PATIN (Charles): Travels. Translated from the French. London, 1697. 12mo.
—— Historia de las Medallas. Madrid, 1771. 8vo. Translated from the Latin.
PINTO: Traité du Credit et de la Circulation. (For Siege-pieces of Tournay.)
POIS (Antoine de): (*See* PISO), Discours sur les Médailles et graveures antiques. Paris, 1579. 4to.
POULLAIN (Henri): Traictés des Monnoyes. Paris, 1621. Another edition, 1709. 12mo.
—— De prix de nostre Escu. Paris, 1613. 8 vo.
PUFFENDORF (Samuel, Baron von): Law of Nature and Nations. London, 1829. Fol.
QUINONES (Dr. Ivan de): Explicacion de unas Monedas de Oro de les emperadores Romanos que se han hallado en el Puerto de Guadarrama. Madrid, 1620. Pamphlet 8vo.
REVUE NUMISMATIQUE for 1862 and 1865. Blois. 8vo.
ROME-DE-L'ILE (Jean Baptiste Louis de): Métrologie. Paris, 1789. 4to.
ROUGE (Viscomte Jacques de): Monnaies nouvelles de Nomes d'Egypte. Pamphlet Paris, 1882. 8vo.
RYMER (Foedera): (For "turneys," see v., 113).
SAIGEY: Traité de Metrologie, par Jacques Frederic Saigey. Paris, 1834. 12mo.
SAINT-CHAMANS: Nouvel Essai sur la Richesse des Nations. Paris, 1824. 8vo.
SAUVAIRE (Henri): Matériaux pour servir a l'histoire de la numismatique musulmanes. Paris, 1882. 8vo., pp. 367.
SAVOT (Louis): Discours sur les Medailles Antiques. Paris, 1627. 4to.
SCALIGER (Joseph Juste): Constantini Imp. Byzantini numismatis argentei expositio, etc. Leyden, 1604. 4to.
—— De Re Nummaria antiquorum dissertatio. 1616, 8vo. 1697. Fol.
—— De Emendatione Temporum. Coloniæ Allobrogum, (Geneva), 1629. Fol.
SCHLUMBERGER (G.): Lead moneys of the Holy Land. Paris, 1878. 8vo.
SINCLAIR (Sir John): History of the British Revenue. London, 1820. 3 vols. 8vo.
SITZGSBER (Christ.): Transactions in der Munchen Akademie. See vol. i., p. 68.
SMITH (Charles Roach): Dictionary of Roman Coins. London, 1889 4to.
SPEED (Joannes): Sigilla et monetæ Regnum Angliæ, etc. London, 1601. Fol.
STANOSA (Don Vicentio Juan de la): Museo de las Medalas desconocidas Espanolas Oscae. 1645. 4to.
STENERSEN (L. B.): Myntfundet fin Graeslid i Thydalen. Christiania, 1881. 4to.
STEVENS (Capt. John): The Royal Treasury of England, or an Historical Account of the Taxes under what Denomination soever from the Conquest to the Present Year. London, 1725. 8vo.
STOURM (René): Les Finances de l'Ancien Régime et de la Révolution. Paris, 1885. 2 vols., 8vo.

STRAHLENBERG (Philip Johan): Northern Europe and Asia. London, 1736. 4to. Translated into English.
THOMSEN (C. J.): Monnaies des Moyen Age. Copenhagen. 3 vols., 8vo.
TILL (William): The Roman Denarius and English Penny. London, 1837. 12mo.
VAN LOON (Gerald): Histoire Métallique des XVII. Provinces des Pays-Bas La Haye, 1732. 5 vols., folio.
VASCO: Essay on Moneys, 1772. (*See* ITALIANI SCRITTORI.)
VATTEL (E. Luis José de): Law of Nations. London, 1834. 8vo.
VELASQUEZ (Luis José): Congeturas sobre las medallas de los reyes Godos y Suevos. Malaga, 1759.
VROLIK (A.): Le Système Monétaire du Royaume des Pays Bas. Utrecht, 1853.
WALTERUS DE HEMINBURGH: See Preface to his work, p. xlv., *re* base coins.
WEX (Joseph): Metrologie grecque et romaine. Traduite de l'allemand, par P. Monet. Paris, 1886. 12mo.
WISSENSCHAFTEN (Kaiserliche Akademie der). Wien. See Bergmann.
YOUNG (Arthur): The Progressive Value of Money in England, with Observations on Sir George Shuckburg's Table of Appreciation. Contained in vol. xlv. of the Annals of Agriculture, London, 1808, 8vo. This volume also has articles on "Wheat from India," "American Premiums offered by the Agric. Soc. of Phila.," "Agric. Statistic of New South Wales, 1792-1801," etc.
ADAMS (Alex., *Revd.*): Roman Antiquities. 18th edition. Edinburgh, 1854 8vo.
BALLETTI (A.): La Questione Monetaria nel seclo xvi. 1882. 8vo.
BASTIAT (Frédéric): Harmonies of Political Economy. London, 1860. 8vo.
BLISS (W. H.): Calendar of Entries in the Papal Registers relating to Great Britain and Ireland. Vol. I., A. D. 1198-1304. London, 1893. 4to.
BULBY (D. T.): Descriptive Coinage of Great Britain and the Colonies. London, 1894. 2 vols., 8vo.
CALCOTT (Lady Maria): History of Spain. London, 1840. 2 vols., 8vo.
CARR (Thomas Swinburne): Roman Antiquities. London, 1836. 8vo.
DOZY (Reinhart, Pieter, Anne): Histoire des Musulmans d'Espagne, jusqu'à la conquête de l'Andalousie, par les Almoravides, A. D. 711-1110. Leyde, 1861. 4 vols., 8vo. Troisième éd.
ECKHEL (Joseph H. von): Doctrina Numorum Veterum. Vindobonæ. 1792 8. 4to.
GARNIER (le Comte Gerinan de): Monnaies de Compte chez les Peuples de l'Antiquité. Paris, 1817. 4to.
HOFFMAN (H.): Monnaies Royale. Paris. 8vo.
KENYON (Robert L.): Gold Coins of England. London, 1884. 8vo.
LETRONNE (M.): Monnaies Grecques et Romaines. Paris, 1817. 4to.
LIVERPOOL (Charles, Earl of): Coins of the Realm. London, 1880. 8vo.
MADOX (Thomas): History and Antiquities of the Exchequer of the Kings of England. Taken from the Records. London, 1769. 2 vols., 4to.
MINTON (Thomas W.): Bibliography of Numismatics. London, 1895. 8vo.
QUEIPO (V. Vazquez): Systèmes métriques et monétaires de Ancien Peuples. Paris, 1859. 2 vols., 8vo.
SABATIER (J.): Monnaies Byzantines. Paris, 1862. 12 vols, 8vo.
SAEZ (Padre Liciiniano): Monedas del Señor don Enrique III. Madrid, 1796. Fol.
———Monedas del Señor Enrique IV. Madrid, 1805. 4to.

HISTORY OF MONETARY SYSTEMS.

CHAPTER I.

ROME.

Supposed silver coins of Servius Tullius—"Romano" coins—A. U. 369, the Nummulary system—A. U. 437, Scrupulum system of gold and silver "Roma" coins—A. U. 485, Centralization of silver coinage and change of ratio—A. U. 537-47, System of the Lex Flaminia—A. U. 663, The Social War; coins of the Italiotes; concession of citizenship; centralization of money at Rome—A. U. 675, System of Sylla—Systems of Julius Cæsar—Augustus—Caligula—Attempted revival of the Republic—Galba—Otho—Caracalla—Aurelian—Diocletian—Constantine—Arcadius and Honorius—The Byzantine systems down to the Fall of Constantinople in A. D. 1204—The Western Systems—Clovis—Pepin—Charlemagne.

SINCE the writing of my "History of Money in Ancient States" many hoards of Roman coins have been discovered, and many important numismatic works have been published and discussed. These throw so much new light on the Roman monetary systems that the subject needs revision. The present chapter is an essay in this direction.

I must begin by assigning a lower value to the monetary evidences contained in Pliny's "Natural History" than was done in my former work. Pliny was far from being well-informed on the subject of Roman money. He wrote hundreds of years after the establishment of those earlier monetary systems of Rome, whose metallic remains have been preserved by the earth to the modern world, but of which no collections appear to have existed in his time. His observations on the subject are gathered rather from grammatical than historical works, of which, owing to the proscriptions of Augustus, but few were extant in Pliny's time. When to these difficulties, which interposed themselves between the Roman encyclopedist and the knowledge which he attempted to acquire and preserve, are added the difficulties of an ecclesiastical and imperial censorship, deeply interested in conserving the religion, history, and chronology invented and bequeathed to it by Divus Augustus, the wonder is, not that Pliny missed, but that he secured so much on this subject as is to be found in his work. Hence, I have treated his observations with almost reverential deference, and have only put them aside where they are contradicted by the numismatic remains or other archæological testimonies.

It has long since been demonstrated that the ecclesiastical and political history of Archaic Rome is fabulous. To this must now be added its early monetary history. That, too, is fabulous. It is quite possible that the earliest money of Rome was the ace grave, or heavy copper brick, held as a "reserve," but "represented" in the circulation by leather notes.[1] It is also possible that this was followed by the ace signatum and afterwards by silver coins. According to Charisius,

[1] Ace is thus spelled by the earlier numismatists, and is preferable to As. It comes from the Sanscrit ayas, meaning totality. The Romans used the word to designate any congeries (Gaston L. Feuardent, in "Am. Jour. of Numismatics," 1878.) The Tarentines gave the same meaning to this word and employed it in similar ways, but spelled it Eis. The same word, bearing the same meaning, found its way from India across the steppes of Russia to the Baltic, where it is still found in the Ies or Jes of the Netherlands (see chapter xiii.) The leather notes of archaic Rome are mentioned by Seneca: "Corium forma publica percussum." Consult my "Hist. Money in Ancient States" for further information on this subject. Some authors trace the Ies to Janus, whose face was stamped on the coins.

Varro wrote: "Nummum argenteum conflatum primum a Servio Tullio dicunt; is quatuor scrupulis major fuit quam nunc est."[1] "It is said that silver money was first made (conflatum means, literally, melted or cast) by Servius Tullius. It was more valuable (or heavier) by four scrupulums than it is now." Varro wrote during the Augustan age, when the denarius contained about 60 English grains of silver; but as he was a bookworm, who gathered his knowledge chiefly from ancient authors, these circumstances go for nothing. The silver coins, alluded to by his authorities as of the present time, "now," were probably the denarii of A. U. 437, mentioned by Pliny (xxxiii., 13), which weighed 78¾ grains, or five grains more than Pliny's inexact "six to the ounce" weight. At that period a scrupulum (as we shall presently see) meant a tenth of anything; so that Varro's statement merely amounts to this, that the most ancient silver coins of Rome were worth four-tenths more than the new ones, namely, those issued after the decline of the nummulary system.[2] The Duc de Luynes had a number of very ancient Roman silver coins in his cabinet, which, relying upon this text, he attributed to the reign of Servius Tullius; but numismatists, while admitting their genuineness, are not disposed to credit them with such great antiquity. Nay, even the existence of Servius Tullius has been disputed. Upon a review of all the evidences connected with this difficult matter, it seems that the Romans struck silver coins at a much earlier date than is commonly believed, that is to say, before A. U. 437, indeed, before the nummulary systems, which preceded that of A. U. 437. The order of systems was, therefore, as follows:—1. Ace

[1] The grammarian Charisius, A. D. 400. Institutionum Grammaticæ, cited by Scaliger, "De Re Nummaria," ed. 1616, p. 42. Queipo, ii, 17.
[2] Queipo, table lix., gives the weights of some of these heavy denarii.

grave, with leather notes; 2. Aes signatum; 3. Silver (and copper) system mentioned by Varro, the silver coins (denarii) weighing each about 118 grains, many specimens of these coins being still extant; 4. A.U. 369, nummulary system; 5. A. U. 437, gold, silver, and copper system, the silver denarius weighing $78\frac{3}{4}$ grains.

When these last-named coins became the principal circulating medium of the Roman State, some of the more ancient denarii mentioned by Varro's authorities, and rescued from subterranean hoards, may have again crept into circulation when they were valued at $1\frac{4}{10}$ denarii each; because, although they contained 50 per cent more silver than the current denarii, they were antiquated, and fit only for recoinage, which involved the loss of a tenth or twelfth for seigniorage. This hypothesis disposes of the passage preserved by Varro and Charisius. It was probably taken from Timæus, and simply meant that ten of the ancient silver coins passed current for fourteen new denarii.[1] Similar valuations are to be found in all ages and countries, many of them in the coinages of the present day.

With regard to the Janus-faced circular copper coins, which Lenormant ascribes to the period of the Gaulish invasion, A. U. 369, or B. C. 384, it is to be observed that although these pieces are now regarded as aces, they may have been nummi, afterwards called sesterces, or pieces of $2\frac{1}{2}$ aces, the figure "1" upon them signifying one nummus instead of one ace, as has been commonly supposed. That these coins were connected with the nummulary system of the Republic there can hardly be a doubt.

Both the examples of the Greek Republics and the

[1] With regard to the practice of seigniorage on Roman coins, Neibuhr denies, while Boeckh affirms it. The coins prove that the latter is right; but neither of these eminent *savants* seemed anxious to discuss the subject.

writings of Plato and other philosophers had taught the Romans the advantages of a limited and exclusive system of money issued by the State, and having little or no worth other than what it derived from its usefulness and efficiency in measuring the value of commodities and services. The proof that the Romans were familiar with such a system of money appears in the writings of Paulus, the jurisconsult, who enunciated its principles long after the system had ceased to exist. Had no such system ever existed in Rome, Paulus would have had no warrant in the Roman law for the monetary principles he laid down. As felted paper was unknown, the symbols of this system could most conveniently be made of copper. Therefore, the means necessary to secure and maintain such a money were for the State to monopolize the copper mines, restrict the commerce in copper, strike copper pieces of high artistic merit, in order to defeat counterfeiting, stamp them with the mark of the State, render them the sole legal tenders for the payment of domestic contracts, taxes, fines, and debts, limit their emission until their value (from universal demand for them and their comparative scarcity) rose to more than that of the metal of which they were composed, and maintain such restriction and over-valuation as the permanent policy of the State. For foreign trade or diplomacy a supply of gold and silver, coined and uncoined, could be kept in the treasury.

There are ample evidences that means of this character were, in fact, employed by the Roman Republic; and, therefore, that such was the system of money it adopted. The copper mines were monopolized by the Roman State, the commerce in copper was regulated, the bronze nummi were issued by the State, which strictly monopolized their fabrication, the designs were of great beauty, the pieces were stamped "S. C.," or *ex senatus consulto;* they were for many years the sole legal tenders for payment of contracts, taxes, fines, and debts; their emission was limited, until the value of the pieces rose to about five times that of the metal they contained,[1] and they steadily and for a lengthy period retained this high over-valuation. The equivalent of four aces signata to the nummus probably marks the period when the nummus was worth four times its weight of copper, for the ace signatum was merely so much metal to the Romans of this period, though it may have had a superior value to the Etruscan and other surrounding nations. The equivalent of two and a half aces signata to the nummus probably marks a further decline in the value of the latter. When the nummulary system broke down entirely, the nummi, which had successively been worth 5, 4 and 2½ aces each, fell to the value of 1 ace, and were thenceforth themselves known as aces. The decadence of this system, that is to say, the precise period when the nummus fell to the value of an ace, is uncertain. If we permit ourselves to be guided by Livy, it was when, the soldiers' stipend ("there being no silver coined at that time") being paid in bronze coins, the immense quantity required for the army was conveyed to it in wagons; in other words, in the year A.U. 402. The introduction, or rather the re-introduction, of silver coins into the monetary system of Rome must, therefore, with the greatest probability, be dated between A. U. 402 and A. U. 437.[2]

Livy (vii., 16; xxvii., 10) mentions a tax called aurum

[1] "History of Money in Ancient States," 257.

[2] Livy, iv., 60. A similar coinage of silver took place in China in 1845, where a somewhat similar system of bronze numeraries had existed, and where, by the way, it still exists (H. M. A., 43). At the present time (1895) silver is being again coined in China for soldiers' pay.

vicesimarium, enacted A. U. 397—an expression which implies the use of gold money in Rome at that early date, or, what is more likely, at a still earlier one. This implication derives corroboration from what we shall presently have to say concerning the "Romano" coins.

Lenormant (i., 316) holds that "it has been established by Mommsen beyond all question that, with perhaps one exception, there exist no gold coins of the Republic but such as were struck by its military generals in the field, or at least elsewhere than in Rome." The exception relates to the aureus of Cn. Lentulus, and even this, it is claimed, was not struck under his civil authority as monetary triumvir, but as urban quæstor, specially commissioned to provide for the expenses of a war. This opinion is based rather upon a theory than a fact. The theory is that the Roman coins of the Republic were struck by virtue of the imperium, that is to say, a military rather than a State prerogative. The answer to this theory is that there was and could have been no prerogative of the imperium other than that derived from the State.

What was the imperium? Supreme military command; the right to do whatever was deemed essential to achieve military success. This right sprang from the people. In the most ancient times it was conferred by the Comitia upon the king after they had elected him, and by virtue of his office.[1] When the monarchy was overthrown the people annually elected two supreme coördinate magistrates, into whose hands were committed all the powers of the State, including the imperium. These were acquired and exercised by virtue of their office. For this reason the consuls were some-

[1] Niebuhr, i., 288; Carr, "Roman Ant.," 108.

times called imperatores.[1] When a general in the field had obtained a notable victory, it was customary for the troops to hail him by this proud title; but it could not be retained after the triumph or the return of the victorious commander to the city. There it fell, of course, to the consuls by virtue of their office.[2] It follows that after the Comitia, the powers of the imperium were derived from the consuls, and were subject to modification or revocation by them. No doubt many of the Roman commanders, during the period of the Republic, struck coins in the field in order to melt down and divide the spoils or pay the troops, but such coinages were, legally, as completely under control of the State as though they had been made in Rome. Indeed, without such legal control and supervision it would have been impossible for generals in the field to adjust their gold coinages with such nicety to the weights of the silver coins and the ratios of value established by the State from time to time between the precious metals, as appear from a due consideration of the coinage systems of this era. Moreover, at the period alluded to by Mommsen, the State had but recently emerged from the use of a bronze currency system, whose efficiency and value had depended largely upon the limitation of its issues by the State, which was, therefore, not likely to have parted with this supernal prerogative. This system had broken down, not from any inherent defect or impracticability, but owing to the circumstances of a war which took place upon Roman soil and threatened the very existence of the Republic. Finally, if there was a department of the government which, more than any other, enjoyed the prerogative of coining gold, it was the pontificate rather than the imperium, for in the

[1] Adams, "Roman Ant.," 91, and authorities cited.   [2] Adams, 322.

ancient times gold was always held to be a sacred metal, and upon it was stamped, not so much the emblems of war as of religion. But that the Roman coins were struck by pontifical authority does not appear to have been suspected by the learned Prussian.

When Mommsen's imperium argument is applied to the affairs of the Empire, it flies in the face of the most illustrious witness whose testimony has been preserved to us from antiquity. Says Tacitus: "Besides the honors already granted Blæsus, Tiberius ordered that the legions should salute him by the title of imperator, according to the ancient custom of the Roman armies in the pride of victory, flushed with the generous ardor of warlike spirits. In the time of the Republic this was a frequent custom, insomuch that several at the same time, without pre-eminence or distinction, enjoyed that military honor. It was often allowed by Augustus, and now by Tiberius for the last time. With him the practice ceased altogether."[1] From this passage we learn that during the empire the title of imperator, and with it necessarily such prerogatives as belonged to the imperium, were granted by the order, permission, or clemency of the sovereign-pontiffs, and that Tiberius granted it for the last time. These replies to the argument of the Prussian *savant* are strengthened by the legends upon the "Romano" coins presently to be mentioned.

The earliest Roman silver coins which are still extant in any number belong to two series, stamped respectively "Romano" and "Roma." Numismatists generally attribute both of these series to the mints of Capua and other cities of Campania, which were then included in Magna Græcia. They date the "Romano" coins from A. U. 412 to 543, and the "Roma" coins from

[1] Tacitus, "Annals," iv., 74.

A. U. 437 to 543. Before giving their reasons for these attributions and dates, I must be permitted to say that several circumstances induce me to regard the "Romano" coins as of an era previous to the Roman nummulary system; in other words, that the silver coins of the "Romano" series are embraced in the heavier and earlier denarii alluded to by Varro. (1.) Many of them weigh half as much again as the "Roma" coins, and, for this and other similar reasons, could hardly have belonged to the same system. Babelon saw this objection, and attempted to avoid its force by supposing the "Romano" denarii to be Greek di-drachmas, but our chapter on Greek moneys proves that the explanation is defective. The "Romano" coins are not heavy enough for di-drachmas of that period, even when the latter are of the lightest weight yet found. (2.) Although the internal dissensions of the Samnites led to the interference of the Romans so early as A.-U. 412, then under the consuls M. Valerius Corvus and A. Cornelius Cossus, yet this interference did not for many years result in any such conquests, on the part of the latter, as would have warranted them in stamping money in the field, or anywhere else, for circulation in Campania; whilst the legend "Romano" forbids the hypothesis that they were stamped for circulation elsewhere than in Rome. Their Grecian type may be simply due to the employment of Greek die-sinkers in Rome.

For these reasons the "Romano" silver coins are regarded as older than the "Roma" series; this view including all the "Romano" coins, whether of gold, electrum, silver or bronze.

The reasons advanced by numismatists for calling both of these series Capuan or Campanian coins are briefly as follows:—(1.) The types of the coins are Greek, not Roman. They follow the coins of Macedon; some of them follow the types of previous Capuan coinages; some are stamped "Capua" in the Oscan letter. (2.) The word "Romano," as employed on the coins, is a Greek rather than a Roman form. (3.) The type of some of the Capuan coins (for example, the casqued Minerva) is apparently copied from the coins of Andoleon, king of Pæonia (in Macedon), about A. U. 470. However, these last are rather late "Roma" coins, about which there is no dispute.

It is quite possible that during the wars of the Romans with the Samnites and other nations in Italy, their generals struck some "Roma" coins in the field; but unless we are prepared to throw both Livy and Pliny overboard, it must be admitted that such coins were also struck in Rome, and that all of them, whether in Rome or elsewhere, were struck under the coinage prerogative of the Roman State—a prerogative which, from the birth to the downfall of their government, the Romans never willingly let slip from their hands.

In A.U. 437 a notable addition was made to the monetary system of Rome by the issuance of a "Roma" gold coin, called the "scrupulum," which was valued at twenty aces, and others of forty and sixty aces—not sesterces, as has been hitherto supposed.[1] Assuming that the denarius of this period contained $78\frac{3}{4}$ grains fine silver and the relation of silver to gold was nine for one, then the scrupulum coins should contain about seventeen and one half grains of gold, which, as is shown in the table below, was the fact.

It should, however, first be explained that in Greece and Rome the scrupulum (not the scripulum, for which it has often been mistaken) was the name of a pawn or

[1] Mommsen, M. R., i., 226, cited by Lenormant, i., 162.

draughtsman, and that the game of draughts was anciently played with nine and afterwards with ten men. Hence the scrupulum at first meant the ninth, and afterwards the tenth part, or multiple, of anything. So also an insect with ten feet was called scrupipidæ, and a measure of land ten feet long and ten feet wide, containing a hundred square feet, was called a scrupulum. At a still later date the game of draughts was played, as it is still played, with twelve men, but these numbers were unknown to the game at the period under review. Hence, in Rome, during the fifth century of the city, a scrupulum meant, not a weight, but the ninth of anything; and in the case of money it meant the ninth of the gold aureus. This is shown in the following table:

Roman coinage system about A. U. 437 *or* B. C. 316. *Ratio of silver to gold,* 9 *for* 1.

2½ bronze aces = 1 bronze sesterce.
4 sesterces = 1 silver denarius, 78¾ Eng. grains.
2 denarii = 1 gold scrupulum, 17.5 grains, stamped "XX."
18 denarii = 1 gold aureus, 157.5 grains.
5 aurei = 1 libra of account, containing 787.5 grains fine gold
Hence 900 aces = 1 libra.

The gold and silver coins were of substantially fine metal. Type of gold coin: obverse, the head of Romulus or Mars, accompanied by numerals, denoting the tale value; reverse, an eagle, with the legend "Roma." Type of silver coins: obverse, female head with winged helmet; reverse, a biga and the legend "Roma."

Pliny (xxxiii., 13) says that the libra was equal to "DCCCC," or 900 sesterces, meaning aces, to the value of which the bronze sesterces meanwhile fell.

From this table of equivalents it will be observed that the scrupulum was not a scripulum weight, nor the libra a pound weight; but that the former was simply one-ninth of the aureus coin, and the latter five aurei.

The scrupulum coins in the British Museum marked

"LX," meaning sixty aces, contain from 52 to 52.7 grains of gold, the theoretical weight being 52⅔ grains. Those marked "XL" contain 34.4 to 34.5 grains, the theoretical weight being 35.106 grains; those marked "XX" contain 17.2 to 17.4 grains, the theoretical weight being 17.5 grains. The denarii contain from 66.5 to 79.9 grains. The lightest of these denarii evidently belong to later systems.

With regard to the "libra" of account, Gibbon says that, besides the libra weight, the Romans used a libra of account, which they called pondo: "Outre la livre pondérale des Romains, ils avoient une livre de comte, qu'ils appelloient pondo."[1] An example in point is shown below. The pound of account was also called the "libra sestercia," or the "sestercium;" that is to say, a thousand bronze sesterces, whether composed of gold, silver or copper coins. Pliny, Ammianus Marcellinus, and the Theodosian Code all assure us that there were five aurei to the "pound" of account during the Empire.

Gibbon supposed that the Romans commenced coining gold at 40 aurei to the libra weight, afterwards (citing Snellius and Agricola) at 42, and gradually more, until, in the time of Caracalla, the number reached 48 (109.38 grains each); "the drachma or denier" always weighing half as much, and valued at $\frac{1}{25}$ of the aureus, a ratio of 12½. But the numismatic discoveries of the present century prove this to be all wrong. The aureus of A. U. 437 was struck 33⅓ to the pound weight; the denier was not always half the weight of the aureus; the ratio was never 12½; there were not always 25 deniers to the aureus. As these errors are only a few, amongst a vast number on the same subject, that ap-

[1] Misc. Works, ed. 1815, iii., 437.

pear in the usual works of reference, they are only noticed here on account of the eminence of the author, and the almost universal acceptance of the great literary masterpiece to which his essay on "Roman Money" formed a preliminary study.

In A. U. 485 a small silver coin was struck in Rome, the fourth of a denarius, called a sesterce. At the same time there appeared a new coinage of aces, of which 10 went to a denarius, of about 73 grains. These coins are shown in the following table of equivalents:[1]

Roman coinage system under the consuls Ogulnius and Fabius, A. U. 485 or B. C. 268.[2] Ratio of silver to gold, 10 for 1.

2½ bronze aces — 1 silver sesterce, 18.229 grains.
4 sesterces   1 silver denarius, 72.9167 grains.
20 denarii   = 1 gold aureus, 145.833 grains.
5 aurei   = 1 libra of acct., containing 729 1-6 grains fine gold.
Hence 1,000 aces = 1 libra.

The gold and silver coins were of substantially pure metal. Coins struck in Rome.

It is in reference to this period that Budæus (lib. 4) says that the pondo of account consisted of 100 denarii, or 400 sesterces (or 1000 aces). The system was purely decimal: for example, 10 aces = 1 denarius; 20 denarii = 1 aureus; 5 aurei, or 1000 aces = 1 libra. This circumstance has a significance which does not belong to the present subject, but which the curious reader may pursue in my "Middle Ages Revisited," index word "Ten." Mommsen holds that in A. U. 485 Rome limited the Latin colonies to the coinage of bronze, and thenceforth monopolized for herself the coinage of silver.

Between the era of this system and the year A. U. 535, when a treaty relative to the exchange of prisoners made during the first was renewed during the second

---

[1] Ernest Babelon ("Monnais de la Republique," i., xxii.) dates the earliest silver sesterce in A. U. 485 (486). It disappeared in 537, reappeared in 665, and finally disappeared in 711.

[2] Pliny, xxxiii., 13; Livy, Ep. xv.

Punic war, the libra of account appears to have been raised from 5 to 10 aurei. There are several testimonies which support this opinion. Plutarch, who alludes to this treaty in his life of Fabius Maximus, fixes the ransom of the prisoners at 250 drachmas or denarii. Livy (xxii., 23), in alluding to the same transaction, computes it at two and a half pounds of money—"argenti pondo bina et selibras." This allows 250 denarii to the libra of account. As the denarius of that period weighed about 70 English grains and the aureus about 160 grains, and the ratio was 10 for 1, it follows that there were 10 aurei to the libra, as appears in the next table. Other testimonies rise from the use of the phrases "libra sestercia" and "sestertium," meaning a thousand sesterces or 2,500 aces to the libra, which could only be the case if the libra was raised to 10 aurei.

Roman coinage system during the second Punic war, A. U. 535 or B. C. 218.
Ratio of Silver to gold 10, for 1.

10 bronze aces = 1 silver denarius, 70 grains.
25 denarii = 1 gold aureus, 160 grains.
10 aurei = 1 libra of account.
Hence 2,500 aces = 1 libra.

The gold and silver were of substantially pure metal. These coins were struck in Rome.

However, this valuation of the libra did not stand long. Before the conclusion of the war the libra appears to have been again valued at 5 aurei, as shown in the following table of equivalents:

Roman coinage system under the consuls Claudius and Livius, A. U. 547,
B. C. 206.[1] Ratio of silver to gold, 10 for 1.

16 bronze aces = 1 silver denarius, 63 grains.
6¼ denarii = 1 quarter-aureus, 39.375 grains.
25 denarii = 1 gold aureus, 157.5 grains.
5 aurei = 1 libra, 787.5 grains.
Hence 2000 aces = 1 libra.

[1] Pliny, xxxiii., 13. Babelon, p. xv., dates this coinage from the Lex Flaminius or Lex Fabius, A. U. 537, the year of the battle of Trasimenus, when Q. Fabius Maximus was dictator and C. Servilius and C. Flaminius were consuls. A discrepancy like this one, of ten years, and a further discrepancy of five years, appears in many instances between the Augustan and Christian chronology. See "Middle Ages Revisited," Appendix, on "Ludi Sæculares."

The gold and silver coins were substantially of fine metal. These coins were struck in Rome. About A. U. 525 the Roman authorities had established branch mints, and authorized the striking of coins for the Republic in the provincial cities of Italy, Cis-Alpine Gaul, and Illyria; but this did not include the right to strike the denarius.[1] In paying the troops a denarius was always reckoned at 10 aces.

One result of the Social war (A. U. 664-6), which was caused by the demand of the rural Italians to share the privileges of citizenship with the Romans, was that the Roman provincial mints in Italy, with the exception of those in Sicily, were all closed, and the work of coinage was removed to Rome. Before this, however, the insurgents issued coins stamped Italia, but as the coins were suppressed with the insurrection, they hardly claim a place in the present brief review. Among the Italiote coins were the aurei of Minius Ieus, weighing $131\frac{1}{4}$ grains.[2]

The period of the Lex Papiria, cited by Pliny, which the older commentators assigned to A. U. 587, has been gradually lowered, until, in the most recent numismatic works, it has been assigned to A. U. 663, when, by the Lex Julia, the rights of Roman citizenship were at length conceded to all freeborn Italians. It is now called the law of Julia and Plautia-Papiria. The original authority for this lowered date is Niebuhr, who has been followed by Mommsen, Lenormant and Babelon. The principal changes which took place in the Roman monetary law at this period will be found embodied in the system of Sylla.

[1] Mommsen, "Rechtsfrage," 18; Lenormant, ii., 234.
[2] Friedlander and Burgon give the weight of the aureus of Minius Ieus at $131\frac{1}{4}$ English grains.

Roman coinage system under Sylla, A. U. 675, *or* B. C. 78   *Ratio of silver to gold,* 9 *for* 1.

 4 bronze aces = 1 silver sesterce, 15 grains.
 4 sesterces = 1 silver denarius, of about 60.6 grains.
 12½ denarii = 1 gold half-aureus.[1]
 25 denarii = 1 gold aureus, of about 168.3 grains.
 5 aurei = 1 libra of account.
  Hence 2000 aces = 1 libra.

The gold and silver pieces were of substantially fine metal. Type of gold coins: MANLIA with biga, or L. SYLLA; on reverse, figure on horseback. Type of silver coins: obverse, head of Ceres, with small head of Taurus; reverse, altar and sacrifice—apparently a concession to the Bacchic cult of Italy.

The gold coins of this series, which are very rare, are believed to have been struck in Asia. The weights of four examples in the British Museum are 169.3, 167.7, 167.3 and 167.2 grains, the theoretical weight being 168.3 grains. The silver coins of the same series are serrated on their edges, and weigh from 55 to 61¼ grains each, the theoretical weight being 60.6 grains. Sylla struck no bronze or copper coins, nor were any struck between his time and the year when Augustus celebrated the Ludi Sæculares, and when M. Sanguinius and P. Licinius Stoto filled the position of monetary triumvirs.

In his earlier coinages Julius Cæsar struck aurei of 142 and afterwards (in U. A. 694)[2] of 131¼ grains, specimens of which are still extant. The ratio of silver to gold in these coinages was probably 10 for 1. In the coinages of A. U. 708 this ratio was definitively—and, as it turned out, permanently—fixed at 12 for 1.

[1] "No smaller gold pieces in use at this period" (Humphreys, 303).
[2] Letronne, p. 75.

Roman coinage system under Julius Cæsar, A. U. 708, *or* B C. 45. *Ratio of silver to gold,* 12 *for* 1

```
4 bronze aces  = 1 silver sesterce, 15 grains.
4 sesterces¹   = 1 silver denarius, about 60 grains.
25 denarii     = 1 gold aureus, 125 grains.
5 aurei        = 1 libra of account.
     Hence 2000 aces = 1 libra.
```

The gold and silver pieces were substantially fine metal. Letronne (p. 84) says that down to Vespasian the aurei were 0.991 to 0.998 fine. Cæsar was the first to stamp the image of a living person (his own) on a Roman coin (Lenormant, ii., 332).

No language is more positive than that of Mommsen and Lenormant in laying down the following institute: that Rome never permitted her vassals to strike gold. "La République se réservait exclusivement la fabrication de la monnaie de ce métal, sans la permettre à ses vassaux."[2] When gold was struck in the provinces—for example, the staters struck by Titus Quinctius Flamininus in Greece and afterwards the aurei of Sylla in Asia, or the aurei of Pompey in Cilicia, A. U. 693—it was always done in the name of Rome and under the prerogative of the State.[3] This practice was continued to the end of the Empire.[4] Lenormant regards it as the jealous prerogative of the imperium.[5] We have discussed this theory already, and shown it to be untenable. But even admitting, for the sake of limiting its place in time, that such was the case during the Republic, it certainly ceased to be so when the Empire was consolidated by Augustus, and all the powers and prerogatives of the State, whether religious, civil, or

---

[1] "These were the so-called 'First Brass,' or, more properly, 'First Bronze,' which took the place of the silver sesterce, the latter thenceforth disappearing from circulation. The half-sesterce, or dupondius, was the 'Second Brass,' and the reduced ace was the 'Third Brass' of the earlier numismatists" (Humphreys, 302, 312).

[2] Lenormant, "Mon. Ant., ii., 120; Mommsen, M. R. iii., 344.

[3] Weight of an aureus of Pompey, 146 grains. Lenormant, ii., 303.

[4] Patin, 35; Lavoix; Procopius; Zonaras.

[5] Pp. 121, 248, 304, 363, etc.

military, were merged in the sovereign-pontiff. The latest of such alleged military coins were the silver denarii and bronze aces struck by T. Carisius, who was Legatus Augusti in Gallia and Lusitania, A. U. 731-2.[1] Augustus united the imperium to the pontificate in A.U. 740, and from this time forward the right to strike gold became the exclusive prerogative of the sovereign-pontiff. That it was regarded a sacerdotal prerogative is proved by the continual repetition of religious emblems on the coins. Lenormant himself notices this: "Pendant longtemps, elles ne portant que des types religieux assez uniformes, arrêtés par les autorités publiques et puises dans la religion de l'état."[2]

In this year the Roman coinage system was permanently organized.[3] The coinage prerogative was divided between the sovereign-pontiff and the Senate, the former retaining that of gold and resigning to the latter that of silver and copper. In a short time, through the virtual subjection of the Senate, the silver coinage also fell to the sovereign-pontiff. In accordance with the ordinance of A. U. 740, the coinage of silver was permitted to the proconsuls, and the pieces stamped PERMissu DIVI AVGusti, that is, "by permission of the divine Augustus." The coinage of bronze always remained with the Senate.[4] However, this prerogative, like that of silver, was virtually in the hands of Augustus; yet it suited his interest not to meddle with it as he did with the coinage of silver.

1 Lenormant, i., 362. 2 Lenormant, ii., 232.
3 "The school of Mommsen hold that a reorganization of the monetary system took place in A. U. 727, when Octavius received the title of Augustus, or in A. U. 738, the date of the Ludi Sæculares and of his (second) attempted apotheosis" (Lenormant, ii., 214, 399). But they fail to offer any proofs which connect the reorganization with these dates. Moreover, their conclusions are vitiated by the unwarranted assumption that the coinage was a prerogative of the imperium—an assumption which is negatived by their own admissions concerning the coinages of Otho mentioned further on.
4 Lenormant, ii., 195, 216, 218.

Roman coinage system of Augustus, A. U. 740 *or* B. C. 13. *Ratio of silver to gold*, 12 *for* 1.

```
4 bronze sesterces = 1 silver denarius, 58.4 grains.
25 denarii        = 1 gold aureus, 121.6 grains.
5 aurei           = 1 libra, 608 grains.
                    Hence 500 sesterces = 1 libra.
```

The gold and silver pieces were of substantially fine metal.[1] In this system the silver sesterce gives way to a bronze one.

The defects of Pliny's history of the Roman money arise chiefly from his too confident reliance upon verbalisms; yet the school of Mommsen follow him without the least misgiving. They gravely inform us that pecunia is derived from *pecus*; that the value of coins is deducible from the names of weights; that the modern pound sterling is from the pound weight of silver, and the marc of money from a mark weight of silver; they talk familiarly of the single and double "standard" under Julius Cæsar and Augustus; and draw conclusions from ancient history, the premises of which cannot possibly be traced in Europe farther back than the coinage legislation of the sixteenth century. Such a school exhibits no claims to be regarded as authorities on either the principles or the history of money. They have been taught to look upon money as so much metal, whereas it is plainly an institution of law. It is as though measures of length and volume were regarded as so much wood, because it has been found most convenient to make yard-sticks, pecks, and bushels of that material. Mommsen's conception of the monetary system of Augustus is that it began with an attempt to establish the "double standard" at a ratio of 15.75, then at 14.29, etc., but that after several trials this system was aban-

[1] Patin ("Hist. Coins," p. 71) says that the Roman gold coins were of fine metal down to the reign of Alexander Severus, when they were alloyed with one-fifth of silver. This alliage, however, was not common, but exceptional. He goes on to say that the purity of coins was restored by Aurelian. On this subject, consult Lenormant, i., 200, 203.

doned as impracticable, and the "single gold standard" was definitely adopted in place of it! The facts are that no such idea as is involved in the phrase of single or double "standard" was dreamed of at that period; that no such attempts were made; that no such ratios are deducible from the Roman coinage systems; that the ratio of the Empire was always 12 for 1; that no change occurred in its monetary system until the reign of Caracalla, and then only a slight one; and that no change at all was made in the ratio for nearly thirteen hundred years.

Gold standard, silver standard, double standard, halting standard, etc., these are terms derived from the legislation of the sixteenth and seventeenth centuries, when, for the first time in the history of the European world, private individuals were permitted to coin money, or, what is the same thing, they were accorded the right to require the government to turn their bullion into money, free of taxation, loss, or expense. This idiotic legislation, euphemistically called "free coinage," deprived government of that control over money which had ever been regarded as an essential attribute of sovereignty and as necessary for the maintenance of opportunities to facilitate a just distribution of wealth. In effect it destroyed money, or nomisma, which is an institution or a measure of value prescribed and regulated by law, and it substituted for money an unknown and illimitable quantity of metal—a substance that, as such, is not amenable to legal control. Hence arose the modern jargon of gold standard, silver standard, etc. So long as money was governed by law, it was the whole number of coins, reduced to one denomination, that determined prices. When money ceased to be governed by law, as was the case after the legislation procured by the Dutch and English East India Companies, it was the whole quantity of metal that determined prices. Before the seventeenth century the "standard," or measure of prices, was the whole number of coins, at the valuation affixed to them by law; after that period the legal valuation (except as to the ratio) formed no part of the measure; and within the last quarter of a century, even the ratio has been swept away. The measure of prices in the Western world at the present time consists chiefly of metal, as such. When that metal is gold, the measure is called the "gold standard;" when it is silver, the "silver standard," etc. But in the days of Augustus this was wholly unknown. There was no individual coinage. The measure of prices was the whole number of coins which were legal tenders, and which circulated, not merely in Rome, but throughout the Empire, after they were reduced to one of the various denominations which were affixed to them by law. Within prudent limits, it made no difference whether the coins were pure or impure, light or heavy, yellow, white or brown. No one could lawfully stamp them except the State. The value they bore was (within such prudent limits) whatever the State chose to stamp upon them;[1] and this principle was so deeply planted in the Roman law and constitution, that it became the groundwork of judicial decisions as to what constituted a good and lawful tender of money, down to and including the period of Sir Matthew Hale.

With regard to the ratios which have been calculated by Mommsen and Lenormant between gold and silver, I have only room to say briefly that they are founded chiefly on two errors. The first one is that of mistaking the "libra" of money, or argenti, which was simply a sum of current aurei, no matter of what weight or

[1] Digest, xviii., i., 1.

alloy, for a pound weight of silver metal; the second one is that of calculating the ratio from anachronical coins, from exceptional coins, or from those of only local currency or limited legal tender. The ratios calculated by Hoffman[1] are of the same defective character. When the ratio is calculated, as it should be, from the full legal tender coins, issued under a given system by the sovereign-pontiff, it will be found to have always been 12 for 1. Although many of the Roman emperors issued debased silver coins, these were never full legal tenders; for example, they were not receivable for tributes or taxes, which were payable either in aurei or in silver coins, or bullion, at the weight ratio of 12 for 1. Lenormant's statement (i., 185) that "Alexander Severus, in order to steady the revenues, decided that all payments into the treasury should be exclusively in gold," is unwarranted by the text to which he refers, which merely says that the emperor "frequently caused his gold and silver to be weighed." This is precisely what is done periodically in all great treasuries.[2] Upon this text Lenormant also builds the unwarranted conclusion that the "standard," or measure of prices, was gold metal. His master, the illustrious Mommsen, also sees in the gradually lessened weight of the aureus, "a virtual demonetization of gold."[3] Whereas, in fact, nothing of the sort is to be seen. The lowering of the aureus (a slight one) was merely an economy of gold metal in the fabrication of Roman money—a measure probably dictated by the necessities of the times, and of no necessary bearing on the position of money in the law, or even upon its power to correctly measure the value of commodities, services or debts.[4]

[1] "Lehre von Gelde," pp. 103, *et seq.*
[2] "Omne aurum, omne argentum, idque frequenter appendit" (Lampridius, in "Alex. Severus," xxxix.)
[3] M. R., iii., 63.
[4] Mill, "Polit. Econ."

Mommsen and Lenormant conclude their remarks on this subject with the statement that the aureus was eventually so much degraded and debased that it ceased to be regarded as money—that it became merely ingots of bullion, and was weighed out with balance in hand. They refer for their warrant to Vopiscus, in Aurelian, 9 and 12, Probus 4, and Bonosus 15. Upon turning to these texts we merely find that certain payments of gold "phillips," or silver "antonines," or copper "sesterces" are mentioned, just as we now say so many Louis d'or, Napoleons, Maria Theresa dollars, etc. Not a word appears in these texts about "ingot-money," or bullion, or weighing in balances. These phrases and inferences are not only unwarranted by the texts, they entirely pervert and misrepresent the condition of money under the Roman law.

From the second coinage of Constantine to the fall of the Empire, a period of nearly 900 years, the aureus was seldom degraded, and but once debased; it never ceased to be regarded as money. There was no ingot-money; there was no weighing of gold coins, they passed then, as they do now, by tale, and, what is more, it was unlawful to refuse, criminal to alter, and death to deface them or to reduce them to bullion.[1] Says Gibbon, of the Roman imperial revenues: "A large portion of the tribute was paid in money, and of the current coin of the Empire gold alone could be legally accepted."[2] Elsewhere he says: "Pendants que dans les tributs il exigeoit toujours l'aureus de Constantin;" *i. e.* while as to tributes, they were always exacted in the aureus of Constantine.[3] He should have added: "Or in twelve times their weight of silver."

Suetonius informs us that upon the death of Caligula

---

[1] Arrian, Epictet, iii., 1; Paul, Sentent. recept. v., 25, 1; Lenormant, i., 237; Digest, xlviii., 13, 1; Suetonius in "Augustus."
[2] "Decline and Fall," ii., 64.   [3] Misc. works, iii., 460.

an attempt was made to re-establish the Republic.[1] Among the acts of the Senate on this occasion was a decree decrying the tyrant's money, and requiring it to be brought into the treasury and melted down, "so that, were it possible, both his name and features might be forgotten by posterity."[2] Nevertheless, there are nearly a hundred different types of his coins still extant. The Senate of this period was republican; but the lower orders of the people, the soldiers, and the priests were in favor of the hierarchy, the former for the sake of the largesses bestowed by the emperors, the latter on account of their benefices, which, ever since the time of Augustus, had been rendered lucrative and permanent. Claudius, the uncle of Caligula, was either so rapid in his movements, or, as the story goes, was so quickly taken up by the prætorian band, that the design of the Senate proved abortive, and it did not have time to issue coins proclaiming the Republic before Claudius succeeded in securing the support of the guards, and was enabled to suppress the incipient rising. It does not appear that the Senate issued any republican coins on this occasion, but, as we shall presently see, coins of such a character were indeed issued some twenty-five years later, when Nero died and before Galba seized the imperial throne.

There were circumstances connected with the reign of Nero which must have encouraged the growth of a revolutionary spirit, having for its object the overthrow of the hierarchy and worship of Augustus, if not, indeed, the restoration of the ancient Republic.

Nero seems to have been rather skeptical about the divine origin which was claimed for Augustus, and but little disposed to offer adoration to him. When Rome

[1] Claudius, 10.
[2] Laurence Echard, "Rom. Hist." ii., 103.

was accidentally burnt, he did not hesitate to rebuild it with funds plundered from the temples in which this profane worship was conducted. By way of retaliation, the enraged priests composed his biography, which they have filled with such horrid crimes as, were the least portion of them true, would render it difficult to understand why the memory of Nero was so dear—as many instances prove that it was—to his countrymen for many ages. If Nero was imbued with any religion at all, it was that of Liber Pater, for it is the effigy of this deity which appears most frequently on his coins. Suetonius also informs us that he sacrificed three times a day to another deity, whose worship was clearly allied to that of Bacchus.[1] Otho, who was one of Nero's favorites, professed the religion of Isis, which was either the same or a similar cult.[2] This was the popular religion of Italy, where some remains of it survive to the present day. It was the religion of the poor and down-trodden, for it inculcated peace and friendship, and promised liberty and immortality. Nero's dislike for the religion of the State and his partiality for the cult of Bacchus, coupled with his neglect of discipline, his condescension, familiarity, and joviality, could hardly have failed to warm those hopes of restoring the Republic, which the example and writings of Brutus and Cicero assure us were deeply implanted in the minds of the Roman patricians. Be this as it may, it is certain that upon the news of Nero's death many people, adopting for the emblem of their hopes the Phrygian cap of Liber Pater, ran wildly through the streets, uttering revolutionary cries, and fomenting an excitement that ended by involving the Senate in their design, and the issuance of an Act proclaiming a Republican Government. Among the first measures of the short-lived

---

[1] Nero, 56.   [2] Otho, 12.

administration was the coinage of money, designed to announce the restoration. It was, perhaps, unfortunate for these patriots that they began by striking gold, this being essentially a prerogative belonging to the pontifical office, and one whose violation, apart from other circumstances, would be likely of itself to array against them, not only the ecclesiastical orders, but the prejudices of all persons of religious pretensions or of superstitious tendencies.

Besides the gold coins, there were struck silver and bronze ones, and so numerous were they that nearly a hundred different types (not merely coins, but types of coins) are still extant. All these must have been struck between June 9, A. D. 68, the date of Nero's death, and July 18, A. D. 69, that of the investiture of Vitellius as sovereign-pontiff. A common type of these coins was a citizen clad in a toga, with a cap of Liberty on his head and a wreath of laurel in his right hand, and the legend LIBERTATI. Reverse: Victory standing on a globe, with crown and palm, and the legend S. P. Q. R. Others have the legends Concordia provinciarum, Concordia prætorianorum, Fides militum, Roma renascens, Libertas, Libertas populi romani, Libertas restituta, Jupiter Capitolinus, Mars ultor, Volcanus ultor, Vesta populi romani quiritium, etc.[1]

The person destined to destroy the ephemeral Republic was Ser. Sulpicius Galba, a member of the Quindecemviral Sacred College, a priest of the Augustals and of the Titii, a man of enormous wealth, who never traveled without a retinue of monks and soothsayers, and who, wherever he pitched his camp, erected an altar, swung a censer, and offered frankincense, sacrificial wine, and costly jewels to the gods.[2] This pious

---

[1] "Revue Numismatique," 1862 and 1865; Lenormant, ii., 375; Cohen, "Mon. Rom."   [2] Suet. "Galba," 4, 8, 9, 18.

Roman enjoyed a proconsulship under Nero in Hispania Tarraconensis, where he appears to have divided his leisure between the celebration of religious ceremonies and the organization of a conspiracy against the throne of his benefactor. When this conspiracy was ripe, he declared it to be a holy war, "sacred and acceptable to the gods." Upon hearing that Nero was dead, Galba proclaimed himself the Cæsar, hung a dagger from his neck, as a token of his bloody intentions, and, attended by his legions and a formidable body of Spanish recruits, made his way to Rome, where an accession of forces had been organized for him by his ecclesiastical friends. Then Galba's dagger came into play. In the course of a few days the Nymphidians, as the Republicans were called, were all put to death or driven into exile; the statues of Bacchus were destroyed, the Phrygian caps were burnt, the power of the sovereign-pontiff was re-established, and the ill-starred Republic came to an end.

The coinage prerogative of the Pontifex Maximus is made the subject of a strange argument by the illustrious Mommsen. We must premise that after a short reign Galba was assassinated. He was succeeded by Otho, who, because he declared it his intention to restore the Republic, was undoubtedly supported by the Nymphidians and opposed by the ecclesiastics. The latter now turned for aid to Aulus Vitellius. This person was the great-grandson of Q. Vitellius, "questor to Divus Augustus," the grandson of P. Vitellius, "a Roman knight and manager of Augustus' affairs," and the son of Lucius Vitellius, who set the example of worshiping Caligula as the living God, and never approached him without covering his head with a veil, turning his body, as was customary in Roman worship, and falling prostrate upon the ground.¹ The piety of his ancestors must have descended to Aulus, who was rewarded with numerous rich ecclesiastical benefices, the gift of three successive princes,² besides the lucrative surveyorship of public buildings, a proconsulship in Africa, and another in Germany. This last office, the gift of Galba, was employed by Vitellius as a means to secure his own elevation to the throne. Indulgence, bribery and promises were employed with success to win the legions under his command. The sword of Divus Julius was taken down out of the temple of Mars and placed in the hands of the ambitious proconsul; the soldiers saluted him as Imperator and Augustus; and a wreath of laurel "most religiously begirt his brow." Sending a powerful army ahead to overthrow his rival, he began his march to Rome. On the way he was informed of a decisive victory at Bebriacum (now Caveto) and of the death of Otho. Arrived in Rome, Vitellius was soon surrounded by "a numerous assembly of priests," who, together with the faction known as the Veneti, appear to have formed the bulk of his party in the capital. He was invested as Pontifex Maximus on the ominous anniversary of the battle of Allia, and after a brief and troubled reign of eight months was assassinated. The previous reign of Otho extended from the death of Galba, January 15th (A. D. 69), to his own death, April 20th, a period of ninety-five days.³

We are now prepared to follow Mommsen's argument. The investiture of the high-priesthood of Rome, after an ancient custom, could only be conferred during the month of March, there being only two instances to the contrary. The coinage of copper, says Mommsen, was the prerogative of the high-priesthood. Otho was

1 Vitellius, 5. 2 Ibid.
3 Lenormant (ii., 416) says April 15th.

invested with the pontificate on March 9th. Within five days of this date he was on his way to meet the troops of Vitellius in Lombardy. Therefore, he had not sufficient time to confer upon the Senate the necessary authority to strike bronze coins. This, in Mommsen's opinion, explains why, although there are gold and silver coins of Otho, there are no bronze ones, except such as were struck in Antioch, and these he accounts for on the supposition that the Antiochians, when they heard of Galba's death and Otho's elevation, presumed that of course Otho would be invested as Pontifex Maximus in March, and, therefore, proceeded at once to strike those bronze coins with his image, which stand in the way of the extraordinary theory propounded by the Prussian *savant*.

To this theory it would be sufficient to reply that if Otho had time to authorize the issue of gold and silver coins, he certainly had time to authorize the issue of bronze ones, and that if the vassal Senate of Antioch could venture to strike bronze coins without Otho's written authority, so could the paramount Senate of Rome. But there is a still further and more cogent reply to make. Mommsen is mistaken in regard to the coinage prerogatives of Rome. His theory is that the prerogative of the gold and silver coinage belonged to the imperium and the bronze coinage to the pontificate. The fact was that the prerogative of gold coinage (certainly from the reign of Julius Caesar) belonged to the pontificate. This is so overwhelmingly proved by the evidence adduced in chapter II. of the present work that nothing further need be said on the subject in this place. In the sweeping interdiction of gold coinage to vassal and subject kings which the Romans maintained for upwards of thirteen centuries, a single exception was made. This related to the kings of Pontus and the Cimmerian Bosporus. The reason of the exception was purely sacerdotal. The kings of Pontus were the guardians of the temples, the oracle, and the mysteries, of that venerated Mother of God, one of whose effigies, piously conveyed to Rome when Hannibal was at its gates, had saved it from impending ruin. Many of the emblems connected with this worship appeared upon the Pontic coins, and this is what saved them from the melting-pot. Augustus merely provided that these coins should bear on the reverse the image of himself as a mark of the suzerainty of Rome. The last coins that were issued by the Ponto-Bosporian kings previous to this regulation are those of Asander, who reigned as governor from A. U. 704 and as king from A. U. 737. These are aurei of 125 grains each. The earliest under the Augustan regulations are those of Polemon I. stamped with his own head on one side and that of Augustus on the other. From this time onward to the reign of Gallien, when the Temple of Ephesus was destroyed by the Goths, the kings of Pontus and Bosporus were permitted to strike a few gold coins, upon one side of which appeared their own images and on the other that of the sovereign-pontiff of Rome, accompanied by the emblems of the Syrian goddess. With Rhescuporis VIII. of the Aspurgian dynasty, A. D. 312-18, this Pontic kingdom, already ruined, came to an end, and with it the feeble series of gold coins struck under these exceptional circumstances. Under Cotys III., a contemporary of Alexander Severus, the Ponto-Bosporian aurei were made of electrum, and from this time onward they became paler and paler, until at last they were made altogether of silver, and, like the Dutch gulden of the present day, were gold coins only in name.

The prerogative of the bronze coinage belonged to the Senate, which, therefore, in the case of Otho, needed no express authority from the pontificate. Whether the silver coinage belonged to the pontificate or to the imperium at this period, is a matter of no consequence in the present connection. Of the gold and silver coins, the former were certainly struck in virtue of Otho's pontifical authority. The bronze coins of Antioch were undoubtedly struck by the Senate of that city in virtue of the authority which had long previously been conferred upon it by the Senate of Rome—an authority which remained in full force so long as it was not abrogated. That no Roman urban bronze coins of Otho are extant may be accounted for either by supposing that such coins were indeed struck but that none have been found, or else by supposing that the Roman Senate had good reason for not striking them. In the latter case the reason is matter of conjecture. The Senate was republican; it was disgusted with emperor-worship; it had but recently engaged in an attempt to restore the Republic; its surviving members, who had returned to Rome, encouraged by the declaration of Otho that his object was to restore the Republic, may have naturally viewed with suspicion his subsequent assumption of the pontifical office and his eagerness to proclaim a continuance of the Empire upon his gold and silver coins, and they may have refrained from lending that sanction to these ambitious proceedings which would have been implied had they stamped bronze coins with his image.

The following tables show the scale of equivalents under Caracalla:—

First Coinage system of Caracalla, A. D. 211-15. *Ratio of silver to gold,* 12 *for* 1.

4 bronze sesterces = 1 silver denarius, of 54 grains.
12½ denarii = 1 half-aureus.
25 denarii = 1 aureus, of 112.5 grains.
5 aurei = 1 libra.
Hence 500 sesterces = 1 libra.

So far as it goes, this agrees with Mr. Finlay's scheme.[1] In addition to these equivalents he introduces a silver argenteus of 60 to the libra weight, valued at 1½ denarii. Between this system and the one next to be mentioned the change in the contents of the pieces was gradual.

Second coinage system of Caracalla, A.D. 215-17. *Ratio of silver to gold,* 12 *for* 1.

4 sesterces = 1 denarius, of 45.83 grains.
6 denarii = 1 gold sicilicus, or shilling.
12 denarii = 1 half-aureus.
24 denarii = 1 aureus, of 100 grains, $\frac{11}{12}$ fine = 91.67 grains fine.
5 aurei = 1 libra.
Hence 480 sesterces = 1 libra.

This system of Caracalla contains all the elements of the decimo-duodecimal, or £. s. d. system, which afterwards became established in the Roman provinces, and still lingers in England and Turkey. The libra, which here contains 458.35 grains fine gold, has since been gradually reduced, until, at the present time, it contains in England but 113.16 grains fine, while the denarius, or penny, which here contains nearly 46 grains, has fallen in England to 7¼ grains, such being the weight of the Maundy money still issued. The relation of copper to silver and of silver to gold varied from decimal (during the Republic) to duodecimal (during the Empire), but from first to last, with two exceptions noticed herein, the relation between aureus and libra was quinquennial.

We have seen that the extension of Roman citizenship to the free-born inhabitants of Italy was marked

[1] Geo. Finlay, "Hist. Greece," ed. 1877, i., 453.

by an important change in the monetary system. So was the extension of the same right to the free-born inhabitants of the provinces, which bears even date with the second coinage system of Caracalla. The tyrant's motive for making this concession was an increase of revenues. One of its fruits was to plant the £. s. d. system wherever the Roman eagles flew.

The argenteus, or, as it was sometimes called, the argenteus antonianus, of Caracalla was a silver coin stamped with the rayed effigy of the sovereign-pontiff, that is to say, he was represented surrounded with a halo of light. In the second coinage system of Caracalla this coin appears to have been substituted for two denarii. Thus, the equivalents appear to be 12 argentei, containing 1,020 grains of silver=1 aureus, containing 91-.67 grains of gold, a ratio of about 11.1 for 1. But, in fact, the argenteus antonianus does not appear to have been a full legal tender coin, and when paid for taxes (due in gold aurei) it was only receivable by weight. The ratio of 12 for 1, therefore, remained unimpaired.

The monetary measures of Aurelian are remarkable for the revolt which they occasioned among the guild of moneyers, who, for this reason, must be supposed to have derived considerable profits from the previous system. Aurelian "took away the privilege of coining (silver) money from almost all the local mints of the empire," and only succeeded in crushing the revolt of the moneyers with a loss of 7,000 troops—a striking proof of the number and organization of the former. Mr. Finlay regards the Roman libra weight, at the time of Constantine, as having fallen to 5,040 English grains, and says that Aurelian struck aurei of 50 to the libra. This would make them contain 100.8 grains each; but, in fact, there are none which contain so much gold. Throughout the present work the libra weight of Rome has been uniformly reckoned at 5,250 grains; but as we have always been guided by the weights of the extant coins, the difference between this assumption and Mr. Finlay's does not affect the weights herein mentioned. The extant aurei of Aurelian weigh from 80.85 to 97.52 grains. Supposing them to be $\frac{11}{12}$ fine, they contain about 74 to 90 grains fine gold. The equivalents are shown in the following tables:

First coinage system of Aurelian, A. D. 270. *Ratio of silver to gold*, 12 *for* 1.

```
5 nummi or minuta  = 1 copper assarion.
4 assarions        = 1 copper denarius, stamped "XX."
20 denarii           1 silver argenteus, 35½ grains fine.
25 argentei        = 1 gold aureus, 74 grains fine.
5 aurei            = 1 libra of account.
```
Hence 500 copper denarii = 1 gold aureus.

Second coinage system of Aurelian, A. D. 274. *Ratio of silver to gold*, 12 *for* 1.

```
5¼ copper nummi = 1 copper assarion.
4 assarions     = 1 copper denarius, stamped "XXI."
21 denarii      = 1 silver argenteus (new), 45 grains fine.
24 argentei     = 1 gold aureus, 90 grains fine.
5 aurei         = 1 libra of account.
```
Hence 504 copper denarii = 1 gold aureus.

Mr. Finlay introduces into this system a "denarius of account" equal to 1 argenteus. This was probably a purse of 20 to 21 copper denarii, used as a means of reconciling the two coinages of Aurelian. This would enable all sums couched in denarii to be reckoned at the rate of either 20 to the old argenteus, or 21 to the new. Mr. Finlay's conjecture with regard to the number of English grains in the libra weight appears to have been derived from the number of copper denarii to the aureus, decupled.

First coinage system of Diocletian, A. D. 284, *Ratio of silver to gold*, 12 *for* 1 (Finlay).

5 copper nummi	= 1 copper assarion.
2½ double nummi	= 1 copper assarion.
4 assarions	= 1 copper denarius.
2 copper denarii	= 1 copper follis.
12 folles	= 1 silver denarius, 45.17 grains standard.
24 silver denarii	= 1 aureus, 90.34 grains standard.
5 aurei	= 1 libra of account.

Hence 576 copper denarii = 1 gold aureus.

The silver denarius of this system was afterwards called the "centenionalis," because instead of 120 to the libra, as in this system, they became worth 100 to the libra. See below.

Second coinage system of Diocletian, A. D. 290 (?). *Ratio of Silver to gold*, 12 *for* 1.

4 copper assarions	= 1 tetrassarion, or copper denarius.
2 copper denarii	= 1 copper follis.
12 folles	= 1 silver denarius, 40 grains, "XCVI."
24 silver denarii	= 1 aureus, 80 grains standard.
5 aurei	= 1 libra of account.

Hence 576 copper denarii = 1 gold aureus.

Third coinage system of Diocletian, A. D. 302. *Ratio of silver to gold*, 12 *for* 1.

4 copper assarions	1 tetrassarion, or copper denarius.
2 copper denarii	= 1 copper follis.
8 copper assarions	= 1 copper follis.
12 copper folles	= 1 silver denarius, 36 grains, "XCVI."
24 silver denarii	= 1 aureus 72, grains.
5 aurei	1 libra of account.

Hence 576 copper denarii 1 gold aureus.

Count Borghesi considers the denarius of Diocletian's *Edictum pretium* to be the copper tetrassarion or four-assarion piece, of which 24 went to the silver denarius, stamped "XCVI," meaning 96 assarions.

If we compare this system with the assumptions of Jacob,[1] it will be found that, erroneously assuming the denarius to weigh 65 grains fine, and that, still further, assuming a wrong equivalent in the money of his own time, he deduced unwarrantably high prices for the whole of Diocletian's schedule.

[1] "Hist. Prec. Met ," ed. Phil. 1832, p. 126.

First Coinage system of Constantine, not later than A. D. 310. *Ratio of silver to gold,* 12 *for* 1.

20 copper nummi = 1 copper follis.
12 copper folles = 1 silver denarius, 36 grains fine.
24 silver denarii = 1 gold aureus, 82.7 grs. standard, say 72 grs. fine.
5 aurei = 1 libra of account.
Hence 5,760 copper nummi = 1 gold aureus.

Nine well-preserved specimens of the earlier aurei of Constantine, now in the British Museum, weigh on the average 82.7 grains.

Second coinage system under Constantine, July, A. D. 325 *Ratio of silver to gold,* 12 *for* 1.[1]

20 copper nummi = 1 copper follis.
12 folles = 1 silver siliqua, keration, or denarius, 35 grains.
2 siliquas = 1 silver miliaresion, 70 grains.
12 miliaresia = 1 gold solidus, or numisma, stamped "LXXII," 70 grains.
5 solidi = 1 libra of account, 250 grains of standard gold.
Hence 5,760 copper nummi = 1 gold aureus.

Type of the aureus: a winged figure with ₽: reverse, the head of Constantine.

These solidi are stamped "LXXII," and, according to Gibbon, Queipo, Finlay and other writers, were struck 72 to the Roman pound weight. The extant coins, in the best state of preservation, only weigh $68\frac{2}{3}$ grains, and I have allowed $1\frac{1}{3}$ grains more to bring them to a round figure of 70 grains. They could hardly have weighed more at any time. The extant miliaresia are of the same weight as the solidi. The copper follis, or purse, consisted of 20 nummi; the silver follis of $2\frac{1}{2}$ argyres, or 250 siliquas, kerations, or denarii, or 125 miliaresia. This was the ordinary donative to the soldiers; it was equal to (about) two libras of account. By a law of A. D. 356,[2] a merchant is forbidden to travel with more than one thousand folles. This means silver folles, one thousand of which were roughly equal to

---

[1] Gibbon (Misc. Essays, iii., 459, ed. 1815) says 14.4, but is mistaken. Consult Queipo, " Sys. Met. et. Mon.," ii , 465; Finlay, "Hist. Greece," vol. i., App. ii.   [2] Cod. Theod. ix., 23; 1

two thousand libras of account. The gleba senatoria, a sum of gold coins, was the annual capitation-tax of that order.

Coinage system under Arcadius and Honorius, A. D. 408(?). *Ratio of silver to gold,* 12 *for* 1.

20 copper nummi = 1 copper follis.
12 copper folles = 1 silver siliqua, 35 grains standard.
2 siliquas = 1 silver miliaresion de sportula, 70 grs. standard
12 miliar. de sport. = 1 gold solidus, 70 grains standard.
4 solidi = 1 libra of account.
   Hence 5,760 nummi = 1 gold solidus.

So far as the copper coins are concerned, this system is constructed by assuming that there were 20 nummi to the follis and 12 folles to the silver siliqua, as in the second system of Constantine. A law of Arcadius and Honorius (A. D. 397)[1] values the gold solidus at 12 miliaresia de sportula, whilst a law of Theodosius II., (A. D. 428)[2] values the solidus at 24 siliquas. Another law of Theodosius II. (A. D. 422) values the libra at 4 solidi, instead of 5, as before.[3] An edict of Honorius and Theodosius II., dated A. D. 418, imposes a mulct of 5 libras of gold upon the members of the provincial council of Gaul for non-attendance at meetings.[4] This evidently means 20 solidi. To regard these libras, as some writers have done, as so many pounds' weight of gold would not only be contrary to usage, but preposterously excessive. The weight of the solidus in the above table was obtained by weighing a number of the best specimens of the extant coins. Those of Arcadius average 68.51 grains; of Honorius 68.05 grains. A slight allowance for wear brings them up to 70 grains. Fineness not known, but apparently $\frac{9}{10}$ to $\frac{11}{12}$.

By a law of Valentinian III. (A. D. 445),[5] there were 7,200 nummi to the solidus, consequently there must

---

1 Cod. Theod., xiii., ii., 1.   2 Cod. Theod., xii., iv., 1; Nov. Majoriani, vii., 16 (A. D. 458).   3 Cod. Theod., viii., iv., 27.   4 "Middle Ages Revisited," chap. xvi., p. 2.   5 Nov. Val. iii., de pretio solidus, xiv., 1.

have been issued a smaller nummus than that of Arcadius and Honorius. Of these smaller nummi there should be 25 to the follis; thus $25 \times 12 \times 2 \times 12 = 7{,}200$ nummi to the solidus.[1] Cassiordorus says there were 6,000 to the solidus, but I cannot make this out, unless Valentinian changed the tale relations of the copper to the silver coins, or the silver to the gold coins, of which no explicit account appears in the texts. As at this period copper coins largely superseded silver ones in the imperial circulation, such changes are by no means incredible.[2]

Coinage system under Anastasius, A. D. 491-518. Ratio of silver to gold, 12 for 1.

5 noumia "A"	= 1 pentanoumion, "C."
2 pentanoumia	= 1 dekanoumion, "I."
2 dekanoumia	= 1 eikosarion or obolus, "K."
2 eikosaria	= 1 follis, either copper "M" or silver (5.83 grs.)
6 folles	= 1 silver keration, or siliqua, 35 grains.[3]
2 keratia	= 1 silver miliaresion, 70 grains.
12 miliaresia	= 1 gold solidus, or nummus, 70 grains.
5 (?) solidi	= 1 libra of account.

Hence 5,760 noumia = 1 gold solidus.

The letters A, C, I, K, M are stamped on the copper coins, and denote 1, 5, 10, 20, 40 noumia respectively.[4] These marks continued until the time of Phocas, when the Greek M was replaced (on the 40-noumia piece) by the Latin XXXX.[5]

Coinage system under Heraclius I., A. D. 610-41. Ratio of Silver to gold, 12 for 1.

40 copper noumia	= 1 copper follis.
6 folles	= 1 silver siliqua, 34.17 grains standard.
12 folles	= 1 silver drachma, 68.34 grains standard.
12 drachmas	= 1 gold solidus, 69.90 grains standard.
5 (?) solidi	= 1 libra of account.

Hence 5,760 noumia = 1 gold solidus.

1 Finlay, i., 444.   2 Ibid.

3 In this coinage system of Anastasius, I have followed Mr. Finlay Sabatier (i., 149) says that in 498 Anastasius made 12 phollerates, or teruntiani, to the siliqua, of which last there were 24 to the solidus. If by phollerates he means eikosaria, or copper oboli, then the system remained the same as shown in the present text.

4 Finlay, i., 445.   5 Humphreys, 371.

The weight of the solidus in this system is that of the extant coins in the best state of preservation. The contents of fine gold in the solidus was 65 grains, and the fine silver contents of the siliqua 32½ grains. It was upon the solidus of this system that the Arabians built their gold dinar. They evidently weighed and assayed a number of the solidi in actual circulation, and finding them to contain exactly 65 grains of fine gold, determined this for the contents of the dinar. In their earlier coinages they also adopted the silver drachma of 65 grains fine and the Roman ratio of 12 for 1; but this was swept away by Abd-el-Melik, and from his time forward nothing except the dinar remained to connect the Moslem coinages with the Empire of Augustus.

Coinage system under Justinian II. (Rhinotmetus), A. D. 685-95, and again 705-11. Ratio of silver to gold, 12 for 1.

40 copper noumia = 1 copper follis.
6 folles = 1 silver siliqua, 34.17 grains standard.
24 siliquas = 1 gold solidus, 68.35 grains standard.
5 (?) solidi = 1 libra of account.
Hence 5,760 noumia = 1 gold solidus.

On this coinage appears the earliest unquestionable Christian legend and the earliest effigy of Christ. These sacred emblems appear on the gold solidus, described by Sabatier: dN. IVSTINIANVS. SERV. ChPSTI. Full-faced bust of Justinian, diademed, with cross on top, the emperor clothed in a tight-fitting robe, ornamented with strings of pearls arranged in squares. In his right hand a "potency" cross on three steps; in his left hand a globe, on which appears the word "PAX," the same surmounted by a Greek cross. Reverse: dN. Ihs. ChS. REX REGNANTIVM. Full-faced bust of Christ. The extremities of the arms of a small cross appear behind the ears and above the head. Under the left arm a book.

There are so few coins extant of this period that, between the reigns of Leo Isaurus and Michael I., or from A. D. 718 to 811, Sabatier, whose work is believed to contain a complete list of all the Byzantine types, only furnishes seventy-three types during the entire interval. As this is an interval of the greatest interest to the Western world, because it embraces the coinage system of Charlemagne, we have endeavored to fill the blank thus left with the system of Nicephorus I. In the table of equivalents we have been guided by Sabatier and the mediæval texts cited in Guerard's "Polyptique d'Irminon" and De Vienne's "Livre d'Argent." Queipo has noticed that the silver coins of Basileus II. (A. D. 962), Romanus I. (A. D. 918), Nicephorus II. (A. D. 963-9), and the emperors of Trebizond are assimilated in weight to the Arabian dirhem or its subdivisions.[1] In like manner, it is to be remarked that the gold coins of all the Byzantine emperors, from Heraclius onward, are closely allied to the Arabian dinar of 65 grains fine. This remark includes the coins of Nicephorus I.

Coinage system of Nicephorus I. (Logothetes), son of Irene, A. D. 802-11.
Ratio of silver to gold, 12 *for* 1.

3 copper folles = 1 silver half-siliqua, 15⅞ grains fine.
2 half-siliquas = 1 silver siliqua, 31¾ grains fine.
1½ siliquas = 1 Arabian dirhem, 46⅞ grains fine.
2 siliquas = 1 miliaresion, 63½ grains fine.
3 miliaresia = 1 gold tetarteron, or sicilicus, 15⅞ grains fine.
4 miliaresia = 1 gold triens, 21 1-6 grains fine.
12 miliaresia = 1 gold solidus, 63½ grains fine.
5 solidi = 1 libra of account, 317½ grains fine.
Hence 12 half-siliquas, or denarii = 1 sicilicus, or tetarteron.
    20 sicilici, or shillings = 1 libra.
    240 denarii, or pennies = 1 libra.

The tetarteron, or gold shilling, appears in both earlier and later coinage systems, for example, in the monetary denominations of Nicephorus II. and Phocas. Tetarteron means the fourth part, and is the Greek equivalent of the Latin *quartarius*, as *quartarius vini*,[2] whence our

[1] Table lxi., vol. ii., p. 464.   [2] Livy, v., 47.

quart of wine, meaning the quarter of a gallon. Tetarteron is also the equivalent of the Latin sicilicus, or fourth part, whence came our shilling, which was the fourth of the solidus and twentieth of the libra, as it is still. Gold shillings or quarter-solidi were struck by many of the Roman sovereigns, and are not uncommon in the great numismatic collections. In the same sense that sicilicus was issued for the fourth of the aureus, scrupulum was anciently used for the ninth and afterwards the tenth of the aureus.

The solidus of the above system is taken from the unique specimens extant attributed to Irene and Nicephorus, both of which are described and portrayed by Sabatier. The former has simply "Irene, Basileus," with her bust and a cross on both sides; the latter has "Nicephorus Basileus," with his bust on one side, and "IhSuS. XRISTVS. nICA," with a potency cross on the other. Nike, Nika, Nica, etc., means the Victor or Victorious, and it appears in the name of Nicephorus himself.

Coinage system under Basil I., A. D. 867-86. *Ratio of silver to gold*, 12 *for* 1.

20 noumia = 1 eikosarion.
2 eikosaria, or oboli = 1 copper follis.
6 folles = 1 silver keration, or siliqua, gross weight 41.46 = 34 grains standard.[1]
2 siliquas = 1 miliaresion, 68 grains standard.
12 miliaresia = 1 gold solidus, 68 grains standard.
5 solidi = 1 libra of account.
Hence 5,760 noumia = 1 gold solidus.

Coinage system under Basil II. and Constantine VIII., A. D. 976-1025. *Ratio of silver to gold*, 12 *for* 1.

20 noumia — 1 obolus.
2 oboli = 1 copper follis.
6 folles = 1 silver siliqua, 41.5 grains gross, or 34 grains standard.
2 siliquas = 1 miliaresion, 68 grains standard.
12 miliaresia = 1 gold solidus, 68 grains standard.
5 solidi = 1 libra of account.
Hence 5,760 noumia = 1 gold solidus.

1 This means when reduced to the same standard as the gold coins.

It will scarcely fail to be remarked that the number of noumia to the solidus exactly corresponds to the number of grains in the troy pound of the Western world—a circumstance that, remembering the common practice of the Romans to apply their subdivisions of money to measures of various kinds, suggests the origin of the troy pound weight. It has been the common method of metrologists to seek for the origin of moneys in weights. The present example, and many others mentioned in my "Middle Ages Revisited," leads to the belief that the converse is the fact, and that the origin of weights is to be found in moneys. In other words, that the first weights were coins, and that weights descended from coins, rather than coins from weights. This consideration, should it hold good, would vitiate a large portion of the laborious metrological work of Boeckh, Mommsen, Queipo and others.

With the system of Basil II. ends our review of the coinages of the Roman Empire, because, from his reign to the fall of Constantinople, they underwent no important changes; indeed, according to Finlay, none at all. The aureus of the succeeding Basilei varied from 68 grains, in the reign of Constantine Porphyrogenitus, to 65 grains in that of John Comnenus, and rose again in that of Eudoxia to 68 grains, where it remained to the end; while the denarius, siliqua, or argenteus, of which 24 went to the aureus, was coined at just half these weights, thus always maintaining the sacerdotal ratio of 12 silver to 1 gold. Even after the Empire fell and the Western States, as Venice, Florence, Amalfi, Aragon, etc., began to coin gold, they maintained the same ratio of 12 to 1 in their coinages, until this ratio came into conflict with the Moorish ratios in Andalusia and the Gothic ratios of the Baltic and Low Countries.

This review would be incomplete without some reference to the Western coinage systems that grew out of those of the Byzantine Empire, and especially the systems of the Meringovinian and Carlovingian dynasties. As a rule, political economists of the present day do not take the trouble to study the history of money; it is much easier to imagine it and to deduce the principles of this imaginary knowledge. Therefore but little information of a reliable character relating to this subject appears in their works. One of the most experienced, and yet the most recent writers of this class, repeats the idle tale to be found in many economical works, that Charlemagne invented the £. s. d. system still used in England.[1] In fact, Charlemagne neither invented the system nor struck the coins requisite to complete it. The libra was a money of account, the solidus he never struck; his coinage began and ended with the denarius, which formed merely the tail end of a system whose beginning belonged to a remote antiquity, and whose principal elements were still firmly held in the grasp of the Basileus.

The prerogative and monopoly of the gold coinage, except as to the Ponto-Bosporian guardians of the Asian temples and mysteries of Greek and Roman veneration, was never parted with, to subject-kings and vassal states, by the sovereign-pontiff of Rome. Even the Roman proconsuls, illustrious and powerful as were many of these officers, were not permitted to exercise this right until it was reluctantly conceded by Anastasius I. to Clovis, the Merovingian king of the Franks, and Amalric, king of the Visigoths of Spain, both of whom were proconsuls of Rome.

In his earlier coinages, Clovis (A. D. 481-512) appears to have adopted a ratio of 8 silver for 1 gold—a con-

[1] Mr. Henry Dunning MacLeod's "Bi-Metallism," London, 1894.

venient mean between the Roman ratio of 12 and the Indian ratios of 6¼ to 6½, which, even at that early period, must have exercised an influence upon the trade of the Baltic.[1] In his later coinages the ratio was 10 for 1.

The principal coins of Clovis were the solidus and triente, both of excellent gold, and both stamped with the effigy of Anastasius. Clovis also coined silver denarii, but at what tale relation to the gold coins is uncertain. The marks of Roman suzerainty which he placed upon his coins were repeated on those of his successors, Clodomir, Childebert I., and Clothaire I. At a later period the coinage of copper was added to that of gold and silver, and the marks of suzerainty were sometimes limited to the gold coins, until in the middle coinages of Theodebert, king of Austrasia (A. D. 534-47), they disappeared altogether, and in their place stood the effigy of the barbarian king and the legend D. N. THEODEBERTVS PP. AUG., or D. N. THEODEBERTVS. VICTOR.[2] This, of course, was a proclamation of defiance to the Basileus, and as such it was resented by Justinian and recorded by Procopius.[3] Notwithstanding the decrepitude of the Empire, its prestige was still so great, and veneration for its sacerdotal claims so widespread, that the example of Theodebert was avoided by his contemporaries, who refrained, with superstitious horror, from the impiety of striking gold without the authority of the Basileus. Yet Theodebert's revolt was not altogether without its influence. Little by little the marks of Byzantine suzerainty upon their rude coinages became fainter, and by the seventh century the Merovingian coins and mone-

---

[1] "Ancient Britain," index word, "Pagan Hansa."
[2] Lenormant, ii., 449.   [3] Procop. "Bell. Goth.," iii., 33.

tary regulations gave evidence of little more than a trace of Roman suzerainty. The following table of weights and valuations is derived from the coins and texts cited by Guerard, Lenormant, De Vienne and others:

Typical coinage system of the Merovingian kings during the seventh century. Ratio of silver to gold, 10 for 1.

12 (?) copper oboli	= 1 silver denarius, 17½ grains.
10 denarii	= 1 gold sicilicus, 17½ grains.
13⅓ denarii	= 1 gold triente, 23½ grains.
40 denarii	= 1 gold solidus, or coronatus, 70½ grains.
5 solidi	= 1 libra of account.

It was to these coronati that Pope Gregory referred when he said that they would not pass in Italy.[1]

The Empire of Gaul, lost by Byzantium, was soon recovered by Rome. An alliance with Pepin the Short ended the Merovingian dynasty, established the temporal power of the Roman bishops, and erected the dynasty of the Carlovingians. The coinage regulations, however, still continued subject to the Basileus, and doubtless formed part of that definitive treaty of partition which was made between Nicephorus I. and Charlemagne at Seltz in 802 or 803[2] Under this treaty it would seem that the coinage of gold was expressly reserved to the Basileus and of copper to the Byzantine Senate; for as a matter of fact from the accession of Charlemagne to the downfall of the Byzantine Empire in 1204, neither gold nor copper coins, but only silver ones, were struck by any Christian prince except the Basileus. The ratio of silver to gold, which the Merovingians had fixed at 10 for 1, was gradually changed by Charlemagne to the sacerdotal ratio of 12. It is this change of ratio which explains the frequently altered weights of Charlemagne's denarii, and his tale

[1] Freheri, 39.
[2] Authorities differ as to this date. Consult "Middle Ages Revisited."

relations of the Byzantine sou d'or, or gold sicilicus (shilling) to the libra of account.

Carlovingian coinage system under Pepin, A. D. 754. *Ratio of silver to gold,* 10 *for* 1.

10 silver denarii, 17½ grains (?) = 1 petite sou d'or, 17½ grains (?).
22 sous d'or = 1 livre de compte.

These sous d'or were coined by the Basileus. Sometimes the worn triente took the place of the sicilicus. The copper coins which circulated in Western Europe were also of Byzantine mintage. The silver coins alone were struck in the West. Pepin not only refrained from the coinage of gold, he forbade it to the princes subject to his authority. In both these respects he was followed by Charlemagne and all the Western "emperors" until the reign of Frederick II.

Carlovingian coinage system under Charlemagne, A. D. 803. *Ratio of silver to gold,* 12 *for* 1.

12 Byzantine coppers = 1 Carlovingian silver denier, 17½ grains.
12 deniers = 1 Byzantine sou d'or, 17½ grains.
20 sous d'or = 1 livre de compte.
Hence 240 deniers = 1 libra.

With regard to the value of gold and silver one to the other, it is to be observed that there are four distinct periods in the history of this relation. These are:

First, the period from the accession of Julius Cæsar to the fall of the Roman or Greek Empire in 1204, during which time the Roman government, by monopolizing the coinage of gold, and fixing the ratio between gold coins and silver, whether coined or otherwise, at 12 for 1, kept it constant and unaltered at that figure. As, during the same interval, the ratio in the Orient and the Arabian States was about 6½ for 1, and in the Gothic States 8 for 1, some variation from the Roman ratio is to be observed near the frontiers of the Empire, but not elsewhere.

Second, the period from the fall of Constantinople to

the enactment of Individual, Private, or Free coinage in Holland, England and other States in the sixteenth and seventeenth centuries. During this interval the various princes of the Occident began to coin gold, each for himself, and they fixed the ratio to suit their own interests or necessities. This period is characterized by the wildest dissonance of the ratio. It was a contest, on the one hand, between monarchs, who alternately raised their gold coins to the value of nearly twenty times their weight in silver (France in 1313), and raised their silver coins to the value of an equal weight in gold (France in 1359); and, on the other hand, their subjects and foreigners, who, until they adopted measures of avoidance or reprisal, were made the victims of these frequent and ruinous changes of value.

Third, the period from the adoption of individual or free coinage to the years 1867-75. The principal States of the Occident ceased to coin silver for individual account at the dates last mentioned. During this interval the ratio of value between gold and silver was the mint price, or the result of a competition between the mints of the principal States. For example, the value of gold in silver, during this interval, never rose above the highest price paid for it at any important mint, and never fell below the price paid for it at any other important mint. In other words, nobody gave more nor less in one metal for the other than the mints gave, and the mints gave whatever the law directed. The so-called "market value" of this period was simply what may be termed an international mint ratio.

Fourth, the period since 1867-75, when, silver being coined by the principal States on their own account alone, there arose in the West, for the first time since the establishment of free coinage, a general market value between gold and silver, entirely distinct from, and having only a remote relation to, their mint value.

CHAPTER II.

THE SACRED CHARACTER OF GOLD.

Coinage the surest mark of sovereignty—Abstention of the Christian princes from minting and coining gold, from Pepin to Frederick II.—Dates of the earliest Christian coinages of gold in the West—Inadequate reasons hitherto given to explain this singular circumstance—Opinions of Camden—Ruding—Father Joubert—The true reason given by Procopius—The coinage of gold was a Sacred Myth and a prerogative of the Roman emperor—Its origin and history—Braminical Code—The Myth during the Roman Republic—During the Civil Wars—Conquest of Egypt by Julius Cæsar—Seizure of the Oriental trade—The Sacred Myth embodied in the Julian Constitution—Popularity and longevity of the Myth—It was transmitted by the pagan to the Christian Church of Rome, and adopted by the latter—Its importance in throwing light upon the relations of the Western kingdoms to the Roman Empire.

THE right to coin money has always been and still remains the surest mark and announcement of sovereignty. A curious proof of this is afforded by the story told by Edward Thomas, in his "Pathan Kings of Delhi," of that Persian commander who, being suspected of a treasonable design towards his sovereign, diverted suspicion from himself to the king's son by coining and circulating pieces of money with the latter's superscription.[1] Says Mr. Thomas: "Some, perhaps many, of the Mahometan coinages of India constituted merely a sort of numismatic proclamation or assertion and declaration of conquest and supremacy." In ancient times such conquest and supremacy often embraced the triumph of an alien religion. Where printing was uncommon and the newspaper unknown, a new gold or silver coinage was the most effective means of proclaiming the accession of a new ruler or the era of

[1] "History Money," p. 89.

a new religion.[1] At the period of the earliest voyages of the Portuguese to India, the same significance was attached to the prerogative of coinage. Says Duarte Barbosa: "There are many other lords in Malabar who wish to call themselves kings, but they are not so, because they are not able to coin money. . . . The king of Cochin could not coin money, nor roof his house with tiles, under pain of losing his fief (to the king of Calicut, his suzerain); but since the Portuguese went there, he has been released from this, so that now he lords it absolutely and coins money." Father Du Halde, in his "History of China," makes a similar statement in reference to that country. Says he: "There were formerly twenty-two several places where money was fabricated, at which time there were princes so powerful that they were not contented with the rank of duke, but assumed the dignity of sovereigns; yet they never durst attempt to fabricate money, for, however weak the emperor's authority was, the coins have always had the stamp that he commanded."[2]

The custom of employing coins as a means of promulgating religious doctrine and official information was adopted by the Romans during the Commonwealth. It may be traced, at a later period, in the otherwise superfluous coinages of the Empire. Julius, Hadrian and Theodoric depicted the principal events of their reigns upon their coins. In the absence of felted paper and printing ink, it was the only means the ancients had of printing and disseminating the most important intelligence and opinions. Addison correctly regarded the Roman coinage as a sort of "State Gazette," in which

[1] Gibbon declared that were all other records destroyed the travels of the Emperor Hadrian could be shown from his coins alone. The Emperor Theodoric the Goth stamped his coins with the view to instruct posterity ("History Money," p. 89, n.)

[2] Duarte Barbosa, pp. 103 and 157; Du Halde, ii., 293.

all the great events of the Empire were periodically published. It had this advantage over any other kind of monument: it could not be successfully mutilated, forged, or suppressed. Especially is the fabrication and issuance of full legal-tender coins the mark of sovereignty. Towards the end of the Republic and during the Empire this attribute belonged alone to gold coins; therefore, to speak of these is to speak of full legal-tender money. Vassal princes, nobles and prelates, under the warrant of their suzerains, everywhere struck coins of silver, which, although legal tender in their own domains, were not so elsewhere, unless by special warrant from the Basileus; but no Christian vassal ever struck gold without intending to proclaim his own independent sovereignty and without being prepared to defy the suzerainty of the Cæsars.

Lenormant, in his great work on the "Moneys of Antiquity," holds similar language. "With the exception of the Sassanian coinages down to the reign of Sapor III., it is certain that the coinage of gold, no matter where, was always intended as a marked defiance to the pretensions of sovereignty by the Roman Empire; for example, during the period of the Republic, about B. C. 86, the gold coinages of Mithridates, in various places over which he had extended his conquests. The supremacy of Rome was so widely accepted both East and West, that for many centuries neither the provinces subject directly or indirectly to the Basileus, nor even the more or less independent States adjacent to the Empire, ever attempted to coin gold money. When gold was struck by such States it was as a local money of the Roman sovereign."[1] As such it yielded him seigniorage; it bore his stamp; its

[1] Lenormant, ii., 427.

use implied and acknowledged his suzerainty, both spiritual and temporal; while its issuance was subject to such regulations as he chose to impose.

Commodus refused to believe that his favorite Perennius aspired to the Empire until he was shown some pieces of provincial money, upon which appeared the effigy of his faithless minister.[1] Elagabalus condemned Valerius Pætus to death for striking some bijoux pieces of gold for his mistress, upon which he had imprudently caused his own image to be stamped.[2] The very first act of a Roman sovereign after his accession, election, or proclamation by the legions, was to strike coins, that act being deemed the surest mark of sovereignty. Vespasian, when proclaimed by the legions in Asia, hurried to strike gold and silver coins at Antioch.[3] Antoninus Diadumenus, the son of Macrinus, was no sooner nominated by the legions as the associate of his father in the Empire, than the latter hastened to strike money at Antioch in his son's name, in order to definitively proclaim his accession to the purple.[4] When Septimius Severus accepted his rival, Albinus, as his associate on the imperial throne, he coined money at Rome in the name of Albinus as evidence to the latter of his agreement and good faith.[5] Vopiscus, in his life of Firmus, asserts that the latter was no brigand, but a lawful sovereign, in whose name money had been coined. Pollion says that when Trebellius was elected emperor by the inhabitants of Isaurus, he immediately hastened to strike money as the sign of his accession to power.[6] When the partisans of Procopius, the rival of Valens, sought to win Illyria to their master's cause, they exhibited the gold aurei which bore his name and effigy, as evi-

[1] Herodian, i., 9.
[2] "Dion. Cass.," lxxix., 4.
[3] "Tact. Hist.," ii., 82.
[4] Lampridinus, in "Diadumenus," 2.
[5] Herodian, ii., 15.
[6] "Thirty Tyrants," xxv.

dence that he was the rightful head of the Roman Empire.[1] Moses of Khorene informs us that "when a new king of Persia ascended the throne, all the money in the royal treasury was recoined with his effigy."[2] Even when countermarks were stamped upon the Roman coins, care was taken never to deface the effigy of the sacred emperor.[3] The interchange of religious antipathy and defiance, which Abd-el-Melik and Justinian stamped upon their coins, is related elsewhere. Indeed, history is full of such instances. The coinage of money, and especially of gold, was always the prerogative of supreme authority.[4] The jealous monopoly of gold coinage by the sovereign-pontiff ascends to the Achimenides of Persia, that is to say, to Cyrus and Darius;[5] in fact, it ascends to the Bramins of India. The Greek and Roman Republics broke it down; Cæsar set it up again.

Assuming the common belief that the Christian princes of mediæval Europe were in all respects independent sovereigns before the destruction of the Roman Empire by the fall of Constantinople, in 1204, it is difficult to explain the circumstance that none of them ever struck a gold coin before that event, and that all of them struck gold coins immediately afterwards. There was no abstention from gold coinage by either the Goths, the Celts, the Greeks, or the Romans-of-the-Commonwealth; there was no abstention from gold coinage by the Merovingian Franks or the Arabians of later ages; there was no lack of gold mines or of gold river-washings in any of the provinces or countries of the West; there was no want of knowledge concerning the manner of raising, smelting or stamping gold; yet we find the

1 "Ammianus Marcellinus," xxvi., 7. 3 Lenormant, ii., 389; iii., 389.
2 Lavoix, MS., p. 12. 4 Lavoix, MS., p. 16.
5 Lenormant, ii., 195, 196.

strange fact that wherever the authority of the Roman sovereign-pontiff was established, there and then the coinage, nay, sometimes even the production, of gold at once stopped. It must be borne in mind that it is not the use of gold coins to which reference is made, but the coinage—the minting and stamping of gold. In England gold coins, except during the early days of the Heptarchy, have been in use from the remotest era to the present time. Such coins were either Gothic (including Saxon), Celtic, Frankish or Moslem, but never Roman, unless struck by or under the sovereign-pontiff. In a word, for more than thirteen centuries— that is, from Augustus to Alexis IV.—the gold coins of the Empire, East and West, were struck exclusively by the Basileus. Again, from the eighth to the thirteenth century, a period of five hundred years, we have no evidence of any native Christian gold coinage under any of the kings of Britain. With the exception of a unique and dubious coin, now in the Paris collection, which bears the effigy of Louis le Debonnaire, the same is true of France, Germany, Italy; indeed, of all the provinces of the Empire whose princes were Christians.

Before pointing out the significance of these circumstances, it will be useful to clear the ground by examining the explanations of others. Camden conjectures that "ignorance" was the cause; but Dr. Ruding very justly remarks that it could not have been ignorance of refining or coining gold, because silver, a much more difficult metal to treat, and one that in its natural state is nearly always combined with gold, had been refined and coined in Britain for many ages.[1] Dr. Ruding and Lord Liverpool both have supposed that coins of gold were not wanted during the middle ages; but this is worse than Camden's conjecture, for it flies in the

[1] Camden's "Remains," art. "Money," p. 241.

face of a palpable fact. That gold coins were indeed wanted is proved by the very common use of gold aurei, solidi, folles, or besants throughout all this period. Not only this, but the Arabian gold dinar, or mancus, was current in all the countries of the North; and either this coin or the gold maravedi was the principal medium of exchange in the trade of the Baltic.

Another explanation which has been advanced is, that the confusion caused by the conquests or revolts of the barbarians resulted in the closure of the gold mines, and rendered gold metal too scarce for coinage into money. Explanations which take no heed of the truth, made either in ignorance or desperation, may be multiplied indefinitely without serving any useful end. The facts were precisely the reverse of what is here assumed. It was the barbarians who opened the gold mines and the Christians who closed them. The heretical Moslem, Franks, Avars, Saxons, Norsemen and English all opened gold mines during the mediæval ages. The moment these people became Christians, or were conquered or brought under the control of the Roman hierarchy, their gold mines began to be abandoned and closed.[1]

All such futile explanations are effectually answered by the common use of Byzantine gold coins throughout Christendom. In England, for example, the exchequer rolls relating to the mediæval ages, collated by Madox, prove that payments in gold besants were made every day, and that gold coins, as compared with silver ones, were as common then as now.[2] If metal had been wanted for making English gold coins, it was to be had in sufficiency and at once. All that was necessary was

[1] "History Precious Metals;" "History Money."
[2] Lord Liverpool does not appear to have perused this valuable and instructive work. For other historical omissions in his Letter to the King, see Sir David Balfour's Memorandum of October 20, 1887.

to throw the besants into the English melting-pot. As for the feeble suggestion that for five hundred years no Christian princes wished to coin gold so long as the Basileus was willing to coin for them, when the coinage of gold was the universally recognized mark of sovereignty, and when, also, the profit, as we shall presently see, was one hundred per cent, it is scarcely worth answering. The greatest historians of the mediæval ages—Montesquieu, Gibbon, Robertson, Hallam, Guizot, etc.—have neither remarked these facts nor sought for any explanation concerning the gold coinage. In their days the science of numismatics had not yet freed itself from the toils of the sophist and forger, and it offered but little aid to historical investigations. It has since become their chief reliance.

The true reason why gold money was always used but never coined by the princes of the mediæval empire, relates not to any circumstances connected with the production, plentifulness, scarcity or metallurgical treatment of gold, but to that hierarchical constitution of pagan Rome, which afterwards with modifications became the constitution of Christian Rome. Under this constitution, and from the epoch of Julius to that of Alexis, the mining and coinage of gold was a prerogative attached to the office of the sovereign-pontiff, and was, therefore, an article of the Roman constitution and of the Roman religion. Although it is probable that during the dark and middle ages the prerogative of mining was violated by many who would never have dared to commit the more easily detected sacrilege of coinage, there are no evidences of such violation by Christians.

The mines of Kremnitz, which contained both silver and gold, and which Agricola says were opened in

A. D. 550, were in the territory of the pagan Avars; the gold washings of the Elbe, re-opened in 719, were in the hands of the pagan Saxons and Merovingian Franks; so were the gold washings of the Rhine, Rhone and Garonne; the gold mines of Africa and Spain, re-opened in the eighth century, were worked by the heretical Moslem; the gold mines of Kaurzim, in Bohemia, opened in 998, were managed by pagan Czechs. Whenever and wherever Christianity was established, gold mining appears to have been relinquished to the Basileus or abandoned altogether. So long as the Byzantine empire lasted, neither the emperor of the West, nor any of the other princes of Christendom, except the Basileus himself, seem to have conducted or permitted gold mining.

With regard to gold coinage the facts are simple and indisputable. Julius Cæsar erected the coinage of gold into a sacerdotal prerogative; this prerogative was attached to the sovereign and his successors, not as the emperors, but as the high priests of Rome; it was enjoyed by every Basileus, whether pagan or Christian, of the joint and Eastern empires from the Julian conquest of Alexandria to the papal destruction of Constantinople; the pieces bore the rayed effigies of the deified Cæsars, and some of them the legend "Theos Sebastos." When emperor-worship was succeeded by Christianity they bore the effigy of Jesus Christ.[1] It would have been sacrilege, punishable by torture, death

---

[1] William Till (p. 39) says that Justin II. (A. D. 565-78) first struck the aureus (solidus, or besant) with the effigy of Christ and the legend "Dominus Noster, Jesus Christus, rex regnantium," and that this practice was observed down to the fall of the Byzantine empire. This statement is erroneous in several respects. The first name of Christ on the Roman coins was never spelled "Jesus," but, successively, "Ihs," "Issus," and "Iesus." The effigy of Christ did not appear on the coins of Justin II. It first appeared on a gold solidus of Justinian II. (Rhinotmetus), who reigned 685-95, and again 705-11 (Sabatier, "Monnaies Byzantines," ii., 22).

and anathema for any other prince than the sovereign-pontiff to strike coins of gold; it would have been sacrilege to give currency to any others; hence no other Christian prince, not even the pope of Rome, nor the sovereign of the Western or Mediæval "empire," attempted to coin gold while the ancient Empire survived.

Says Procopius: "Every liberty was given by the Basileus Justinian I. to subordinate princes to coin silver as much as they chose, but they must not strike gold coins, no matter how much gold they possessed;" and he intimates that the distinction was neither new nor its significance doubtful. Theophanus (eighth century), Cedrenus (eleventh century), and Zonaras (twelfth century) state that Justinian II. broke the peace of 686 with Abd-el-Melik because the latter paid his tribute in pieces of gold which bore not the effigy of the Roman emperor. In vain the Arabian caliph pleaded that the coins were of full weight and fineness, and that the Arabian merchants would not accept coins of the Roman type. Here are the exact words of Zonaras: "Justinian broke the treaty with the Arabs because the annual tribute was paid, not in pieces with the imperial effigy, but after a new type, and it is not permitted to stamp gold coins with any other effigy but that of the emperor of Rome.'" The "new type" complained of probably had as much to do with the matter as the absence of

1 From the period A. D. 645, when their conquests deprived the Roman empire of the bulk of its Asiatic and African possessions, to about the beginning of the eighth century. the Arabians struck coins with the effigy of the Roman emperor and the emblems P and the cross. At that period they struck coins still with these emblems, but in place of the emperor's effigy, that of Abd-el-Melik with a drawn sword in hand. Like the maravedis of Henry III. (1257) and the nobles of Edward III. (1344), the issue of these coins amounted to an assertion of independent sovereignty, and as such was resented by Justinian. To the nummulary proclamation of the Arabian: "The servant of God, Abd-el-Melik, Emir-el-Moumenin," the Roman replied: "Our Lord Justinian, servant of Christ."

Justinian's effigy. That new type was the effigy of Abd-el-Melik with a drawn sword in his hand, and the Mahometan religious formula: a triple offense—an insult, a defiance and a sacrilege.

The privilege accorded to subject-kings with regard to silver was extended to both mining and coinage. Silver mining and coinage was conducted by all the Western princes, the Western emperor included. The pope disposed of a few coining privileges to new or weak States, or dependent bishoprics, the Western emperor disposed of others to the commercial cities; but for the most part silver was coined by the feudal princes, each for himself, and not under any continuing prerogative of the empire, whether ancient or mediæval.

The following table shows some of the earliest gold coinages of Christian Europe:—

1225. NAPLES (Amalfi).—Aurei, or augustals, of Frederick II.; 81 to 82 English grains fine.

1225. LEON.—Gold ducats of Alfonso, gross weight 54½ English grains, with the following inscription in Arabic: "In the name of the Father, Son, and holy Ghost, God is One. He who believes and is baptized will be saved. This dinar was struck in Medina Toleitola, in the year 1225, month of Saphar."[1] Here is a curious mixture of doctrines and dates.

1225. PORTUGAL.—Gold ducats of Sancho I., weighing 54½ grains gross.

1226. FRANCE.—Louis IX. Pavillon d'or, De Saulcy, "Documents," I., 115—25.

1241. FAENZA, Siege of.—Leather notes issued by Frederick, payable in gold augustals. Yale's "Marco Polo."

[1] Although this can hardly be deemed a Christian coin, I have included it in the table. Heiss publishes a gold coin with "Ferdinand" on one side, and "In nomine Patris et Filii Spiritus sanctus," on the other, which he ascribes to Ferdinand I. (II.), 1157-88; but Saez is positive that it is a sueldo of Ferdinand II. (III.), 1230-52. There is about the same difference of time between the Julian and Christian eras. The next gold coins, after those of Alfonso, were either the sueldos of Barba Robea, in the thirteenth century, or the Alfonsines struck by Alfonso XI., of Castile, 1312-50. The latter had a castle of three turrets on one side, and a rampant lion on the other. Gross weight 67.89 English grains (Heiss (i., 51; iii., 218).

THE SACRED CHARACTER OF GOLD 77

1250. FRANCE.—Gold agnels, or dinars, struck for Louis IX, by Blanche, his mother. Weight 63⅓ grains gross.[1]
1252. FLORENCE.—Republican zecchins or florins, 56 grains fine.
1252. GENOA.—Gold "genovinas."
1257. ENGLAND.—Pennies, or maravedis, of Henry III., 43 grains fine.
1265. FLANDERS.—Mantelets d'or. De Saulcy.
1276. VENICE.—Zecchins or sequins, 55¾ grains fine.
1300. BOH. AND POL.—Ducats of Veneslas, 54½ grains gross.
1312. CASTILE.—Alfonso XI. Doblas, valued at 100 pesetas.
1316. AVIGNON.—Sequins of Pope John XXII., 54½ grains fine.[2]
1325. GERMANY.—Louis IV. Ducats.
1336. ARRAGON.—Pedro IV. Florines.
1339. HOLLAND AND HAINAULT.—Ducats.
1340. GUELDERLAND.—Duke Rainhold. Ducats.
1342. LUBECK.—Patent from Louis IV. Ducats.
1344. ENGLAND.—Edward III. Nobles.
1356. HOLLAND.—William V. Ducats.
1357. FLANDERS.—Louis II. Ducats.
1372. NUREMBERG.—Frederick, under patent from the Emp. of Ger. Ducats.
1496. DEN. AND NOR.—Eight-mark piece of John, 240 grains gross.[3]

That Christian Europe abstained from coining gold for five centuries because such coinage was a prerogative of the Basileus, is an explanation that may not be acceptable to the old school of historians; but this is not a sufficient reason for its rejection. The old school

[1] Baron Malestroict ("Inst.," p. 4.) ascribes the first gold agnel to Blanche of Castile, as regent of France during the minority of Louis XI. Patin ("History of Coins," p. 38) repeats that they were struck by Blanche as regent, but says nothing more. As Blanche was regent a second time (during the sixth crusade, 1248-52), these coins were probably struck in 1250 to defray the expenses of that war. Louis' ransom of 100,000 marks was probably paid in silver. "There were sent to Louis in talents, in sterlings, and in approved money of Cologne (not the base coins of Paris or Tours), eleven waggons of money, each loaded with two iron-hooped barrels" (M. Paris, sub anno 1250, vol. ii., pp. 342, 378, 380). Humphreys (p. 532) ascribes these agnels to Philip le Hardi, 1270-85; but there is no reason to doubt the earlier and more explicit authority of Malestroict, Le Blanc, and Patin, nor the more recent judgment of Lenormant ("Monnaies et Médailles," p. 228) and Hoffman ("Monnaies Royale").

[2] This pope is responsible for a treatise on the transmutation of metals, the prolific exemplar of many similar works.

[3] The eight-mark piece and its fractions, of King Hans (John), A. D. 1481-1512, are in the Christiania Collection. The type of these coins is evidently copied from the nobles of Edward III., minted from 1351 to 1360.

would have been very greedy of knowledge if they had not left something for the new school to discover.

In his "Science des Médailles" (i., 208-11), Father Joubert, and after him other numismatists, observing the strange abstention of the Christian princes from coining gold, and perhaps anxious to supply a reason for it which would have the effect to discourage any further examination of so suggestive a topic, invented or promulgated the ingenious doctrine that the Roman emperors from the time of Augustus were invested, *in like manner*, with the power to coin both gold and silver. If this doctrine enjoyed the advantage of being sound, it would deprive the long abstention from gold coinage by the Western princes of much of its significance; because, assuming that the coinage of gold and silver stood upon the same footing, and remembering that all the Christian princes coined silver, their omission to coin gold might, with some reason, be attributed to indifference. But that Father Joubert's doctrine is not sound is easily proved.

I. With the accession of Julius Cæsar was enacted a new and memorable change in the monetary system of Rome. The gold aureus was made the sole unlimited universal legal-tender coin of the empire; the silver and copper coins were limited and localized in legal tender; the ratio of gold to silver in the coinage was suddenly—and in the face of greatly increased supplies of gold bullion—raised from 9 silver to 12 silver for 1 gold; and the mining and commerce of gold were seized, controlled, and strictly monopolized by the sovereign-pontiff; whereas the mining of silver was thrown open to subsidiary princes and certain privileged individuals.[1] With the production of gold thus limited to pontifical

[1] The exportation of gold had been previously controlled by the Senate. Cæsar made it a prerogative of the sovereign-pontiff.

control, and that of silver thrown open to numerous persons, the coinage of the two metals in like manner, or under like conditions, was totally impracticable and historically untrue.[1]

II. As will presently be shown more at length, the imperial treasury—which was kept distinct from the public treasury, and known by another name—was organized as a sacred institution; its chief officer, then or later on, was invested with a sacred title; the coinage of gold, which was placed under its management, was exercised as a sacred prerogative; and the coins themselves were stamped with sacred emblems and legends.[2] On the contrary, the coinage of silver was a secular prerogative; it belonged to the emperor as a secular monarch, and as such it was thrown open to the subsidiary princes, nobles and cities of the empire, while that of copper-bronze was resigned to the Senate. These are not like conditions of coinage, but, on the contrary, very unlike ones.

III. From the accession of Julius to the fall of Constantinople, the ratio of value between gold and silver within the Roman empire, whether pagan or Christian, was always 1 to 12; whereas, during the same interval, it was 1 to $6\frac{1}{2}$ in India, as well as in the Arabian empires, in Asia, Africa and Spain; and it was 1 to 8 in Freisland, Scandinavia, and the Baltic provinces. It is inconceivable that one single unvarying ratio of 1 to 12 should have been maintained for centuries by the innumerable and irreconcilable feudal provinces of the Roman empire, if the freedom to coin silver, exercised by the feudal princes, was in like manner extended to gold.

[1] See "History Money," chapter xxv., for further consideration of this subject.
[2] The officers of the sacred fisc, who were stationed in the provinces to superintend the collection of gold for the sacred mint at Constantinople, are mentioned in the Notitia Imperii.

IV. The authority of ancient writers is conclusive on this subject. Cicero, Pliny, Procopius, and Zonaras, though they lived in distant ages, all concur in representing that the coinage of the two precious metals was not conducted in like manner nor under like conditions.

V. The authority of modern writers, for example, Letronne, Mommsen, and Lenormant, is to the same effect. This absolutely closes the subject, and completely disposes of Father Joubert.

The sacerdotal character conferred upon gold, or the coinage of gold, was not a novelty of the Julian constitution; rather was it an ancient myth put to new political use. Concerning the testimony of witnesses, the very ancient Hindu Code says: "By speaking falsely in a cause concerning gold, he kills the born and the unborn"—an extreme anathema. Stealing sacred gold is classed with the highest crimes.[1] A similar solicitude and veneration for gold occurs elsewhere throughout these laws. The Budhists made it unlawful to mine for, or even to handle gold, probably because the Bramins had used it as an engine of tyranny. According to Mr. Ball, this superstition is still observed in some remote parts of India. It is possible that, in some instances, the sacerdotal character attached to gold by the Bramins belonged only to such of it as had been paid to the priests, or consecrated to the temples, and that when the priests paid it away it was no longer sacred; but the texts will not always bear this reading. For example: "He who steals a suvarna" (suvarna, a gold coin) "dies on a dunghill, is turned to a serpent, and rots in hell until the dissolution of the universe," (*vide* Braminical inscription found on copperplate dug up at Raiwan, in Delhi).[2] The same superstition occurs

[1] Halhed's "Gentoo Code," viii., 99; ix., 237.
[2] "Jour. Asiat. Soc. Bengal," lvi., 118.

among the ancient Egyptians, Persians and Jews. There are frequent allusions to it in the pages of Herodotus. For example, Targitaus, the first king of Scythia, a thousand years before Darius, the sacred king of Persia (this would make it about B. C. 1500), was the divine son of Jupiter and a daughter of the river Borysthenes or Dneister. In the kingdom of Targitaus gold was found in abundance, but being deemed sacred, it was reserved for the use of the sacred king. In another place Herodotus relates that in the reign of Darius, B. C. 521 (of whom Lenormant says, in his great work on the "Moneys of Antiquity," that he reserved the coinage of gold to himself absolutely), Aryandes, his viceroy in Egypt, struck a silver coin to resemble the gold darics of the king. Possibly, to make the resemblance greater, it was also gilded. For this offense Aryandes was condemned as a traitor and executed.[1] Josephus makes many allusions to the sacredness of gold. A similar belief is to be noticed among the ancient Greeks, whose coinages, except during the republican era, were conducted in the temples and under the supervision of priests. Upon these issues were stamped the symbolism and religion of the State, and as only the priesthood could correctly illustrate these mysteries of their own creation, the coinage—at least that of the more precious pieces—naturally became a prerogative of their order. Rawlinson notices that the Parthian kings, even after they threw off the Syro-Macedonian yoke, never ventured to strike gold coins.[2] The reason probably was that in place of the Syro-Macedonian yoke they had accepted the Roman, and that the Roman (imperial) law forbade the coinage of gold to subject-princes.

[1] Mel., 7, 166; Lenormant, i., 173.
[2] Geo. Rawlinson, "Seventh Monarchy," p 70.

Whatever credit or significance be accorded or denied to these ancient glimpses of the myth, its significance becomes clearer when it is viewed through the accounts of the Roman historians. The Sacred Myth of Gold appears in Rome at the period when the history of the Gaulish invasion of A. U. 369 was written. The story runs that after the eternal city had been saved from the barbarians, it was held by the Roman leaders that to the gold which had been taken from the mass belonging to the temples should be added the gold contributed by the women towards making up the ransom, or indemnity, of a thousand pounds weight, and that all of it should thenceforth be regarded as sacred. Says Livy: "The gold which had been rescued from payment to the Gauls, as also what had been, during the hurry of the alarm, carried from the other temples into the recess of Jupiter's temple, was altogether judged to be sacred, and ordered to be deposited together under the throne of Jupiter."[1]

At this period, according to Pliny, the Roman money was entirely of bronze. If this is true, all offerings of money to the temples must have been in bronze coins. If the object of conferring a sacerdotal character upon gold was merely to preserve the ecclesiastical treasure from violation, it is inexplicable that the same sacred character was not also conferred upon the current bronze money. It is far more consistent with the grossly superstitious character of the age to believe that the Romans (of the period when this legend was penned) were taught to regard all gold, except such as was worn upon the person, as sacred; and that the object of pronouncing the gold in the jewels contributed by the Roman women to be sacred, was to prevent its ever being again worn as jewelry. This gold had saved

[1] Livy, v., 50.

Rome, for although it is said it was not actually paid to the Gauls, the delay attending the weighing of it had given time for Camillus to advance to the rescue of the beleaguered citadel and drive the barbarians away. There was no less reason for rendering sacred the gold in the jewels, whose weighing had saved the city, than the geese whose cackling had contributed to the same happy event. However, it is possible that, as yet, a sacred character was only attached to such gold as had been consecrated to the gods.

The social, servile and civil wars of Rome were characterized by great disorders of the currency, and during the latter, that is to say, in B. C. 91, Livius Drusus, a tribune of the people, authorized the coinage of silver denarii, alloyed with "one-eighth part of copper," which was a lowering of the long established standard. As the civil wars continued, a portion of the silver coinage was still further debased, and the denarius, whose legal value had long been 16 aces, was lowered to 10 aces. Later on we hear of the issue of copper denarii plated to resemble those of silver. It is possibly to these debased or plated coins that Sallust alludes when he says that by a law of Valerius Flaccus, the Interrex, under Sylla (B. C. 86), "argentum ære solutum est," *i. e.* silver is now paid with bronze. Valleius Paterculus explained the operation of this law differently, in saying that it obliged all creditors to accept in full payment only a fourth part of what was due them. These explanations afford a proof that at this period the gold coins were not sole legal tenders. The discontent produced among commercial classes by this law of Valerius Flaccus, induced the College of Prætors (B. C. 84) to restore the silver money to its ancient standard by instituting what we would now call a trial of the pix. Sylla, enraged at this interference with the coinage and the political designs connected with it, annulled the decree of the prætors, proscribed their leader, Marius Gratidianus, as a traitor, and handed him over to Catiline, by whom he was executed.[1]

Sylla's lex nummaria (B. C. 83), which prescribed the punishment of fire and water, or the mines, to the forgers of gold and silver coins, implies that at this period the immunity which perhaps previously, and certainly afterwards, attended gold coins, was not yet secured. About B. C. 82, Q. Antonius Balbus, an urban prætor, was authorized by the Senate, then controlled by the partisans of Marius, to collect the sacred treasure from the temples and turn it into coins. This money was employed in the struggle with Sylla. It is to this period, doubtless, that Cicero afterwards referred when he said: "At that time the currency was in such a fluctuating state, that no man knew what he was worth."[2] After Sylla's triumph over Marius, and his resignation of the dictatorship (B. C. 79), the ancient standard of silver coinage was restored; and the opulent citizens, in order to express their approbation of this measure, erected full length statues of the unfortunate Marius Gratidianus in various parts of Rome. About B. C. 69, Cicero alluded to the public treasury as the "sanctius ærarium." This expression, in connection with the coins struck by Antonius Balbus, from consecrated treasure and the statues erected to Marius Gratidianus, all point to this period as that of the adoption of the sacredness of gold in the Roman law.

About this time the Jews appear to have again acquired some share in that lucrative trade with India

[1] Modern writers on money have expended a great deal of false sentiment on Gratidianus. Cicero, who was his relative and possibly knew him better, proves him a liar, cheat, demagogue, and traitor (Off., iii., 20.)

[2] Off., iii., 30.

which they had formerly shared with the Greeks, and which has ever been a source of contention and hatred among the states of the Levant. The principal channel of this trade was now by the Nile and the Red Sea, and was in the hands of the Ptolemaic rulers of Egypt. A portion of it, however, went overland by Palmyra; and from this portion Jerusalem derived important commercial advantages. Such as they were, these advantages were lost to the Jews and acquired by Rome, when, in B. C. 63, Pompey and Scaurus snatched Judea from the contentious Maccabees, and established over it a Roman government.[1] In B. C. 59 Cicero said: "The Senate, on several different occasions, but more strictly during my consulship, prohibited the exportation of gold." (Exportare aurum non oportere cum sæpe antea Senatus tum me consule gravissime judicavit.)[2] Cicero was consul four years previously, that is to say, in B. C. 63. "Exportation" here seems to mean transmission from one province of the Roman empire to another, because elsewhere, in the same pleading, Cicero says: "Flaccus" (a proconsul of Syria) "by a public edict prohibited its exportation" (that of gold) "from Asia." The introduction of the word "Italy" in Cicero's plea for Flaccus, can only be regarded as a means of enlisting the prejudice of the judges. Here is the passage in full: "Since our gold has been annually carried out of Italy and all the Roman provinces by the Jews, to Jerusalem, Flaccus, by a public edict, prohibited its exportation from Asia." The Jews probably bought gold (with silver) in the provinces between Judea and India, because it was cheaper in those places than in

---

[1] The Maccabees struck the earliest Jewish coins. These were called sicals or shekels, the same name given to coins by the ancient Hindus, with whom sicca meant a mint, or "minted," or "cut." The Arabians of a later period also borrowed the same term.

[2] "Orat. pro L. Flacco," c. 28.

Europe. They may have bought silver in Greece or Italy, but unless their commercial pre-eminence is a trait of altogether modern growth, it is hard to believe that they bought gold in Italy, when it could have been obtained nearer by, at two-thirds the price. The penalty which this unlucky people have paid for their ill-starred attempts to share in the Greek and Roman profits of the oriental trade has been more than two thousand years of oppression and ostracism.

The conquest of Egypt by Julius Cæsar (B. C. 48) threw the whole of the oriental trade into the hands of Rome. Canals connecting the Mediterranean and Red Seas had been constructed successively by Necho,[1] Darius and Ptolemy; and shortly after the Julian conquest, one of these canals was used for the voyages of the Indian fleet.[2] A century or so later Pliny recorded the fact that a hundred million sesterces' worth of silver (equal in value to one million gold aurei) was annually exported to India and China.[3] The numerical proportions of the gold and silver ratios in Europe and India indicate that this trade was not a new one, and that a similar trade had been conducted by the Ptolemies and by the Babylonians and Assyrians upward to a remote era of the commercial intercourse between the Eastern

---

[1] Herodotus, Clio, 202; Eut., 158; Mel., 39.

[2] Strabo. At a later period the inter-oceanic canal became clogged with drifting sand, and was reopened by Trajan or Hadrian. probably the latter. It was kept open by the Byzantine emperors. See Marcianus in Morise' "Orbis Martimus," and Anderson's "History of Commerce." It v reopened by Amrou in A. D. 639, during the reign of the cal' The Ptolemaic (and Roman) route was by Alexandria, the Nile, the Canal, Berenice, Sabia, and Muscat. It is fully described in the "Periplus maris erythræi" of Arrian.

[3] Minimaque computatione millies centena millia sestertium annis omnibus India et Seres peninsulaque illa imperio nostro adimunt. Tanto nobis deliciæ et feminæ constant ("Nat. History," xii., 18.) In another place (vi., 23) he puts it at half this sum, "Quingenties I. I. S.," for India alone. The "feminine luxuries" imported in exchange included gold, silk, and spices. Numbers of the silver coins exported to India at this period have been found during the present century buried in Budhist topes.

and Western worlds.[1] During the Ptolemaic period the ratio was 10 for 1 in Europe, and 12½ for 1 in Egypt, whilst it was 6 to 6¼ for 1 in the Orient. In other words, a ton weight of gold could be bought in India for about 6¼ tons of silver, and coined, in Egypt, into gold pieces worth 12½ tons of silver.[2] The profit was therefore cent per cent, and even after the Romans conquered Egypt, the rate of profit on exchanges of Western silver for Eastern gold was quite or nearly as great. This explains what seems so abstruse a puzzle to the industrious but uncommercial Pliny: he could not understand why his countrymen "always demanded silver and not gold from conquered races."[3] One reason was that the Roman government knew where to sell this silver at a usurer's profit. When this profit ceased, as it did when the oriental trade was abandoned, the Roman government entirely altered its policy. During the middle ages it preferred to collect its tributes in gold coin.

When the enormous difference in the legal value of the precious metals in the Occident and Orient is considered, and that, too, at a period when maritime trade between these regions was not uncommon, it is impossible to resist the conviction that the superior value of gold in the West was created by means of legal and, perhaps, also sacerdotal ordinances. This method of fixing the ratio may even have originated in the Orient.

Colebrook[4] states that the ancient Hindus struck gold

[1] "Hist. Money, Ancient," p. 71.
[2] Lenormant, i., 146-51.
[3] Equidem miror P. R. victis gentibus in tributo argentum imperitasse non aurum ("Nat. Hist." xxxiii., 15).
[4] "Asiat. Researches," London, 1799, v., 91. Meninsky, in his "Thesaurus Ling. Orient.," p. 1897, voc. "Chœsrewani," says that, in the time of Chosrœs (A. D. 531-79), the Persians worshiped the dirhems of that monarch. If we read "venerated" for "worshiped," and "dinars" for "dirhems," we shall probably get nearer to the truth. Chosrœs the deified was so successful in his wars against Justinian, that the latter

coins, which were multiples of the christnala, the latter containing about 2¼ English grains fine. According to Queipo,[1] five christnalas equaled a masha of 11¼ grains and 80 christnalas a tola, or suvarna, of 180 grains. This system appears to have originated at two different periods, the octonary relations belonging to the remote period of the Solar worship, and the quinquennial to the Braminical period. Dished gold coins (scyphates) of the type afterwards imitated in the besant, called "ramtenkis," and regarded as sacred money, were struck in India at a very remote period. The usual weights were about 180, 360 and 720 English grains (1, 2 and 4 tolas). One example weighed 1,485 grains, and was probably intended for 8 tolas sicca. The gold being alloyed with silver gave a pale appearance to the pieces. The extant coins contain no legible dates or inscriptions, and are much worn by repeated kissing. The emblems upon them are the sacred ones of Rama, Sita and Hunuman. They were evidently held in high veneration by the Bramins. Facsimiles of these coins have been published in the "Journal of the Asiatic Society of Bengal."[2] In the Braminical coinages the value of silver seems to have been lowered from 4 (to 5) for 1 gold; and though in later coinages the value of silver was again lowered, as before stated, to about 6¼ for 1 gold, the general tendency in the Orient was to maintain the value of silver, and in the Occident to raise that of gold. So that, although the

was obliged to pay him an annual tribute of forty thousand pieces of gold (sacred besants). These were most likely the pieces that, upon being recoined in Persia, were venerated by its subservient populace Von Strahlenberg (p 330) says that the Iestiaks or Ocs-tiaks, near Samarow, venerated a cufic coin of the Arabians, from whom they had captured it. In a tomb near the river Irtisch, between the salt lake Iamischewa and the city Om-Iestroch, a flat oval gold coin that had evidently been used as an object of worship, was found and delivered to Prince Gagarin, the governor of Siberia (about A. D. 171).

1 Queipo, i., 449-52.   2 "Journ. Asiat. Soc. Bengal," liii., 207-11.

system of deriving a profit from the device of altering the ratio was probably of oriental origin, the practical operation of this system—certainly at the periods embraced within the Greek and Roman histories—was precisely opposite in the Western world to what it was in the Eastern. The governments of Persia, Assyria, Egypt, Greece and Rome made a profit on the coinage by raising the value of gold, while those of India, China, and perhaps also Japan, made their profit by maintaining, or enhancing, the value of silver. In the last named State silver was valued at 8 (some say at 4) to 1 of gold, at one of which ratios it stood so late as 1858.

It is evident that, by continuing the use of this myth, or by attaching a sacerdotal character to the coinage and coins of gold, which in Italy may hitherto have only been attached to consecrated deposits of gold—a character which the conqueror, who was also the *pontifex maximus* of Rome, was quite competent to confer upon it—he would not only acquire the means to republish upon its coins the mythology and religious symbols of the empire, altered to accord with his own impious pretensions of divine origin, but he would also be enabled to reap profits equal to those which the Ptolemies had derived from the oriental trade. Indeed, in this respect Cæsar made another innovation: he increased the Roman ratio from 9 to 12 for 1, and there it remained fixed, in consequence of his ordinance, for thirteen centuries.

That Cæsar attached a sacerdotal character to the gold coins of Rome, and that Augustus and his successors, both the pagan and Christian sovereign-pontiffs of the empire, continued and maintained this sacred character is so abundantly evidenced that it has never been disputed. It is only in assigning reasons for the measures that numismatists have differed. Evelyn believed that the gold coins were rendered sacred to preserve them from profanation and secure them from abuse.[1] Others have found the origin of this regulation in the desire to preserve the most precious monuments of Roman antiquity from the melting pot, and they point to the numerous coinage restorations of Trajan as a proof of the Roman anxiety on this subject. The reasons herein suggested as the true ones are, first, the usefulness of coins to proclaim monarchical and pontifical accessions, and to disseminate religious doctrine; and, second, the profits of the oriental trade, which could only be secured by means of an ordinance enjoying the sanctity of religious authority. These reasons even receive confirmation from the contrary regulations adopted by the Arabians. Whether in scorn of the Roman mythology, or else to enhance the value of the immense silver spoil which they had derived from the conquest of the Roman provinces in Asia, Africa and Spain, or because they were unable or unwilling to continue that pretense of sacredness, partly by means of which so artificially high a valuation of gold had been created in Europe, it appears that when the Arabians came to permanently regulate the affairs of the conquered provinces (reform of Abd-el-Melik) they swept away the mythological emblems upon the coins for all time, and for several centuries they destroyed the sacred character of gold. They issued plain coins of constant weight and fineness, and reduced the ratio to the Indian level (then) of $6\frac{1}{2}$ for 1.

Whatever reasons induced Cæsar to enhance the value of gold, there can be no doubt of the fact. In the scrupulum coinages of A. U. 437 the ratio was 10

[1] Evelyn, "Medals," 224-7.

silver for 1 gold; in the coinage system of Sylla (A. U. 675) the ratio was 9 for 1. Cæsar raised the value of his gold coins by a double jump to 12 for 1; in other words, without changing its value in silver coins, he gradually lowered the aureus from 168⅓ to 125 grains fine, and this alteration he sanctified and rendered permanent by stamping upon the coins the most sacred devices and solemn legends. If this great politician of antiquity endeared himself to the masses by thus lowering the measure of indebtedness, he secured for his empire the approval of the patrician and commercial classes by securing its stability, for the ratio which he adopted and solemnized was never changed until Rome dissolved into a mere name—a name by which ambitious princes afterward continued to conjure, but which at that late period really belonged to a dead and powerless empire.

In that admirable review of the Byzantine empire which forms the subject of Gibbon's seventeenth chapter, he declares that by law the imperial taxes during the dark ages were payable in gold coins alone.[1] We now know the reason of this ordinance—the oriental trade was gone. The custom of the period was that when gold coins were not paid, silver coins were accepted instead, at the sacred weight ratio of 12. In the reign of Theodosius the officer entrusted with the gold coinage was the *Comes Sacrarum Largitionum*, or Count of the Sacred Trust, one of the twenty-seven *illustres*, or greatest nobles, of the empire. His powers supplanted those of the former *quæstori præfecti ærarii* and other high officers of the treasury. His jurisdiction extended over the mines whence gold was extracted, over the mints in which it was converted into coins, over the revenues which, being payable in

[1] Same, in his Misc. works, iii., 460.

gold coins, kept the latter in use and demand, and over the treasuries, in which gold was deposited for the service of the sacred emperor or in exchange for silver. Even the woolen and linen manufactures and the foreign trade of the empire were originally placed under the control of this minister, with the view, no doubt, to regulate that exchange of Western silver for oriental gold, of which some remains existed at the period of these elaborate and subtle arrangements.

It is the peculiarity of sacerdotal ordinances that they long outlive the purpose intended to be subserved by their enactment. In the hot climates of India, Egypt, Palestine and Arabia the interdiction of certain meats for food may possibly have been originally founded upon hygienic considerations—a fact that may have commended this ordinance to local acceptation, but certainly did not earn for it that general and continued observance which it owes to the Braminical, Jewish and Mahometan religions. It is not to be wondered that Justinian I. rebuked Theodoret the Frank for striking heretical gold coins, nor that Justinian II. proclaimed war against Abd-el-Melik for presuming to pay his tribute in other heretical gold; but it certainly seems strange to find this myth observed in distant ages and among distant nations—for example, to witness the pagan Danes of the mediæval ages solemnizing their oaths upon baugs of sacred gold; to find Henry III., of England, after plundering the Jews of London, receiving the gold into his own hands, but the silver by the hands of others; and to discover that Philip II., of Spain, attempted to re-enact in America this played-out myth of idolatrous India, Egypt and Rome.[1]

[1] Procop. "Bel. Got.," iii., 33; Lenormant ii., 453, 454; Du Chaillu, "Viking Age;" Matthew Paris, i., 459; "Recopilacion de Leyes de los Reynos de las Indias," law of 1565.

The importance of this myth, in throwing light upon the political relations of the Roman provinces toward the Byzantine and Western or mediæval empires, does not depend either upon its antiquity or the reasons of its adoption into the Roman constitution, nor upon its general acceptance or popularity. It is sufficient for the purpose if it can be shown that, as a matter of fact, the sovereign-pontiff alone enjoyed the prerogative of coining gold throughout the Empire, and that the princes of the Empire respected this prerogative. It is submitted that concerning this cardinal fact the evidences herein adduced are sufficient.

CHAPTER III.

POUNDS, SHILLINGS AND PENCE.

This system appears in the Theodosian Code—Is probably older—Its essential characteristic is valuation by moneys of account—Advantages—Previous diversity of coins—Danger of the loss of numismatic monuments—Exportation of silver to India—Difficulty of enforcing contracts of coins of a given metal—£. s d. as an instrument of taxation—As an historical clew—It always followed Christianity—Sidelights to history afforded by the three denominations—£. s. d. and the Feudal system—It saved the most precious monuments of antiquity from destruction—Artificial character of the system—Its earliest establishment in the provinces—In Britain—Interrupted in some provinces by barbarian systems—Its restoration proves the resumption of Roman government—This rule applied to Britain.

SEARCHING for the beginning of a custom is like tracing a river back to its source: we soon discover that it has not one source but many. When brevity is preferable to precision, it is sufficient if we follow an institution to its principal or practical source.

We have elsewhere shown the marks of chronological stratification in Roman history—originally decimal and afterwards duodecimal—which resulted from a change that, it is assumed, took place in the method of measuring the solar circle. This, we are persuaded, was originally divided into ten parts, each of 36 degrees; hence the archaic Roman or Etruscan year of ten months, each of 36 days, and the week or *nundinum* of nine days. At a later period the zodiac was divided into twelve parts, each of 30 degrees, whence the year of twelve months, each of 30 days.[1] In these two sys-

---

[1] By some writers the year of 360 days has been erroneously called a lunar year, but in fact a year contains nearly thirteen lunar months. The year of twelve months was originally solar, and was always astrological. Many of the early institutes mentioned by Livy, Pliny, and Censorinus were evidently taken from the laws of conquered and obliterated Etruria, and falsely attributed to Romulus, Numa, and other creations of Roman fancy. Among these institutes was the change from ten months of 36 days to twelve months of 30 days to the year (Livy, i., 19).

tems we have the basis of the decimal and duodecimal methods of notation, which are so strangely intermingled in all Roman numbers and proportions, and which also appear in £. s. d. Thus the number of solidi to the libra was five, and the number of sicilici to the libra twenty, both of which are decimal proportions.[1] On the other hand, the number of denarii to the sicilicus was twelve, and the ratio between the metals was twelve, which is duodecimal.[2]

Those writers whose researches into monetary systems are bounded by the narrow conclusions of Adam Smith's "Wealth of Nations" or Tooke's "History of Prices" usually attribute the origin of £. s. d. to William the Norman or to Charlemagne, and their explanation of the system is commonly confined to that of the £., which they regard as the symbol for a pound weight of silver, or else a pound weight of silver coins. The different books in which this delusion is repeated are probably sufficiently numerous to stock a good sized library; yet it can be demolished in a few words. Neither the contents of the Norman or Carlovingian nor of any other coins sustain this theory, neither is

[1] The "pound" of money is to be discerned during the decay of Attic liberty. The Romans used the term "pondus" to mean 100 drachmas, and the Greeks used the "talenton" of money before them. Twenty drachmas (silver) equaled in value one stater, and five staters were valued at a talenton, which the Romans called a pondus. The Greek ratio was 10. Most of the confusion on this subject has resulted from the refusal of numismatic writers to recognize—what their own monetary systems of to-day attest—that every name of a weight also meant at the same time a sum of money, which had no relation to such weight. Humphreys, Chambers and Putnam all furnish confused references to the pondus of 100 drachmas. The Persians in the time of Cyrus appear to have had a system of £. s. d. very like what the Romans afterward had.

[2] A remarkable custom, which, it may reasonably be conjectured, originated in the changed subdivision of the zodiac, prevailed among the Goths. With them the ten meant twelve, and an hundred was six score. The custom still prevails in Essex, Norfolk and Scotland (Sir Francis Palgrave, i., 97). Some vestige of the score system still lingers in the French names for numbers. Curiously enough, too, the method of counting by scores was employed by the Aztecs (Prescott, p. 35).

it sustained by the texts of the Carlovingian or any other period. The libra of money (not the whole triad of £ s. d.) is at least five hundred and may be fifteen hundred years older than Charlemagne, being clearly defined in the Theodosian Code (lib. xiii.,tit. ii.,11), of which the following is the text and literal translation:—
"Ita ut pro singulis libris argenti quinos solidos inferat" —"So that for each libra of money five solidi are to be understood."[1] This portion of the code is attributed by some commentators to the constitutions of Constantine, by others to a law of Honorius and Arcadius (A.D. 397);[2] but, as shown elsewhere, the libra of five gold pieces is older than either. It was used for five gold aurei by Caligula, Probus and Diocletian. It frequently occurs in the texts of Valens,[3] Arcadius and other sovereign-pontiffs of the fourth to the eighth century, where, except in one instance, it always means five solidi. According to Father Mariana ("De Pondéris et Mensures"), the sicilicus—known in a subsequent age as the gold shill-

[1] It is from this passage in the Theodosian Code that the learned Boeckh, Rome d'Lisle, and Bodin regarded the libra as a weight, and deduced the supposed ratio between silver and gold of 14.4 to 1. It is needless to say that if the libra was a money of account and not a weight, the deduction is erroneous. There is no instance of such a ratio of 14.4, or thereabouts, in Roman or Greek history—a fact which by itself should have rendered these erudite persons more cautious. The Code of Justinian (liber. x., tit. lxxvi., de argenti pretio) also gives the ratio, "pro libra argenti, 5 solidi."

[2] Queipo, ii., 56.

[3] The cupidity of the Duke of Moesia induced him to withhold provisions from the Gothic refugees, whom Valens, the sovereign-pontiff, had permitted to enter that province, so that a slave (*mancipium*) was given by the Goths for a loaf of bread (*unum panem*) and ten libras (of money) for a carcass of meat (*aut decem libras in unum carnem mercarentur*). It is evident that ten libras meant precisely what the law declared it should mean, namely, 50 solidi (equal to the contents of about 32 English sovereigns), for ten pounds weight of gold would contain as much as 464 English sovereigns. Gibbon avoids the difficulty by saying "the word *silver* must be understood;" but such was not the custom of that time, any more than it is now. When silver was understood it meant *money* and not metal. Said the law: "So that for each libra (libris argenti) five solidi (of gold) are to be understood" (Jornandes, "De Getarum," c. xxvi.; Gibbon, ii., 597, 4to ed.)

ing—was struck as early as the first century of our era, for he states that in his own collection were gold pieces of this weight, struck by Faustina, Augusta, Vespasian and Nero. Others of Justinian, weighing 16 grains, are now in the Madrid collection. The denarius of the early empire, of which 25 in value went to the aureus, tallied in weight, though not in fineness, with the half-aureus. In the reign of Caracalla 24 denarii went to the aureus, the ratio of value between the metals remaining unchanged. Such is briefly the genesis of £. s. d.

The translation of "argentum" into "money" needs no explanation to Continental readers, for in all the Continental languages—French, Spanish, Italian, etc.—"silver" means money. This custom is derived from the Romans of the Empire, with whom "argentum" meant money, as the following examples sufficiently prove:—Argentariæ tabernæ, bankers' shops (Livy); argentaria inopia, want of money (Plautus); argentarius, treasurer (Plautus); argentei sc. nummi, or money (Pliny, xvi., 3); ubi argenti venas aurique sequuntur (Lucretius, vi., 808); cum argentum esset expositum in ædibus (Cicero); emunxi argento senes (Terrence); concisum argentum in titulos faciesque minutas (Juvenal xiv., 291); tenue argentum venæque secundæ (*ibid.*, ix., 31). The Romans in turn got this term from the ancient Greeks, whose literature they studied and whose customs they affected. One of the Greek names for money was "argyrion," from *argyros*, silver. The Hebrew word for money was *caseph*, literally silver, alluding to the coined shekels of the Babylonians. The same custom, *i. e.*, using the term "silver" for money, is to be found in the most ancient writings of Egypt and India.

In a letter of Honorius and Theodosius II. to the Prefect of Gaul, written in our year of 418, after suggesting the formation of a council to regulate the affairs of that province, the emperors proposed, in case its members failed to attend the meetings, to subject them to fines of three and five "libras of gold" each. It is evident that the "libras" here mentioned are moneys and not weights, for five Roman libras weight of gold are equal to the quantity contained in 232 English sovereigns of the present day, and this would have been a preposterously heavy mulct for mere non-attendance. On the other hand, a libra of account represented by five gold solidi, would not have contained more than one-fourteenth of this quantity of gold, and it is evident that this is what was intended.

These researches into the origin of £. s. d. were necessary in order to determine its essential characteristics as a system of valuations and proportions. The names of the subdivisions of money have in all ages been used to denote the relative proportions or subdivisions of other measures, as of weight, area, capacity, etc., and it is this practice which is responsible for much of that confusion on the subject of money that distinguishes economical literature. For example, £. s. d. were at one time used as proportions of the pound weight for weighing bread, at another time as proportions of the acre for measuring land. In the former case £. represented a pound weight of bread, s. an ounce, etc.; in the latter £. meant one and a-half acres and d. a rod of land.[1] Sir Francis Palgrave (i., 93) says that many instances of this practice are to be found in charters of the sixth century. The mischief of it lies in the insinuation it conveys that because a "pound" weight can be the unit, integer, or standard of weight,

[1] Statute 51, Henry III. (1267); Fleetwood's "Chronicon Preciosum."

and a "pound" measure (one and a-half acres) can be the unit of superficial area, so a "pound" sum of money can be the unit of money, which in the last case is physically impossible. The unit of money can never be one "pound," but must necessarily be all the "pounds," under the same legal jurisdiction, joined together. In other words, the unit of money is and must necessarily be all money.[1]

Taking the essential character of £. s. d. to be a system of valuation by moneys of account, as distinguished from a system of valuation by coins, it must have possessed merits that rendered its adoption highly necessary and advantageous. We shall find that this was actually the case. Previous to the adoption of £. s. d. there was commonly but one denomination of money and—except in the peculiar monetary system of the Roman Commonwealth—it usually related to an actual coin. With the Romans this coin was successively the ace, denarius, sesterce and aureus. Even when two of these kinds of coins circulated side by side—as the ace and the denarius, or the sesterce and aureus—sums of money were always couched in one denomination, never in both. We now say so many pounds and shillings and pence, perhaps combining some of each denomination in one sum; or we may say so many dollars and cents, or so many francs and centimes. Down to the era of £. s. d. the Romans, in expressing sums of money, only used one term. So long as only one or two or three kinds of coins were current at the same time, there was no inconvenience in this custom; but when coins came to be made of different sizes and weights and of several different metals—bronze, silver and gold—some of them of limited tender and highly over-valued, like the bronze

[1] See chapter on this subject in the author's "Science of Money."

coins of to-day, one term for money became inexact and inconvenient. This is one of the reasons that led to the adoption of £. s. d.

In the last quarter of the third century the Roman empire was divided between four Cæsars, to whom was afterwards added he whom Sir Francis Palgrave has rather effusively termed "our own Carausius." Even before this division took place, the diversity of bronze and silver coins was so great as to produce confusion. With four emperors almost daily adopting new designs for coins, and several thousand unauthorized moneyers expelled from Mount Cælius and other places to ply their trade in every province of the Roman empire, the confusion became intolerable. Without some device by aid of which this maddening variety of types and weights could be readily harmonized and valued, it became impossible to carry on the operations of trade. Such a device was £. s. d.

The infinite diversity and number of local and imperial silver coins had long since broken down that fragment of the fiduciary system of money which was attempted to be revived by Augustus; it had effaced all the influence of mine-royalties; it had nullified all the effects of mint-charges and seigniorage. The relative value of coins, which Rome was formerly content to read in the edicts of her consuls or emperors, she was now almost compelled to determine with a pair of scales. The imperial government could scarcely have observed this symptom of popular distrust without grave concern. In proportion as such coins lost fiduciary value, and rested upon that of their metallic contents, so did the empire lose importance to the provinces and the proconsuls to the local chieftains. Furthermore, when money ceased to derive any portion of its value from limitation of issue or from sacerdotal and imperial authority, why might not the proconsuls feel at liberty to issue circulating money as well as the sovereign-pontiff? why not the under-lords as well as the proconsuls? why not foreigners as well as citizens?—why not anybody or everybody?

Besides this, it is to be remembered that the coins of Rome were designed to illustrate its mythology and history, and that they constituted its most precious and enduring monuments. Upon them were stamped the story of its miraculous origin, the images of its gods, demi-gods and heroes, the symbols of its religion, the spirit of its laws, and the dates of its most glorious achievements. All these now threatened to disappear in the melting-pot. The monuments had come to be regarded only as so much bullion, and every provincial governor or barbarian king would be tempted to reduce them to metal, in order that, upon recoining them, his own upstart image might shine in the glass that had once reflected a Romulus, a Cæsar, or an Augustus. There was but one way to stop such a calamity, and that way was monopoly of the coinage and arbitrary valuation; but this had to be done through some new device, for the old ones were worn out, and would be seen through and rejected at once.[1] The efforts to save the old monuments would justify a slight discrimination of value at the outset in favor of certain precious issues, and this discrimination might be extended and enlarged as time went on. Rome had hitherto kept its most sacred numismatic monuments from the furnace by means of a golden myth, a fixed ratio, and the restric-

---

[1] In a less superstitious age perhaps not even the device of £. s. d. would have allayed the fear that the valuations would be changed, or have kept the coins from the melting-pot. But to the Romans that law was a sacred one, which forbade the melting down of old coins (Digest i., c. de Auri pub. prosecut.; lib. xii., 13; Camden, "Brit.," p. 105).

tion of exports. Without disturbing either of these arrangements, it was now proposed to supplement them with the device of £. s. d.

The diversity of coins, and the hope of restoring some of their lost fiduciary value, furnished reasons for the adoption of a triad of monetary terms, in the place of that single term in which the Romans had hitherto couched their valuations and contracts; but the same considerations do not explain why these denominations were essentially ideal ones, nor why they remain so still. The explanation is simple enough. It will be found in the physical impossibility of adding together quantities of various materials and producing a quotient of one material. If £. means a piece of gold, s. a piece of silver, and d. a piece of bronze, then as a matter of fact it is impossible to add them together and produce a sum which shall represent a quantity of any one of these metals. Hence these denominations are essentially ideal. However, as logic seldom stands in the way of practical legislation, we may be sure that it was not this difficulty which compelled the Romans, when they adopted £. s. d., to make them ideal moneys, or moneys of account, that would logically add together; it was the practical difficulty of enforcing contracts payable in coins of a particular metal. Numbers of the mine-slaves had revolted, or escaped, to swell the armies of the Goths and other malcontents; the produce of the Roman mines had become irregular; the oriental trade had absorbed vast quantities of silver.[1] A contract to pay sesterces meant so many silver coins, and the name sesterce had been so long wedded to a silver coin that it was found easier to establish a new denomination than divorce sesterce from silver. The same may be said of the gold aureus. £. s. d. being

[1] Pliny, "Natural History," vi , 23, and xii., 18.

imaginary moneys, might be represented by either gold, silver or bronze coins at pleasure of the government, and as best suited the convenience of the times or the equity of payments.[1]

It is scarcely necessary to turn from the public to the private influences which urged the adoption of £. s. d. upon the imperial and pontifical mind. A monetary system which by insensible degrees might be made to slip away from all metallic anchorage or limitation, needed no further recommendation to a needy treasury. Yet it still had another one. The diversity of races that constituted the population of the Empire and a nascent feudal system both stood in the way of any uniform system of taxation, while the distance between Rome and the capital of each province greatly multiplied frauds upon the treasury, and threw too much power and profit in the hands of the provincial vicars or proconsuls and the greedy farmers of the revenues. The facility to regulate the value of various coins which the adoption of £. s. d. promised to afford, placed in the hands of the sovereign-pontiff the means of levying a tax that could neither be evaded nor intercepted.

Thus many reasons and interests combined to recommend the system of £. s. d. It brought into harmony the diversity of coins and coinages; it promised to restore some of the lost value of bronze and silver coins, and to conserve or obliterate (at pleasure) the ancient and sacred types; it offered to remedy the difficulties produced by the irregular supplies of the mines, and by the heavy exports of silver to India; it placed a

[1] In 1604 the Chief Justices of England decided that £. s. d. were imaginary moneys, and meant concretely whatever coins the sovereign from time to time might decree they should mean. They deduced this conclusion, not only from the spirit of the common, but also from the principles of the civil law; and there can be no doubt that such was its legal significance at the period of its original adoption in Rome (State Trials, ii., 114; Digest, xviii., 11).

future choice of other remedies in the hands of the emperor; and, finally, it was competent, at a pinch, to solve the problem of suddenly recouping an empty treasury. Under the system of £. s. d. any coin or piece of money could be legalized or decried at pleasure of the government, and any value could be put upon it that seemed expedient or desirable. All that was needed was a brief edict of the supreme sovereign, and at once, with military precision, this or that piece of money took its allotted station among the £. s. d., and there it served in the capacity and with the rank assigned to it by its imperial master.[1]

In the fourth century the d. was represented by a silver coin, and the s. by a gold coin containing about 18 (afterwards 16) grains of fine gold, and the £. by five large solidi (afterwards called besants), each containing 72 (afterwards 64) grains of fine gold.

If we follow the adoption of £. s. d. in the various provinces of Europe—for example, Gaul, Britain, Spain or Germany—it will be found that it never preceded, whilst it invariably followed, the establishment of Roman Christianity. It therefore furnishes a valuable guide to the date of such establishment, and to the restoration of Roman government. £. s. d. was adopted in Gaul by Clovis, in a part of England it was established by Ethelbert, whilst in other parts it was rejected by the unconverted Gothic kings, his contemporaries.[2]

[1] On different occasions the same coin has ranked as a penny three-half-pence, two-pence, and even three-pence. A shilling was at one time represented by a gold coin, at another by a silver coin. Examples of this character often occur in the ordinances of the mediæval kings of France; and there is reason to believe that the sovereign-pontiffs of Rome more than once altered the legal value of their silver and bronze issues.

[1] The name of the sicilicus, which is evidently derived either from the fourth of the aureus or else from the fifteen-grain gold pieces of Sicily, was applied to the Norse aurar in the laws of Ethelbert (Sections 33-35). From the context it is evident that fifty scats are less in value than three

So the Arian Goths of Spain, down to the close of Roderic's reign, refused both the Roman religion and the Roman system of money, and the Saxons would have none of either until Charlemagne bent their stubborn necks to the yoke of the Roman gospel.

Another valuable historical sidelight is derived from £. s. d. The arithmetical relations of these moneys of account were originally, but have not been always, 12×20=240. Sometimes they were 5×48=240, or 4×60=240, or even (exceptionally) 5×60=300. Whenever this is observed it affords a sure indication of grafting. The Gothic ratio between the precious metals was 8, the Arabian ratio 6½, and the Roman ratio 12. Consequently, when the Roman arithmetical relations of £. s. d. were grafted on Gothic or Arabian, or Gothic-Arabian, monetary systems they had to be modified to suit the local valuation of gold and silver.[1] For example, in the eighth century in Roman Christian Gaul (ratio of 12) it took 12 silver pence, each of 16 grains, to equal in legal value 1 gold sicilicus of similar weight, whilst in the Gothic parts of Britain, where the Arabian ratio prevailed (ratio of 6½), 5 silver pence, each of 20 grains, sufficed; so that if, as convenience dictated, the newly introduced £. was still to consist of shillings, hence that the purely silver scat of five to the gold shilling was not yet in use, and that the scats alluded to were the old rude ones of composite metal, weighing 7½ grains and upwards, and of varying and uncertain metallic contents.

The shilling of Ethelbert's laws is the earliest mention of that coin in England. There was as yet no Norse analogue, either for the libra or the penny; in other words, there was no twelfth of the aurar nor any twenty-aurar piece, hence there was no further application of £. s. d. at that time to Gothic coins. The Roman "pounds, shillings and pence" had yet to be fully established in England. Some of the gold sicilici of the heretical Roger II., of Sicily, bear the legend in Arabic: "One God; Mahomet is His Prophet." On the other side is the phallic sign. A specimen, somewhat worn, weighed by the writer, contained 15 grains gross. These shillings were evidently copied from older Sicilian coins of the same weight and type.

1 The system of Offa, king of Mercia, was Gothic-Arabian, and, as is elsewhere shown, some of his coins had Arabian inscriptions upon them.

240 pence, it would have to be valued at 48 shillings of account, and this was accordingly done.[1] Modifications in the weights of the silver penny, and efforts to harmonize the two principal conflicting ratios—the Roman and Arabian—will explain, not only the remaining variations of £. s. d. above alluded to, but also many other obscure problems connected with the early monetary systems of England.

We have seen how £. s. d. arose out of the circumstances of a decaying empire; we shall now see how it accommodated itself to those circumstances, so as to promote the very disease it was in part designated to remedy. The empire was falling to pieces, splitting into many parts. First, it had one Cæsar, then two, three, four or more. Even when it got rid of its Thirty Tyrants, and reduced the number to six, the diversity of coins and coinages was too bewildering for practical purposes. To harmonize and regulate these coins, as well as for other reasons, £. s. d. was adopted. Yet by accommodating itself to a diversity of moneys, this system prevented the evil from righting itself through the simple and efficacious means of re-coinage. Dispensing with the necessity of uniformity, it encouraged heterogeneity by rendering it less intolerable, and thus facilitated that splitting up and subdivision of the coining authority which characterized the matured feudal system, and lent it strength and support. Devised in part to unify moneys and centralize authority, it became no insignificant aid to decentralization and feudalism. On the other hand, but for its influence the Roman coins, and with them the memories which they invoked and the sacred myths they perpetuated, would have been destroyed, and the modern world would have had to read the history of the past in the unmeaning baugs of

[1] System of Ethelbert, king of Kent, 725-60.

Scandinavia, the saigas of Frakkland, or the composite scats of the Anglo-Saxon heptarchy.

Returning to the historical clew afforded by the adoption of £. s. d., the reader will scarcely fail to have been impressed with the extreme artificiality of this system. Hundreds of books have already been written upon it, and hundreds more will probably yet be written upon it before its true character, mischievous bearing, and incongruity with the modern age of progress will be recognized and acted upon. Allusion is here made, not merely to a system of three denominations, as £. s. d., nor to a mingled bi-decimal and duodecimal notation, nor to its character as money of account, but to the mingling in this system of imperial with provincial and municipal or other coins; of seigniored with non-seigniored coins; of coins with various degrees of legal tender; of coins of local with others of extensive legal tender; of native with foreign coins made legal tender; of redeemable with non-redeemable coins; of governmental with private (bank) issues of various degrees of legal tender; and of non interest-bearing with interest-bearing legal-tender issues. In these respects and others the principles of all the monetary systems of the present day originated in the Roman imperial system of £. s. d., and so far as they follow it they interpose important obstacles to the practice of equity, the just diffusion of wealth, and the progress of civilization.[1]

The £. s. d. system was as much unfitted for the Gothic kingdoms or fiefs of the dark ages as it was suitable for the Empire. In a former work it was shown that there existed a natural harmony, or tendency toward harmony, between systems of government and systems of money, just as there is between social phases

[1] "Science of Money," chapter vi.

and language. For example, if one of the sentences of Cicero or Tacitus were imputed to a savage orator, no matter how eloquent or renowned, the unfitness of the phraseology, and its lack of harmony with the social phase of the speaker, would a once expose the blunder or imposture. Similarly, if an £. s. d. system of money were attributed to a tribe of Zulus, the incongruity of the collocation would immediately stamp it as untrue. For not only are three denominations of money too artificial a means of valuation to fall within the mental compass of a barbarian tribe, one of them (the £.) was always an ideal money, and all of them were maintained, and could only be maintained, by a mint code of extreme complexity, and covering mining, minting, seigniorage, artificial ratio between the precious metals, and a hundred other subjects, concerning which neither Zulu nor Goth ever had a clear conception. For these various reasons the artificial system of £. s. d. furnishes an unerring clew to historical researches during the dark ages. In a previous chapter similar clews were found in the golden myth and the sacred ratio of twelve; in the present one we shall follow the clew of the three denominations.

The text of the Theodosian Code implies the use of £. s. d. at Rome and in all the Christian provinces of the Empire. The non-Christian provinces were those parts of Gaul and Britain which, at the time of the promulgation of this code, were temporarily under the control of Anglo-Saxon, Frankish and other barbarian chieftains. The letter of Honorius and Theodosius II. (A. D. 418) implies the use of £. s. d. at that date in southern and perhaps central Gaul. From 496 to 561, during the governments of the Roman patricians Clovis and Clothaire I., the £. s. d. system was probably established throughout the whole of Gaul, except Brittany, Burgundy and Provence. The Roman coins found buried with the body of Childeric,[1] and more especially the Roman offices and titles accepted by the Merovingian Frankish princes down to the sixth century, when image-worship was insisted upon, or, still worse, when the assassin Phocas was worshiped at Rome, imply the continuance of Roman government in Gaul until that period. After this time, and until the reign of Pepin, many of the provinces forgot their allegiance.[2] Over and over again the Franks had professed and evinced their willingness to live under Roman law and Roman government, and they proved their sincerity and good faith in these professions by accepting Roman ecclesiastics as the administrators of that law and the representatives of that government. So long as Rome inculcated the worship of a heavenly deity the Franks continued loyal to the empire, but when the Roman pontiff fell at the feet of Phocas, and the detested religion of emperor-worship seemed about to be revived in the very fane of religion, they turned upon the Empire.[3] From Theodebert to Pepin the Short the Roman monetary system was interrupted in Gaul. Its place was partly filled with a Frankish system, in which the relative value of gold and silver, no longer kept in place by the sacred myth of Rome, fell back to the old Druidical (and Etruscan) ratio, or else obeyed, to a certain extent, the influence of the Moslem mint-laws of Spain and Southern Gaul, for it became 1 to 10 instead of 1 to 8. The gold sou, or solidus,

[1] His tomb was opened in the seventeenth century (Morell, 67).
[2] The Merovingians struck gold under authority of the Basileus until the reign of Theodebert, who struck gold for himself. Yet even after this period many of the Merovingians coined under authority of the Basileus.
[3] Charlemagne, at the Council of Frankfort (794), denounced the worship of the imperial images.

was valued in Merovingian laws at 40 silver deniers, or denarii; the little sou, or sicilicus, was valued in the same laws at 10 silver deniers, the sicilicus and denier containing the same weight of metal. The first fact is from the texts of the period, the last from the coins themselves. The establishment of this system was the mark of Frankish independence from the empire. It lasted about a century and a half; after that Gaul again became a Roman province.[1]

In short, the monetary system of £. s. d. was established wherever Roman government prevailed—in Italy, Greece, Asia Minor, Armenia, Egypt, Carthage, Spain, Gaul, Britain and Germany. It was not established by any state or people not subject to Rome, never by the pagan Angles, Jutes, Saxons, Franks, Sclavs or Huns, and never by the Moslem, whether in Arabia, Egypt, Africa, Spain, France or Persia. After the dry bones of the sacred Empire fell into the hands of the Turks, in the fifteenth century, the latter, in order to accommodate their nummulary language, so far as practicable, to the customs of the conquered Greek provinces, employed the £. and the d. to mean—not indeed what they formerly meant—but something that suggested it, and this practice afterwards found its way into other provinces of Turkey; but it had no essential connection with the £. s. d. system, and employed only two denominations instead of the characteristic three.

Although it is probable that the libra of money (not the £. s. d. system) continued to be used in the Roman cities of Britain from the Roman period down to the time when these cities fell into the hands of the Anglo-Saxons, we have no certain evidence of the fact. The

[1] The earliest rehabilitation of the Roman system appears in the capitulary of Pepin and Carloman, A. D. 743, wherein the sol is valued at 12 deniers (Guizot, iii., 27).

earliest implication of the £. s. d. system in any document now extant occurs in the barbarian laws of Ethelbert, A. D. 561-616 (ss. 33-5), where certain fines are levied in shillings. No "libras" are mentioned; and no denarii for twelfths of the Norse aurar;[1] hence no entire adoption of the system can be positively inferred. The shilling of Ethelbert was probably either a Latin name for a coin identical in weight with the Norse aurar, or an anachronism, inserted by copyists at a later date.[2] In neither case would this text afford any certain indication when the £. s. d. system was re-introduced into Britain; and there is no other evidence that can be relied upon of an earlier date than the reign of Ina, which was toward the end of the seventh century.

Measured by the clew of £. s. d., the Anglo-Saxon chieftains interrupted the continuity of Roman government in some parts of Britain during an interval of more than two centuries, that is to say, from a date somewhat later than the edict of Arcadius and Honorius to the reign of Ina. In other parts there was scarcely any interval at all, for many of the Roman cities of Britain held out long after the legions departed, and even then, they capitulated on terms which involved, if they did not expressly admit, the imperial supremacy of Rome.

So far as it goes, the clew of £. s. d. harmonizes with the myth of gold and the sacred ratio, and they all corroborate those other evidences which proclaim that except during a comparatively brief interval, which was probably no greater in Britain than in Gaul, the former

---

[1] See Roman gold coin of Canterbury mentioned in my "Ancient Britain," ch. xix.

[2] Bishop Fleetwood ("Chronicon Preciosum," pp. 52-4) gives examples from Brompton's translations of the laws of Ethelstan and Ina, in which the terminology and valuations of money were changed to suit the circumstances of the translator's times. Guerard and De Vienne give examples of similar alterations in the ancient texts of the Frankish, Lombardian, Frisian, and Burgundian codes of law.

remained a province of the empire from the reign of Claudius down to a much later period than is commonly supposed.[1]

[1] Mr. Freeman deemed it probable that at the end of the sixth century there were still Roman towns in Britain tributary to the English chieftains, rather than occupied by them. Sir Francis Palgrave (i., vi.) extends the Roman occupation of some British cities down to the seventh century. Du Bos, Savigny, and Gibbon concur in a similar belief with regard to some of the cities of Gaul.

CHAPTER IV.

GOTHIC MONEYS.

Proofs that the earlier sagas were altered in the mediæval ages—Among these is their frequent mention of baug-money: an institution which did not survive the contact of Norsemen and Romans—Progressive order of Norse moneys—Fish, vadmal, and baug moneys—The baug traced from Tartary to Gotland, Saxony and Britain—Gold baugs acquired a sacerdotal character—This was probably immediately after Norse and Roman Contact—Subsequent relinquishment of baug-money and the adoption of coins—Proof that Cæsar encountered Norse tribes in Britain, derived from his mention of baugs—This view corroborated by archæology and philology—Subsequent Norse coinage system of stycas, scats, and oras—Important historical conclusions derived from this study.

It needs but a cursory examination of the earlier sagas to be satisfied that they have been grossly mutilated. They jumble together events hundreds of years apart; they mingle details which belong to communities as yet ignorant of Roman customs with the affairs of communities well acquainted with them; they resurrect the Turkish or Scythian forefathers of the Norsemen, and set them down in the midst of mediæval Christian saints; they omit all mention of Rome or Roman affairs, or the Roman religion, or the causes of difference between the Norsemen and the Empire; they eschew dates, ignore the calendar, and commit the pagan festival to oblivion. The silly explanation which has been offered to us of this disorder is that the sagas were popular songs,[1] which were repeated by word of mouth for centuries before they were committed to writing, and that this custom produced the confusion, omissions, anachronisms, and other defects which now characterize them. There might have been a time when such an

[1] Tacitus ("Germania," iii.) mentions the folk-songs of the Northern tribes.

explanation was sufficient, but the class of people who offer them forget that the world grows and that knowledge is cumulative. We now know that language without a written literature to fix its terms and meanings is too ephemeral to last for centuries, indeed, that a few generations mark the utmost time during which it will remain unaltered. It was reliance upon this principle that led to the distrust of Macpherson's forged "Ossian," and that compels us to regard as mutilations the Eddas as produced by Saemund Sigfusson and Snorri Sturlason.[1]

In the present connection the liability of unwritten language to rapid mutation proves one of two things— either that the earlier sagas are mediæval fabrications in Latin, translated into the mediæval Norse and re-translated into the vernacular, which is precisely the case with Macpherson's spurious "Ossian;" or else they are mutilations of early Gothic or runic originals. Their repleteness of historical materials and local coloring belonging to the earlier centuries of our era, leads at once to the conclusion last named.[2] It is this local coloring which marks the distinction between a mutilation and a forgery out of the whole cloth. Macpherson had no historical dates before him, therefore he was forced to forge his entire work; Sigfusson found plenty of history in the old written sagas, so he merely mutilated them, and, with the sobriquet of "The Learned," achieved that immortality which is ever the reward of virtue and fidelity. If any further proof than that afforded by the nature of language itself were needed to corroborate these views, it will be found in the frequent mention of anachronical moneys in the sagas. An

[1] The historian of Iceland (A. D. 1056-1133) and his foster-grandson (A. D. 1178-1241).
[2] Charlemagne made a collection of these sagas, but these are now "lost" (Note to Murphy's Tac. "Germ.," iii., probably from Eginhard).

example of this sort will be quoted in the present chapter from the Egil Saga; others will appear as the argument develops.

The evolution of Norse monetary systems, whether in Iestia, Saxony, Scandinavia, Frakkland, Britain, Russia or Iceland, usually proceeded in the following manner:—First, fish and vadmal (cloth) money; second, baug, or ring-money; third, imitations of pagan Roman coined money; fourth, Norse pagan coinage system (partly derived from the Roman system) of stycas, scats, and oras; fifth, intrusion of Moslem coinage system of dinars, maravedis and dirhems; sixth, replacement of the last by Christian Roman coinage system of £ s. d. This progression did not occur simultaneously in the various countries named, because the Goths used coined money in Britain before they employed fish-money in Iceland; it was the usual order of progression in each country or petty kingdom by itself. From the period of their original settlement in Britain down to that of their contact with the Brigantes, the Norsemen used no coined money; indeed, they had little or no commerce, and lived chiefly by hunting, fishing and plundering. After each raid upon the enemy the plunder was "carried to the pole" and there divided. It is evident, from numerous analogous examples in the sagas, that in case of dispute the rival claimants fought it out at once, and the survivor took the lot. This is a custom, not of trading communities, but of predatory bands.

The first money of the Norsemen in Britain was probably fish, as was the case in Norway[1] and in Iceland down to the close of the last century. Sild, hring, or herring, is still used to mean money,[2] and the scad or scat (corrupted to scot), a fish of the same genus,

---

[1] Frostathing Laws, xvi., 2.
[2] Poole, "Anglo-Saxon Coins," i., 7.

has the same meaning in North Britain.[1] There are suggestions of fish-money in the expressions "Rome-scat," "scot-free," "scot-and-lot," etc. Following fish, the money of the Norsemen in Britain was vadmal, a homespun cloth, measured by the arm's length; still later they used baugs, or ring-money. It was not until after all this that they began to strike coins.

Baugs were anciently that money of Scythia, northern China and northern India of which a reminiscence still survives in the baugle or bangle.[2] At a remote period baug-money was introduced from Scythia into Egypt. Representations of it appear upon the stone monuments of Thebes. As for dates, Egyptian chronology has been so ruined in the various attempts made to fit it successively into the mythologies of Assyria, Greece and Rome, that no reliance can be placed upon it. The baugs engraved at Thebes are round rings, which are represented as being placed in the scales to be weighed. No peculiarity of form and no stamp-marks distinguish them in the sculptures—facts that, coupled with the weighing, led the author in a previous work to doubt that they were money. Since that time "dozens of rings (stamped), with the names of Khuen-Aten and his family, and molds for casting rings" have been found in the ruins of Tel-el-Amarna.[3] It cannot now be doubted that such rings were money, and we may also feel tolerably confident that they formed the principal circulating medium of Egypt during the time of the Hucsos or Scythian kings. From Egypt baug-

[1] According to Mr. T. Baron Russell's "Current Americanisms" (London, 1893) "scads" is still used for "current coin" in some parts of the United States.
[2] The pinched bullet-money of Cochin China also appears to be a modification of the baug.
[3] Address of Dr. Flinders Petrie, before the Oriental Congress, London, September 6th, 1892. Khuen is evidently the Tartar "kung," or king. Ridgway mentions the baugs of Mycenæ found by Dr. Schliemann, while Madden alludes to the baugs of Syria, mentioned in the bible.

money made its way down the eastern coast of Africa, where the early Portuguese and Spanish navigators found it, the latter giving to the rings the name of manillas or manacles. They were used in Darfoor (latitude 12° north, longitude 26° east) so late as 1850, for Mr. Curzon saw several chests full of gold baugs from that country at Assouan in 1854. They are still used on the West coast, from whence the present author had one of copper, shaped like the letter C, that is to say, with the two ends of the ring left apart.[1] Another line of baugs is traceable from Scythia to Gotland, where they are mentioned in sagas, which, although in their present form belonging to an era subsequent to the employment of baugs for money, are evidently mutilated versions of more ancient texts.[2] Egil having been paid two chests of silver as indemnity for his brother, "recites a song of praise," in which he alludes to the indemnity as "gul-baug," or gold rings, meaning money.[3]

The suspected mutilations of the sagas are corroborated by the known mutilations of the laws: "If a hauld wounds a man, he is liable to pay 6 baugar to the king, each worth 12 oras; if an arborin-madr wounds a man, he has to pay 3 baugar, and a leysingi (freedman) 2, a leudrman 12, a jarl 24, a kning 48, 12 oras being in each baug, and the fine shall be paid to those to whom it is due by law. All this is valued in silver."[4] The text of this law proves that it assumed its present form at three different dates. The first belongs to the

---

[1] "History of Money," 133. Baugs, or ring-money, are mentioned by Pliny ("Nat. History," xxiii., 1).

[2] Baugs appear to have been also used by the tribes of the Baltic coasts after the Goths conquered or assimilated with them, for the term was employed by the Salic Franks, and is still employed in French to mean rings.

[3] Egil Saga. The Dutch still give the name of "gulden" to certain silver coins. [4] Frostathing Laws, iv., 53; Du Chaillu, i., 549.

barbarous period, when the indemnity was fixed in Gothic baugs; the second to the Roman period, when the baugs were valued in heretical oras, or Roman sicilici; and the third to the period when the oras were valued in Christian silver pennies. The original baug appears to have weighed about as much as three sovereigns of the present day.

A C-shaped figure, like that of the African baug above mentioned, is twice repeated on a stone slab from the Kivikgrave, near Cimbrisham, a monument assigned by archæologists to a very remote period. Whether it represents the baug or not cannot at present be determined,[1] but there is some reason to think it does, from the fact that gold baugs seem to have been clothed with a sacerdotal character. For example, Egil fastened a gold baug on each arm of the dead Thoroff before he buried him,[2] and a gold baug was paid for his bride.[3] Bagi was also the Parthian name for divine or sacred; it appears on all the coins of the Arsacidæ.[4] The originals of the Frostathing laws may have descended from the period before the Goths revolted from Roman control.

Specimens of Gothic baug-money are still extant. Gold, silver and iron baugs will be found in the collections of Bergen, Christiania, Newcastle, York and other centers of Norse antiquities. There are Gothic gold baugs (about one inch in diameter) and copper and iron baugs in the London and Paris collections. During the last century " a vast quantity of small iron ring-money was exhumed in the west of Cornwall, and one of these was deposited by Mr. Moyle in the Pembroke collection."[5] After the era of baugs the Goths used

---

1 Fig. 28, in Du Chaillu, 88.   2 Du Chaillu, ii., 476.
3 Frostathing Laws, vi., 4; Du Chaillu, ii., 16.
4 Geo. Rawlinson, "Seventh Monarchy," p. 66.
5 Walter Moyle's works, i., 259.

coins. Says Du Chaillu: "A barbaric imitation in gold of a Roman imperial coin was found with a skeleton at Aarlesden in Odense, amt Fyen," a district and island about 86 miles from Copenhagen.[1] A barbaric imitation of Byzantine coin of the fifth century was found in Mallgard, Gotland.[2] A barbaric gold coin, falsely stamped with the image of Louis le Debonnaire, was found in Domberg, Zealand, and is now in the Paris collection.

When, several centuries before our era, the Celts came into contact with the Greeks, whether in Spain, Gaul or Britain, they began to strike Celtish coins in imitation of Greek originals. In like manner, after the Goths came into contact with the Romans, or rather after they had learnt to abhor the religion of the Romans and despise their arms, whether in Moesia, Saxony, Zealand or Britain, they began to strike Gothic coins in imitation of Roman originals. Such imitations are found in the uninscribed stycas, scats and oras of early Britain—a fact which is deduced as well from the Latin name of the ora as the general type and composition of all the pieces.

When Goth and Roman first met in Britain was when the ring-money was still used by the former—a period clearly established by the following passage from the principal work ascribed to Julius Cæsar. Speaking generally of the tribes whom he encountered in Britain (B. C. 55), Cæsar says: "Utuntur aut ære, aut nummo aureo, aut annulis ferreis, ad certum pondus examinātis pro nummo"—"They used either bronze (money) or gold money, or iron rings of a certain (determined) weight for money." The bronze metal, Cæsar

[1] Du Chaillu, i., 262.
[2] Du Chaillu, i., 275.

adds, was imported.¹ It is evident that this ring-money was not used at the time by the Celtic or Gaelic tribes of Britain, because these tribes used coined money, which, as a measure of value, is more precise and convenient than baugs. The Celts also came from Gaul and Belgium, where coined money was already in use. Their productions and commerce were too varied for the employment of so rude a measure of value as baugs. Cæsar says their numbers were countless, their buildings exceedingly numerous, their wealth great in cattle and cultivated lands, and their industry diversified, including not only pasturage and agriculture, but also mining for tin and iron.² Baugs had not been used by the Celtic tribes for nearly three centuries, that is to say, not since they had learnt the superiority of coins from the Greeks. On the other hand, their use among the Norsemen at this time or, perhaps, even a later period is proved by the sagas,³ and the conclusion that the ring-money found in Britain by Cæsar belonged to the Norse tribes in the remoter parts of the island, and indicated their presence there, seems to be well sustained.⁴ When added to the evidences of archæology, customs and language, adduced by Wright, Stillingfleet, Pinkerton, Du Chaillu, Hawkins, Evans and other

1 "De Bell. Gall.," v., 12. Several readings of this important passage are given in Henry's "Hist. Brit.," ii., 238. The reading in the text is from a MS. of the tenth century. Mr. Hawkins discovered that this passage had been materially corrupted in later copies (Hawkins, "Silver Coins," p. 8, and Ch. Knight, "Hist. England," i., 15, citing remarks on ancient coins in "Moneta Historica Brit.," p. 102).

2 Even after Cæsar had ravaged their lands, the Belgians were able to send him supplies of corn to Gaul ("De Bell. Gall.," v., 19, 20).

3 The pagan Norse kings who ruled in Ireland used baug money until they were driven out of that country in the twelfth century. This is what Sir John Lubbock, in his article on Money in the "Nineteenth Century," loosely called the "ring-money of the ancient Celts."

4 Cæsar (v., 9 and 11) alludes to the civil wars which preceded his arrival in Britain, and which, since the Celts were all of one religion (the Druidical), we may reasonably surmise were occasioned by the encroachments of the heretical Norsemen.

writers on the subject,[1] the body of proof that the Norse settlement of Britain antedates its Roman settlement becomes difficult to overthrow.

The Norse-British coinage system consisted of stycas, scats and oras. The styca was a small bronze coin, struck from the composition derived probably from the melting down of bronzes, and containing about 70 per cent of copper and 20 of zinc, the remainder consisting of tin, silver, lead and a minute proportion of gold. The extant stycas are confined by numismatists to Northumberland, but a coin of similar description, and used as a divider for the scat, must have been employed in Kent and elsewhere. The scat was an electrum coin, struck from the composition resulting from the melting down of gold and silver jewelry. The ora was a coin of pure or nearly pure gold. Originally containing about 30 grains of gold, it fell successively to $22\frac{1}{2}$, 20, 16 and even 13 grains. The electrum scats weighed about the same as the oras. The early oras are known among modern numismatists as gold scats. Sometimes the scats were stamped with the svastica, or with runes —a peculiarity that does not appear upon any coins issued by the southern kings of the heptarchical period. Eight stycas went to the scat, and eight scats to the ora. Owing to the composite nature of the scats, the ratio between gold and silver is indeterminable. Judging from the numerical relations between scats and oras, the ratio was intended to be 8 for 1. The coin ora must not de confused with the weight ora, which was afterwards the eighth of the mark weight; nor must the money of account, called the mark (of which more anon), be confused with the weight mark.

There is a remarkable similarity between the Gothic

[1] Doom-rings and numerous other Norse antiquities have been found in Britain.

coinage system and that of ancient Japan. There, too, coins were made respectively of gold, electrum, and bronze; the gold and the electrum coins were of the same weight, and the relative value of these even-weighted coins indicated that of the metals which composed them.[1] On the other hand, the Norse-British systems were distinctly non-German. Styca and scat are Norse terms, and were not used in Germany; mark is also a Norse term, and, according to Agricola, it was employed by the Goths many centuries before it was known in Germany. The runic letters and svastica are both Gothic and pagan. The Germans did not strike gold coins. The ratio of 8 for 1 is Gothic; that of Germany followed the Roman law, and down to the thirteenth century was either 12 for 1 or some mean between this and the Gothic ratio. Finally, the independent issues of gold and electrum coins were essentially Gothic, because the Goths, down to the eighth, ninth, or tenth centuries, were pagans, and refused to acknowledge the pope; whilst the Germans from the date when their country was made a province of the Empire, had invariably bowed to its ecclesiastical authority.

The Anglo-Saxon coins were not issued by any central authority, but by each local chieftain independently of the others. For this reason the valuation of the coins, and of the metals of which they were made, probably greatly varied. More important than all, the whole number of coins was uncertain and subject to the vicissitudes of war. A successful attack upon the Romans, who, down to the sixth or seventh century, still held many of the walled towns of Britain, might in a

[1] The Japanese system is fully described in "Money and Civilization," chap. xx. The reader must, however, not argue too much from this resemblance. In the ruder societary life of the Anglo-Saxons exchanges were comparatively few and simple, and the monetary system was of minor importance; in the refinement of modern Japanese life, it affected the foundations of equity and civil order.

single day have doubled the entire circulation of a given kingdom; whilst a repulse, followed by Roman pursuit and reprisals, might as suddenly have reduced the circulation to a moiety.

The reader will bear in mind that the ora described above was the original Gothic ora, afterwards called the gold shilling (gull skilling), not what the ora became in later ages. As time went on it continually fell in weight; the ratio of silver to gold changed from 8 for 1, to 6½ and 7½ for 1, then to 10 for 1, then to 12 for 1; the number of scats—or, as they were afterwards called, pennies—to the ora, changed from 8 to 5, then to 4, then to 20, 12, 20 and 16.[1] In one instance there were 15 minutæ to the ora. "Ora, vernacula aura, Danis öre, fuit olim genus monetæ, valens, 15 minuta."[2] These may have been, not copper coins, but silver half-pence.[3] It would be tedious to explain the endless combinations to which the changes in the three terms—viz., weight, ratio and value—gave rise. Eventually the ora became a money of account, and as the ora weight was one-eighth of the mark weight, so the ora of account was valued at one-eighth of the mark of account, which, during the Norman and Plantagenet eras, consisted of five gold maravedis, each weighing two-thirds of the Roman solidus. This mode of fixing the value of the ora gave rise to new and still more perplexing numismatic problems, all of which, however, are readily solved by the guides herein offered. For example, in the time of William I. there were still some actual gold oras extant, or mentioned in unexpired leases. These were valued in Domesday Book at 20

---

[1] Domesday Book; Ruding, i., 315. The relation of four scats to the ora was enacted prior to the middle of the tenth century ("Judicia Civitatis Londoniæ;" Ruding, i., 309).

[2] Dolmerus, in Du Fresne, in Fleetwood, p. 27.

[3] The minuta of the Netherlands was the Ies, or Es (Budelius).

pennies, because their namesake, the ora of account, was in England one-eighth of the mark of account, and the mark of account was two-thirds of the libra of account. As the latter then consisted (in England) of 240 actual silver pennies, so the mark was valued at 160 pence, and the gold ora was valued at 20 pence.

If this mode of calculation, which was employed in England after the Norman conquest, be applied to the ancient Gothic system, in which the gold ora was of the same weight and value as one-fourth of the gold solidus or mancus, it would follow that the mark of account consisted of two mancusses instead of five maravedis. Thus, if an ora is 20 pence and a mark is 160 pence, then there are eight oras to the mark. If there were four oras to the mancus, there were consequently two mancusses to the mark. The fallacy of this mode of calculation, which some numismatists have used, arises from the employment of the ora in two senses—firstly, as a money of account, which it was in the eleventh century; and, secondly, as an actual gold coin, which it was probably from the second to the seventh or eighth century.

CHAPTER V.

MOSLEM MONEYS.

The empire of Islam—Conquest of the Roman provinces in Asia, Africa, and Spain—Administrative policy of the Moslem—Monetary regulations—Numismatic declaration of independence—Origin of the dinar and dirhem—Singular ratio of value between silver and gold—Probable reasons for its adoption—Its worth as a historical guide—As a monetary example—Permanence of the tale ratio between dinar and dirhem—Moslem remains in the Western and Northern States of Europe: Spain, France, Burgundy, Flanders, Britain, and Scandinavia—Coinage system of Abd-el-Melik—Prerogative of coinage vested in the caliphate—Individual coinage unknown—Emir coinages—These substantially ceased with the reform of Abd-el-Melik—Legal tender in Egypt, Spain, and India—Weights and fineness of the dinar in various reigns—Same of the dirhem—Frontier ratios between gold and silver.

ISLAM, like Rome, was a sacred empire; the sovereign was both emperor and high-priest, but with this remarkable difference, that whilst the Roman emperor demanded to be worshiped as a god, the Commander of the Faithful unswervingly directed all worship to be made to an incorporeal deity. Mr. Freeman perceives another difference. The Roman emperor, he says, was pontiff because he was emperor, whilst "the Prophet, from a spiritual teacher, gradually became a temporal lord, consequently his successor is only emperor because he is pontiff."[1] I confess myself unable to follow this author, either as to the fact or its significance. The first Augustus was emperor for several years before the death of Lepidus enabled him to reunite the two offices in one person. After that time the Augustus or Basileus was the emperor, and the emperor was the Augustus. Those who were proclaimed by the army were neces-

[1] Freeman's "History of the Saracens," p. 62.

sarily emperors before they could be invested as chief-pontiff. On the other hand, those who became sovereign-pontiffs by adoption or descent were both emperors and chief-pontiffs at the same time. With respect to the Moslem, Mr. Freeman's inaccuracy is still more glaring. Mahomet was never a temporal lord; whilst several temporal lords, or emirs, ruled the empire which he did so much to erect, before Abd-el-Melik proclaimed himself an independent sovereign, and, uniting the pontificate to the throne, took the title of caliph and Emir-el-Moumenin, or Commander of the Faithful. Spain emancipated herself from the temporal but not from the spiritual control of the Arabian caliphs so early as A. D. 756; Egypt followed suit in A. D. 868. Abd-el-Raman I. was therefore an independent sovereign before he became a pontiff; indeed, he never became one. Says Lavoix: "The Ommiades of Spain always respected the supremacy of the caliph." This was true down to the reign of Abd-el-Raman III., but not afterwards. The previous caliphs of Spain never styled themselves Emir-el-Moumenin, but he did. He was not only Commander of the Faithful, he was also En-Nasr-li-din-Allah, or "Servant of the Religion of God."

As usual, the coinage decides the point. The Arabian emirs or caliphs, call them what you will, struck no independent coins before Abd-el-Melik. Their coins bear the stamp of Roman suzerainty; the emblems of the Roman religion; the legends of Roman superstition. These are proofs that until Abd-el-Melik the Arabian caliphs were not independent sovereigns. But the coinage proves more than this: it proves that the temporal sovereignty of the caliphs did not arise from their spiritual authority. This existed from the time of

Mahomet, while the temporal sovereignty only began with Abd-el-Melik. Another proof of the correctness of this view is derived from the coinage of gold, which, with the Arabs as with the Persians and Romans, was a sacerdotal prerogative. This prerogative belonged to the caliph as the sovereign-pontiff of Islam. The early emirs struck no gold, not even with Roman devices, and when Abd-el-Melik struck gold, the sovereign-pontiff of Rome, who was aware of its significance, immediately declared war upon him. It was the same in Spain. The Spanish caliphs struck no gold before Abd-el-Raman III. Until then the gold coins used in Spain were struck by the Arabian caliphs as Commanders of the Faithful. In Egypt it was the same. When the first Fatimite King struck gold in that province he meant it to be understood, and the caliphs so construed it, that he regarded himself as independent of the caliphate, and was prepared to take the consequences of that declaration.

The spiritual and temporal attributes of the caliph, and the important bearing which this dual character had upon the development of the Moslem empire, is best shown by the historian Dozy. The empire rose by the strength which it derived from this union of the spiritual and temporal powers; it fell by the weakness which invariably follows such a union. The strength was born of religious enthusiasm; the weakness resulted from the impractical features of hierarchical government.

The demands of space forbid us to follow this subject any further. Our object is not to trace the history of Islam, but of its monetary systems in Europe. We can, therefore, only glance at the events connected with the establishment of Moslem government,

It is a common mistake to confound the rise of Saracenic power with the advent of Mahomet. Three centuries before his time the frontier tribes of Arabia had ventured to resist the authority of Rome, and under their goddess or queen Mania[1] their strength had been sufficient to defy and overthrow an imperial army. Their religion had also taken form. Sozomen, describing the Arabs of the fourth century, says: "They practice circumcision, refrain from the use of pork, and observe many other Jewish rites and customs." It may be added that they observed many religious rites and customs which were afterwards adopted by the Roman church.[2]

However, the establishment of Islam is certainly due to Mahomet and his successors, and to their conquests of Persia, Syria, Egypt, Africa and Spain. It is through this last-named country that France, England, Germany and America are interested in the progress of the Arabian monetary systems.

At the time of Mahomet and the emirs the Arabs numbered about 120,000 fighting men. These constituted that army of invasion which accomplished its work with so much courage and energy. After repelling the forces which had confined them to the desert, they burst out upon Rome and Persia, at that time the two most powerful States of the Western world. In less than ten years they subdued Irak, Mesopotamia, Syria and Egypt, and turned these countries into "the dwelling of the Arab race, the kernel of the empire, the garden where Religion and Victory were born together."[3] The attack was so rapid that the conquest proceeded almost without administrative organization.

[1] Rufinus calls the Arabian queen Mania; Socrates and Sozomen call her Mavia. The name is probably the same as Maia, Maria, etc.
[2] Stanley's "Sabean Philosophy," p. 800.   [3] Ibn Kaldoun.

Locally this was left entirely in the hands of the conquered races. In Persia the conquerors, who were rough soldiers and awkward in clerkly duties, employed Jewish or Persian writers and accountants. The native language was retained. In Syria the principal servants of the Arabian government down to the reign of Abd-el-Melik were "Arian" Greeks. For example, one Sergius, a Greek, was superintendent of finances, or collector of taxes. But in the reign of Abd-el-Melik all was changed. The civil government of Irak was taken from the Persian writers and given to Arabians. The Domesday Book of Syria was translated into Arabic; the registry of the treasury, the tax lists, and the text of the laws all became Arabic.

It was the same with the coinage. During nearly sixty years following the conquest, this privilege and function was exercised by local emirs, who employed Persian, Greek or Hebrew moneyers. The sizes, types and inscriptions of the coins, their weight, fineness, value, legal function, and other characteristics were copied with precision from the current coins and monetary systems of the subdued nations.[1] Under Abd-el-Melik this was all reformed. The coins became wholly Arabian, and among the characteristics which they acquired was one which was carried westward, and continued to influence the coinages of Europe until after the discovery of America. This was the peculiarly Arabian valuation of silver to gold of $6\frac{1}{2}$ for 1. But before explaining this subject, let us first briefly follow the Arabian conquests through Africa to Spain.

[1] From Abd-el-Melik the Arabs seldom omitted an opportunity to proclaim upon the coins the unity of God. The ordinary motto was, "There is no God but the one God." Upon the bilingual coins it varied; for example: "In Nomine Domini Misericordis. Unus Deus." . . . "Non est Deus nisi Solus Deus cui non socius Alius." . . . "Non est Deus nisi, Unus cui non Deus alius similis." The coinage of the emirs began as early as A. D. 638; cf Ali 660; Abd-el-Melik, 685.

An interesting relic of antiquity, communicated to the world in recent years, assures us that the Arabian policy in Egypt was the same as in Persia and Syria—the local administration was at first left entirely in the hands of the conquered nation.[1]

John of Nikios, after describing the anarchical condition of the religious community in Egypt, the dissensions which distracted it, the persecutions instituted by the sacred emperor Heraclius, and the joy with which the inhabitants forsook the Roman for the Moslem yoke, notices the wisdom of the Arabian policy in retaining native administrative officers. Says John: "After the Moslem conquest a man named Menas, whom the Emperor (of Byzantium) made præfect of Lower Egypt, and who despised the Egyptians, was, nevertheless, retained at his post. The Moslem also chose another Greek, named Sinoda, as præfect of the province of Rif, and another, named Philoxenos, as præfect of Arcadia or Fayoum." Even when Menas was removed from the government of Alexandria, the Moslem replaced him by John of Damietta, a Greek who had also been a præfect under the Emperor, and who, moreover, had successfully exerted himself to save the city from injury by its Arabian conquerors. This was his recommendation to them.

The conquest of Africa was very different from that of Persia, Syria and Egypt. In these countries the worship of Cæsar had deeply disgusted the inhabitants with Roman rule, and even where "Christianity"[2] had

[1] "Chronique de Jean, évêque de Nikiou" (Nikos), texte Ethiopien, publié et traduit par H. Zotenberg, Paris, 1883. This bishop lived in Egypt during the latter half of the seventh century, that is to say, at the time of the Arabian invasion.

[2] It is hardly necessary to remind the intelligent reader that the so-called "Christianity" of the seventh century bore but slight resemblance to the Christianity of the present day.

supplanted emperor-worship, the people never became wholly reconciled to the religion of their conquerors. The Berbers of Africa, being more remote from Byzantium, were less troubled by religious disputes. Neither the worship of Augustus, nor Bacchus, nor of the reigning emperor, gave them much concern. They were strangers to both the Latin and Greek tongues, and came but little into contact with the officials, either secular or sacred, who had been appointed over them. Hence they were not divided by schism, and were far from being disposed to welcome the new race of religious enthusiasts and conquerors. The conquest of the other provinces of Rome had been effected by the Moslem in campaigns, which, ending with the battle of Nevahend (A. D. 641), had lasted less than ten years. The conquest of the African provinces of that empire cost them half a century of fighting. The country which lay before them comprised Tripoli to the Tingitane, Central Maghred and Western Maghred. Two races occupied it; the seaports were in the hands of the Byzantines, who also possessed, in the interior, military posts defended by strong garrisons. The Byzantine legate reigned at Carthage; Gregory, the patrician, governed at Sufetula; the rest of the country was filled by the warlike Berbers, chiefly in Auras, Zab and Hodna, where they had established themselves during the contests between the Romans and Vandals.

After a series of preliminary raids and skirmishes, during which the Moslem established bases of supplies at Zaoueilah and Barkah, they prepared for a more extended campaign in A. H. 49. This was under the chief command of Akbar-ben-Nafi, who, in A. H. 50, founded the city of Kairoun. At the end of twelve years' hard fighting Akbar had penetrated westward so far as Ceuta, then commanded by Count Julian. From the flanks of this fortress Akbar first beheld the limitless ocean of the West and the towering Rock of Hercules, Calpe (or Gibraltar), beyond which lay the famed land of gold and silver. Leaving Ceuta on his right, Akbar marched straight on to Tangier. Here, while separated from his army, and defended by only 300 cavaliers, he was ambushed and massacred by the enemy.

Zohair-ben-Kais, and after him Hasan, having succeeded to the command of the Moslem forces, other campaigns followed, in which Carthage was won, then lost, and then won again. With its second winning the Roman garrisons in Africa were virtually subdued. The natives, however, were far from being conquered. Under their queen, Kahinah, they held the Arabians in check, and eventually defeated them. Africa seemed unconquerable. After this defeat—the most terrible that the Moslem had ever sustained—Hasan received orders from the indomitable caliph to renew the war. This time Kahinah was defeated and Kairoun retaken. The Moslem armies again took up the march for Ceuta. Hasan was now replaced by Mousa-ben-Nosier, under whose vigorous command Ceuta was secured, and (A. D. 704) the arms of Arabia were carried to the Western Ocean.

Five years later Abou-Zoriah-Tharik-ben-Zaid (better known to us as Tarik), under the orders of Mousa, passed the Straits of Hercules with one hundred horse and four hundred foot soldiers, debarked at the Rock, captured and sacked the town, as well as the neighboring cities of Carteia and Algeciras, and then returned to Africa rich with spoils. Next year Tarik landed with a larger force, better equipped, and boldy advanced to meet the Gothic army of King Roderic. Except when the Saracenic vassals of the empire, whom Valens in 378 had called to the defense of Constantinople, and whose savage valor had avenged his death by bloodily repulsing the Goths from the suburbs of the capital, this was the first occasion when the Moslem and the Gothic arms came into conflict, and here, again, victory was with the Arabs. The immediate consequence of the action was to open the road to Toledo, and in an incredibly short space of time nearly the whole of Spain fell into the hands of the invaders. The fame of this extraordinary exploit aroused the jealousy of Mousa, who, crossing from Africa, hastened to complete the conquest of Spain, and share the vast spoils of Tarik. By A. H. 94 (A. D. 712) the conquest was completed, and Mousa, like Cortes at a later period, found himself master of an empire greater and richer than that of the caliph his master.

In every country that fell beneath their sway the policy of the Moslem was the same: they imposed a tribute (usually of about one dinar per capita per annum) upon the inhabitants, but only so long as they remained kafirs or infidels. The moment they accepted the Moslem formula—"There is but one God"—the tribute was taken off, and they became Mahometans and freemen. The civil administration of Spain was entrusted to native (Gothic) clerks and leaders. The coinage, which began in each country from the moment that victory was assured, was always an exact imitation of the previous local coinage. No change at all is perceptible at first. For example, Mousa commenced to strike coins from the moment that the conquest of Spain was effected, and one of these pieces is still extant.

In A. H. 37 (A. D. 658), during the civil contest between Ali and Moawiyah, the latter "bought peace of the Emperor Constans by a round sum of ready money and the payment of a daily tribute." In A. H. 59 (A. D. 679), after his repulse from the walls of Constantinople, Moawiyah was fain to purchase peace from Constantine Pogonatus by an annual tribute of 3,000 libras of gold, fifty slaves, and fifty Arab horses.[1] In A. H. 67 (A. D. 686) Abd-el-Melik, being at that period involved in civil war with the Mardaites, bought peace of Justinian II. (afterwards called Rhinotmetus) by the payment of a tribute of 1,000 gold solidi or dinars per annum for ten years. Down to this time these coins were struck by Abd-el-Melik, with Roman emblems and legends upon them. Six years later the Arabian caliph, having disposed of the Mardaite trouble, determined to assert his independence of Rome, and by a token understood of all the world. He struck gold coins with his own effigy, holding a drawn sword, as afterwards did Edward III. when he renounced the same dread authority. Abd-el-Melik's dinars bore this challenging legend: "The Servant of God, Abd-el-Melik, Emir-el-Moumenin." These coins Justinian refused to receive, because, says Zonaras, "It is not permitted to stamp gold coins with any other effigy but that of the emperor of Rome."[2] Whereupon a war was declared by Justinian, which lasted until the latter was driven from his throne by a civil revolt, which occurred in A. D. 695. Justinian was banished by his successor to the Crimea, where he married the daughter of a Mongol chieftain. He afterwards escaped to Bulgaria, where he married the daughter of a Gothic chieftain. Then, in A. D. 705, he appeared before Constantinople with an army of barbarians, and re-entered it in triumph. Among his first

---

[1] Freeman (pp. 90, 91) says "pieces" of gold, or dinars.
[2] Consult Theophanus (pp. 751-818); Cedrenus (eleventh century) and Zonaras (twelfth century) on this subject.

acts was the striking of a gold solidus, with which he hurled back the religious challenge of the Arab. Upon this solidus appears the legend: "Our Lord Justinian, the Servant of Christ."

The monetary system of Abd-el-Melik consisted of coins of purely Arabian type and legend. The ratio between silver and gold was that oriental valuation of $6\frac{1}{2}$ for 1, which marked for several centuries the line of separation between the Moslem and Christian States of Europe. The Arabian ratio was fixed by striking dinars, each of approximately 65 grains, and silver dirhems of approximately 43 grains, and valuing ten of the latter, in the law, at one of the former. Unless the purely economical considerations, which will presently be adduced, are deemed sufficient, it is difficult to discern the reasons for establishing this peculiar ratio; yet practical politicians will assure us that economical considerations have never been the principal influence which determined the policy of nations.[1]

The ratio of $6\frac{1}{2}$ may have been a reaction from the coinages effected under the ratio of 13, mentioned by Herodotus concerning the ancient Persian tributes;[2] or it may have been due to the fact that in all the western countries conquered by the Moslem, silver was chiefly in the hands of the people, whilst gold was in those of their rulers; and the great alteration which was made in their relative value was a covert bribe to gain the suffrages of the former and reconcile them to Moslem government and religion. But it is far more likely to have originated in a simpler and straightforward manner.

[1] "The events of the last few years on both sides of the Atlantic have proved that men are not now, any more than they ever were, chiefly governed by calculations of material profit and loss" (Bryce, "Holy Roman Empire," p. 301).

[2] Thalia, p. 95. Some warrant for this hypothesis is afforded by the Brazilian milreis, which, though derived from that of Portugal, contains only half the same quantity of fine metal ("Hist. Money and Civilization," chap. xii.)

The Athenian, Persian, Egyptian and Roman governments had successively absorbed a large portion of the profits derived from the Indian trade, by lowering the value of silver (in which their tributes were chiefly received) in the Occident to half its value in the Orient. By making the bullion trade a strictly governmental monopoly, as Cicero informs us was the case with Rome, that hierarchy obtained twice as much gold for silver in India as it paid for it in Europe. This policy, except where it was swept away by the influence of Islam, was pursued until the Roman empire expired. The Arabian government was more considerate of its merchants: it threw open the oriental trade to all true believers; it imposed no restrictions; it was averse, at least at that period, to the imposition of covert exactions. During the seventh century of our era the ratio in India was about $6\frac{1}{2}$ for 1, and this high valuation of silver in India continued substantially unchanged until the fifteenth century. It was at the Indian ratio that the Moslem struck their coins of gold and silver.

Whatever the true reason of this policy, it was certainly more profitable for the Moslem conquerors than had they adopted the contemporaneous Roman ratio of 12 for 1. A brief computation will serve to measure this profit. After consulting those Arabian authors who have treated the subject, and making allowances for instances where exaggeration seems to have been employed, we have ventured to roughly estimate the Moslem spoil of the precious metals, including the tributes exacted from the conquered nations during the first eighty years of the conquest, at about five million marks' weight of gold and about one hundred million marks' weight of silver.

In determining at what relation of value of one to

the other metal this mass of gold and silver should be coined, Abd-el-Melik may be reasonably supposed to have indulged in some such considerations as the following:

"We have a vast treasure before us to coin. At what ratio of value between silver and gold shall we coin it? Our armies are invincible; the populations are tired of Roman rule; our conquests will extend. Arabia is a commercial country, watered by three oceans—the Mediterranean connects it with the West, the Euxine with the North, and the Red Sea with India and China. The influx of the precious metals, due at first to our arms, will be continued by means of trade. In the Roman empire and its feudatories the coinages have hitherto been conducted on the basis of 12 weights of silver for 1 of gold; in the Orient the ratio is 6 or 7 for 1. It is evident that the most profitable, perhaps also the most important, part of our commerce will be with what we soon hope to call our Indian empire; and it is more desirable that our moneys should harmonize with the Indian than with the Roman coinages. It must also not be forgotten that to conform with the Roman coinages would involve us in pecuniary loss, whereas to follow the oriental ratio would afford us a profit. Judging from the proportions of the metallic spoil thus far captured, we shall secure about twenty times as much (in weight of) silver as gold, and assuming that we eventually secure 100,000,000 marks of silver, and coin it at the Indian ratio, our fund will amount to 1,120,000,000 dinars; whereas if we coin at the Roman ratio, it will only come to 746⅔ millions. Let those who are learned in the art of arithmetic make the calculation for themselves. The only questions left to consider are these: **Can we permanently maintain this** ratio of value—so different from that established by the coinages of the Roman empire, a large portion of which, however, is already subject to our arms? Will not our gold dinars flow out and silver metal come into Arabia to take its place? and, if so, will not this prove injurious to our affairs? These questions can be answered very readily. As we have already gained control of the Egyptian, and, please Allah, will soon have control of the Spanish mines, from what other country is the silver metal to come which is to buy our gold dinars? Answer—No country. As we have driven the Romans from the Mediterranean, and will soon control the commerce of maritime Europe, whither could our gold dinars go outside of the influence of our own trade? Answer—Nowhere. If, nevertheless, such an unlikely thing should come to pass, how much should we lose were our 280,000,000 of gold dinars to flow out and we received for them 280,000,000 dinars' worth of silver at our own ratio of valuation? Answer—Nothing. Then what is the objection to the adoption of such a ratio of value between silver and gold as best suits our present interests and our probable future trade with India? Answer—None whatever."[1]

Encouraged, more than likely, by reflections of this character, the Arabians commenced, under Abd-el-Melik, that system of purely Arabian coinages which continued until the center of their empire was virtually removed to India, and they had lost control of both the mines and the commerce of Europe.

These coinages were for several centuries conducted on the basis of $6\frac{1}{2}$ weights of coined silver as the equivalent in value of 1 weight of coined gold. This was

[1] At the ratio of $6\frac{1}{2}$ there would be 56 dinars and 84 dirhems struck from the mark weight; at the ratio of 12 there would be 56 of each coin struck from the mark weight. The difference in the total sum would amount to $373\frac{1}{3}$ millions of dinars.

not only a peculiar ratio; it differed so greatly from the Roman one of 12 for 1 that it can never fail to be recognized wherever and whenever it existed—whether in the countries of Islam or elsewhere. Moreover, when found elsewhere, it is an infallible sign of Moslem connection or influence. As in the remains of antiquity the presence of silk and porcelain denotes commerce with China; of spices, with India; of tin, with Britain; of amber, with Iestia; and of papyrus, with Egypt, so, in the monuments of the mediæval ages, does the establishment of this peculiar ratio of value between silver and gold in coins denote intercourse with the Arabians. Wherever this ratio was adopted merely by giving currency to Arabian coins at Arabian values, the intercourse with Arabians may have been limited to commerce. Where the ratio was established by means of local coinages, based on the Moslem valuation and supplemented by the use of Moslem types, the former implies the presence of Moslem artificers. Where to the Moslem ratio and types was added the Moslem religious formula, "There is but one God," this definitively bespeaks the presence of Moslem influence, and a formal protest against polytheism. All these will be found in some mediæval States—the Moslem ratio, type, and religious formula; hence their historical significance.

When it is borne in mind that the Moslem empire was a sacred one, that the Moslem coinages, like the Roman or Byzantine, were employed as a means of disseminating religious doctrine, and that, also like the Roman, the legal ratio of value between coins of the precious metals, once fixed, remained unchanged for centuries, the importance of the Moslem ratio for solving other historical problems will be better understood. For example, how far did the Moslem conquest and occupation of France extend? and how long did it last? are questions to which a far more reliable answer will be found in the Merovingian coinages than in the popular story of Martel's victory.[1] To what extent, at a given era, was Christianity established in Gothic countries, is a problem to be solved much more satisfactorily by means of the coinages and valuations which prevailed in those countries than by listening to the airy fictions of the Quindecemviral College.

We find Moslem remains or else marks of Moslem influence in the antiquities of England, Scandinavia, the Netherlands, Frakkland (Burgundy), Spain, and other Gothic or semi-Gothic States of the seventh and eighth centuries. In Sicily Moslem marks continue to the twelfth century, and in Spain to the fifteenth. Whenever we find them we have not far to look for the frontier-line of Christianity. Since the Julian era, in whatever country the ratio of 12 prevailed, that country may be safely regarded as having been first under Roman-pagan, and afterwards under Roman-Christian domination; in whatever country west of India the ratio of 7 or 6½ prevailed, it may be regarded as having been under Moslem influence. But for the influence of the archaic Gothic ratio of 8, explained elsewhere, it might also be concluded that wherever any intermediate ratio between 6½ and 12 prevailed, that place was at or near the frontier-line between the spheres of Roman and Moslem influence.

To those to whom the ratio of value between the precious metals appears due to any other circumstance than the arbitrary laws of national mints, or to those whose attention to the history of this recondite subject has now been drawn for the first time, the ratio may

[1] One of the earliest Arabian dinars, now in the Paris collection, was found at Autun, with two Merovingian coins (Lavoix's Catalogue, No. 26).

seem a strange or inadequate criterion of political or religious domination; but it is precisely in such obscure relations between great and little things that an all-wise Creator has sheltered the truth of history from man's destructive powers. The forgery of books, the defacement of monuments, the perversion of evidences, the extermination of nonconformists, the invention of fabulous cosmogonies and superstitious fictions—all are made in vain to conceal or crush the truth so long as a blade of grass or a breath of air remains on earth to reveal it; for all Nature is united in a mysterious harmony, and to even approximately master one branch of science is to gain a key which, with patience and industry, may eventually unlock for us all the others.

The Moslem systems of money were based on the dinar coin, whose weight was called a mithcal, this word meaning literally "any weight with which one weighs;" in other words, the mithcal of money was the weight of the dinar, which was theoretically a symbol, a money of account, forming part of a monetary system, but palpably a single coin, containing 65 grains fine gold, this having been the average contents of the Roman solidus at the period of the first Arabian coinage.[1] In the earliest Moslem system (period of Mahomet) the mithcal was divided into 96 parts, as follows: 96 barleycorns=48 habbeh=24 tussuj=6 danik=1 mithcal. The ratio of silver to gold in this system was 12 for 1. Hence the silver drachma, of which 12 went to the gold dinar, contained 65 grains fine silver.[2] In the system established by Abd-el-Melik, about three-fourths of a century after the Hegira, the mithcal was divided into 100 parts, as follows: 100 barleycorns=20 karats=1

[1] The extant solidus of Heraclius I. weighs 69.9 grains, about 65 grains fine.
[2] Esh Shafy and Ibn Hanbal both affirm that the ratio was 12 in the time of the Prophet.

mithcal. Hence a barleycorn of this system weighed 0.65, or about two-thirds of a grain, and a karat 3¼ grains. Both the Roman binary weights and the Roman ratio of silver to gold were now dropped. The weights became decimal. The gold dinar remained unchanged, but the principal silver coin was modeled upon the average Sassanian dirhem of 14 karats, or seven-tenths (in weight) of the dinar, and it took the name of its Sassanian prototype. Hence the dirhem theoretically contained seven-tenths of 65 grains=45½ grains. The dinar was valued at 10 dirhems—a valuation derived from the ordinances of the Prophet, and one which it would have been sacrilegious to alter. The law of the Prophet levies a tithe on all possessions of the precious metals, amounting to 5 oukias, or 200 silver dirhems, or 20 gold dinars.[1] Here the dinar is valued at 10 silver dirhems, and it remained so until the tenth century. This ratio had nothing to do with the value of billon, potin, copper, or glass dirhems, of which we have had to speak elsewhere; it related only to gold and silver coins of fine, or substantially fine, metal.

Had both the gold and silver coins of the Mahometan mints continued the full theoretical weight of metal, and had they been of like standard, alloy, or fineness, the weights given above would have made a ratio of 7 silver=1 gold; but the actual circumstances were different. The dinars weighed 65 grains (0.979) fine; the dirhems weighed 43 grains (0.960 to 0.970) fine. Hence the ratio of value between silver and gold in the coins was 6.52 for 1.[2]

There has been a good deal of confusion and misunderstanding on this subject, and it is essential to clear it up in this place. El-Hassan, an Arabian writer (A.

[1] The Koran, as revised by Othman or Ali.
[2] "Money and Civilization," p. 22.

H. 22-110), calculated the theoretical ratio of value between the precious metals in the coinage at 3½ for 1, which is just half of the true theoretical ratio. Bergmann, a recent writer, doubled the theoretical ratio, and made it 14 for 1. Queipo doubled the actual ratio, and made it 13 for 1. These errors probably arose from mistaking the number of dirhems to the dinar. El-Hassan may have assumed 5 to be the correct number; Queipo and Bergmann certainly assumed the number to be 20. The correct legal number was 10.[1] M. Sylvestre de Sacy supposed that, because there were 10 dirhems to the dinar, the ratio was 10 for 1.[2] This would be true if the weights and fineness of the two coins were alike, but not true as the case stood.

The average gross weight of 2,222 whole dinars now extant, and dating from A. H. 76 to 132, is 65.3 grains; that of 6,982 whole dirhems of the same period is 43.36 grains, all of them being coins in the best state of conservation.[3] The legal valuation of 10 dirhems to the dinar will be found repeatedly confirmed in the works of Makrisi, de Sacy, Queipo, Lavoix, Sauvaire and Poole. The standard, or fineness, of the coins is given by Sauvaire. The conclusion that the ratio was (approximately) 6½ for 1 therefore stands upon very solid grounds.

Coinage system of Abd-el-Melik, A. H. 73 (A. D. 692). *Ratio of silver to gold*, 6.52 *for* 1.

6 copper fels = 1 silver dirhem, 41.495 grains fine.
10 dirhems = 1 gold dinar, 63.635 grains fine.
4 dinars = 1 oukia.
5 oukias = 1 nisab.
Hence 240 fels = 1 oukia.

Ed. Bernard ("Mens. et Pond.," p. 188) gives also the equivalent of 700 mithcals, or dinars, equal 1 talent; but whether this applies to Abd-el-Melik's time or not

[1] Sauvaire, pp. 49—55.   [2] Sauvaire, p. 55.
[3] Sauvaire.

is uncertain. The talent appears to have had only a local meaning, which varied from five dinars to almost any number. The original word for it in the Koran is "quintar." "There are some who if thou entrust them with a talent (quintar) give it back to you; and some if thou entrust them with a dinar will not return it" (Imran's Family, iii.; Medina, v. 60).

Reverting to the subject of the ratio, because of its great importance, both from the numismatic, the monetary, and the historical point of view, Sauvaire, in his "Materiaux," gives 57 eccentric valuations of the dirhem to the dinar, which are repeated by Poole in the "London Numismatic Chronicle" for the year 1884. Of this number thirty-one (or more) belong to Egypt, and only one to Spain. These commence in A. H. 363-5, and vary from 50 in the fourth century of the Hegira to 13¼ in the sixth century. They relate not to silver, but to billon dirhems, some of which—for example, the *nukrah*—contained but 10 per cent of silver, the rest being copper. In another instance (A. H. 815) the relation is between the dinar and the so-called "pure dirhem, each weighing a half-dirhem." It is evident that no correct ratio of weight and value between the dinar and dirhem can be deduced from coins of this character. The other examples are equally useless. From the era of Mahomet to the fourth century of the Hegira there are no examples at all except one for A. H. 225, which is probably a corrupted Fatimite date. In this example there are 15 dirhems to the dinar. Some examples relate to copper coins, as the Delhi *tankah* dirhems of A. H. 823 (800 dirhems to the dinar); nearly all of them bear the impress of miscalculation, and none of them state the fineness of the coins. With the exception of the 12 for 1 in the time of the Prophet and the 10 for 1 in Bagdad (A. H. 632), I regard them as entirely worthless for the purpose of deducing the ratio of value between silver and gold.

The Moslem always respected the 10 dirhems for 1 dinar, just as the Romans respected the 12 silver for 1 gold, and from similar motives. The relation of the dirhem to the dinar was ascribed to the law of the Prophet; the relation of 12 silver for 1 gold was fixed by Julius Cæsar. The former was not altered while the empire of Islam lasted; the latter remained unchanged until the throne of the Cæsars was overturned.

The prototype of the dinar has been mentioned; it was the Roman solidus. The dirhem, according to Sauvaire's translation of El Damiry, was based upon an average of the three sorts of silver coins then circulating in the Persian dominions. Those with the effigy of the king and the legend NOUCH KHOR, or "Feast in Health," weighed one mithcal. Of the Samarys dirhems there were two sorts, one weighing six-tenths of a mithcal, the other half a mithcal. The inscriptions on these coins were in Pehlvic. An average of the three sorts made seven-tenths of a mithcal, and accordingly this was the weight of the Arabian dirhem adopted by Abd-el-Melik. In A. H. 1276 (A. D. 1859) a Persian, named Djevad, paid into the postoffice at Constantinople a dirhem struck at Bassora in A. H. 40. This dirhem is now in the Paris collection. Its weight is 36.13 English grains, but it is somewhat worn, and it may have originally weighed seven-tenths of a mithcal. It has been submitted to Mordtmann, Rogers, Longperier, Sauvaire, Waddington, and other competent judges, all of whom pronounced it genuine, the only dissentient voice being that of Mr. J. Stickel.[1] If genuine it rather discredits the Arabian account of the manner in which

[1] J. Stickel, in "Handbuch zur Morgenlandischer Munzkunde," p. 51.

Abd-el-Melik got the weight of his dirhem, for it belongs to the reign of Ali, and the averaging of the three sorts of dirhems, if it was done at all, must have been done by him. This view is sustained by the tale equivalents cited from the Koran, a work revised in the reign of Othman or Ali. However, the Bassora coin may have followed the Samarys dirhem of six-tenths of a mithcal, in which case its original weight was 39 grains.

The prerogative of coining became vested in the caliphate from the moment of its inception. "I have left to Irak its dinar and to Syria its dirhem" is a boast ascribed to Mahomet, and which, whether true or false, and whether uttered by Mahomet or somebody else of the same era, implies control of the coinage from some center of administration, either religious or civil. This is a point which will be discussed farther on. During the conquest, before the central administration was organized, the emirs or commanders in the field struck coins. This was merely to facilitate the distribution of the spoil, for these coins were exact fac-similes of those already in circulation, including their religious emblems and legends. The division of the spoil was regulated by the Koran; in all cases one-fifth of it went to the hierarchy. "Whenever ye seize anything as a spoil, to God belongs a fifth thereof." (Spoils, viii.; Medina, v. 40.) This is the origin of the Royal Quinto, which the Spanish monarchs afterwards exacted from the conquerors of America.[1] The coins of the emirs extend from about A. H. 5 to A. H. 60. In a few instances such coinages continued after the administration was centralized by Abd-el-Melik, but they were gradually suppressed until the entire system was brought under the control of the

[1] See my previous works for full discussions on this subject.

caliph. We have the assurances of the Arabian numismatists and the corroboration of Lavoix that such control was rigidly exercised and jealously guarded.[1] No private individual dared strike a coin; no individual had the right to require the government to strike a coin for him; it was a felony for any person or corporation other than the State either to fabricate or destroy a coin.

In respect to the emir coinages the policy of the Arabians was similar to that of the Romans during the Punic wars, when the State, for reasons of convenience, permitted its commanders in the field to strike coins. Such was the whole foundation of that imaginary "prerogative of the imperium," with which Mommsen and Lenormant have enlivened the pages of their works on the Roman monetary system. In the Roman empire all suggestions of such a prerogative must certainly cease from the time when Augustus organized the administration; in Islam they disappear with the coinage reforms of Abd-el-Melik. In both cases the coinage was really the prerogative of the State, and was only exercised by the imperatores, emirs, or commanders in the field, under the actual or anticipated authority of the State. In both cases the coinage became the prerogative of that hierarchy into which the State developed. In both cases the coins were employed, not merely for money, but also as means to proclaim accessions and to promulgate and disseminate religious doctrine.

But here the analogy ends. The Roman hierarchy continued down to the time when Constantinople was overthrown by the troops and allies of the Latin pope; until that event the coinage of gold was exercised solely by the Basileus.

Says Freeman: "That the caliph of the Prophet

[1] Henri Lavoix, "Catalogue des Monnaies Musulmanes," 1891, 4to.

was the lawful lord of the world no true believer thought of doubting; but who really was the caliph of the Prophet was a question on which opinions might widely differ."

It was the same with the Roman government. That the Augustus was the lawful lord of the world no one presumed to question; but who was the lawful Augustus was often a matter of vital dispute. The difference between the Roman and Arabian hierarchies—at least so far as such difference affected the monetary system—was of another character. In the Roman empire the right to coin gold always remained with the sovereign-pontiff, and was never exercised by any other authority; in the Arabian empire, after the revolt of Spain and Egypt from the authority of the caliph, it was lost by the latter, and became vested in the independent sovereigns of those States, and was exercised by them and by other Moslem sovereigns who had thrown off the same authority. A belief in the unity of God is not favorable to the maintenance of a hierarchy.

According to Lavoix the gold dinar was the only full legal-tender coin of the Moslem in Egypt. This may have been the case elsewhere in the Arabian empire, but so far as we can determine, not in Spain nor in India. In those States both gold and silver coins seem to have been clothed with the full legal-tender function. This only ceased to be true when the latter were adulterated.

CHAPTER VI.

EARLY ENGLISH MONEYS.

Sterling standard—Type of the penny—Arabian coins in Gotland—Offa's dinar—The mark—The mancus—Arabian moneyers in England—Arabian ratio—Arabian metallurgists—The Gothic-Arabian monetary system.

OUR account of English moneys begins with the Moslem remains which have been found in England. This does not allude either to the Moorish troops whom the Romans stationed at Watchtowers nor to the reputed Arabian remains in the Yorkshire Tyke (Tyrkr) dialect, but to the numismatic monuments of the mediæval age.[1] For reasons which will presently be adduced, we venture to regard the sterling standard of England as practically of Moslem origin. By sterling standard we mean, not the nummulary terms £. s. d., but the metallic composition of the silver sterlings—the alliage of all the best silver coins now extant of mediæval England. The mancus and carat are certainly Moslem. The peculiar ratio of value between the precious metals in mediæval England was either wholly Moslem or largely due to Moslem influence. There is reason to believe that the sterling alliage was also Moslem.

Although we have no Gothic-Arabian coin with an Arabian inscription earlier than Offa, and only one of that prince, it is probable that other Arabian types of

[1] Muratori III. (Dissert. xl., pp. 686-708) prints some rhymes embodying the medical precepts of the Arabians, which were addressed by a student at Bagdad to Edward Confessor, Rex Anglorum. The English words admiral, algebra, alkali, almanac, cotton, cypher, damask, damson, sheriff, and many others are well known to be Arabian. What is alluded to in the text is an obscure dialect only spoken in Northumberland.

coins were introduced into England during the seventh century; for that period coincides alike with the earliest mention of the Arabian mancus in England and with the appearance of flat, thin coins of nearly pure silver (and Arabian type), in place of the lumpish ones of composite metal which preceded them.

The Moslem monuments of England may be conveniently described under the several heads of: Type of the so-called penny; Arabian coins found in Scandinavia; Offa's dinar; Arabian moneyers in England; Arabian ratio in England; Arabian pre-eminence in the metallurgical arts; and the practically Arabian origin of sterling.

Type of the so-called Penny.—This piece is a flat, thin, round silver coin, about three-quarters to seven-eighths of an inch in diameter; in weight, from 17 in the earlier, to $21\frac{1}{2}$ grains in the later, ages. It roughly coincided with both the Byzantine half-siliqua, or quarter-miliaresion, and the Norse scat, but it differs from them in size, composition, and design. These last-named pieces, especially the scats, are thicker and smaller, the diameter of the latter being usually about half an inch. The standard of the so-called penny is 0.925 to 0.960 fine, that of the quarter-miliaresion is about 0.900, and of the scats of this period indeterminable, because they were not made of refined silver, but of old jewelry. Pieces of the type of the so-called penny, and known at the time as half-dirhems, were coined by the Arabians in the seventh century, and carried by their armies to the coasts of the Caspian and, during the eighth century, into northern Africa, Spain, and France. Whilst the Moslem were in possession of a large portion of France, Charles Martel struck coins of the same size, weight, and composition as their dirhems, while Pepin the Short imitated their half-dirhems. Modern numismatists call these last-named pieces deniers, or pennies. The design of the half-dirhem was simply a few lines of writing with arabesque work. Such, also, was the design upon the so-called pennies of the Norse or Anglo-Saxon kings of England. Afterwards they stamped their own effigies on one side; but this was not a Moslem practice, for with them it was strictly forbidden both by law and custom.

Although the use of the Arabian gold mancus in England during the seventh century, and the hoards of Arabian silver coins—some of them bearing an equally early date—which have been found in Gotland and in many other places in Scandinavia, afford reason for believing that the silver dirhem and half-dirhem were employed in England at the same period, yet the first certain appearance of what we have ventured to regard as the half-dirhem type in England was during the reign of Ethelbert II., king of Kent, who struck a silver coin of that description. It circulated side by side with the gold mancus of unquestionably Arabian origin,[1] thus leaving but little room to doubt the Arabian parentage of the former. Locally, however, the coin was not known as the half-dirhem, but variously as the scat and the penny, according to the local prevalence of Gothic or Roman nomenclature. At a later period it was appropriately called the "sterling."

Arabian coins found in Gotland, &c.—More than 20,000 Moslem coins have been found in various parts of Scandinavia, chiefly in Gotland, some dated so early as A. H. 79, others so late as A. H. 401. The presence of

[1] Keary assigns the first coins of this type to a still later date. ' The pennies of Offa, struck about the year 760 were the first ever struck in England. Their artistic beauty was not equaled for many centuries, not until the period of Henry VII " ("English Coins," p. xxii.) These so-called pennies we regard as half-dirhems. The penny, or Roman denarius, was of a different size, thickness, and metallic composition.

such large numbers of these coins evinces an extensive commerce with Arabians, and implies the currency of their coins and familiarity with their ratio in Scandinavia, and probably also in Mercia and Northumbria—in short, Scandinavian England, or all England north of a line drawn between the Severn and the Wash.[1]

Offa's Dinar.—In every country which fell beneath their sway, whether Syria, Irak (Persia), Egypt, Barbary, Spain, or Sicily, the Arabians struck bilingual coins of the denominations and partly of the type of those which they found in circulation. "I left to Irak its dinar, to Syria its dirhem," boasted Mahomet. His successors took care to observe this wise policy. From the reign of Abd-el-Melik coins were struck by Arabian moneyers after the type of the dinars and dirhems which he prescribed. A gold dinar of this character belongs to the reign of Offa, king of Mercia,[2] and its type is only to be accounted for upon the supposition that that prince was obliged to employ Arabian moneyers. On this coin appears, in Arabic, the words "In the name of God. This dinar was struck in the year 157" (A.D. 774). The reverse has: "Mahomet is the messenger of God, who sent him with the doctrine and true faith to prevail over every other religion," and, "There is no other God than one God—He has no equal." Between the lines, in Latin, appear the words "Offa Rex." A description of this coin by Adrien de Longperier is published in the London Numismatic Chronicle," iv., p. 232, and in Kenyon's "Gold Coins of England,"

[1] At the period mentioned Kent formed part of the Mercian kingdom. Arabian coins of gold and silver have also been found eastward, in the Gothic province of Novgorod, and in Great Permia. Hundreds of round bronze coins with runic characters have been found in graves between the Irbyht and Toboll rivers. A cut of one appears in Von Strahlenberg's valuable wok, p. 408; see also pages 110 and 409.

[2] Murcia was one of the names of Venus and the name of one of the provinces of Spain. The gold maravedi was sometimes called obolus de Murcia.

1884, where a fac-simile also appears in the frontispiece. The coin itself was in the collection of the Duc de Blacas, who obtained it in Rome about the year 1840. It contains about 60 English grains of fine gold. Its genuineness has never been doubted. It has been asserted that towards the end of his life Offa declared or pretended fealty to the pontificate, and was summoned to Rome, where he performed homage and entered into an obligation to pay to the Holy See 365 mancusses a year as Rome-scat. The conversion and the pilgrimage to Rome are doubtful. Longperier believes that the bilingual dinar was the sort of coin stipulated. Its heretical inscription, which, although in Arabic, could not have remained long unread, supplies a reason for its early suppression and present rarity.[1]

The Mark.—The origin of the mark has ever been a mystery to the metrologists. Agricola says it is mentioned in the earliest annals of the Cimbrian peninsular.[2] This carries it back to the third century. Queipo deduces it from the half-rotl of Ptolemaic Egypt; De Vienne, following the German metrologists, traces it from Etruria; whilst Saigey discovers it in a weight which he imagines was sent by Haroun-al-Raschid to Charlemagne before the year 789. These metrologists must have overlooked Agricola; they also forgot the common custom of antiquity in using coins for weights.[3] Instead of seeking the origin of this weight, as they have done, by means of mere literary coincidences, had they placed in a scale two-thirds of the silver coins rep-

[1] We are informed that upon Offa's return to England he built a monastery at Holmhurst, near St. Albans, another at Bath, and a church at Off-Church in Warwickshire, and that he was buried at Bedford (Speed, p. 362, ed. 1650, fol.) Perhaps.
[2] Bircherod, "Moneta Danorum," ed. 1566, p. 7.
[3] See Herodotus, i., p. 65, where hair is weighed with a silver coin in Egypt.

resenting a Roman "libra" they would have found the mark at once. In the first place it is quite evident that the name "mark" is neither Egyptian, Etruscan, Gaulish, nor even Arabic, but Gothic. Among the Saxons it meant a collective number of men or things—a community, a society, a clan, a market. Applied to money, it meant precisely what the Roman "libra" of the Theodosian code meant, namely, five gold aureii, or else their equivalent value in silver. Among the Romans this equivalent was twelve times the weight of the gold; among the Northmen it meant eight times, because the ratio in Gothic coins was 8 for 1; hence the mark of money was always two-thirds of the "libra" of money, not of the Roman libra weight. During the third century, between the reigns of Caracalla and Probus, the aureus was degraded to 90 English grains fine; consequently a "libra" of money contained 450 grains of gold. The Roman equivalent of this weight of gold in the silver coins with which the barbarians paid their tribute was 5,400 grains. The Saxon equivalent of a gold libra of this period was (at 8 for 1) 3,600 grains, which is the Saxon mark weight.[1] In short, the mark was originally the Gothic equivalent at the ratio of 8 for 1 of a Roman libra.[2] From this mark of money descended the mark weight, and from the mark weight the *livre poid de marc* (two marks) of King John of France.

The mark of money is mentioned in the reign of

[1] Bishop Fleetwood ("Chron. Prec.") regards the mark of money and the mancus coin as identical, but in this instance the learned and venerable numismatist is hopelessly wrong. Among other proofs the lawyer's fee of half a mark is still extant to refute him.

[2] These were the marks alluded to by Louis IX. in his reply to the Moslem demand of ransom. But, as a matter of fact, in the various temporary valuations which were made in the course of changing from the Moslem or the Saxon to the Roman ratio, the mark of account was not always valued at two-thirds of the libra of account. There are instances when the valuation was 150 pence to the mark, and at the same time 240 pence to the "libra."

Osbright, or Osbercht, the Norse pagan king of Northumbria (848-67); in the Alfred-Guthrum Treaty of 878; in the "Formanna Sogur," vi., p. 271 (a work ascribed to the tenth century); and in many other Norse writings.

The Mancus, Quarter-mancus and Half-dirhem.— The gold dinar or mancus contained at first 65 grains, 0.979 fine, say 63¾ grains fine, afterwards about 60 grains fine. Two heretical and exceptional mancusses (so-called) of 54½ and 51½ grains gross weight are mentioned elsewhere. In purity and color the mancus resembled no other coin of the Western world; hence it always retained the Arabian name of mancoush, or, as Latinized, mancus.[1] Such was not the good fortune either of the gold quarter-mancus or of the silver half-dirhem. These being smaller and less valuable coins, their superior purity and slightly different weight went unheeded, and in the intercourse between Goth, or Anglo-Saxon, and Roman, which took place in England, they passed respectively for the gold sicilicus and silver denarius. Although there was a difference in their purity, there was substantially none in the net contents of the mancus and besant, and these also passed for one another. As greater precision was obtained in refining the precious metals, and in striking coins of uniform weight, this practice gradually fell into disuse, but not until it had left the nummulary language of the period in great confusion. However, much of this disappears when the weights and fineness of the two classes of coins, Arabian and Byzantine, are contrasted in tabular form. It is then perceived that while there was disagreement between the gross weights of the

---

[1] Wex, "Métrologie," p. 114; De Vienne, "Livre d'Argent," pp. 43—56. Without agreeing with the conclusions of either of these writers, their works contain much incidental information on this difficult subject.

one set and those of the other, there was little or none in the fine contents of the gold coins, and also that each set of coins was by itself harmonious.

Arabian coins, 0.960 to 0.980 fine

	Gross. Eng. gr.	Net Eng gr.
Gold dinar or mancus[1]	65.00	63.75
Gold quarter-mancus	16.25	16.00
Silver half-dirhem (0.925 to 0.960 fine)	21.50	20.00

Byzantine coins under Heraclius, about 0.900 fine.

	Gross. Eng. gr.	Net. Eng. gr
Gold solidus, or besant	70.00	63.00
Gold sicilicus, or skilling	17.50	15.75
Silver quarter-drachma, or whole denarius, or penny	17.50	15 75

Arabian Moneyers in England.—Among the moneyers of the Norse and Anglo-Saxon kings, and afterwards of other kings of England, are many whose names are clearly Arabian. These names are: Ahlman, Ahlmund, Almuth, Alchised, Alchred, Abenel, Adulfere, Alghere, Alvyda, Abba, Aldruri, Baba, Babba, Beriche, Bosa, Baee, Bofa, Bora, Buga, Buiga, Dealla, Diar, Diola, Duda, Dela, Dia, Deid, Diora, Eckber, Eoba, Eaba, Eana, Elda, Enodas, Gineef, Heaber, Hussa, Hdiraf, Ibba, Idiga, Iaia, Lulla, Liaba, Ludic, Lil, Messa, Nom, Osmund, Osyaef, Ohlmund, Oshere, Osmere, Oba, Osmune, Oeldai, Tatel, Teveh, Tevica, Tata, Tila, Tisa.

Five centuries later than this period, Edward I. was obliged to send to Marseilles and Florence for artists skilled in refining and coining the precious metals.[2] Indeed, this was a common practice in England down

[1] The dinar was probably struck sixty to the mark weight, then of 1,600 to 3,777½ grains, while the besant was struck seventy-two to the Roman libra of, say, 5,250 grains; the sicilicus 288 or 300 to the libra, and the quarter-miliaresion 288 to the libra, or one-fourth of the whole miliaresion de sportula, which was ordered to be struck seventy-two to the libra (M. de Vienne).

[2] Lowndes on Coins, p. 94.

to the fifteenth century; and it is not too much to suppose that the princes of the heptarchy sent in like manner for Arabian moneyers.

Arabian Ratio in England.—As will be seen in another place, the ratio of value between gold and silver was fixed by the coinages of Ethelbert, king of Kent, and Offa, king of Mercia, and perhaps other early English princes, at $6\frac{1}{2}$ silver for 1 gold. This was a distinctly Arabian ratio, that of the Byzantine Empire being always 12 for 1. The coinages of those Merovingian kings of France who spurned the authority of Rome must be classed, like Offa's, with the Arabian. The following table affords a view of various ratios of silver to gold prevalent in England from the early portion of the eighth to the twelfth century. Pepin le Bref adopted the Roman monetary system in 754 or 755, from which date he refrained from striking gold. The ratio of valuation between his silver coins and the gold solidi of the Empire was 12 for 1, for the solidus is valued in the texts of the period at 40 silver pence, and the quarter-solidus, or *petite sou d'or*, at 10 pence. The ratio being 12 for 1 in France, it is difficult but not impossible to believe that, at the same period, it was successfully and permanently kept at $6\frac{1}{2}$ or $6\frac{3}{8}$ for 1 in England. However, there is no reason to doubt the ratios deduced in the table. The influence of Pepin's 12 for 1 is seen in the coinages of our Alfred.

Ratio of silver to 1 gold in the moneys of England from the eighth to the twelfth century.

Period A. D.	Ratio	Remarks
650— 750	6½	East Indian, Eastern-Arabian, and Spanish-Arabian coins of seventh and eighth centuries.
725— 760	6⅔	Coins of Ethelbert II., king of Kent.
758— 796	6½	Coins of Offa, king of Mercia.
800— 836	6	Valuations of Egbert, king of Wessex.
852— 874	6⅔@7½	Coins of Burgred, king of Mercia.
874— 878	7½	First coin valuations of Alfred.
878— (?)	10	Second " " "
(?)— 901	12	Third " " "
925— 941	12	Valuations of Athelstan, son of Edward, elder.
978—1016	10¾	" Ethelred II., king of Wessex.
1016—1033	9	" Canute.
1024—1066	8@12	" Edward Confessor.
1066—1087	12	" William I.
1087—1100	12	" William Rufus.

The Arabian ratio was adopted in England during the seventh century. It lasted without any substantial alteration until the second valuation of Alfred—a period of about two hundred years, and this in spite of its great variance with the Roman ratio.[1]

Arabian pre-eminence in the Metallurgical Arts.— Except the Byzantines and Arabs, there were few or no moneyers in Europe during the seventh and eighth centuries who were able to reduce gold or silver to the uniform fineness requisite for the coinages of new and, as yet, untried mints and governments. Mr. Keary's assays of the early Norse scats fully prove this view with regard to English moneyers. The cutting of steel dies was another mechanical difficulty. To the Gothic mints of the dark ages it was substantially insuperable.

The earliest coinages of mediæval England are later than those of France. Dr. Ruding's flourish about the pontificate of pope Hadrian I. cannot weaken the assertion that, down to nearly the beginning of the seventh century, no Anglo-Saxon coins, other than the rude, unlettered products of the early mints, were struck in

[1] For further information on Arabian ratio and coinages, consult "Money and Civilization."

England. The Moslem occupation of Spain and southern France, so long as it lasted, put an end to the exercise of the coinage prerogative of the Byzantine emperors in those countries. The last triente struck by Roderic of Spain was coined under Byzantine authority, and this was followed, with scarcely any interval of time, by the bilingual coins of Mousa-ben-Nozier. The refining of the precious metals and the cutting of steel dies for the West now fell wholly into the hands of the Arabians, and, taking into account the Gothic aversion to the Byzantine hierarchy, it would be difficult to advance any valid proofs that the nearly pure mintages of pagan gold and silver, which appeared in England during the seventh and eighth centuries, could, under the circumstances, have been effected without the aid of Arabian artists and moneyers.

Practically Arabian Origin of Sterling.—This term is now applied to distinguish coins, or bullion, of a standard fineness, or alliage, of metal, equal to that of certain sterling or easterling coins, or "sterlings" of the middle ages. This standard, afterwards called "old sterling," was 0.995 for gold and 0.925 for silver.[1]

There have been many explanations of the term sterling, none of which, however, are free from objection. There certainly existed during the eighth century an important traffic along the Gothic zone, which, bounded by the 50th and 60th parallels, extended from Mongolia to Britain, and found its chief emporia in Novgorod and Vinet, the eastern and western portals of Iestia.[2] The money chiefly employed in this trade, as we know from the vast quantities of it which have been dug up in modern days, was Arabian half-dirhems. This was the current money of Iestia, whose cities were all destroyed and whose records and monuments all

[1] Lowndes on Coins, p. 18.   [2] Von Strahlenberg.

perished under the proscriptions of Charlemagne and his successors. The earliest mention of Iesterling money which occurs in Western literature appears in the laws of the Ripuarian Franks. Hovenden, as cited in Hollingshed, attributes the term sterling (indicating a coin) to the reign of Osbright, the pagan king of Northumberland (A. D. 848-67).[1] It also occurs in the Alfred-Guthrum Treaty, still meaning a coin. It does not occur in Domesday book, where "libra arsa" and "arsura" are used to indicate the metallic fineness of money, and denarius to indicate the coin in common use, which, to the Arabians, was a half-dirhem, and to the Gothic races, as we are persuaded, was known as the iesterling or esterling. Ordericus Vitalis, an author born during the reign of William I., uses the expression, XVlibr sterilensium," meaning, doubtless, £15 in silver pennies.[2] The word sterling, meaning a certain coin, crept into extant texts during the reigns of the Norman and Plantagenet kings, and in the dealings of the Christian Hansa of the thirteenth century. The origin of its present meaning is not entirely clear; but, as the degree of fineness indicated, is precisely that of the Arabian coins contemporaneous with the heptarchy, and was not that of any other coins (unless we go back to the Roman coins of the third century), it is all but certain that sterling meant, first the Arabian half-dirhem, and afterwards the Arabian standard for coins. The only people who struck such coins at this date were the Arabians, whether in Arabia, Africa, Spain, France, Persia, Parthia or Scythia; and not only did they adopt a high standard for coins, they struck such immense quantities of them as to fill the channels of commerce, and render the standard well known and typical.

[1] Chambers's Encyc.
[2] Samuel Pegge, in "Gent.'s Mag.," 1756, p. 456.

Finally, they adhered to this standard for several centuries, and thus caused it to be depended upon and regarded as reliable, which, except as regards the besants of the sacred Empire, is more than can be said of any other coinages of the dark ages.

These marks of Moslem influence upon the early monetary types of England are submitted to the indulgent criticism of archæologists. Before the discovery of these evidences it appeared strange to the author that, during a period when Arabian industry and commerce and Arabian art and literature dominated the Western world, no traces of Moslem civilization were to be found in England—a country always famous for its maritime proficiency and the intimate knowledge of other maritime States which such proficiency promoted. These evidences bring to the surface a link in the chain of English history, whose long subversion finds ample explanation in the circumstances of the age to which it relates, and whose recovery, like a guide through a labyrinth, may enable us in future to outline with more assurance the still obscure history of the heptarchical era.

Grafted upon the Gothic monetary system, described in a previous chapter, the Moslem coins and types produced a hybrid system, which differed from its predecessor chiefly in the weight and composition of the scat and in the number of scats to the ora, also in the weight of the latter. At first the Gothic-Arabian system embraced the following coins and scale of equivalents, but as time went on several of these were modified:

Gothic-Arabian system (eighth century). Ratio, 6½ for 1.

Coins.	Money.	Value in scats.
8 stycas (bronze)	1 scat (silver)	1
3 scats	1 thrimsa	3
5 scats	1 ora (gold)	5
4 oras	1 mancus, or dinar	20
8 oras	1 double dinar (dobla)[1]	40
20 oras	1 mark of account	100

Under the Salic law,[2] as it was remodeled by Clovis, the gold sou, solidus, or besant, then of 68 English grains weight, was valued in Gaul at 40 silver deniers (scats), then of 17 English grains each—a ratio of 10 for 1. This was a mean between the Roman and Gothic ratios.

The etymology of styca, scat and thrimsa is uncertain. Lye derives styca from the Saxon sticce, but to this Ruding objects that the word sticce cannot express value distinct from magnitude; and again, why not sticce from styca, rather than styca from sticce? It is much more likely to be derived from the oriental word for a cutting instrument. Sicca (Indian), sycee (Chinese), styca (Gothic), saiga (Frankish), siccal, or shekel (Chaldean and Hebrew), zicca (Arabian), and sequin (Venetian) are evidently the same word and meant the same thing; that is to say, an instrument or tool for clipping coins, and, by metonym, a mint, a coin, etc. In fact, most of the coins of this period were finished with the shears. As the thrimsa was valued at three scats, its name was probably derived from the Latin trium. The etymology of scat, scad, or shad, has been already treated. During the dark ages the Roman

---

1 Abd-el-Raman spent on the mosque of Cordova over 600,000 doblas or "double pieces," of gold (Calcott's "Spain," i., p. 152).

2 The law of the Salian Franks (from the river Sala, Ies-sel, or Yessel) is believed to have been compiled after the Franks were established in the Netherlands. None of the extant compilations are of an earlier date than the seventh century. The original compilation was in Latin; in the later copies there are some German words, those copies containing the most German words being the most recent of all (Wiarda, "Histoire et Explication de la loi Salique"). Upsala (Sweden) appears to be another form of Ober Ies-sel (Holland).

imperial fisc in Gaul was obliged to accept its revenues and make its payments in rations.[1] If the Romans were obliged to use rations for a measure of value there is nothing improbable in supposing that the Norsemen used herrings. Ora, or aurar, is obviously from the Latin equivalent for gold. The term is still employed in the monetary systems of Scandinavia. Mancus is from the Arabian mancoush, coined money, and this from the verb *macasha*, to strike. Marcrus, manenco, etc., are corrupted synonyms.[2]

The scat, or properly half-dirhem, of this period was nearly of pure silver, thin and flat, but larger and heavier than the composite scat which preceded it. It contained $21\frac{1}{2}$ grains, 0.925 to 0.960 fine. The term scat is, of course, a name given to these pieces by modern numismatists, by some of whom they are termed pennies; but, for the various reasons herein adduced, these flat, thin pieces must be regarded typically as half-dirhems, and of Arabian origin. Owing to their superior weight and uniform standard, these scats were now reckoned at five to the ora instead of eight, as their namesakes had previously been reckoned. The thrimsa (it was not long in use) was either a coin or money of account, valued at three scats, and therefore worth three-fifths of the ora of five scats, or three-fourths of the later ora of four scats.

The ora of this hybrid system was identical both in weight and fineness with the Arabian quarter-dinar. It contained about $16\frac{1}{4}$ grains of gold, 0.960 to 0.979 fine, or nearly 16 grains fine, and it so closely tallied in contents with the sicilicus, or gold skilling, as to pass, at least in the south of England, for the latter. It is called a scilling in the Christian chronicles, and at a later period it found its way by the same Roman name

[1] Guizot, "Hist. Civ.," i., p. 351.

into the Norse sagas. "Olaf (1015-28) went southward across the sea from England and defeated the Vikings before Williamsby. He captured Gunnvaldsborg (in Seljopollar) and levied a ransom on it and the jarl of 12,000 gull skillingar."[1]

The gold mancus, or dinar, has been already described. That this coin circulated in the Norse kingdoms of England the frequency of its mention in documents of the seventh and eighth centuries leaves no room to doubt. The only Gothic-Arabian mancus extant is the unique coin of Offa, and this is stamped a "dinar." Of the doblas, or double dinars, there are no English specimens extant, although there are plenty of Spanish Arabian ones. The ratio of value between silver and gold in this system is indicated by dividing the fine contents of the ora (about 16 grains) into that of its legal equivalent of 5 scats, say 104 grains, the quotient being $6\frac{1}{2}$. Whilst this was the ratio in both the Indian-Arabian, Spanish-Arabian and Anglo-Arabian monetary systems of this era, it must not be forgotten that in the coinages of Byzantium the ratio was always 12; in other words, that the Christian valuation of gold (in silver) was nearly double that of the Moslem.

Such are the Moslem remains yet to be found in England—remains which, being traced upon monuments that the impassioned eyes of superstition failed to perceive, fortunately escaped its merciless proscriptions. To point out their significance and bearing upon English history is a task that belongs to the philosopher rather than the historian.

[1] Olaf's saga, c. 16.

CHAPTER VII.

MONEYS OF THE HEPTARCHY.

Summary of historical evidences furnished by the materials of this chapter—No coins of the Anglo-Saxons exist earlier than Ethelbert—Pagan gold coins—Gothic coins of Ethelred—Interpolations in ancient texts—Moslem coins of Offa the Goth—Rome-scat, or Peter's pence—Egbert adopts the Roman system of £. s. d.—Danish invasions—Burgred is defeated and interned in a monastery—Guthrum is baptized and reigns as Athelstan II.—Alfred of Wessex—Mingling of Gothic and Christian coins and denominations—Changes of ratio—Edward the Elder—Athelstan—Edmund I.—Eadred—Leather moneys—Ethelred II.—Danegeld—Canute the Dane—Harold the Dane—Edward Confessor—Harold II.—Evidences derived from these researches.

THE monetary systems of the various Anglo-Saxon States were of such essentially different structure as to denote the existence of different governments and religions, some Gothic, others Roman, some pagan, others Christian. After the era of baugs these States employed oras, scats and stycas, that is to say, native coins of gold, electrum and bronze, all of somewhat irregular weights, bearing no marks of a common authority, and issued by pagan chieftains owning no superior or overlord. The tale relations were octonary, and the ratio of silver to gold was 8 for 1. At a later period some features of the Arabian monetary system were grafted on the Gothic: the mancus and half-dirhem—coins of sterling fineness and regular weights—were issued or circulated in the various States, the tale relations exhibit the influence of the Arabian decimal system, and the ratio was $6\frac{1}{2}$ for 1.

When they successively adopted Christianity these States received their monetary systems from Rome.

The coins now used were besants (5 to the libra), shillings and pence; the denominations were £. s. d.; the weights were accommodated to these tale relations, which, as between shillings and pence, were duodecimal; the ratio of silver to gold was duodecimal; and the coinage prerogative, as to gold, was exercised exclusively by the emperors of Rome, and granted by them to the English princes as to silver—practices that are held to denote both the feudal form of government and the Roman religion of the vassal States. Of these various features of money the abstention from the coinage of gold by the converted princes, and the marked difference between the Christian, Gothic and Moslem ratios between the value of gold and silver, are the most significant.

It will simplify the subject to observe: first, that with few exceptions, which will be noticed as we go along, the only English coins now extant of the heptarchical period are silver scats, half-dirhems and pennies, all of which, being of somewhat similar weight, are usually, though erroneously, classed as pennies;[1] second, that as the Roman ratio was always 12 for 1, the denarii (of which 40 went to the Roman aureus, when the latter was struck 60 from the pound weight of standard gold) weighed 26¼ grains gross; third, that the denarii (valued at 40 to the aureus, solidus or besant, when the latter was struck 72 from the pound weight) weighed 21⅞ grains gross; fourth, that the denarii (when valued at 240 to the £., or 48 to the solidus) weighed about 19¼ grains gross, or 18¼ grains fine. There were also lower weights to the denarius, explained elsewhere. As this was the prevailing system of valuation in Christian States of the period answering to the heptarchy, it fol-

[1] There is nothing but historical inference to prove what these pieces were respectively called at the date of their issue.

lows, fifth, that when any so-called denarii, or pennies, belonging to such period, and being in good condition, are found to contain more metal than is here indicated,[1] they were either struck under the Gothic or Gothic-Arabian systems, and were really silver scats, or half-dirhems, or else, if of Christian stamp, they were valued in the law, at the time of their issue, at more than a penny each—a practice concerning the prevalence of which we have the testimony both of Bishop Fleetwood and M. Guerard. It does not, however, follow from this rule that a scat, or half-dirhem, containing more silver than a penny was worth more than the latter, because, as Christianity and "pennies" gained ground, and paganism with scats and dirhems lost ground, the latter, even when heavier, were accorded a lower value in the law.

The earliest coin of the heptarchical kings now extant is a certain unique one stamped "Ethelbert," containing about 20 grains of fine silver. Some writers ascribe this monument to Ethelbert I., but there is not sufficient evidence to warrant the inference. It is very much more likely to have been an issue of the second Ethelbert, king of Kent (748-60), replacing the composite scat, which by this time was disappearing in the refining crucibles of the Arabian moneyers. Mr. Keary prefers, indeed, to attribute it to Ethelbert, king of the East Angles, who died in 792 or 793, and, moreover, hints that its genuineness is not above suspicion. Of this class of coins twenty went at this period to the gold mancus, or solidus, of 60 grains fine, and five of them to the gold ora or shilling—a ratio of silver to gold of $6\frac{2}{3}$ to 1, thus $20 \times 20 = 400 \div 60 = 6\frac{2}{3}$. In some Anglo-Saxon coinages of this period the ratio was $6\frac{1}{2}$ to 1, in

[1] In applying this rule some allowance must be made for the unskillfulness of early mints in striking coins of a uniform weight.'

others 6 to 1. In other words, gold in England was valued as in Asia and Arabia, that is to say, at half the price (in silver) at which it was maintained by the sacred empire of Rome. The adoption of the oriental ratio in England, though probably due directly to the influence of the Arabian coinages of Spain, may also have been superinduced by the Gothic-Arabian trade of this period through Russia and the Baltic. Whatever the cause, the fact is believed to be indisputable, and as its acceptance solves many of the otherwise inexplicable problems of this period, it is commended to the careful consideration of the reader. Similar ratios of 6, $6\frac{1}{2}$ and $6\frac{2}{3}$ for 1 will be found in the contemporaneous coinages and valuations of Spain and southern France.

Hawkins and Keary both intimate that during the reign of Ethelbert II. there was a silver penny of twelve to the shilling, and leave it to be inferred that there was either a silver shilling coin or a shilling of account employed in England at this period. A silver shilling coin is hardly worth discussing; there is none extant and there is no evidence that such a coin ever existed until the reign of Alfred, and even then it is by no means certain. At all previous dates the shilling, whenever embodied in a coin, was made of gold. With regard to a supposed silver "penny," of which twelve went to the shilling of account, this is an inference drawn from extant copies of the laws of Ethelbert, in which such denominations are mentioned. But as it is quite unlikely that two coins, namely, the scat and the penny, of nearly similar weight and contents, circulated in the same kingdom side by side, the one five, the other twelve, to the shilling, we must regard the latter as an anachronism introduced into copies of the law at a later period, when there were indeed twelve pence to the shilling.

Ethelbert's laws are unique in being written in English, but the MS. is Anglo-Norman of the twelfth century, and the original laws have evidently been frequently altered.[1] Bishop Fleetwood has proved several anachronisms in the monetary terms employed in the earlier English texts of laws. The ratio of 9 silver to 1 gold, assumed by Keary for the coinages of Ethelbert's reign, rests upon this same literary and probably anachronical penny, and must stand or fall with it. It will probably be found difficult to overthrow the ratio of $6\frac{2}{3}$ derived from the Anglo-Saxon valuation of 20 silver pence to the besant. Some of the other conclusions of Mr. Keary—for example, that the thrimsa was a tremissis, that the pound or livre of money always consisted of 240 pence, and that the mark weight was (in England) half a pound weight—will incidentally receive consideration as we proceed.

The tax of Peter's pence was first collected in England by the Roman pontificate from Ina of Wessex.[2] It is also alleged that after the conversion of Offa (about 790) it was levied upon that prince, who testified his submission to the pope by going to Rome in 793, and paying him homage in person; but this is doubtful. At this period Charlemagne was at the height of his power. France, Germany, Saxony, Hungary, Italy and even a portion of Spain acknowledged his sovereignty. Pope Hadrian I. had vowed himself Charlemagne's liege subject and vassal, and governed in his name. If Offa acknowledged the suzerainty of the pope, it is not clear whether he intended to admit or ignore that of Charlemagne, the pope's political superior or suzerain. Egbert, a Christian king of Wessex (800-36),[3] had been

1 Sir Francis Palgrave, i., p. 44.
2 For examples of Rome-scat, see Ruding, ii., pp. 205, 210, 212, 218, 230, 366, etc.   3 Not Egbert, or Egfrid, son of Offa, who died in 796.

for three years a soldier in the army of Charlemagne. He obtained his kingdom through the good offices of that emperor, to whom he swore fealty and did homage. When Charlemagne died (814), and the weak-minded Louis le Debonnaire was brought under the domination of the pontificate, the latter seems to have at once claimed Egbert as its vassal; but there are no evidences—at least not of that period—that the latter conceded this claim. The slender remains of Egbert's coinage system throw no certain light upon the question. The only coin of his reign extant is the silver penny of fifteen grains fine. The mutilated texts of the period mention a shilling of five-pence and a pound of sixty shillings, both of which may be anachronical, and supplied by the copyists of the extant MS. If the shilling was an actual coin, it was probably the old ora of $12\frac{1}{2}$, worn down to 11 1-6, grains fine. At fivepence to the shilling, this would give the Arabian ratio of $6\frac{1}{2}$ for 1—a result that would hardly tally with the Christian attitude ascribed to Egbert, for no Christian prince, except the Basileus, could lawfully coin gold, and he only coined it at 1 for 12 silver.

Following Offa on the Mercian throne were Egbert, his son (heterodox, died suddenly, 796), Coenwlf, or Kenulph (706-18,) Kenelm, Coelwlf, Beornwlf, Ludica, Wiglaf (interned), Berthwlf, Burgred (interned), and Coelwlf, the last of the line. The church had employed excommunication, female influence, monastic internments, and other resources to reduce the Mercian and Northumbrian princes to submission, but without definite success. The Danish invasion served its ends better. London was taken in 851, York fell in 867, Guthrum, the East Anglican, was baptized in 878,[1] and

[1] There are reasons for believing that Guthrum was a Christian before this time. In 875 he succeeded in dividing the Anglo-Danish army, of which a portion, under Halfdane, took possession of Northumberland and applied themselves to agriculture.

both Mercia and stubborn Northumberland were at length brought beneath the dominion of Rome. From 831, when the seven kingdoms of England were merged into the three kingdoms of Wessex, Mercia and Northumberland, until the date of the Alfred-Guthrum Treaty of 878, the intrigues of the pontificate and the military operations of the Danes were incessant. Gotfried, king of Denmark, having been poisoned in 819 and Harold installed in his place, the latter was baptized at the court of the conqueror, Louis le Debonnaire. Ridding himself of Regenfroy, his pagan rival for the throne, Harold made preparations to continue on a large scale the war against the English kingdoms, which had been inaugurated a quarter of a century previously by Ragnar Lodbrok, under king Sigurd Snogoje. This circumstance, together with the suddenness of Harold's conversion, and the fact that his expedition was mysteriously directed from the south of England against the not yet converted kingdoms of the north, warrants the suspicion that papal intrigue was at the bottom of the entire project.

In 832 the Danish forces landed on the isle of Sheppey; in the following year they overran the coasts of Dorset, and in 835 those of Cornwall. At this juncture died Egbert of Wessex, yielding the crown to his son, Ethelwolf, at that period a subdeacon of the cathedral at Winchester. In 844, at the Council of Winchester, upon the instigation of the bishop of Sherborn and the bishop of Wilton, and perhaps also influenced by the menaces of the Danish commander, Ethelwolf, as king of the West Saxons, made a donation to the church, by which he granted to it "the tenth part of the lands throughout our kingdom in perpetual liberty, that so such donation may remain unchangeable and freed from all royal service and from the service of all secular claims."[1] This embraced the Three Necessities—building bridges, fortifying and defending castles, and performing military service. So soon as this grant was duly executed the Danish forces disappeared.

A few years after this happy relief—that is to say, in 854—Ethelwolf went to Rome, where he did homage to the pope, and presented him with a crown of pure gold weighing four pounds, a sword adorned with pure gold, two golden images, two golden vessels, a service of plate, and a donation of gold to the clergy and of silver to the people of Rome. On his return from this pilgrimage, he married Judith, the daughter of Charles the Bald, of France. In the following year (855) the bishop of Sherborn played Ethelbald, one of the king's sons, against the father, and won from the latter another donation to the church, which donation was to last—to quote its own terms—"as long as the Christian faith shall flourish in the English nation."

Bearing in mind the fact that a ratio of 12 for 1 during this period was always a mark of Roman government, an attentive examination of the tables of ratios in a previous chapter will afford a tolerably correct indication of the dates when Roman domination was thoroughly re-established in the various provinces or kingdoms of Britain. However, the new domination, though practically the same, was not altogether identical with the ancient one: its appearance was changed, as though viewed through a defective glass. The ancient domination of Rome, so far as Britain is concerned, was in great measure a military one; the re-established domination was practically an ecclesiastical one. Both brought in their train the benefits of the ancient Roman civilization and the ancient arts. This civilization dur-

[1] "Anglia Sacra," i., p. 200.

ing its banishment had borrowed something, both from the anti-hierarchical spirit of the Norsemen and the scientific spirit of the Arabians. It bore a new aspect: it lacked the refinement of the old imperial civilization, but it was fresher, healthier and stronger. To the student and philosopher who contemplates the mediæval ages, the civilization that accompanied Christian government must have appeared like the face of a friend whom ill-health had banished to remote climes, but who had returned after a long absence—his frame the same, his features bronzed, his gestures coarse, but his step vigorous, and his eye animated with a new and hopeful vitality. Such seems to have been the character of that Roman civilization which, cleansed in the fire of Christianity, had returned to regain its wonted influence upon the Western world.

Resuming our consideration of the heptarchical monetary systems, the appearance of the extant coins and the study of the valuations accorded to them in the texts, make it evident that Burgred struck silver coins of 15 grains fine, which were valued by Christians at one penny each, with five pennies to the shilling. This gives a ratio of 6 silver for 1 gold, but owing to the varying weights of Burgred's coins, the ratio was in fact more commonly 6⅔ to 7½ for 1.[1] In 874, after Burgred was driven from his throne by the Danes, he repaired to Rome, where he was quietly interned in the convent of St. Mary's,[2] from which, it is perhaps need-

---

[1] In Schmid's "Gesetze der Angelsachsen" the scale of monetary equivalents relating to this period is confused and defective. Comparing the anachronical money "pound" of sixty shillings, mentioned in the texts of Egbert's reign, with the contemporaneous money mark of thirty shillings, mentioned in those of Guthrum's reign, he deduces a money pound of two money marks. Whereas, in point of fact, whenever the mark and pound were contemporaneous and belonged to the same system, whether they were moneys of account or weights, the former was two-thirds of the latter.   [2] Henry, ii., p. 71.

less to say, he never emerged alive. We next turn to Guthrum, several of whose moneyers (like those of Offa and other Gothic kings of England) were Arabian. It does not appear whether these officers were retained or not after Guthrum's public avowal of Christianity. If his monetary system accorded with the valuations in his treaty with Alfred, it embraced the Saxon gull-skilling (now reduced to 10 grains), the Arabian gold mancus of 60 grains as the equivalent of 30 silver pennies (each of 15 grains), and the mark of gold (a money of account) as the equivalent of 30 Saxon shillings. The ratio was 7½ for 1.[1]

Table of supposed moneys of Guthrum, afterwards Athelstan II.

Moneys.	Contents, or value, in fine metal.	
	Gold, gr.	Silver, gr.
Penny, silver coin	2	15
Saxon shilling, or ora, gold coin	10	75
Quarter-mancus, gold coin	15	112½
Mancus, gold coin	60	450
Mark, money of account	300	2,250

The monetary systems of Alfred of Wessex exhibit a curious mingling of Arabian, Gothic and Roman influences. The standard of fineness and the old mancus coin were Arabian, the ora was Saxon, the £. s. d. system and the ratio of 12 silver to 1 gold, in his third system, was Roman. It will be remembered that after the immense benefice which Ethelwolf granted to the church of Rome, the Danes disappeared from Wessex. This maneuver appears to have occasioned some dissatisfaction in Denmark, for we hear no more of Harold the Christian, who, in 850, was succeeded by Eric the pagan. Under this monarch preparations were made to conquer England for the Danes, and in 851 a fleet of

---

[1] An eminent English numismatist says of this period that the mancus was "one-thirtieth of the pound, or thirty pence." The mancus was, indeed, thirty pence, but there was no pound, and if there had been, it would not have been valued at 30, but at 7½ mancuses. The equivalent in silver coins was not 900, as our authority would argue, but 225 pence.

350 vessels landed an army on the Isle of Sheppey, which soon afterwards captured and plundered Canterbury and London. In 853 the Danes invaded Mercia, and upon the accession of Eric II. (pagan) in 854, they landed an expedition on the northern coast of Britain. In 858 Ethelwolf died, and Ethelbald, his eldest son, married Judith, his step-mother. This, and some other scandalous acts of the new prince, seem to have rendered the English nobles indifferent to the progress of the Danes, who (in 867) took York, and thus gained control of Northumbria. Two years afterwards the conquerors occupied the county of Fife in Scotland; in 871 they defeated the Anglo-Saxons at Merton, in Surrey; in 875 they divided into two armies, led severally by Guthrum and Halfdane the Black; in 876-7, although previously repulsed at sea, they invaded Alfred's dominions by land, and before they were checked took Wareham, Exeter and Chippenham. In 878 Guthrum publicly accepted baptism, and made a treaty with Alfred, by which Britain was virtually divided between these princes. In 885 Alfred turned the River Lea, where a number of pagan Danish warships were lying, and compelled their abandonment. In the following year he occupied, rebuilt and strengthened London. In 893 the famous viking, Hastings, with 300 ships, one of which was commanded by Rolla, seized Appledore and Melton-on-Thames. In 894 Alfred defeated Hastings' forces at Farnham, and captured that leader's wife and children. In 897 the pagan Danes were defeated at sea, near the Isle of Wight, and although their forces afterwards roamed through Mercia, and even invaded Wales, they gave for a time a wide berth to Alfred's dominions, and made no substantial progress in their conquest of England. However, a very considerable portion of the island was already in

their hands, and, evident as was Alfred's desire to submit his kingdom in all respects to the ordinances of Rome, it can hardly be supposed that, so far as his monetary system is concerned, he could bring this at once into harmony with the Roman system, while the very different system of the Danes was employed so close to his frontiers.

In arranging the coins of Alfred, Mr. Hawkins says that "they seem to fall into four principal divisions, struck, apparently, at different periods of his reign."[1] This opinion is corroborated by a study of the tale relations of his different moneys, which cannot be harmonized without admitting at least three different coinage systems. The Arabian mancus was certainly in use, or else its value was well understood, down to a certain period of Alfred's reign, for the king himself, writing of his translation of the pastoral of Gregory, says: "I sent a copy to every bishop's seat in my kingdom, with an aestel, or handle, worth 50 mancuses."[2] The Guthrum Treaty and the writings of Ælfric the Grammarian both testify that the mancus at this period was valued at thirty pence. Dr. Ruding has deduced a silver mancus of about the year 838, but no silver mancus has been found, and its existence is doubtful. A silver coin, possibly a two-shilling piece of this reign, is mentioned farther on.[3]

Of the silver scats or pennies of this reign there are

[1] "Silver Coins of England," 2nd edition, p. 121.
[2] Spelman, in Henry, vol. ii., p. 58.
[3] Both the mark and the ora are mentioned in the Edward-Guthrum Treaty of between 901-24 (Ruding, i., p. 314). Keary says that the ora is first mentioned in Guthrum's Laws, vii., and is there valued at 2½ shillings. In the earliest Anglo-Saxon coinages and valuations, the ora and shilling, both gold coins, were of like weight and value. The shilling afterwards lost weight. The difference in the value of the ora probably arose when the shilling, no longer made of gold, was represented by a sum of silver pennies, the ora of gold still surviving and the ratio being changed to 12.

two sorts extant—one containing 19 to 20 grains, the other about 15 grains, of fine silver. The Alfred-Guthrum Treaty values the mark of account at thirty shillings; Ælfric the Grammarian valued the shilling at fivepence. In another text[1] he says "they are twelve shillings of twelve pennies." These last are regarded as coins and valuations which belonged to Alfred's third system. Bearing in mind Mr. Hawkins' opinion that the light pennies of Alfred were of his first coinage, his first monetary system, about 874-8, appears to have been precisely the same as that supposed above of Guthrum. The contents of 60 grains fine, accorded to the mancus, is a measure derived from the contemporary dinars of Abd-el-Raman II., of Cordova.[2] There is a silver coin of Alfred, now in the British Museum, $\frac{15}{16}$ of an inch in diameter, and weighing 162 grains gross, presumably containing about 150 grains fine—a measure which would exactly answer for that of a two-shilling piece in this system. Humphreys and Hawkins regard it "more in the light of a medal than of a coin"— a convenient if not a convincing method of avoiding a practical contradiction of their theory of the ratio, the ratio being the significant and political feature of the whole matter.

Alfred's Second System.—This may be conveniently dated about the year 878. The principal features were the coinage of sterlings, containing about 20 grains fine silver, and an enhanced valuation of the foreign gold coins, in such sterlings. The Arabian mancus of 60 grains fine was still valued at 30 standard silver pennies, but as the latter were 5 grains heavier than the previous penny, this valuation makes a ratio between silver and gold of 10 for 1. The mark (money of account) of 5

[1] His translation of Exodus xxi., 10.
[2] The dinars of Al-Mostain-Billah were of the same weight.

mancuses was valued at 150 standard silver pennies.[1] The shilling was represented by 5 sterling pennies. If the "pound" was in use it consisted of 45 shillings, or 225 pence.

Alfred's Third System.—This must be dated some time between 878 and 901. Its principal features were the adoption of the modified Roman system of 5×48=240 pence to the pound of account, and the definite relinquishment of gold coinage. This meant the eventual acceptance of the Byzantium gold coins and ratio of 12. By this time all gold coins, except old and greatly worn mancuses, had probably disappeared from circulation. Assuming that these mancuses (really zecchins) contained about 50 grains fine gold, the ratio was now 12, as follows:—5 standard pence=1 shilling of account; 6 shillings of account=1 mancus or zecchin; hence 600 grains of coined silver equaled in value 50 grains of coined gold, or 12 for 1.

In the earlier portion of the reign of Athelstan III.,[2] Christian king of Wessex (925-41), the Byzantine shilling was valued at 5 silver pence, in the latter portion it was altered to 4 pence.[3] This involved an alteration in the value of the Gothic thrimsa, which before was 2½, and was now rated at 3 scats. It also involved a change from 5×48=240 to 4×60=240 pence to the £., while the mark of account was valued at 160, instead of 150 pence as before.[4] There can be little doubt that

[1] During the mediæval ages, the English mark of account is valued variously at 80, 100, 150 or 160 actual scats or pennies. It would seem that the mark of account was always two-thirds of the pound of account; it was also, from the analogy of weights, counted as eight oras of account, and from this it was also, though erroneously, reckoned at eight times the value of the gold coin ora. The ora of 2½ shillings has been mentioned in the text.

[2] There were three Athelstans or Æthelstans. The first was a son of Ethelwolf by his first wife. His father made him king of Kent, Sussex, and Essex, in the year 836 (Henry, ii., p. 65). The second was the converted Guthrum. The third was the son of Edward the Elder, and the victor at Brunanburg.

[3] Hawkins, pp. 268, 269. [4] Fleetwood, p. 23.

this adjustment was made by Athelstan. At this period the terms "mark" and "pound of account" were chiefly employed in the valuation of "retts," taxes, and fines, all of which went to the king. The adjustment, therefore, was in favor of the crown. The ordinary transactions of trade were conducted in pennies, or scats and stycas, and these were not affected by the changes mentioned. Guthrum had been the first English prince to assume on his coins the pretentious title of "King of England." Athelstan III. improved on this style by stamping his coins "Rex toticus Britanniæ." It was after the battle of Brunanburg, when flushed with triumph and backed by an overwhelming display of power, that he was most likely to have adopted this measure. In one of his edicts Athelstan orders that no coins except those struck or authorized by himself shall pass current in England, that none shall be struck except within the precincts of a town, and that no names, titles, nor effigies shall be placed upon the coins except those of himself. It is evident that coins were being struck by rival princes independent of his authority, and that the object of his edicts was to prevent the chieftains whom he claimed as vassals from striking coins in the name of such rival princes.

Because the extant texts of the period mention but few alterations in the value of coins and moneys of account, we are not at liberty to assume that no others occurred. On the contrary, from the appearance of the various coins, it is probable that many changes occurred, the only uncertainty about the matter being the precise date and manner of their occurrence. The weight of the penny, the proportion of alloy in this and other coins, the composition of the scat, the relation between penny and scat, the number of pennies and scats to the shilling, the number of scats to the mark, or pennies to the pound of account, and the ratio of value between silver and gold in the coins, were all altered. The kings of the heptarchy were no less ready to exercise the prerogative of "coining moneys and regulating the value thereof" than were the Romans before or the Normans after them. There were but few princes, form Offa to William 1., who hesitated to avail themselves of some from of this financial resource.

A later monetary scale of Athelstan shows a further intrusion of the Roman system into the moneys of Northumbria and Mercia. It consisted of Roman £. s. d. in the numerical proportions of 4×60=240 pence to the £., and of the following Gothic coins and moneys of account:—8 stycas=1 scat; 3 scats=1 thrimsa; 7 thrimsas=1 ora; 8 oras=1 mark; 1½ marks=£1. The foregoing two classes of moneys were united by the following scale of equivalents:—4 1-6 scats= 4 pennies, or 1 shilling; 160 pennies=1 mark. Hence, 250 (exactly 252) Gothic scats, or 240 Christian pennies= 1 "pound" of account. Hence also, 20 pennies to the ora, "Denar qui sunt XX in ora," as mentioned in Domesday Book, vol. i., fol. i. The styca of this reign was a small brass coin, the scat a small lumpish silver coin containing about 17 grains fine, the penny contained about 18 grains fine, or 22 grains alloyed, the sterling, or half-dirhem, was slightly heavier than the penny. The ratio of fine silver to gold in the coins of Athelstan was 12 for 1.[1]

During the reign of Edmund I., king of Wessex (941-46), the silver pennies contained from 16⅓ to 22⅓ grains fine.[2] We are aware of no alterations in the val-

---

[1] The mark of silver was reduced to two gold mancuses, whereas previously it was worth five. This was mainly due to the rejection of the Arabian and adoption of the Byzantine valuation of gold, an act which lowered the value of silver to a moiety.

[2] Ruding, i., p. 292.

uation of money during the reign of Edred, king of Wessex. The reign of Edgar, king of Wessex, is marked by the issuance of leather moneys and an effort to unitize the numerous and heterogeneous coinages of England—an effort which proved futile. The sterlings of this prince contain 18 to 20 grains of fine silver, but we do not know at what valuations they passed. Many of these coins were surreptitiously reduced by clippers to half their weight. After executing a batch of these criminals, a new coinage was ordered, and it was probably to fill the void thus temporarily created in the circulation that the leather moneys were issued. [See table on page 182.]

Ethelred II. (the Unready) has left us silver "pennies" of three different weights, containing respectively 20, 25 and $18\frac{1}{2}$ grains fine, which were struck respectively about A. D. 978, 990,[1] and 1016, and valued respectively at five, four and twelve to the shilling, there having been three systems of £. s. d., with respectively forty-eight, sixty and twenty shillings to the pound of account, the latter payable with five gold besants. When the last-named system of £. s. d. was fully established the heavy penny, or scat, of 25 grains fine, and belonging to the $4 \times 60 = 240$ system, undoubtedly went for three halfpence.

Contemporaneously with these systems, Gothic-Arabian moneys were employed by the Danish population (which, previous to the massacre of St. Bride's, had become very numerous), and valuations in such moneys were employed in the laws, treaties and other texts of the period, also for the payment of Danegeld. In Brompton's translation of the laws of this reign, fines

[1] The type of this coin (silver scat) is said to have been imitated by Haco of Norway (977-95), and for this reason we have dated the issue by Ethelred at about 990.

Table of Leather Moneys of the North.

Year.	Ratio and Country of Issue.	Description of Moneys.	Authorities.
B.C.			
140—117	Woote, emperor of Han dyn., China	Stagskins, a foot square	"Hist. Money," p. 24, 25.
A.D.			
806	Heen-tsung, emperor of China	Facsimile by Terrien	Ibid., p. 25.
862—879	Ruric the Goth, Novgorod[1]	Stamped leather	"Mon. and Civ.," p. 294.
959—975	Edgar, king of Wessex	Leather money	Ruding, i., p. 361.
998	Olaf I., king of Norway	Leather money	Greijer.
1060—1103	Philip I., king of France	Leather with silver náils	"Mon. and Civ.," pp. 29, 53, 64, 189, 192, 294.
1122	Doge Michieli, at Tyre	Stamped leather money	Ibid.
1154	William the Bad, king of Sicily	Leather money	Ibid.
1215	John, king of England	Leather money	Anderson, i., p. 297.
1226	Louis IX., king of France	Leather money	"Mon. and Civ.," p. 192.
1235	Frederick II., at Milan, etc.	Leather money	Ibid., p. 53.
1285	Edward I., king of England	Leather money	Ibid., p. 64.
1364	John II. (Charles V., regent), France	Leather money	Ibid., pp. 65, 192.

1 Down to the tenth and eleventh centuries the Norse fleets traded in England, Spain and Russia. An animated description of the Great Fair of Novgorod appears in the Flateyjarbok, i., p. 577; Du Chaillu, ii., p. 234. This cannot be later than A.D. 1050-60. Gyda, daughter of Harold II. of England, is said to have been married to "king" Vladimir, in Holmgard. Holmgard is the same as Novgorod, or Novgard.

are expressed not only in £. s. d., but also in marks, oras and scats. These appear to have been related as follows:—8 bronze stycas=1 silver scat (probably the heavy "penny" mentioned above); 8 scats=1 Danish gold ora; 3 oras=1 Arabian mancus; 5 mancuses=1 mark.[1] The "mancus" of this scale was evidently not a mancus, but a gold zecchin, or ducat, weighing 50 to 54 grains. There is a specimen of this coin extant, with the effigy of Ethelred, weighing $51\frac{1}{2}$ grains. It is heretical, and was probably struck without authority of the king.[2] In this system thirty (light) pence went to the zecchin.[3] Regarding the penny as containing $18\frac{1}{4}$ grains and the zecchin $51\frac{1}{2}$ grains, this would imply a ratio of $10\frac{3}{4}$ for 1.

There is little room to doubt that the middle term shilling was changed from forty-eight to sixty, and afterwards to twenty, to the pound of account. The first proportion rests upon the authority of Fleetwood (p. 23) and Anderson (i., p. 98), and the third upon Ælfric Grammaticus, the translation of Exodus xxi., 10, and the "Historia Eliensis." Both Guerard and De Vienne testify to the same practice at the same period in France. Shifting the middle term affords the best proof that the ora was now too valuable to pass for a shilling, and that the latter was merely a money of account, payable in silver pennies.

Canute, the Christian but anti-papal king of Denmark and England, has left us a greater variety of coin-types

[1] In Anderson's "History of Commerce," Mr. Lampard, the antiquary, is relied upon to prove that a thrimsa of this period was valued at three shillings; but this is evidently a blunder and means three scats.

[2] Zikkah, the Arabian word for stamp, die, coinage and mint, gave the name to the zecchin, sequin, ducat, florin, etc., all of which were different names for a gold coin, varying from 50 to 54 grains, something between the ancient dinar and the maravedi. The standard varied from 22 to 23 carats fine.

[3] Ælfric the Grammarian.

than any other English prince before the Plantagenet dynasty. His Gothic coins and valuations were 8 scats=1 ora; 3 oras=1 mancus; 5 mancuses=1 mark of account. His Christian coins were valued in £. s. d. on the scale of 5×48=240 pence to the £.[1] The pence vary in weight from 12 to 18, and the scats from 20 to 24 grains each, and are all about eleven-twelfths fine, the lighter weights, or the pennies, greatly predominating. The intervaluation between the two systems was 30 silver pence, each of 16 grains fine, equal to 1 "mancus," really a zecchin, of 50 to 54 grains, bespeaking a ratio of about 9 for 1. However, his Danish coinages render this ratio uncertain.

The accession of Edward Confessor marks the decline of Danish power and influence in England—an event long celebrated by the Catholic portion of the population in the religious festival of Hokeday. This prince's friendship for Normandy and his fealty to Rome manifested itself in the appointment of Norman favorites to office, in the quarrel with Godwin, the incarceration of Edgitha, the welcome which he accorded to William of Normandy, and his removal of Godwin's hostages (his son Ulnoth and grand-nephew Haguin) to William's court. Although the quarrel with Godwin was patched up, the hostages remained in Normandy. After Godwin's death (in 1053), when his son Harold, now the head of the family, sought to recover these hostages, he was refused by William. Upon the death of Edward (in January, 1066), Harold usurped the throne, and until the fatal battle of Hastings reigned for a brief period as Harold II.

The following scale of equivalents will illustrate Edward's system of moneys:—Five light silver pennies containing variously from 12½ to 18½ grains fine=1

[1] "Chron. Preciosum," p. 23.

shilling, and 48 shillings equal 1 pound of account; four heavy silver pence (scats), containing from 20 to 25, but for the most part about 20, grains fine=1 shilling; and 60 shillings=1 pound of account. The shilling of four pence appears to have survived that of five pence. Thus there were successively two classes of pounds, shillings and pence, and it is not improbable that there were three, the third consisting of the factors $12 \times 20 = 240$ pence to the £., and based on a degraded penny containing about $8\frac{1}{2}$ grains fine silver. Edward's coins were of uneven and oft-changed weights, and owing to the disturbed state of the government, they were also of uncertain and fluctuating value. The gold besant of Constantinople was in circulation, and, according to Dr. Henry, was valued at eight shillings, each of five silver pence. During another portion of Edward's reign the besant was valued at nine shillings.[1]

There is some reason to suspect that about this time the payment of Danegeld by the people to the king's officers was made in the degraded coins above mentioned, but the evidences are not sufficiently conclusive to entirely warrant the inference. However, the imposition of this tax was abolished by Edward, and it was not imposed again until the reign of William I. The Gothic moneys of Edward Confessor were valued as in Canute's reign. There is too much uncertainty about the weights and value of coins in this reign to make any reliable inferences concerning the relative valuation of gold and silver. The gross weight of a heretical zecchin ascribed to this reign, as given by Kenyon, is $54\frac{1}{2}$ grains. The ratio may have been any figure between $7\frac{1}{2}$ and 11 for 1. It was probably often changed.[2]

[1] Henry's "Hist. Brit.," ii., p. 275.
[2] For allusions to mint laws of Edward Confessor, see Kemble, pp. 67-9; for "Treasure Trove," see Ruding, i., p. 390.

Harold II. only reigned nine months, yet his coins are very numerous, nearly one hundred varieties of moneyers' names having been found upon them. It is quite probable that in the confusion of the times the chieftains and the prelates who supported Harold's pretensions to the crown took occasion to coin money for themselves, the profit upon such coinage varying from a twelfth to a tenth of the metal coined, sometimes more. Harold's silver scats weigh about 22 grains, and contain about 20 grains of fine silver. There is no reason to believe that he changed the previously existing system of £. s. d., nor that any of the coins previously in circulation—such as the Arabian zecchin, the besant and its fractions, or the Gothic stycas, scats and oras—were decried or interdicted.

CHAPTER VIII.

ANGLO-NORMAN MONEYS.

Norman, Anglo-Saxon, early Gothic, Moslem, Byzantine, and other coins circulating in England—Difference in the silver value of heretical and orthodox gold coins—Scats, sterlings, and pennies—Efforts of the Norman princes to escape the monetary supervision of Rome—Receipts and payments made in different moneys—Counterfeiting—Barter—Permutation—Fairs—Taxes and rents in kind—Bills of exchange—The monetary systems of the Norman princes exhibit a strange condition of political affairs.

DURING the Norman dynasty the coins in circulation consisted chiefly of five classes, namely: Norman, Anglo-Saxon, early Gothic, Byzantine and Moslem.

Norman Coins.—These "sterlings," or flat, thin, silver coins of the half-dirhem type, containing about 20 grains of silver 0.925 fine, or about $18\frac{1}{2}$ grains of fine silver. In modern numismatic works these are always called "pennies." No less than twelve thousand of the "pax" sterlings of William I. were discovered at Beaworth, in Hampshire, in 1833, besides other large hoards elsewhere. Twelve of these sterlings went to the Norman shilling.

It has been assumed by numismatic writers that the sterlings were always valued at one penny each; but in face of a contrary practice in France at this period, where the sterling was sometimes rated at three half-pence, two pence, etc., and of the twopenny sterlings, and threepenny sterlings cited elsewhere in the present work, this is by no means certain.

Anglo-Saxon Moneys.—The best Anglo-Saxon silver sterlings (scats) were valued at four to the Saxon shilling of account, while sixty Saxon shillings were counted to the pound of account. These relations were not disturbed by William, who continued to employ them in all payments under the Anglo-Saxon laws, or in reference to Anglo-Saxon rents and contracts. There were, therefore, two moneys of account employed during his reign, namely, the Norman $12 \times 20 = 240$ pence to the pound of account, and the Saxon $4 \times 60 = 240$ pence to the pound of account.

Early Gothic Moneys.—The ora is valued in Domesday Book at 20 pence, from which it would appear that Edward the Confessor's base pennies were meant, or else that William's sterlings actually went for twopence each. It has been suggested that the ora here meant was either the ora weight of 45 grains (one-eighth of the Gothic mark), or else a gold coin of about that weight, say the Moorish obolus de Murcia or maravedi,[1] but in 37 Henry III. (A. D. 1252), the maravedi of Moorish Spain was valued at 16 pence[2]—a fall in value which, if it related to a weight of gold bullion, would be difficult to account for, but which, if to an actual gold coin, might have been due to its having been reduced by abrasion or "rounding," or else to its heretical stamp. But, in fact, at the period of Domesday Book, the maravedi was a new coin; therefore we regard the first hypothesis as more reasonable. The composite or electrum scat had disappeared; the silver scat is mentioned under the name of a penny. The brass stycas, so common during the Gothic era, do not appear to have remained in circulation during the Norman one, for no mention is made of them in extant texts. They were replaced by Roman bronze coins.

Moslem Moneys.—The Spanish-Arabian dinar (60 to 66 grains fine) and the zecchin (50 to 55 grains fine),

---

[1] The maravedi of this period weighed about 43 grains (nearly) fine.
[2] Ruding, i., p. 316.

circulated in England under the misnomers of besant and mancus. Norman sterlings of the half-dirhem or sterling type, and containing 18 to 20 grains fine silver, had taken the place of the half-dirhems coined in Arabian-Spain. Valued in these Norman sterlings, the dinar was worth 34 to 36 sterlings, and the zecchin 30 to 31 sterlings—a ratio of 9 or 10 for 1. The mark of 5 zecchins, afterwards of 5 maravedis, was valued at 160 sterlings. The other Moslem coins which circulated in England during this period were the gold half-mithcal and a few of the old silver dirhems and half-dirhems.

Byzantine Moneys.—These were the gold besants of 65 grains, valued at 40 sterlings—a ratio of 12 for 1.[1] The besant of this period was a thin and slightly "dished" gold coin, or "scyphus," with a rayed image on one side. It was the direct descendant of the sacred aureus of Augustus and the sacred solidus of his successors, the sovereign-pontiffs or emperors of Rome.

Other Moneys.—Besides these coins the circulating money of England included the silver coins of France, Venice and other States. These were rated, by official proclamation, at something near their bullion value. Roman bronze coins of varied types and designs also circulated among the common people, and, according to Sir John Lubbock, they continue to circulate among them, in the remoter parts of England, at the present day.

The legal status, history and tale value of bronze or copper coins, and an investigation of the authority under which they were struck, during the interval between the establishment of Christianity in the provinces and the fall of the Sacred Empire in the thirteenth century, is a domain of numismatics upon which so little certain

[1] It results that the ratio for Moslem or heretical gold was 9 or 10 silver, and for Byzantine or orthodox gold, 12 silver.

light has hitherto been shed, that it would perhaps be unsafe to make it a basis for historical induction. There is strong reason to believe that the Roman Senate never parted with its authority to strike copper, and that during the dark and mediæval ages the Christian provinces were supplied with copper coins struck by moneyers appointed by the Senate, first of Rome and afterwards of Constantinople. It is certainly a remarkable fact, one well worthy the profoundest attention, that, except when at rare intervals they ventured to disregard the authority of the Empire, the Christian princes of England struck no copper coins until after the fall of Constantinople.

The Anglo-Norman kings coined no gold at all. The coinage of gold ceased when Christianity was introduced, and the last gold coins known to have been struck in England previous to the reign of Henry III. were the dinars of Offa, before his alleged submission to the yoke of the gospel.[1]

A good deal of learning has been spent upon that passage in the Black Book of the Exchequer (ascribed to William of Tilbury, in the reign of Henry II.), which states that a custom was introduced by William I. of requiring payments into the treasury to be made *ad scalam* (by weight). Lowndes treats this custom as general, and ascribes it to the universal prevalence of clipped and counterfeit coins; but this explanation, in view of the valuations based on the Byzantine ratio, and in view of the large hoards of full-weighted sterlings which have been found in modern days, is not satisfactory. Madox—who if less concise, is more practical—assures us that coins were received in the exchequer by deducting sixpence from each twenty shillings, for

[1] Two or three heretical exceptions to this rule have been already mentioned.

light coins: this was payment *ad scalam*. When the coins were unusually light they were only received as standard bullion: this was payment *ad pensum*. When their purity was in question they were received as crude bullion and sent to the refiners and assayers: this was payment by *combustion*. In brief, this means that payments *into* the exchequer, when made in light or debased coins, were, as nearly as possible, subjected to precisely the same regulations that they are to-day.

There is no reason for supposing that the phrase "payments into the treasury" meant anything more or less than what it literally conveys. Notwithstanding the theory of Lowndes, it may be asserted with confidence that it did not include other payments, such as payments *out* of the treasury, nor payments between merchants, nor between merchants and nobles. For all these classes of payments the king, at times, assumed the right to prescribe different sorts of moneys—a right which he invariably relinquished when admonished by the sacred college that he was exceeding his powers. In view of this tendency of the crown it would be absurd to suppose that when clipped or counterfeit coins were received at the treasury by weight, they were re-coined or paid out by weight. Nothing of the sort. The revenues came from comparatively few sources, whilst payments were made to a vast number of people; and payment by weight would have been simply impracticable. On the other hand, if the clipped and counterfeit coins received into the treasury had been re-coined, it would have taken but a comparatively short time to reform the entire currency; but no such reformation appears to have been undertaken. The fact is that the crown practically legitimized clipped and counterfeit coins, not by receiving them into the treasury *ad scalam*, but by paying them out of the treasury *ad numero*. Some of the numismatists have patriotically paraded one custom, and carefully suppressed the other; but the evidences of its practice appear plainly enough in the course of this work to satisfy the ordinary demands of reason. The power that scrupled not to receive and pay by different weights, would scarcely have hesitated to receive and pay with different coins, and it may be confidently believed that this was the practice.[1]

The sterlings assigned by numismatists to William Rufus are slightly heavier than those supposed to have been struck by his predecessor, and described at the outset of this chapter. The fineness is the same, and the two types and designs are so much alike that none but the most expert can distinguish them. No other coins are known of the reign of William Rufus.

The sterlings of Henry I., are of about the same weight as those of William I. but not quite so fine. These were followed by emissions of debased pieces, which it was afterwards pretended were counterfeits. Upon instructions—no doubt from the Roman pontificate—a re-coinage was ordered in 1108, and the severest sentences were threatened to false coiners. In 1123, to lend effect to these threats, the power of Rome was invoked in aid of the crown, and the penalties of the canon law were added to those of the civil. It is the indifference that was manifested toward these solemn injunctions, coupled with circumstances mentioned elsewhere, which leads to the suspicion that much of the base coining was done by a class of people who knew too much about the *crimen majestatis* to stand in fear of impeachment.[2]

[1] This practice (elsewhere) is alluded to and condemned in the Koran.
[2] In 1362 the abbot of Missenden was convicted of coining and clip-

In 1125 the current coins had become so corrupt that a large proportion of them would not pass even from hand to hand, and ninety-four accused persons, among them several privileged moneyers, underwent mutilation for false coining. Some of the numismatic writers have credited Henry I. with "abolishing the oppressive tax of moneyage;" but the fact is that he had no right even to levy such a tax. . Its abolition must be credited, not to Henry, but to his suzerain, the pope.

The only coins of Stephen are the sterling pennies of the regular Anglo-Norman weight and fineness. There were debased coins struck in Stephen's name, but they cannot be traced to the royal mints. Other debased coins were struck by Stephen's illegitimate brother, Henry, bishop of Winchester; by his illegitimate cousin, Robert, earl of Gloucester; by his two sons, Eustace and William, as well as by Roger, earl of Warwick, and numerous other prelates and nobles. In 1139 the sum of forty thousand marks, probably in debased silver pennies, was captured in the castle of the Devizes, from Roger, bishop of Salisbury. In 1181 silver coins, nominally valued at eleven thousand pounds, and foreign gold coins, amounting in value to three hundred pounds, were found in the treasury of Roger, bishop of York.[1]

Ratio.—In the reigns of Stephen, Henry II., and John, embracing the period 1140 to 1216, there occur several entries in the Exchequer Rolls where silver bullion appears to have been paid for gold bullion at the ratio of 9 weights for 1, and this ratio is supposed by some writers to have been adopted in the coin valuations of the first three Norman kings; but such is not

ping groats and sterlings; in 1369 the canon of Dunmore was accused of counterfeiting gold and silver coins; and in 1371 the canon of St. Gilbert de Sempingham was charged with secretly conveying coins the fact—the coin ratios were 12 for 1.[1] In France, also, during the same period, the ratio of silver to gold in the official valuations of coins was always 12 for 1, and the constant valuation of the mark coin in England at 13s. 4d. affords reason to believe that the Roman ratio of 12 to 1 was reflected in the legal valuations given to other coins in England.

In dealing with this period it should not be forgotten that there were but four classes of people who had anything to do with public affairs—the imperial authorities, the royal authorities, the nobles, and the ecclesiastics. The adulterations of money were committed chiefly by the two last-named classes. During the reign of Stephen castles, monasteries and fortified retreats sprang up on all sides, some of them supplied with implements to fabricate counterfeit money. A large number of these retreats—called in official language "robbers' dens"—were destroyed by the first Plantagenet king, but no mention is made of counterfeiting, and it was probably not common.

"Up to the year 958 the Flemings, Germans and Sarmatians dealt mostly by permutation of merchandise." In 959 Baldwin III., earl of Flanders, observing that the scarcity of money was an obstruction to the trade with France, established markets and fairs, at which merchandise could be permuted without money, and declared trade free of export or import dues.[2] Fairs

---

[1] See entry in the Exchequer Rolls 17 John, 1215, where certain besants of Constantinople were valued at 3s. 6d. silver each (Madox, ii., p. 261). Making allowance for difference of standard between the gold and silver coins, and for the probably abraded condition of the former, this evidently means a ratio of 12 for 1. At the same time the ratio for bullion was 9 or 10 for 1. We are not here alluding to the compromise ratios in the coinages of the Gothic kings of the heptarchy, shown elsewhere. but to the actual ratios for bullion, in 5 Stephen, 2 and 16 Henry II., and 15 and 17 John (Madox, i., p. 277 and ii., 261 n.) The subject has already been alluded to.

[2] "Annales Flandriæ," year 958, printed at Frankfort 1580, cited in Anderson's "Commerce," i., p. 98.

were held in England throughout the entire period of the Roman empire; they were encouraged in 1071, tallaged in 1195 (or before); they fell gradually into disuse after the discovery of America, and were abolished during the present century as "nuisances." The still lingering fairs of Beauclaire, Leipzig, Nijni Novgorod, etc., are moribund examples of this now almost extinct but once indispensable institution of European industrial life. Nor do we believe with some authors that the permutation practiced at fairs was simply barter. The exchanges were too numerous and important to be made by barter. It therefore seems likely that permutation was a system of clearings. The goods were bought and sold on a credit which was to last during the fair. The prices were couched in £. s. d. or other moneys, and when the fair closed the clearing was made, thus obviating the use of any other money than the final sums needed to effect a balance.

It is commonly asserted by continental writers that bills of exchange are of mediæval origin, and were first used in England during the reign of Henry III. This is entirely erroneous. There are examples of their use in India and China backward to remote historical eras; in ancient Babylon; in Pontus during the fourth century before our era; and probably also at the same time in Greece; in Athens and Rome (*tempo* Cicero) and probably also for centuries before and afterwards; in Constantinople and Carthage about the year A. D. 321; at Alexandria, Venice, Amalfi, Sienna, Florence, Barcelona, etc., during the Arabian epoch; and in all the cities (including the English "staples") of the pagan and Christian Hansas. Bills of exchange were in common use in Hamburg in 1188, and it can scarcely

1 Madox, i., p. 703.

be doubted that they were known at the same time, and indeed long before, in England.[1]

Blanqui says that at least the device of endorsement was unknown during the middle ages; but this is also incorrect. An instance of assignment by means of written endorsements is given in Madox, i., p. 242, and relates to a transaction between two Jews in 18 Edward I., year 1289. It appears on the ancient Exchequer Rolls relating to Jewry, and is not mentioned as a novelty. Being written upon the dorsal portion of a "membrane," or parchment, it afterwards came to be known as an endorsement.[2]

Sir Matthew Hale ("Sheriffs' Accounts") proves that during the Norman era farms were let variously upon a money rent (*numero*) or a bullion rent (*blanc*), but that in both cases the actual payments were made in kind. Even the payments into the exchequer—which Madox would lead us to infer were always made in silver *ad scalam*, *ad pensum*, or by *combustion*—were often made with goats and pigs. Lord Liverpool's researches led him to the same conclusion. He says (chapter x.) that in the reigns of William I. and William II., and during a great part of the reign of Henry I., the king's rents, arising from his demesnes (which formed at that time an important part of the royal revenue) though reserved in money, were really answered in cattle, corn and other provisions, because money was then scarce among the people.[3] The rents

[1] On the early use of bills of exchange consult Lenormant, "La Monnaie," i., p. 118; "U. S. Com. Rel.," 1858, p. 311; M. Courcelle Seneuil, "Dict. Polit. Econ.,"1853, art., "Lettre de Echange;" Savary; Blanqui; Garni; Thompson's "Polit. Econ.;" Del Mar's ";History of Money in Ancient States," pp. 26 and 106; Eggleston's "English Antiquities," p. 122; Cicero's Letters; Anderson's "Hist. Com.," i., p. 171; Eusebius. "Ecc. Hist.," x., c. 6.

[2] The expression "dorse of the membrane" is twice used in Madox, i., p. 239.

[3] However, they were commuted for money by Henry I. (And. "Com." i., p. 248-55) This was probably after his various coinages had rendered money sufficiently plentiful.

of private landholders continued to be paid in kind down to a still later period. The best evidence with respect to this matter is given by the writer of the Black Book, or Liber Niger Scaccarii, cited elsewhere, who avers that he had conversed with men who saw the rents brought in kind to the king's court.

Such are the monetary monuments, and such were the monetary systems, of the Anglo-Norman kings. That attempts were made to harmonize the diverse materials of which they were composed—Roman, early Gothic, Moslem, Anglo-Saxon, Carlovingian and Byzantine—is proved by the intervaluations of Domesday Book, and the gradual suppression and disappearance of some of these materials, chiefly the early Gothic and Moslem; but it is equally evident that the attempt was only partially successful, and that there yet remained— as, for example, in the mark and pound—an incongruous medley of pagan and Christian denominations, and in the divided authority to coin—for example—to the Basileus gold, and to the kings, nobles and prelates silver (upon conditions)—another medley, which faithfully reflected the general confusion of a period whose history was one of personal wars, personal combats and personal displays of heroism, chivalry or religious devotion. Cœur de Lion is its false ideal; Froissart was its true historian; and all attempts to deduce from such materials an independent national existence or policy for France, England, Germany or Spain during this early period have been both unsuccessful and misleading.

CHAPTER IX.

EARLY PLANTAGENET MONEYS.

Purity of the coinage before the fall of Constantinople—Corrupt state afterwards—The change was due to the destruction of the sacerdotal authority, the disappearance of the sacred besant, and the assumption of certain regalian rights by the kings of England—Whilst contracts could be made in gold besants, there was no profit in tampering with the silver coinage—Afterwards it became one of the commonest resources of royal finance—Coinage systems of Henry II.—Richard I.—John—Henry III.—Edward I.

THE evidences which will be brought together in this chapter may be conveniently formulated as follows:—Previous to the fall of Constantinople there were but few tamperings with the English coinage, afterwards such tamperings became numerous and continual—a proof that some event had occurred meanwhile to render them practicable and profitable, such event having been, in fact, the acquisition by the king of the coinage rights which the Basileus had lost. Previous to the fall of Constantinople no king of England had ventured to strike a gold coin, whereas soon after that event, and following the example of other princes of the West, a gold coin was struck by Henry III.; and although this coin was recalled and melted down, it was followed by another one struck by Edward III. The issuance of this coin, the gold noble, or half-mark, is regarded as the definite declaration of England's independence.

Reference to other portions of this work must convince the reader that from William I. to Henry II.—an interval of nearly a century—the coins issued by the kings of England were substantially free from degradation and debasement. In other words, the Norman kings rarely tampered with the coinage. The coins were all of one class—silver pennies, sometimes including half-pennies, but usually pennies only. These did not constitute the only money in circulation, but the only money issued by the king. In addition to the silver pennies, there were coins issued by the nobles and ecclesiastics, commonly base silver coins, of local course and circulation, and the gold coins of the Basileus, valued by the Basileus always at one for twelve weights of silver, and made and accepted as legal tender for any sum in all parts of the kingdom.[1] Other foreign coins had only a permissive circulation, at valuations announced from time to time by the king; the gold coins of Constantinople constituted the backbone of the circulation, and kept the rest of it straight. So long as contracts could lawfully be made in these coins, the king could make no profit by tampering with the silver pennies; accordingly he struck the latter, as nearly as he could, to contain exactly the same quantity of fine metal as the gold shilling, or quarter-besant, of the Empire. As previously shown, the besant contained about 73, afterwards 65, grains fine. The gold shilling, therefore, contained $18\frac{1}{4}$, afterwards $16\frac{1}{4}$, grains fine; and this was exactly the contents of silver in the two classes of silver pennies of the heptarchy and of the Norman kings; twelve such pennies being valued at a shilling and forty-eight at a besant.

With the reign of Henry II. (Plantagenet) commenced those tamperings with money which announced the advent of independent sovereign power in England, and presaged the extinction of imperial control. Plantagenet inherited from his mother the States of Normandy and Maine, and from his father Touraine and

[1] The subject of Roman copper coins during the mediæval period is alluded to in the last chapter.

Anjou; from his wife Eleanor, who had been divorced from Louis VII., he received Poitou, Saintonge, Angumois and Aquitaine; in a word, he became possessed of the entire western half of France from the Channel to the Pyrenees. After adding these domains to the crown of England, he acquired Northumberland by treaty with the king of Scotland. Ireland he acquired by a grant from Pope Hadrian IV., in 1154. The productions and trade of these extensive domains, together with his share of that additional trade and wealth, which, in common with other Christian princes, the king of England derived from the suppression and spoliation of the Spanish-Arabian empire, are indicated to some extent by the vastly increased revenues of crown and mitre, the splendor of the court, and the number and wealth of the churches. To this period belong some of the finest specimens of ecclesiastical architecture yet existing in England. Yet the monetary monuments are still those of a vassal and feudal State. An important part of the coinage was struck, valued and made part of the circulation by one foreign prince (the Basileus), whilst an important part of the revenues were collected and enjoyed by another (the pope). The influx of besants, the efflux of Peter's pence, the defiant issues of baronial and ecclesiastical mints, which included leather and tin coins, all betray the impotency of the king to preserve the national measure of value from degradation and derangement.

Of old sterlings there were probably few or none in circulation when Henry II. came to the throne; whilst of the base and adulterated coins issued by the robbers and forgers, who flourished during the weak reign of Stephen, there were many. Among Henry's early cares was the suppression of these moneys and the issuance in their place of a new coinage (about the year 1156). This coinage in violation of the king's commands was made below the standard—a fault for which he severely punished the moneyers.

About the year 1180[1] Henry II. sent to Tours for Philip Aymary, a French moneyer, and committed to his charge the striking of a new stamp of sterlings. These were issued, and the previous sterlings retired. After executing this work, Aymary was himself charged with fraud, and dismissed to his own country; yet the appearance of the coins supposed to have been minted under his superintendence, great numbers of which are extant, afford no support to this accusation. The pieces are indeed badly executed, and may thus have formed a ready temptation to rounders and clippers; the weights are also irregular. Perhaps it was on these accounts that the foreign artist was so summarily treated.

The rates of exchange established by the mint between the new sterlings and the old ones—whether the base ones of 1156, or the rounded and clipped ones is uncertain—prove that the latter were inferior in value to the former by about 10 per cent; at all events, this rate probably marks the degrees to which clipping extended at this period. For £375 3s. 9d. of old clipped money the mint paid £343 15s. 6d. of new; for £100 old, £89 6s. 8d. new; for £100 old, £83 6s. 8d. new, and so on (Madox, i., p. 278). This *nova moneta* is known to numismatists as "short-cross pennies," and these became so popular that they continued to be struck in the name of "Henri" until the middle of the reign of Henry III. (1247), although the reigns of Richard I. and John Lackland intervened. This, however, does not necessarily imply that Richard and John struck such

[1] "The Norman Chronicle" states that the new sterling money was struck in 1175 (Madox, i., p. 278).

coins. The extant coins of Henry belong solely to the last issue. A hoard of these coins was found at Roylston in 1721. Other pieces, to the number of 5,700, were found at Tealby, in Lincolnshire, in 1807. They were as fresh as when they left the mint. According to Keary, the fineness is 0.925, and the contents in fine silver of the most perfect specimens, 18¼ grains. Dr. Ruding's valuable but antiquated work gives what seems to be a wholly different account. He says that 5,127 of them weighed 19 lbs. 6 oz. 5 wts. This is an average of 22 grains each, or (assuming the fineness as equal to sterling) 20¼ grains fine; but as he says nothing of the remaining 57 pieces found at Tealby, it may be that the average of the whole corresponded with Keary's assays.

With regard to tin money of the nobles, mention of albata, or white money *(argentum blancum)* occurs in the Exchequer Rolls pertaining to the fourth year of this reign, where it is expressly distinguished from silver money *(argenti)*. In the fifteenth year Walter Hose paid one shilling in the pound for the *blanco firmæ* of Treatham; in the seventeenth year twenty shillings were paid in *argento blanco;* in the twenty-third year Walter de Grimesby forfeited a lot of the same metal; in the twenty-sixth year the sheriffs of London and Middlesex paid in, from the effects of a coin clipper, £9 5s. 4d. in silver pennies and five marks in "white money." In order to determine the meaning of "white money," it is to be remarked that the term "*argento blanco examinato*" was used when silver bullion was meant. For example, in the thirtieth year of Henry II. the sheriff of Devonshire paid 8s. 9d. in bullion *(argento blanco examinato)*, made up of divers old coins, and in the thirty-third year the same sheriff paid twenty-six pennies in bullion *(argento blanco examinato)*, made up of numerous coins dug up from the earth. Sir Charles Fremantle was of opinion that the trial of the pix mentioned in the Lansdowne MS. related to this reign.[1] In this opinion the author finds himself unable to concur, but believes that it relates to the reign of Edward I. Some consideration of this subject will appear further on.

Turning from the monetary system of Henry to that of his successor, we find it marked by the same characteristics—a full legal-tender gold coinage issued by the Basileus, and constituting the basis of the system; a silver coinage (pennies) issued by the king, as nearly as practicable of even weight with and exactly one-twelfth the value of the Byzantine sicilicus; and a base coinage of local circulation, issued by the nobles and ecclesiastics, the gold coinage being never, the silver coinage rarely, and the base coinage frequently, altered.

Although there are no native coins extant of Richard I., the evidences that he exercised the usual coinage rights of provincial kings are so numerous as to leave little room to doubt the fact. In 1189, upon his accession to the throne, Richard weighed out more than 100,000 marks from his father's treasure at Salisbury; in an ordinance of the same year moneyers at Winchester are mentioned; in the same year he granted a local coinage-license to the bishop of Lichfield; in 1190, while at Messina on a crusading expedition, he found it necessary to command and exhort his followers to accept his money—a tolerably sure indication of coinage; and in 1191, Henry de Cornhill was charged in the exchequer accounts with £1,200 for supplying the cambium, or mints of England (except Winchester),

[1] British Mint Report, 1871, p. 12.

and with £400, the profits of the cambium for a year. The names of Richard's moneyers in his mints at Warwick, Rochester and Carlisle appear in several texts relating to his reign. Coins which were struck in Poitou under his authority are still extant. Finally, as will presently appear evident, he granted and revoked licenses to nobles and ecclesiastics to strike tin and other base coins. All these prerogatives were such as were common to provincial kings; but Richard struck no gold, and made no attempt either to interdict the circulation of the Imperial coins or to alter the sacred valuation of gold and silver which was laid down in the constitution of the Empire.

With regard to his ransom, the inference of new coinage is totally wanting. In 1192 Richard was taken prisoner on the continent, and handed over to Henry VI. of Germany. In 1194 he was ransomed for about the same amount of money that he is said to have inherited from his father. This ransom was collected in England and from the possessions of the English crown in France. From the particulars of its collection—to be found in the pages of Madox—it appears to have been contributed in coins. Caxton says that plate "was molten and made into money." Stowe makes a similar statement. Altogether ten ancient texts agree in stating that the ransom was paid in money, and that the same was answered in "marks weight of Cologne," which latter was natural, that being the standard of weight with which the German emperor was most familiar. Notwithstanding this testimony, it may be safely conjectured that there was no new coinage, for such an operation would have been needless, tedious and expensive. The old coin and bullion was probably melted down, refined, cast into bars, assayed, weighed, and delivered to the German emperor's legate—a supposition that precisely agrees with Polydore Vergil's account of the affair.

In this same year (1194), according to Trivet and Brompton, the king decried the divers coins of the nobles and ecclesiastics which remained in circulation, and ordained one kind of (silver) money to be current throughout his realm.[1] Among these various coins were those of tin. Camden would have us believe that the coinage of tin was a term used to denote merely the payment of that forty shillings per one thousand pounds weight which was the heirloom of the dukes of Cornwall; but this can only relate to a subsequent period, for there were no dukes of Cornwall in the reign of Richard I.

In 1196 Henry de Casteillun, chamberlain of London, accounted to the king for £379 1s. 6d., received for fines and tenths on imported tin and other mercatures, also for 16s. 10d., the chattels of certain clippers.[2] In the same year £1 19s. 1d. were allowed to Odo le Petit in his account for the profit of the king's mint for erecting therein a hutch and forge *(fabrica)* and utensils for making "albata silver," or albata money *(dealbandum argentum)*, also £2 4s. for a furnace and other devices for working the same. These coins, though struck in the royal mint, were not of royal issue, and could have had only a local and limited course within the domains of the noble for whom they were made. In the same year the sheriff of Worcestershire accounted for £40 13s. 6d. albata, or album, money, the balance

---

[1] In this same year (1194) occurs what has been regarded as the earliest mention in extant texts of the mark, valued at 13s. 4d. (Fleetwood, p. 30, from M. Paris); but, as shown in a previous chapter, the mark of 13s. 4d. is three or four centuries earlier. The mark of 1194 was composed of five gold maravedis; 13s. 4d. was its value in silver, at the Christian ratio of 12.

[2] Madox, i., p. 775.

of his ferm of the county. Of this sum he had paid £12 in album money to the archbishop of Canterbury, and owed £28 13s. 6d. in album money to the exchequer, besides enough more to make up the difference between £12 silver money and the like sum album money, paid to the aforesaid archbishop. In explaining the use of the term "*blanc*," Madox confuses *blanc* silver and *blanc* money. The former was silver bullion, the latter a white money, sometimes called album, made wholly or for the most part of tin. The meaning of album money is clearly indicated in several of the Exchequer Rolls, which he himself cites.[1]

In the same year (1196) the king granted a coinage license to the bishop of Durham. In 1198 William de Wroteham accounted at the exchequer for the yearly ferm and profits of the mines of Devonshire and Cornwall, partly in money and partly in tin bullion. This bullion appears to have been sold for tin marks, for in the 13th and 14th John, who succeeded Richard I., this same William de Wroteham accounted to the king both for his ferm and for the marks obtained from the tin *(de marcis provenientibus de stanno)*. It may be safely inferred that in all cases these base coinages were issued by the nobles or ecclesiastics, and were of limited course.[2]

The albata money of Richard's time was either a composition of tin and silver—a good deal of tin and very little silver—or else merely tin coins blanched with silver. The clippers, whose chattels were confiscated to the exchequer by Henry de Casteillun, must have practiced their art upon the royal coins, for there could

---

[1] Madox., i., p. 280
[2] The writers who allude to these corrupt coinages are Tindal ("Notes to Rupin," i., p. 258); Leake ("Historical Account of English Money," p. 58); Nicholson ("Eng. History," lib. i., p. 254); and the modern special writers on tin and base coins.

have been but small profit from exercising it upon those of the nobles.

Although, immediately after the payment of his ransom, Richard decried all other coins but his own, his edict became a dead letter; indeed, he was probably glad enough to see the base coins remain in circulation. The population of England and Plantagenet France during the reign of Richard I. was probably not over four or five millions, and the total money not over as many shillings, or, say, £250,000. Richard's ransom therefore stripped the kingdom of probably one-third or one-fourth of its measure of value, and but for the album money of his nobles, this circumstance might have brought on far greater calamities than the release of the king was expected to avert.

The main defect of the tin coins was not the low cost of the material of which they were composed. The gold and silver obtained from the spoliation of the Moslem and the Jews were cheaper than tin, for they cost nothing to produce beyond the labor of cutting so many pagan and infidel throats, whilst tin ore had to be discovered, excavated and reduced to metal. But there was no world-wide demand and no world's stock in hand to enhance and steady the value of tin, whilst as to gold and silver there was; and this is chiefly what has always rendered these metals preferable for coins. Tin coins were also easily counterfeited, the material was exposed to rapid oxidation, and the condition of society and government was wholly unfitted for the use of coins of any material which could not conveniently and without substantial loss be buried in the earth, or otherwise hoarded for use in future and safer times.

There are no English coins extant of John. It is stated[1] that this king sent for certain Easterling artists

---

[1] Anderson's "History Commerce," i., p. 199.

to refine his silver coins. These may have been the coins he struck in Ireland, as lord paramount of that country, specimens of which still remain. On the other hand, they may have been English sterlings, of which no specimens have yet been found.[1] John lost most of his French possessions to Philip II., and thus, almost at the outset of his career, gained the name of Lackland. His return to England was marked by the imposition of fines and aids, which, because they extended to the monasteries, earned for him the curses of the archbishop of York and a defamation of character which extends to the present time. This being probably in great measure unjust,[2] should enjoin caution in weighing the events of his reign. Camden ascribes to this period the leather money attributed to John, but though belonging to his reign, it may have been issued by his vassals; at all events it wholly failed to secure public appreciation. In 1205 John publicly decried all coins which were clipped more than an eighth; severely denounced and threatened all clippers, particularly the Jews, whom he affected to believe were the chief offenders; forbade the re-blanching of old pennies, which could have been none other than the tin coins of his nobles; and fixed the rate for exchanging "fine and pure silver at the king's exchanges of England, and at the archbishop's exchange of Canterbury, at sixpence in the pound." This could not have meant the exchange of new coins for old ones by tale, because the latter were much worn and clipped. It probably meant the exchange of new coins, weight for weight, for old ones.

1 The "Encyc. Brit.," art. "Coin," states that since Richard I. all coining has been confined to the Tower of London and the provincial mint of Winchester. This is a double error. Sir Matthew Hale's account of this matter is the correct one.
2 Anderson's "History Commerce," i., p. 193.

More important, however, than the king's coins were those of the Basileus. The form used in expressing large sums of money proves the still common use of gold besants and Byzantine trientes and shillings. For example, in the previous reign, where £100 of old coins are bought for £83 6s. 8d. of new, the sum is thus written in the Great Roll of the Exchequer: "quartor XX l & lXVj, s. & Viij d." meaning four score libras, sixty-six solidi and eight denarii. The former were evidently composed of actual besants and thirds, and quarter-besants. In the Magna Charta of this reign (Art. 2), where "centum solidus" is mentioned as the price of a knight's relief (a sort of succession duty), it is usually translated as "one hundred shillings." Were these shillings merely moneys of account, as is commonly held, it would be difficult to explain why they were not expressed in "libras" or pounds of account, like the sums which precede them in the same text. They were evidently actual quarter-besants, or shillings, and, therefore, belonged to the gold issues of the Basileus. The vassalian coinage of tin, which characterized the preceding reigns of Plantagenets, appears to have been also permitted by John, for in the thirteenth year of his reign (1211) William de Wrotcham paid into the Exchequer £543 5s. 0d., and in the following year (1212) £663 12s. 9d., for the money which he was permitted to strike from the tin of Cornwall and Devon.[1] The meaning here given to this record finds corroboration in the allowance of one-eighth for clipped coins, contained in the decree of 1205, which would have been excessive and impracticable in relation to sterling silver, but which, when applied to tin or albata coins, was reasonable.

Two years after John had taken his humiliating oath

[1] Provenientibus de Stanno Cornubiæ et Devoniæ Madox, ii., p. 132.

of vassalage to the pope he revolted from his servitude, and in the Great Charter which he sealed at Runnymede, June 15, 1215, he assumed powers which only belong to an independent monarch. With the fickleness that marked his entire career, he violated this charter in the following August, and in September it was formally annulled by his master, the pope. Soon after this John was poisoned to death. He was a weak prince, but brief though his reign and irresolute his purpose, he earned the glory of executing an instrument which has served as the model of every Bill of Rights won by Anglo-Saxons from that day to the present. Though disclaimed by John and denounced by the pope, Magna Charta was not dead, but lived on, and both in its inception and repeated confirmation it marks the slow and toilsome steps by which our race has won from hierarch, king, and noble its present inestimable liberties.

The only silver coins of the reign of Henry III. now extant are the sterlings struck in 1248, originally of the usual weight and fineness, but for the most part much worn, rounded and clipped. In addition to these issues, certain base coins were in circulation, which are reputed to have been of foreign fabrication; but which are more likely to have been struck by or for English nobles and ecclesiastics. Some of these were probably coined in the abbey of St. Albans. When complaint was made of them, the transgressors were permitted to avail themselves of a technical defense, and so escaped punishment.[1] Herne states that he had one of these base coins in his possession, and describes its composition.[2]

The presence of tin money, also struck by the nobles and ecclesiastics, is evinced by several contemporaneous

[1] Madox, i., p. 759, note x.
[2] W. Henningford, preface, p. xlv., cited in Ruding, ii., p. 74.

references which point to the use of the metal for coinage. The following passage from Matthew Paris (sub anno 1247) is an example:—

"As the money was now adulterated and falsified beyond measure, the king began to deliberate on some remedy for this, namely, whether the coins could not be advantageously altered in form or metal; but it seemed to many wise persons that it would be more advantageous to change the metal than to alter the shape, since it was for the sake of the metal, not the shape, that the money was subject to such corruption and injury." As a matter of fact, however, the king did not change either the metal or the shape.

In the 30th Henry III. the sheriff of Devonshire paid into the exchequer 25s. 1d., the profits of his contract for mining the black metal *(nigra minera)*, which we take to be tin, that being its usual color in the ore (oxide). He also accounts for 79s. received from the sale of dealbanda and tin. Dealbanda seems to have been a composition of tin, like album or albata. He also accounts for £6 13s. 8d., profit upon an issue of small coins, and of £54 15s. 3d. upon an issue of large coins *(de exita majoris cunei)*, both of which were evidently of tin, and were emitted by some local magnate. The comparatively small profit thus derived by the crown from the issue of tin coins in one of the principal tin-mining districts of England, implies a dwindling of this coinage. It is true that we have no accounts from Cornwall, and none from the mints, of tin coined during this reign, so that quantitative conclusions drawn from this single entry are apt to be misleading.

Although, as is shown in another chapter, this reign is marked by the issue of a native gold coin—the first one ever struck by a Christian king of England—the issue was almost immediately retired, and matters remained apparently as before; so that the besants of the sacred mint continued to form the basis of the English monetary system. But though in shrinking from the coinage of gold the king was afraid to definitively repudiate the suzerainty of the sacred Empire, the nobles and the burghers were not. The General Council of 1247 resolved to lower the standard of royal silver coins—an act which by itself is almost sufficient to mark the fall of the sacred Empire, and the declining authority of Rome.[1] Corrupt coins made their appearance in all directions—counterfeit coins at St. Albans; tin coins in Cornwall and Devon; base and clipped coins everywhere.[2] It is now evident that at this juncture the besant began to disappear from circulation, and that its agency in regulating the English monetary system was sensibly diminished; but in the era of the Plantagenets no such explanation offered itself. In that age the solution of all monetary problems was found in torturing the Jews. Henry had resorted to this measure before the decision of the General Council.[3] He now resorted to it again. It was a pretty theory, a furtive belief in whose efficacy is not yet wholly effaced from the minds of men; but it did not work. With the second persecution of the Jews, the besants became still scarcer, and as, for lack of besants, contracts could no longer be discharged with them, the use of other coins was rendered unavoidable, and the multiplication of base or over-valued ones was thus encouraged. One of the last contracts in which the consideration is specifically expressed in besants is still extant. It is a Hebrew bond and mortgage executed during the reign of Henry III., a complete English translation of which, by Dr. Samuel Pegge, the anti-

[1] The profits of this coinage are shown in Ruding, ii., p. 67.
[2] Ruding, ii., p. 74.   [3] The second massacre of the Jews was in 1264.

quarian, appeared in the "Gentleman's Magazine," 1756, p. 465. The besants are therein called Iaku of gold, in allusion to the rayed figure which is stamped upon them, Iaku being the Hebrew form of the Greek Iacchus and Roman Bacchus.

The division of the pound of account into twenty parts, and each of these into twelve, was in this reign extended to the pound weight, used for the assize of bread. Still more strangely it was imitated in the sub-divisions of the agrarian acre. By the Act 51 Henry III. (1266) it was provided, among other things, that "when a quarter of wheat is 12d. per quarter, then wastel bread of a farthing shall weight £6 16s.;" by which we suppose was meant $6\frac{2}{3}$ pounds weight.[1] A similar enactment was made as to acres. The acre was divided into 160 pence, or 320 halfpence, or 640 farthings, so that it tallied with the subdivisions of the mark of account.[2] Thus *denariatus terræ* (a penny of land) meant a rod or perch, for the perch was the 160th part of an acre, as the penny was the 160th part of a mark. So the obolus, or half-penny, of land meant half a perch, and the quadrante, or farthing, of land, meant a quarter of a perch, or $4\frac{1}{4}$ square feet. The expression 40 perches of candles" quoted in Anderson's "History of Commerce" (i, p. 178), and the use of "shillings" for ounces in the mint accounts of Henry III., are puzzling.[3] This application of the divisions of moneys to weights and measures was not peculiar to England. It is to be found in all the kingdoms which grew up from

---

[1] Martin Folkes' "Table of English Silver Coins;" Harris on Coins, i., p. 51.   [2] "Chronicon Preciosum," p. 40.

[3] Ruding, i., p. 179. The term "shilling" appears to have been also used in the mint accounts of this reign for an ounce weight (Fleetwood, p. 23; Ruding, i., p. 179, etc.) The origin of this practice is obscure. Twelve sterlings (value one shilling) weighed less than half an ounce, so it could not have been derived from this analogy. Perhaps it was due to the use of tin or albata pennies, of which twelve may have roughly weighed an ounce.

Roman provinces; for the custom is as ancient as the Empire itself. Wine measures were based on the Roman ace, which was the integer, and consisted of twelve cyathi. Thus a cup of two cyathi was called a sextans, three cyathi a triens, four cyathi a quadrans, etc., after the names of Roman coins.[1]

Many modern economists and writers on money have argued that because by this law a £ meant a pound weight, as applied to bread, therefore it meant a pound weight of silver as applied to coins; that because an *s* meant the twentieth of a pound weight as applied to bread, therefore it meant the twentieth of the pound weight of silver as applied to coins; and that as a *d* meant the two-hundred-and-fortieth part of a pound weight as applied to bread, it meant the two-hundred-and-fortieth part of a pound weight of silver as applied to coins. This mode of reasoning, if applied to the sub-divisions of the acre, would lead to very startling results. For example, because by law a mark meant the whole and a penny the one-hundred-and-sixtieth part of an acre, therefore when applied to coins the mark meant an acre of silver, and the penny a perch of that metal!

Another fallacy of money—one of practical importance at the present time—derives its origin from the monetary issues of this period. Jevons, in his "Money and Exchange," avers that the "standard" of England, from the reign of the Plantagenets to that of the House of Brunswick, was silver, and afterwards gold. This is one of a host of modern sophistries which have sprung from the Act of 1666, and which no one before that period ever stumbled upon. It will be found in Harris's "Essays on Money and Coins," printed in 1757, and possibly in somewhat older books, although

[1] Adams, p. 396. The custom is accounted for by M. de Vienne.

neither so old as the Dutch prototype of the Act of 18 Charles II., nor as that story of the disputative knights and the shield, which on the one side was of yellow metal and the other of white. In the case of money, the shield was neither of one metal nor the other. The term standard, as here used, can only mean measure, and neither gold nor silver metal was ever the measure of value in England until 1666, while since that date it has been such only to a limited extent, and under the operation of that Act as affected by subsequent legislation. Down to 1666 the "standard" of England was the whole number of £. s. d. in the kingdom, whether of gold, silver, tin, copper or leather, and the whole number of £. s. d. was whatever the combined coinages of Basileus, king, barons and prelates happened to make it. In the course of this history many instances have been given when the king altered the measure or "standard" of value by simple decree, and without increasing or diminishing the quantity of either gold or silver—an irrefragable proof that the standard was not either of those metals, nor any other metal, but merely the whole number of £. s. d., whether coined or existing by the king's will. Had either gold or silver been the standard of value, that standard would have been beyond the power either of Basileus, pope or king to alter. It needs but a cursory perusal of the annals of the time to be convinced that such was not the case, and that, in fact, gold and silver metal had very much less to do with measuring value than the imperial and royal constitutions and edicts.

Edward I , Longshanks, found the coinage of England in great confusion and very corrupt. The sterlings of Henry III., badly executed, and so much worn and rounded or clipped that they contained but half their original weight of silver; the base silver coins of the nobles and ecclesiastics, which had in great degree replaced them in the circulation; the gold besants and maravedis, which the Jews and goldsmiths hoarded for export; and the numerous foreign silver coins which had crept into the circulation, combined to form a melange of money which was impossible to replace and troublesome to improve. Before making any effort in this direction, the king commenced to fill his treasury by robbing the Jews and the goldsmiths, putting great numbers of the former to a cruel death, and throwing the latter into prison. In the reign of Edward III. there were few or no Jews left to kill, so the king robbed the Lombards; in that of Charles I. there were no Lombards, so the king robbed the goldsmiths. Edward Longshanks' apology for slaying the Jews was that they circulated base money; but, in fact, everybody did this, including the king himself, for there was at one period practically little other money in circulation. Their real crime was the hoarding of gold, which the king coveted.

Edward's raid upon the Jews and goldsmiths was made in 1279, the eighth year of his reign. As a makeweight to this transaction, he affected great concern for the purity of the silver coins purchased with this innocent blood. In the ninth or tenth year of his reign, he ordered the barons of the exchequer to "open the boxes of the assay of London and Canterbury, and to make the assay in such a manner as the king's council were wont to do."[1] Nothing is said in these instructions about the base coins minted at St. Albans, nor the coinage of tin in Devon and Cornwall, nor the issue of leather moneys at Conway, Caernarvon and Beaumaris, nor the pollards and crockards valued in other royal edicts,

---

[1] Madox, i., p. 291.

nor the light coins, called from their devices mitres and lions, nor the cocodones, rosaries, stepings and scaldings,[1] nor the three sorts of copper coins which this king issued after cunningly plating or washing them with silver. Lowndes, with some intemperateness, attributes to this reign "the most remarkable deceits and corruptions found in ancient records to have been committed upon coins of the kingdom." Nothing is said of these matters in Edward's instructions concerning a trial of the pix; and nothing is said of them in modern numismatic works.[2] Yet these corruptions of money have the highest historic value. Just, as in after times, the New England shilling first announced the stern resolution of her people to be free, and the "Continental" note proclaimed and asserted that freedom, so did the leather notes and base coins of Edward's[3] reign mark the parting of that mighty cable which held the province of Britain to the sinking ship of the Empire. The laws of politics, like those of pathology, are not gained by study of the healthy or the normal, but by observing the diseased and the abnormal.

In 1289 an indented trial-piece of "old sterling" (0.925 fine) was ordered to be lodged in the exchequer, and "every pound weight troy was to be *shorn* at twenty shillings and three pence, according to which the value of the silver in the coin was one shilling and eightpence farthing an ounce." So says Lowndes (p. 34), citing the Red Book of the Exchequer, but this citation only conveys part of the truth, the remainder being supplied by Dr. Ruding. This conscientious author states, with reference to sterling coins, that from the Conquest down to the year 1527, the royal mints of England bought bullion by the pound troy (5,760

---

[2] Fleetwood, pp. 39, 47.
[3] For leather issues of this reign, consult Ruding, ii., p. 130, and "Money and Civilization," p. 64.

grains), and sold it by the pound tower (5,400 grains); so that even when the buying and selling price was the same, there remained to the crown a profit of about 7 per cent.[1] The weight of Edward's sterling pennies, many of which, in a perfect state of preservation, are still extant, corroborate this statement. If we assume with the Red Book that Edward paid 243 sterling pence per pound troy for sterling silver bullion—which is doubtful, for there were probably deductions made from this price to cover the cost of coinage—the coins prove that he sold it at 260 pence per troy pound, or, which is the same thing, 280 pence per tower pound. According to Keary's assays, the extant sterling pennies weigh $22\frac{1}{2}$ grains, eleven-twelfths fine, equal to about $20\frac{3}{4}$ grains net; but these are exceptionally heavy specimens.

In the same year (1289), says the Black Book, Edward sent for foreign moneyers, to teach him how to make and forge moneys. Forging here means simply striking. It does not relate to the forged coins which were current in this reign, and which Edward's apologists imputed to the foreigners and the Jews, but which, it is much to be feared, were made with the connivance and for the profit of that ingenious prince. However, the Jews suffered for the forgeries all the same, for in the very next year Edward plundered and banished the remainder of them from the kingdom.[2] In 1298 (27 Edward I.), it was commanded "that all persons, of whatever country or nation, may safely bring to our exchanges[3] any sort or sum of good silver coins or bul-

---

[1] The statute of the Pillory and Tumbrel and of the Assize of Bread and Ale, 51 Henry III. (1266), provides punishment for those "that sell by one measure and buy by another"—a proof that the royal example had become contagious.

[2] See forgery, confession, and pardon of Sir William Thurington, in reign of Edward VI.

[3] Offices in the mint for exchanging coins (Madox, i., p. 291).

lion, which shall be valued or reduced by the assayers according to the 'old standard' of England. Silver bullion, when assayed and stamped with its value[1] at our exchanges, may be used as a medium of barter—that is to say, as money." This was similar to a Spanish-American regulation of the sixteenth century,[2] and it proved quite as impracticable and futile. It was also provided by 27 Edward I. "that no bullion shall be exported out of the country without special license." This prohibition was repeated by Edward II., in 1307, thus implying that it had meanwhile been successfully evaded. This, and some other acts of the Plantagenets, which encroached upon the imperial prerogatives of Rome, must be recognized as efforts on the part of these kings of England to throw off their allegiance to the Empire. But it was not yet thrown off entirely. In 1299 (28 Edward I.) it was provided "that silver plate shall be of no worse standard than coins. Gold plate shall be no worse than the 'touch' of Paris. All plate shall be assayed by wardens of the craft, and marked with a leopard's head. The wardens shall visit the goldsmiths' shops, and confiscate all plate of a lower standard." This was a new exercise of royal authority.

With regard to the pollards, crockards and other base coins of the reign, Dr. Ruding assumes (apparently because they were base, or because their coinage does not appear to be provided for in the laws or mint indentures) that they were of foreign fabrication and surreptitious circulation; but this does not follow. Base issues were the rule, not the exception, of this reign. It is mere prejudice to heap them upon Phillip le Bel and other French kings, and omit them from the records of the English monarchy. Base coins were quite as common

[1] This could only mean the value with reference to gold, which the coins of the Basileus still imposed.
[2] "Money and Civilization," pp. 17, 78, 146.

in England as in France; they were due to similar circumstances; they were attended by similar social phenomena; they had similar results; and no good can come of their suppression, concealment or false ascription by modern historians. Pollards and crockards appeared in the circulation so early as 1280. In 1303 (32 Edward I.) the custodes of the ordinance for the money at Ipswich were charged upon the Exchequer Rolls with £14 4s. 11d. for pollards and crockards.[1] If these were foreign and unlawful coins it is difficult to account for their use in the royal treasury and their appearance and recognition in the royal accounts. In 2 Edward II. there is an entry of a relief granted to the king's sheriffs and bailiffs who had received these coins at a penny each, which "by the king's proclamation were fallen from a penny to a half-penny."[2] Does this look like a reference to foreign or discredited coins? The king's officers are first required to receive them at a penny and afterwards at a half-penny each, and royal relief is granted to them for such of this class of coins as had accumulated in their hands during the royal alteration in their legal value. That they were in use during the whole of the reign of Edward I., and part of that of his successor is of itself almost sufficient proof of their legality. Sir Matthew Hale says that they were decried in 1300 (29 Ed. I.) It is possible that this was the date when they were lowered by proclamation, but the entries above quoted prove that they actually continued in use for years afterwards. As to their omission from the laws and mint indentures, there are no such instruments extant. With a fragmentary and unimportant exception, all instruments relating to the coinage previous to 18 Edward III., if any existed (which is doubtful), have been lost or destroyed.

[1] Madox, i., p. 294.   [2] Ibid., i., p. 294.

The extant sterlings ascribed to the first and second Edwards are not distinguishable one from the other. Numismatists assign those with the name composed of the fewest number of letters, as "Edw.," to Edward I.; those with more letters, as "Edwa.," to Edward II.; and those with the full name, "Edwardus," to Edward III. This classification is attributed to Archbishop Sharpe, a numismatist of the last century, whose reasons for its adoption are, however, far from convincing.[1] In respect of the groats, Bishop Sharpe's capricious arrangement was as capriciously reversed, for there the full-spelt "Edwards" are ascribed to Edward I., and the abbreviated Edwards to his successor. For the reason that Lowndes' citation from the Red Book merely relates to the buying price of silver at the exchequer, and as there is no certainty that any of the extant coins were struck by Edward I., and, finally, because it is incredible, in such a condition of society as existed during this reign, that sterlings should have remained in a circulation filled with tin, copper and leather coins, we should deem it quite likely that no sterlings at all were issued during this reign were it not for a circumstance recorded by Bishop Fleetwood, namely, that Edward's sterlings were valued at the time at two, three, or four pence, or sterlings, each—a custom quite common, both in England and France, during the whole period from the thirteenth to the fifteenth centuries, but commonly ignored or suppressed by modern writers on the subject.[2]

Among his other issues Edward struck silver coins weighing 80, 85, 92, 116 and 138 grains each, which are regarded by various writers as groats, shillings, medals, etc., but which might have passed as half-

[1] Ruding. ii., p. 123; from "Bib. Top. Brit.," No. xxxv, p. 25. Per contra, see Leake, p. 8, and Folkes.
[2] Fleetwood, pp. 34, 35, 39, etc., and "Present State of England."

marks, or even marks, for all that can be learnt from the few records now left of his numerous issues and their capricious valuations. The whole sum of money coined during this reign is estimated by Dr. Ruding at less than £16,000, but as this calculation leaves out of view the enhanced legal valuation of the sterlings, it is of little worth.[1] The native mines produced some small amount of silver in this reign. Those of Martinstowe, in Devonshire, yielded 370 lbs. weight of silver in 1294, 521 lbs. in 1295 and 704 lbs. in 1296, after which time they seem to have been abandoned as unprofitable.[2] An assay of silver from the mine of Byrlande, in Devon, was made in 24 Edward I.[3] The assumption of control over the mines which the rendition of these accounts implies, was also a new exercise of royal authority.[4] The system of £. s. d. remained unchanged, but what constituted a pound of account was now quite within the king's newly assumed powers to determine at pleasure. The king's prerogative to raise or lower moneys, or to enhance or diminish their value, or to reduce them to bullion—a prerogative which had only been assumed by Henry II., when the sacred empire drew to its close, and was only asserted after it had expired—developed during the course of Edward's reign into a very practical form.

[1] Consult Humphreys, p. 140; Sir M. Hale in Davis' Reports, ed. 1674, p. 18; Drier's Rep., 7 Ed. VI., fol. 82; Madox, i., p. 294; "Money and Civilization," p. 65; Ruding, ii., p. 129.
[2] Jacob, "Hist. Prec. Met.," Phil. ed., p. 195.
[3] Madox, i., p. 291.
[4] Mines Royal were first asserted in Spain by Alfonso in the "Partidas." Cuesta, "Castilla practica," Burdeos, 1838.

CHAPTER X.

LATER PLANTAGENET MONEYS.

No mint indentures prior to Edward I.—No statutes of any kind previous to Magna Charta—Sudden beginning of frequent monetary changes in the reign of Edward II.—Significance of this movement—Progressive assumption of regalian rights—Lowering of pollards and crockards—Interdiction of commerce in coins and bullion—Lowerings of sterlings—Establishment of a maximum—Coinage of base money by the king—His death—Accession of Edward III.—New monetary ordinances—Black money—Mercantile system—Tin money—Review of the gold question—The maravedi of Henry III.—Preparation of Edward III. to issue gold coins—Permission from the emperor—Convention with Flanders—Authority of parliament—Issue of the double florin—Its immediate retirement—Fresh preparations—Issue of the gold noble or half mark—Its great significance.

No written annals so plainly mark the steps by which England gradually developed from the provincial to the national phase of its existence as those which are stamped upon the coinages of the second and third Edward. Before describing these issues, one or two observations are necessary.

With the exception of the statute 28 Edward I., already cited, not a single indenture of the mint, from 1066 to 1346, is extant at the present day, nor is there any reason to suppose that any ever existed. If negative evidence were admissible in an inquiry of the present kind, this fact would be conclusive. It furnishes the inference that, down to the era of the Plantagenets, the princes of England did not enjoy control of the coinage, and had neither occasion nor authority to prescribe its regulations. The continued coinage and circulation of the gold solidus by the Basileus, its recognition by the Latin pontificate, and the prescriptive ratio of 12 silver for 1 gold, rendered the coinage of silver by the king a mere perfunctory act. The silver penny coined by Christian princes had to be of the same weight as the gold shilling coined by the Basileus. When the penny failed to conform to this rule, it failed to circulate; and the sacred college had the power to seal the prejudices of the public with its official condemnation of the heretical coin. But no sooner was the power of the Basileus extinguished than all this began to change; and every prince of Christendom stretched out his hands to grasp the coveted prerogative of coinage. The Gothic and Saxon princes, as usual, were the foremost. It was a Gothic prince of Leon who, next after the emperor Frederic, struck the first Christian coin of gold, and a Gothic prince of Denmark who first openly repudiated the suzerainty of pontifical Rome.[1] It need hardly be added that in such a cause the Saxon kings of England were not behind their compeers. Gold coinage began with Henry III., and mint indentures with Edward III.

Not only are there no mint indentures before the fourteenth century, there are no national laws of any kind previous to the fall of Constantinople. The earliest entry in the Statutes at Large is an altered copy of Magna Charta, not drawn from any official registry, but fished out of an antiquarian collection. Hardly more creditable is the appearance of the ordinances which follow it down to the reign of Edward III.[2] They have all the appearance of having been "restored" in modern times. If the kings of England previous to Edward III. were not vassals, why have we none of their ordinances? and if the pope or the Emperor was not their suzerain, why do the marks of the latter's

[1] See letter of Waldemar in the preface to Boulainvillier's "Life of Mahomet."
[2] These ordinances are not in the English, but the Roman language.

superior authority appear in this, as they do in every kind of literary record, except, indeed, upon the pages of recently written history?

However, it is not alone upon literary evidence that the argument relies; it stands also upon the far more certain evidence of coins and the nummulary grammar. Many of these evidences have been already adduced. Those which will now be furnished relate chiefly to the sudden and frequent alterations of money which began after the fall of Constantinople, and culminated in the reign of Edward III. There are, indeed, many modern writers who either affirm or assume that no such alterations took place; but the evidence on the subject is overwhelming. From the accession of Edward I. to the coinage of gold by Edward III. is a period which corresponds with the reigns of Philip le Hardie, Philip le Bel, Louis Hutin, Philip le Long, Charles le Beau, and Philip Valois, when, we are taught, that hundreds, almost thousands, of alterations were made in the monetary system of France, of which country a part still remained subject to the kings of England. In 1346 (reign of Philip Valois) there are recorded no less than ten alterations of the ratio between gold and silver in the French coinage. As to the debasements and degradations of Philip le Bel, every historical work is full of them. Yet all this time, while a furious storm of monetary changes and financial shifts was raging across the Channel, and whirling into every nook and corner of the English possessions in France, the political economists assure us that England lay in the midst of a dead calm, and that nothing of the sort happened there. How utterly unfounded is the inference upon which they rest so confidently will be seen when the positive evidence of the extant coins is unfolded.

The wave of monetary alterations which distinguishes this period began in Gothic-Spain, whence it flowed into France and England. The changes which began in France with Philip le Hardie and became so numerous under Philip le Bel and his successors, have rarely been correctly described and never fully understood. Even Mr. Hallam, one of the ablest and most impartial of historical writers, must have failed to grasp the significance of these transactions when he stigmatized them by the coarse names of fraud and robbery. "The rapacity of Philip le Bel kept no measure with the public. . . . Dissatisfaction and even tumults arose in consequence. . . . The film had now dropped from the eyes of the people, and these adulterations of money, rendered more vexatious by continued re-coinages of the current pieces, upon which a fee was extorted by the moneyers, showed in their true light as mingled fraud and robbery."[1] The fidelity of this description is discredited by Mr. Hallam himself, who elsewhere says "these changes seemed to have produced no discontent"—an admission that ill-agrees with the imaginary dissatisfaction and tumults above set forth. That the crux of the situation is misunderstood is evident from the absence of all allusion to the fall of the Empire, and the recent acquisition of its coinage prerogatives by the Christian states of the West.

If we turn from Mr. Hallam's condemnation of Philip le Bel to his approval of his contemporaries, the princes of England, we shall find even less cause to be satisfied with his opinions on this subject. In the former case they find some apology in the defamation with which the mediæval ecclesiastics pursued Philip for curtailing their privileges and restraining their rapacity;

[1] Hallam's "Middle Ages," chapter ii.

in the latter, he is left with the poor defense of patriotic partiality. Says the historian: "It was asserted in the reign of Philip le Bel as a general truth that no subject might coin silver money. The right of debasing the coin was also claimed by this prince, as a choice flower of the crown." Whilst, a little farther on in the same paragraph, he says: "No subject ever enjoyed the right (I do not extend this to the fact) of coining silver in England without the royal stamp and superintendence—a remarkable proof of the restraint in which the feudal aristocracy was always held in this country." If, in fact, the nobles and ecclesiastics of England exercised the privilege of coining silver, as we know they did, it is difficult to see wherein they were under greater restraint than the same classes elsewhere. But this is not all; Mr. Hallam's flourish goes farther. It implies that the right to coin, which he represents to have been so sadly abused by Philip, was more rightfully or more justly exercised by his contemporaries, the English princes.

Such is not the opinion of the earlier English writers. Our Matthew Paris says that the coins of his own time were adulterated and falsified beyond measure. Holinshed (ii., p. 318) says that, notwithstanding the baseness of the father's coins, the son, Edward II., proclaimed them to be good and current money. Stowe (p. 326) says that Edward II. ordered that his father's base coins should not be refused on pain of life and limb; and Carte prefers a similar accusation.[1] Indeed, the text of the proclamation (4 Edward II.) which contains this mandate is extant, to justify the mediæval chroniclers. Lowndes (eighteenth century) says that the greatest deceits and corruptions known to history

[1] History England, ii., p. 308.

were committed in the coinages of Edward I.; and Lord Liverpool—who wrote during the present century—reluctantly confesses, in a letter to the king, the adulterations of money which were inaugurated by the Plantagenets.[1]

We shall presently offer even better testimony than the opinions of historians, namely, the evidence of the coins themselves. It will then be seen, not only that England fully kept pace with France in the wildest excesses of a now unrestrained right to coin, but also that these excesses, in which Mr. Hallam only perceives fraud and robbery, really constitute our most valuable proofs of England's approach toward national autonomy. They are the unsteady steps of tutelage, which preceded the firm march of an actual and independent sovereignty.

The year 1307 (1 Edward II.) is the most probable date when the value of the pollards and crockards was lowered one-half. In effect it was decreed that that which was yesterday a penny, to-day shall be but a half-penny, and that which yesterday constituted a pound, shall be to-day but ten shillings.[2] In the same year was also enacted an explicit interdict against the exportation of either coined money or bullion from England.[3] A similar interdict was made in 1326.[4] It does not appear to have occurred to the crown that the Jews, banished to the continent, had it largely within their power to prevent the shipment of foreign moneys to England by paying for English merchandise with bills of exchange, drawn against foreign merchandise shipped to England. In this way they could, and doubtless did, intercept and prevent the shipment to

[1] Letter to the King, chapter ix.
[2] Madox, i., p. 294.
[3] Eggleston, "Antiq.," p. 196.
[4] Ruding, ii., p. 136.

that country of some of the coins or bullion which would otherwise have been remitted to it to pay for its exports. Many people, even at the present day, similarly fail to comprehend the operation of exchange. Their view is that unless every nation makes its money of the same material as other nations, it will place itself in the position of being unable to pay its foreign debts. A lesson from practical bill-drawers would greatly tend to alleviate such an apprehension.

In 1310 the Commons petitioned and represented to the king that the coins were depreciated (meaning probably, not in value, but in contents of silver) more than one-half.[1] Nevertheless, the king made proclamation the same year that the coins should be current at the value they bore under Edward I., and that no one should enhance the price of his goods on that account. This is the edict of which Holinshed, Stowe, and Carte, complain. Mr. Jewitt[2] says that the petition of the Commons set forth that coins (probably meaning the old sterlings) were clipped down to one-half. This was very likely, because unless the silver coins were cut down so as not to contain any more silver than the base coins of like denomination, they would probably have disappeared. But this time it could not have been the Jews who committed the offense, for there were no Jews now in England. Nor should the Caursini, Peruchi, Scali, Fiscobaldi, Ballardi, Reisardi, or other Roman clans or families, who filled their places in the English marts and exchanges, be suspected, for these were all good Catholics, and therefore presumably loyal subjects. Clippers and counterfeiters had been condemned to excommunication by the Council of the Lat-

[1] Rolls of Par., i., app. p. 444. Consult 4 Edward II., m. in 12 dors. (Ruding, ii., p. 133.)
[2] "Antiq.," p. 146.

eran in 1123, and were subject by a statute—attributed to Edward I.—to the penalty for treason.[1] Earth denounced such sacrilegious criminals, and heaven forbade them to approach its holy precincts. We are therefore at a loss to look for the transgressor, unless, indeed, he was to be found in the royal sanctuary itself. It may have been with the object to more effectually keep his base money afloat that the king, by proclamation in 1310, forbade, under heavy penalties, the importation of false moneys. If these false moneys were close imitations of the king's base coins, and contained the same proportion of fine silver, the practice of importing them infers that prices had not risen to the level of the debasement.

In 1311 the Lords Ordainers enacted that no changes should be made in the value of the coins without consent of the barons in parliament assembled. This startling declaration amounted to a claim on the part of the nobles for a share in those regalian rights which the king was daily acquiring from the falling power of Rome, but it was successfully resisted by Edward, who, in 1321, repealed the ordinance, at York. There are no records relating to its operation in the interval. According to the Roll of 9 Edward II. the king commanded Richard Hywysh, sheriff of Cornwall, by writ, to pay on his account £372 14s. 4d. to Antony di Pessaigne of Janua, out of the profits of the tin coinage *(coignagio stagminis)*.[2] Indeed, tin money and gold money appear to have been struck by the Western princes at the same time, and owing to the same parent event, the fall of the Basileus. There being then a great deal of false money in circulation, a writ was issued in 1318 to the barons of the exchequer, com-

[1] Ruding, ii., pp. 214-226.
[2] Madox, i., p. 386.

manding them to order the sheriffs of England to make proclamation that "no man should import into the realm clipped money or foreign counterfeit money, under great penalties, and that such persons as had any clipt money in their hands, should bore it through in the middle, and bring it to the king's cambium to be recoined."[1] This proclamation must have had some other than its professed object, for in the same year Edward complained to Philip le Bel of France that "merchants were not permitted to bring any kind of money out of France into England, for that it was taken from them by searchers." When it is remembered that the coins of Philip le Bel were greatly debased and overvalued, it appears more likely that the clipped and "foreign" counterfeit coins mentioned in the proclamation were fabricated in England. This view finds further corroboration in the fact that, in 1318, "an assay was made of the money minted in the exchanges of London and Canterbury . . . to wit, of £40,730 minted in the said exchanges within the said time" (about two years), and "upon this assay it was found that the said money was too weak and of a greater alloy than it ought to have been by £258 5s. 10d."[2]

The classification of bullion into domestic and foreign first occurs in the reign of Edward II., and was continued in that of Edward III., after which no traces of it appear in the mint records. Nature does not admit of such classification, because all bullion of the like metal and when refined is alike. Domestic metal cannot be distinguished from foreign. It was clearly impracticable to prevent foreign bullion from being imported, indeed, the complaint of the times was that foreign clipped and counterfeit coins were imported,

[1] Madox, i., p. 294; "Statutes at Large," vol. i.
[2] Madox, i., p. 291.

and if practically coins could be imported, so also could bullion. Nor was it the policy of the crown to prevent the importation of bullion; on the contrary, it did everything in its power to promote such importation. It is therefore difficult to see what object was aimed at by classifying silver into *cismarinum* and *transmarinum* (Ruding), except a further assertion of that newly acquired imperial prerogative of entire control over the coinage and the materials of coinage, which the king had in his mind and seemed determined to proclaim to all the world. Whatever his plans, they were defeated by the rebellion of his wife, Isabella, and the nobles whom he had previously curbed and restrained. These, fleeing to France with the infant son of the king, there organized an expedition, which landed in England during the autumn of 1326, defeated and captured the king, threw him into a dungeon, and there dispatched him.

Edward III. was crowned January 25th, 1327. To the numerous and sudden alterations of money which, like an exhibition of fireworks, celebrate the emancipation of the Western princes from the thraldom of Cæsar's empire, but introduced the greatest confusion into nummulary denominations and relations, England contributed an additional element of confusion. At all events, it was far less common in other countries. This was a marked difference between the contents of a coin as provided by law or mint indenture and its actual contents, as found by weight and assay, of perfect specimens still extant. For example, the mint indenture of 1345 provided that the pound tower of silver, 0.925 fine, should be coined into $22\frac{1}{2}$ pennies. This would make the gross weight of each penny 24 grains, and the contents of fine silver 22.2 grains, whereas the actual coins in good condition weigh but 20 grains, and contain but 18½ grains of fine silver. Similar differences are to be found in other coins of the period.

In choosing between the conflicting evidences of the statutes, the mint indentures, and the actual coins, the author has observed the following order of preference:— first, the actual coins; second, the mint indentures; third, the Acts of Parliament, which in many instances were only intended for show or deception, and in such cases were practically a dead letter. Even in the actual coins there is room for error, because they vary considerably. Mr. Keary's weighings are those of the heaviest, and because this practice is regarded as misleading, we have not always been guided by that author. Among the earliest statutes of the new reign were those of 1327, against the importing of light and counterfeit coins, and of 1331, against the exportation of either coins or bullion. The penalty for the latter was at first made death and the forfeiture of all the offender's profit, but two years afterwards it was lessened by proclamation to mere forfeiture of the money so attempted to be exported, and in 1335 the Act was extended to "religious men" as well as others. The conviction which must enforce itself upon all persons in authority that such ordinances can never be practically executed, the actual failure of similar ordinances in the preceding reign, and the language and tone of the present ones, all combine to produce the impression that the latter were intended as a cover, to account for the melting down of the "old sterlings" in the king's mints, and to furnish an apology for that emission of black money which soon afterwards made its appearance, and was probably fabricated at the king's behest. That he was not above the art of issuing insincere edicts is strikingly proved by his proclamation of 1341, wherein he avows that in his previous Interdict of Usury he "dissembled in the premises" and "suffered that pretended statute to be sealed," which he now revokes and declares void.[1]

Dr. Ruding naively enquires if the Turonensis nigri, mentioned in the statute of 1335 as being "commonly current in our (the king's) realm," meant copper coins struck at Tours? We think not. There are no proofs that copper coins of Tours circulated in England at this period, but many proofs that English black money did; for in the same statute it was provided that all manner of black money in circulation should cease to be current in one month's time after it is decried.[2] Yet but a short time afterwards the king's council in parliament at York authorized new black money to be made, containing one-sixth part of alloy.[3] In 1338 various proclamations were made, which denote that black money was still in circulation, and in 1339 one was made which authorized the circulation of black "turneys" (Tournois) in Ireland.[4] Black money was not peculiar to Edward III., but had been used by both his father and grandfather. Edward I. (in 1293) agreed to pay to the emperor Adolphus 300,000 "black livres tournois," and in 1297 to certain nobles of Burgundy 30,000 "small black livres tournois."[5] To the earl of Guelders Edward promised to pay 100,000 "black livres tournois,"[6] and it is not likely that at this period he

---

[1] "Statutes at Large" (Ruding, ii., p. 251).
[2] "All manner of black money which hath been commonly current of late in our realm" shall cease to be current within a month after it is decried ("Statutes at Large," 9 Edward III., 1335).
[3] A great part of this statute is not printed in the modern editions of the "Statutes at Large." Consult 9 Edward III. in Statutes folio ed. (1577), black letter.
[4] Consult 4 Edward III., pt. ii., 35 dors (Rymer, "Fœdera," v., p. 113).
[5] Anderson's "History Com.," i., p. 250; 'Fœdera,' ii., p. 778.
[6] Anderson, i., p. 251; Rymer's "Fœdera," ii., p. 675.

would have stipulated to pay so large a sum in a coin which he did not himself fabricate.

In the royal ordinance authorizing the establishment of a mint at Calais, after the capture of that city in 1347, the king (Edward III.) commanded "white money" to be made there similar to that which was struck in England.[1] In 1354 the moneyers of Aquitain were allowed threepence in the mark for all money coined by them for the king, whether "white or black," except gold.[2] We repeat that these black moneys, which the historians usually evince much anxiety to keep out of view, are really the proofs of England's dawning independence; for while she remained a fief of Rome, and the mints of the Basileus supplied her with besants, nobody was obliged to use silver, and the fabrication of black money would have brought the king no profit, and therefore none was coined. The coinage of black money and the abrogation of the sacred besant mean the same thing—the refusal and rejection of any further allegiance to the Empire.

In 1341 a great mass of sterling coins and silver-plate was collected in London by private parties for exportation. In 1342 a similar event occurred at Boston.[3] It is difficult to see the motive for these attempts to export silver, unless the circulation consisted of royal money overvalued, and unless there was no further use for sterlings and silver bullion in the hands of private owners. In 1342 the king's rents in Guernsey, Jersey, Sark and Alderney were exacted in sterlings, while his payments were made in light coins worth but ten shillings in the "pound."[4] This may have been clipped coins or black money, of which each penny piece had

1 Rot., France, 22 Edward III. m. 19 (Ruding, ii., p. 182, n.)
2 Rot., Vasc., 28 Edward III. m. 1 (Ruding, ii., 195).
3 Ruding, ii., pp. 150-2.   4 Ibid., ii., p. 152.

but a half-penny's worth of silver in it, and therefore the nominal "pound" but ten shillings' worth.

In 1343 the council in parliament advised the king to issue what would now be termed a Convention gold coin, to be current, with permission of the Flemings, both in Flanders and England, that no silver should be carried out of the realm except by noblemen, and that these should be limited to the carrying out of silver plate for use in their houses. The first part of this proposal introduces one of the most important subjects connected with the regalian rights of the English crown. Down to the year 1204, or practically to 1257, the gold coins lawfully circulating in England had been supplied exclusively by the Basileus, and consisted as before stated, of the besant and its fractions. When in that year Henry resolved to invade the prerogative of the Sacred Empire, he struck, not a solidus nor a fraction of a solidus, but a Moorish maravedi—a piece which commerce with the Spanish-Arabians had rendered familiar to Englishmen under the various names of "maravedi," "new talent," "obolus de Murcia," "gold penny," etc. The maravedi of that period contained 40 to 43 grains of fine gold; it circulated in England, not, like the besant, by force of law and immemorial usage, but merely because it was a justly-minted and well known coin of regular weight and fineness, and preferable to the adulterated and clipped coins which had made their appearance when the besants began to disappear in the reign of John. The maravedi had filled the circulation in continually increasing proportions. Its low valuation in silver (10 for 1) proves that it had no standing in the law. As the common circulation of the maravedi in England may seem incredible to a certain class of numismatists, it has been deemed useful to bring together some of the texts in which it is mentioned. It will be seen at a glance that its era agrees substantially with that of the Plantagenet dynasty.

Table showing the texts which mention the maravedi, or obolus de Murcia, as circulating in England.

Year when circulated.	Regnal period.	Remarks.
1176	23 Henry II.	Madox, ii., p. 367, valued at 20 sterlings.
1193	5 Richard I.	Madox, i., p. 278, valued at 10 for 1.
1215	17 John.	Madox, ii., p. 261, valued at 21 sterlings.
1250	35 Henry III.	Madox, re Philip Lurel.
1252	37 Henry III.	Ruding, i., p. 316, valued at 16 sterlings.[1]
1257	41 Henry III.	Weight 41½ grains fine, coined by the king, valued at 20 sterlings.
1269	53 Henry III.	Same, valued at 24 sterlings.
1283	12 Edward I.	Madox.
1293	22 Edward I.	Madox.
1347	21 Edward III.	Sir M. Hale, in Davis' Reports.

The maravedi was first coined in Spain, during the dynasty of the Almoravedis, hence its name. One of these coins, struck in Murcia, A. H. 548 (A. D. 1153), during the interregnum between the Almoravedi and Almohade dynasties, is called by Queipo a "Mourdanish," which we are inclined to believe is a misnomer. This piece, in a very good state of conservation, is now in the cabinet of Gayanos, and weighs 44⅛ English grains. It tallies in weight with the siliqua weight, or the $\frac{1}{120}$ part of the Egypto-Roman pound of 5,243¾ English grains, with the gold maravedi, with the silver dirhem and with two sterling pennies.[2] The true Mourdanish should rather be found in the half-mithcal, a specimen of which, struck during the first years of the Almohade dynasty, is now in the cabinet of Cerda. This coin is also published by Queipo, who accords it its true name, the "Mourdanish of Murcia,"

[1] From Henshaw's translation of Domesday Book, vol. i., fol. i. The pence were light ones.

[2] The siliqua weight must not be confused with the siliqua coin, which weighed scarcely more than a third as much.

and gives its weight at 34¾ grains, the state of conservation being very good. The use of the gold mithcal in Spain can be traced back to the eighth century, when Hachem I. settled upon his brother Suleiman a life annuity of 70,000 "mithcales or pesantes" as an equivalent for his estates in Spain.[1] In the tenth century the mithcal was called by the Christians the "dobla," probably in reference to its being the double of the more popular and better known half-mithcal or "Mourdanish."[2] Abd-el-Raman III. (912-61) settled a life annuity of 100,000 "doblas of gold" upon Ahmed-ben-Saia for his capture and plunder of Tunis.[3] The annual revenues of Alhakem II., besides the taxes in kind, were "twelve million mithcals of gold."[4] The piece we are considering is therefore not the half-mithcal, but the maravedi, and its period is not that of the early but of the later caliphs of Spain, the contemporaries of the Plantagenets.

The weight of Henry's gold coins was 43 grains (0.965 fine), equal to about 41½ grains fine. They were probably intended to weigh exactly the same as one gold maravedi, or two silver sterlings. These coins he called "oboli," and ordered them to pass for twenty silver sterlings, or half-dirhems—a ratio apparently of 10 for 1, but really of 9 for 1, because his sterlings weighed less than 20 grains, and were only 0.925 fine. It is alleged that these gold coins were objected to, on commercial grounds, by the merchants of London. This is hardly credible, because the coins were really undervalued. They could be bought with nine

[1] Calcott, i., p. 139.
[2] The contents of the dobla de la vanda in "Money and Civilization," p. 93, deduced from the assumption that the castellano coin was as heavy as the castellano weight, are given erroneously. In other words, the dobla of the period mentioned above was a heavy dinar; afterwards it was a double maravedi.
[3] Calcott, i., p. 223.   [4] Ibid., i., p. 249.

weights of pure silver, whereas they were worth twelve, which was the ratio of the time in all Christian States. This conclusion is strengthened by the circumstance that these same "oboli," after being temporarily demonetized, were raised, by Henry's command in 1269, to 24 pence —a ratio of 12, and that at this ratio they actually passed current without objection. As to their mechanical execution, the author is able, from personal examination, to declare that they were far superior to any other coins, English or French, of that day. The only valid reason that can be assigned for the objection made to them was the superstitious repugnance to accept gold coins not stamped with the authority of the Sacred Empire. This repugnance may have been enhanced by the fear that the coins would not be currently accepted in England, or, if in England, not in other Christian states.

Bearing in mind the example and failure of Henry III., Edward did not venture to strike coins of gold until he had acquired that full degree of sovereignty which the Basileus had involuntarily bequeathed to the Western princes. In November, 1337, Edward was appointed, and he accepted the appointment of Vicar-General to the German emperor, with power to coin gold and silver. Though this formality now seemed needless, yet that it was entered into with the view to prepare the way for the coinage of gold is evident from several circumstances. In 1340 the king's council in parliament enacted that all shippers of wool should undertake to bring in for each bag two marks' worth of gold or silver (Ruding, ii., p. 149). Again, in 1342 the king ordered still more pointedly that all corn exported to foreign countries should be sold for gold coins or bullion. Another preparation—a futile one to be sure—consisted in employing Raymond Lully, or some other alchemist, for whom a laboratory was fitted up in the Tower, which should enable that impostor to transmute gold from baser metals. Was it an excess of caution, lest the great step he meditated might miscarry at the last moment, that the king found a means to prompt the advice of his council in parliament that he should coin gold? At all events, such seems to be the character of the insinuation that the Flemings sold their goods only for Flemish gold florins, which were valued so highly in English silver coins as to render payment in the latter unprofitable to English merchants. "In other words," said the king, "by paying gold florins with silver coins our merchants continually lose; let us, therefore, enable them to pay with gold ones."

Such appears to have been the genesis of the famous ordinance of 1343. Upon the king's information, the king's council advised the king, in case the Flemings were willing, to issue a convention gold coin, and it was provided, in such event, that such coins should be unlimited legal tender between merchant and merchant, "as money not to be refused;" that all other persons, great or small, might accept them if they pleased, but not otherwise; that all other (foreign) gold coins should be melted down; and that no silver should be carried out of the realm, except by noblemen, and then only silver-plate for use in their houses. This advice was carried into effect in 1344 by the coinage of a gold double-florin, weighing 50 to the pound tower and 23½ carats 0.979⅙ fine, the old "standard" for gold.[1]

[1] As this was the first issue of gold coins by any Christian king in England, or any king of all England, except the abortive maravedis of Henry III., the expression "old standard" in the mint indenture could only refer to the Byzantine or the Arabian standard. The former was about 0.900, the latter was 0.979 1-6 fine (23½ carats). Therefore, "old standard" in reference to gold meant the Arabian standard.

Thus, each piece would contain $105\frac{7}{8}$ grains fine. It was ordered to be current at six shillings (each of 12 sterlings). Two or three specimens of this piece are extant, both found in the river Tyne. The best one weighs 107 grains gross. There were also florins and half-florins of the same issue, now extremely rare. At first—and differing from the advice of the council in parliament—the double-florins were made full legal tenders, in "all manner of payments," afterwards optional legal tenders, and finally they were demonetized all within the same year. They were the first English coins of any kind upon which were stamped the words "Dei gratia."[1] Down to that time the kings of England coined by the grace of Cæsar, or, as in John's case, the pope, his successor. Edward III. first coined by the grace of God.

Previous to 1344 the sterlings of Edward III.[2] contained $20\frac{3}{4}$ grains 0.925 fine $= 19\frac{1}{4}$ grains fine silver. Hence the ratio between the double-florin and sterling was about 12.6 for 1—too high for gold and too low for silver. As the Flemings were evidently unwilling to accept gold at this valuation, and the double-florins found no welcome with the merchants, the king, bent upon the successful issuance of this significant proclamation and token of national independence, ordered a new gold coin to be struck, and he decried the first one. The second issue, which was made in the same year as the first, was of nobles weighing $39\frac{1}{2}$ to the pound tower, same fineness as the double-florins, hence containing 133.8 grains fine, and valued at 6s. 8d.—a ratio of 11.06 for 1. These were made legal tender for all sums of 20s. and upwards, but not for any sum below. The obverse of this coin represents the king

[1] Ruding, ii., p. 212. [2] "Old Sterlings" (Lowndes).

standing in a ship in mid-channel, obviously in allusion to its international character. Some of the numismatists, however, make it typify the strength of the English navy in 1359, fifteen years later date; others a victory over corsairs in 1347, three years after; and others a naval victory over the French in 1340, four years before. Mr. Keary gives the weight of an extant noble of this issue at 138½ grains standard. This is evidently exceptionally heavy. He also gives the weight of the later issues of 1346 at 128⁴⁄ grains standard, and the still later ones of 1351 to 1360 at 120 grains standard, the legal value being always 6s. 8d. The king's seigniorage upon these coins was £1 for each one pound tower weight of gold, and the charge of the Master of the Mint was 3s. 4d.—together, £1 3s. 4d. As the tower pound weight was coined into £13 3s. 4d. of account, the merchant received back but £12, or scarcely more than 91 per cent of the gold deposited at the mint. In the following year the merchant's proportion of the £13 3s. 4d. coined out of his pound weight of gold was raised from £12 to £12 13s. 4d., thus leaving to the Crown and mint only 4 per cent.[1]

When the Crown came to deal with the Flemings it found that people less compliant than it had wished. They agreed to accept gold nobles provided they were coined (under the king's letter of authority) in Flanders, and also provided they could agree upon a proper division of the profits from the coinage.[2] To determine this proportion and superintend the issuance of the coins, commissioners were sent to Ghent, Bruges, and

[1] Ruding, ii., pp. 165, 174.
[2] Ibid., p. 194. The Flemish ratio of the time was evidently 10 for 1; and to warrant the acceptance of the gold nobles in Flanders at Edward's valuation, the Flemings must have demanded the entire abandonment of the seigniorage, to which, of course, the English commissioners would not assent.

Ipre, but the result of the negotiations is not definitively known. Froissart and Grafton both state that gold coins with the name of Edward were struck at Antwerp in 1337, but such coins are not extant; neither are there any of the Anglo-Flemish gold coins proposed in 1344. In a mint indenture of 1345 the weight of the noble was reduced. The pound tower of gold, 23½ carats fine, was to be coined into 42 nobles, each valued at 80 sterlings. In 1351 the noble was reduced to 120 grains standard without alteration of nominal value, which continued as before at 6s. 8d., or 80 sterlings.

One thing more. This coin convention with the Flemings is the earliest, or among the earliest, international monetary treaties known to history since the establishment of the sacred Empire. If the "kingdoms" of France, Spain, Portugal, England, Burgundy, etc., were as independent as the modern historians of those countries would fain pretend, why is it that they have not been able to produce the evidence of any international conventions between them previous to the fall of Constantinople, and why is it that such conventions took place immediately after that event, and have continued to take place down to the present day?

Down to the issuance of the gold nobles, the monetary systems of the English monarchy belonged to the Empire: they conserved no local or national principles; they contain no lessons for Englishmen. But from this moment they assume an entirely different phase and bearing: they become imbued with life; they partake of the spirit which had begun to animate the nation to which they belong; they occupy a distinct position in the British constitution; and they bear upon them the marks of those endless struggles and vicissitudes through which the Anglo-Saxon races have borne the standard of religious and political liberty.[1]

[1] If it be asked why I have not continued the history of money in England beyond the Plantagenet period, the answer is that it was my design to illustrate the development of money in one of the Roman provinces during its provincial and inchoate national period. until its autonomy was established beyond all question. The subsequent development of money is deemed to be sufficiently illustrated in the monetary histories of the various States included in my former works and in that of Scandinavia, Germany, the Netherlands, etc., included in the present one.

CHAPTER XI.

EVOLUTION OF THE COINAGE PREROGATIVE.

Impetus afforded to the development of British national independence—The great Interregnum—Assertions of British sovereign authority—Assumption of royal or national control over the precious metals and money—Assumption of Mines Royal—Assumption of treasure trove—Royal coinage of gold—Interdict of the besant—Trial of the pix—Royal monetary commission—Suppression of episcopal and baronial mints—Export of precious metals prohibited—First complete national sovereignty of money—Prohibition of tribute to Rome.

THE gold coinage of Henry III. proclaimed an assumption of sovereign power which Henry's weak and faithless character was not fitted to support by force of arms. It bears about the same relation to England's declaration of independence as the coinage of Pine Tree shillings did to that of America: it was the trumpet-sound of a coming event; not the event itself. The latter was embodied in the magnificent gold coinage of 1344, upon which Edward is portrayed with drawn sword, and standing on the deck of a man-of-war asserting his readiness to defend the new-born liberties of his country if necessary against the world.

The interval between the coinages of Henry and Edward was filled with significant events. Prominent among these was that Great Interregnum[1] which marked the fall of the German mediæval empire, and the dissolution of that political partnership, which had joined the prayers of Leo III. to the dripping swords of Pepin and Charlemagne. Frederick II. died in 1250, and, as Mr. Bryce pithily remarks, "with Frederick fell the

[1] The name given to the interval between the death of Frederick II. and the acceptance of the so-called "imperial crown" by Rudolph of Hapsburg in 1293.

empire." The brief and eventless reign of Conrad IV., and the assassination of Conradin, by the connivance and with the approval of Clement, ended the Suabian line of "emperors," but furnished no basis for a new dynasty. In vain did the See of Rome urge Richard of Cornwall, Alfonso of Castile, and others, to fill its puppet-throne of empire. In vain did it urge upon the Western princes the necessity of choosing an imperial sovereign. It met with nothing but respectful apathy. Edward was not the only prince who, during or shortly after the Interregnum, drew an independent national sword. The church had extinguished both the Basileus and the "emperor;" there was no longer any Empire, neither sacred nor holy, neither Eastern nor Western. The edifice which Cæsar had erected had often given way, and had been as often propped up, patched, and repaired. This time it went to pieces, and many of these pieces disappeared in the void of the Interregnum. The pope remained master of the field, but the field was a desert. The princes of Europe, the pro-consuls, dukes, and kings of the Roman provincial states were free. Nay, more; the people were also free, and the Commons once more assembled together as a political body, with political rights and functions.

Yet, though long since condemned by the united voice of Europe, though dismembered and past all hope of resuscitation, there was still enough vitality in the empire to make a show of authority. The pope of Rome, who had been its executioner and was now its legatee, was anxious to revive its prestige, in order that he might inherit that as well. He possessed sufficient resources to make a strong effort in this direction, and resolved to embark them in a contest with the Western princes. This struggle did not come to a close until the reigns of Philip le Bel and Edward III. Boniface VIII. had written to Philip, claiming him as "a subject both in spirituals and temporals." To this Philip replied, "We give your Foolship to know that in temporals we are subject to no person."[1] And with this contemptuous retort was blown out the last spark of Cæsar's empire.

From this period commenced a new era in the development of European liberty. Previously the movement against Roman suzerainty was directed against the "emperor" and the pope, and, therefore, was divided and weakened. It had now only to contend against the pope, and the result was that it won many important victories.

Among the great political signs which mark the birth of the independent English monarchy was the assumption by the Crown of entire control over the precious metals. This was accomplished by various steps—the assertion of mines royal; treasure trove; coinage of gold; demonetization of the Imperial besant and other coins; control over the movement of the precious metals; the suppression of episcopal and baronial mints; the trial of the pix; the regulation of the standard; and the doctrine of national money. All these steps were accomplished at this period.

Control over such supplies, as mining and commerce afford, of the material out of which money is to be made by the sovereign power, is a necessary corollary of the sovereign right to create money, and the two prerogatives will always be found in one hand.[2] The doc-

[1] Brady, "Clavis Calendaria," ii., p. 84.
[2] Consult my "Money and Civilization" on this subject A proper adjustment of the rights of governments to mines of the precious metals, both in England, France, Spain, and America, still awaits the dispassionate consideration of this great principle.

trine of mines royal holds that all mines producing such materials belong of necessity to the Crown. Down to the fall of the sacred Empire the only material out of which the princes of Europe could lawfully create money was silver;[1] after that period such material or materials included gold. The earliest extant assertion of the doctrine of mines royal, including gold as well as silver, by any Christian king was made by Louis IX. of France. He was followed by Henry III., who in 1262 asserted, for the first time in England, a similar doctrine and prerogative. But Henry—though in this, as well as in other respects, he frequently assumed an attitude of independent sovereignty—was easily bullied out of it by the effrontery and swagger of the pope; so that, according to Matthew Paris, the independence of England was asserted and surrendered many times during his weak reign. The heroic example of Frederic II., in defying the impudent claims of the Vatican, was thrown away upon this superstitious and faithless voluptuary, who saw his country again and again led captive to the foot of a foreign throne rather than brave a single curse from the lips of a scheming pontiff. The prerogative of mines royal was, therefore, practically abandoned until the period of the issue of gold coins by Edward III., when, without any formality, it again came into force, and has so remained, with apparently little change, down to the present time. However, in point of fact, the institution of private coinage has dragged the prerogative of the mines down with that of the royal coinage.

The prerogative of treasure trove was adopted, held, and subsequently relinquished by the sovereign-pontiff of Rome, who, in the reign of Hadrian, equitably divided

[1] With regard to copper, see elsewhere herein.

it between property and discovery. This right afterwards fell into the hands of the Roman proconsuls, vassal kings, and great lords. What disposition they made of it does not appear in the chronicles of the mediæval ages, but we need no chronicle to inform us. The chance discovery of a hidden treasure was not, like the opening and working of a mine, a public and onerous enterprise, involving outlays of capital, the coöperation of numerous persons, and the permission of the State authorities. On the contrary, the finding of hidden treasure was of a secret and furtive character, and in the mediæval ages treasure trove belonged to him who could keep it. The earliest public notice of the subject in England relates to Edward Confessor, who declared that all of the gold and one-half of all silver treasure trove belonged of right to the king. It will be borne in mind that the England of this prince embraced only a portion of the present kingdom. We next hear of treasure trove in the reign of Louis IX. of France (1226-70), who declared: "Fortune d'or, est au roi; fortune d'argent, est au baron," thus claiming gold treasure trove for the Crown and relinquishing silver to the nobles.[1] The same doctrine in England belongs to the reign of Henry III., and it was not until the following century that the Crown claimed both the gold and silver of treasure trove.

The coinage of gold, first timidly attempted by Henry, then boldly and resolutely begun by Edward, has been sufficiently treated in this work. It is only necessary to repeat that it forms, and has always formed, practically the most striking, notorious and unequivocal assertion which it is possible to make of sovereign authority and power, and that its entire re-

[1] "Etablissements," liv. i., chap. 15.

linquishment and avoidance by the Western Christian princes is to be accounted for on no other sufficient grounds than that the Basileus was universally conceded by them to be the lawful successor of Constantine, and therefore the lawful suzerain of the Empire to which in certain respects they owed fealty.

An intermediate step between the acts of Henry and Edward III. was taken by Edward I., who in 1291, or thereabouts—the date being uncertain—ordered that no foreign coins should be admitted into the kingdom except such as might be in use by travelers and others for casual expenses; and as to these, he provided public offices where they might be exchanged. This law may have been intended to include and aim at the besant, then the most important "foreign" coin in circulation: for, with regard to other foreign coins, they appear to have been as numerous and as commonly employed in England after this enactment as before.[1]

The policy of regulating, or attempting to regulate, the import and export movement of the precious metals, which, as we may see from Cicero, Pliny, and other authors, was systematically pursued by the Roman State, both as it approached, and after it had assumed, the condition of an Empire,[2] was also first adopted by the king of England during the Plantagenet period. It is true that Mr. J. R. McCulloch was of opinion that this policy was pursued in England before the Norman Conquest;[3] but as he has offered no proofs to support it, and the coinage and other legislation respecting gold contradicts it, the author is compelled, though with reluctance, to differ in this instance from that distinguished economist.

[1] Jacob, "Hist. Prec. Metals," p. 204.
[2] At that period, for reasons which the readers of this work will understand, it was confined to gold.
[3] "Polit. Econ.," p. 27.

The same policy of regulating the movement of gold and silver, now erroneously known as the mercantile system, was assumed by all the States that rose on the ruins of the empire, but not until they had shaken off its claims to their allegiance. The sudden assumption of this regalian right implies a previous interval of over thirteen centuries, during which, save the Empire itself, there was no permanently independent sovereign State within the domain of Christendom with power to exercise it.[1]

Analogous to this right was that of purging the kingdom of episcopal and baronial mints, with the view to concentrate the prerogative of providing a unital measure of value for the whole kingdom, and placing it in the hands of the sovereign. Such right was evidently attempted to be exercised by means of the Monetary Commission of 1293 (22 Edward I.), which was appointed to examine the various coins employed throughout the kingdom, and report the same to the king. The text of the instructions to this commission is preserved in Madox's "History of the Exchequer," i., p. 293, note F.

Another assertion of regalian rights during this period was the trial of the pix, which is first specifically mentioned in the Exchequer Rolls relating to the 9th or 10th Edward I., about 1280 or 1281.[2]

[1] This view is amply supported by Mr. Bliss in his recently published 'Papal Registers."
[2] The regulation of weights and measures—an obscure subject awaiting elucidation at the hands of scholars—seems to have been in ancient times connected with the coinage, and exercised as an ecclesiastical function. With the organization of the Roman empire it fell into the hands of the sovereign-pontiff, and continued to be exercised by his successor, the pope. The ninth decree of the council assembled by Athelstan, at Gratanlea, forbade the holding of fairs on Sundays, while the tenth exhorts the bishops "to keep the standards of the weights and measures of their respective dioceses, and take care that all conformed to these standards." The acts of this council, or parliament, were evidently made in conformity with orders or advices from Rome. (Henry, "Hist. Brit. II.," i., p. 262).

The regulation of the standards of weight and fineness is necessarily connected with the prerogative of coinage. So long as the sacred Empire remained, the coinage prerogative of the Basileus—which the princes of Christendom had never presumed to violate—acted as a continual check upon any desire or tendency on their part to adulterate or lower the coinage. Anybody could balance a quarter-besant against a silver penny, and so settle out of hand the question of weight. That of fineness, though not susceptible of so satisfactory a solution, was almost as readily determinable with the aid of the touchstone. By these means the tendency of the vassal princes of the Empire to adulterate their silver coinage was effectually defeated. That such was their desire and tendency, and that they often attempted to indulge it, has been abundantly proved; and to rid themselves of the serious restraints which the ancient prerogatives of the Basileus imposed upon their fiscal operations, they would probably have been glad to enlist in a dozen crusades, instead of five. But whilst the *fainéant* Empire of the Basileus actually lasted—and this it did so long as the pope hesitated to destroy it—the Christian princes had to return sooner or later to the ratio of value and the standards of weight and fineness imposed upon them by its senile but venerable authority. The moment the Empire fell all restraint flew before the winds. The standards then, and for the first time, began to permanently vary, and they continued to vary until all sight of the originals was lost. Indeed, nothing more curiously, yet unerringly, marks the emergence of the Christian princes from the position of vassals to that of independent monarchs than the open, flagitious, and radical alteration, debasement, and degradations of the coinage which began in all parts of Europe after the fall of Constantinople, and which, unlike all previous alterations, parted completely from the original Roman standards and never returned to them.

In all its aspects money is the most certain indication of sovereignty, but in none of them so absolutely as in the practical and continued assertion of the principle that that is money which the State declares to be money. This principle was asserted by the ancient Commonwealth, preserved by Paulus, and enshrined forever in the Digest of the Civil Law. It was practically observed and employed by every sovereign of the Empire, but, until the downfall of the Empire, by no other prince of Christendom; then, like all the other prerogatives left by the defunct Basileus, this one was assumed by the princes who had shaken off his ancient but dishonored claims of suzerainty, and we first hear of it in England during the reign of Edward III.[1]

If we turn from the prerogatives of the Basileus to those of the pope, to mark the end, as we have already marked the beginning and progress, of those practical assertions of sovereignty which constitute the birth of the independent monarchy of England, we shall find it in 1366, the fortieth year of the glorious reign of Edward III. In that year it was ordered that Peter's-pence should no more be gathered in England nor paid to Rome.[1]

[1] Plowden's "Com.," p. 316; Polydore Vergil; Parl. Rolls, 21 Edward III., fol. 60; Chief Justice Hale's opinion in "State Trials," ii., p. 114.
[1] Cooper's "Chronicle," fol. 245; Stowe, p. 461; Fabian's "Chron." 40 Edward III., in Nicholson's "Hist. Lit.;" Statute, 25 Henry VIII., c. 21 (1533); Ruding, ii., p. 205.

CHAPTER XII.

SAXONY AND SCANDINAVIA.

Fish, vadmal, baugs, and coins—Ratio—The mark—Imitations of Roman Coins—The pagan Hansa—Charlemagne—The Christian Hansa—Great fair of Novgorod—Ruric—Harold Härdrade—Christian II.—The tyrant's "klippings,"—Massacre of Protestants—Mons-Gustavus Vasa—"Klippings" of freedom—Marks, talents, and dalers—Private coinage—Rundstyks—Copper plates—Assignats Transport notes—Bank of Stockholm—Goertzdalers, or mynt-saicen—State notes—Banks of Copenhagen—Inconvertible notes—Silver dalers—Demonetization of silver—Gold "standard" of 1872.

ANCIENT Saxony consisted of the southern shores of the Baltic and North Seas. It was situated between Germany and the ocean. Its inhabitants were Goths, that is to say, a mixture of the Sacæ and the native tribes whom they had conquered, and with whom they had amalgamated. Their original seat of government was Vinet or Julin. In the eighth century the Goths were destroyed or dispersed by Charlemagne. Those who survived an almost exterminating war, escaped for the most part to the Cimbrian and Norwegian peninsulars, where they united the fylkis, and founded new kingdoms. The principal ones were Danmark, Gotland, Upsala, and Halgoland, now called Denmark, Sweden and Norway. Collectively these are known as Scandinavia.[1]

In very early ages, and in later ages among the more remote, isolated, or primitive communities of ancient Saxony and Scandinavia, fish, cattle, vadmal, and linen-cloth were used as money; but as society became more numerous and its affairs more complicated, the equity

---

[1] Scanda was the name of a Getic city in Colchis, and Scandea that of a Getic seaport at the extremity of Cythera, a large island off the southern coast of Greece. Pausanias in "Laconics," 23.

of exchanges, rentals, and heritages demanded a measure of value more refined than commodities; and this —as appeared in the customs and institutes of China and India to the eastward, and Greece and Rome to the southward, with all of which States the Goths were in communication—was money. The earliest moneys found in Saxony and Scandinavia are coins of Tyre and Sidon. After these come native baugs and Greek and Roman coins. Between the era of baugs and the ninth century the Goths were obliged to use foreign moneys, and they often compelled captured cities to strike coins for them.[1] During this period they successively used five classes of moneys, only two of which were of native fabrication. First, native baugs; second, oriental coins; third, Greek and Roman coins; fourth, native and rude imitations of Roman coins. For example, a Gothic imitation of a Roman imperial gold coin was found with a skeleton at Aareslen, in Odense, amt Fyen, an island about 86 miles from Copenhagen; while a similar imitation of a Byzantine coin of the fifth century was found at Mallgard, in Gotland.[2] Fifth, Moslem coins of the seventh and eighth centuries, of which immense numbers have been found all over Scandinavia and the shores of the Baltic, from Esthonia to the Netherlands. It is possible there was a sixth class, silver sterlings, struck in Saxony before the Carlovingian period; but there are none in the British Museum collection nor in the collections of Paris, Copenhagen, or Christiania.[3]

[1] Thompson's "Social Science," p. 157.
[2] Du Chaillu, i., pp. 262, 275.
[3] The Gothic kings struck coins in Spain from the Roman to the Moslem period, that is to say, from A. D. 411 to 711. Other Gothic kings struck coins in England from Ethelbert II. to Harold, that is to say, from A. D. 748 to 1066. Specimens of these coins are extant ("Ancient Britain," chap. xix.) Under such circumstances it is difficult to believe that the Goths of the Baltic struck no coins before the Carlovingian era; yet this is what some numismatists maintain.

Baug means literally a ring or bracelet. In the former sense the term is still used in France; in the latter sense it is retained in the bangles of India. Baugs were used as money in the Northern lands at a very remote date. They were mentioned by Cæsar as being in use when he landed in Britain; and they have been found in graves of apparently a far higher date. On the other hand, they continued in use long after coins were introduced, and only disappeared when the superior efficiency of the latter, as a measure of value, was universally recognized, or else when the use of the former was forbidden. As baugs thus passed from use as money, they were employed as relics and ornaments—a circumstance which appears quite plainly when the texts of the sagas are examined with attention.

Egil, having been paid two chests of silver as indemnity for his brother's life, returned thanks in a song, in which he calls the indemnity a "gul-baug."[1] In this passage "gul" cannot mean, as "argentum" did in Latin and "argent" does in French, money generally, because it is coupled with "baug;" nor can it mean gold money, because it was actually paid in silver. It can only mean a money payment, that perhaps was once made with gold baugs, and was now commuted with silver coins, of which a "chest" was a known number.

"If a leudr-man wounds another he has to pay 12 baugr, each of 12 aurar, valued in silver."[2] Twelve aurar to the baug is an alteration of rather low date. Aurar was the name of the Gothic ounce weight of 450 English grains, derived from the weight of a "libra" of gold, or five Roman aureii, of the time of Caracalla to Probus. It was also the Gothic name of a gold coin,

[1] Egil's saga; Du Chaillu, ii., pp. 16, 476-7.
[2] "Frothstathing Law," iv., 53.

the sicilicus, or skilling, containing from 30 down to 16 grains. Still later it became the name of a Gothic silver coin, eight times the weight of the gold one. Du Chaillu (i., p. 549) regards the aurars mentioned in the last passage as weights. If they were, it would follow that the indemnity for wounding a man was equal to 18 marks weight of silver, which at the period of this law would have been a preposterous penalty. They are far more likely to have meant gold skillings, payable in silver coins.

"Olaf II. (1015-28) went southward across the sea (from North Britain or Norway to the continent), and defeated the vikings before Williamsby. He captured Gunnvaldsborg, in Seljopollar, and laid ransom on it and the jarl of twelve thousand gull skillingar. This was paid by the town."[1]

Gold baugr have been found at Baugstrop, with Roman coins of the third and fourth centuries—a circumstance that marks the contemporaneous use of baugs with Roman imperial coins.[2] Some of the baugs found in graves consist of small spiral rings, strung upon a large loop, like keys upon a modern key-ring. If the spiral rings were used as money, the loop was probably the "silver aurar." But I am inclined to believe that these particular baugs were not money.

In the following passage the baug was evidently used for sacerdotal or ceremonial purposes: "Egil fastened a baug on each arm of the dead Throlf, and then buried him."[3] "A baug was paid for a bride."[4] King Olaf the Holy (A. D. 993-98) sent a large gold baug from England to Queen Sigrid in Sweden. He wanted to marry her. She had the ring broken, and found that the inside consisted of brass."[5] This was the same

[1] St. Olaf's saga, c. 16; Du Chaillu, ii., p. 485.
[2] Du Chaillu, i., 245.   [3] Egil's saga.
[4] "Frostathing," vi., 4.   [5] "Olaf Trygvaeson, 65-6.

Olaf who is said to have established Christianity in Norway, and who helped Sveyn to conquer Northumbria.

Although the Goths employed moneys so diverse, as are shown in the five classes stated above, they accorded to them a valuation (as between the gold and silver ones), which was peculiarly their own; and as in this valuation, and its connection with passages in the sagas, there are locked up many precious fragments of a buried history, it is worth while to explain it at length.

What the Romans called a feira, or fair, the Goths of Holmgard and Iestland called a merk, or market, possibly from mir, a community, the term being still used in Russia.[1] Gatherings by this name were held in villages once a week, when the people came together and exchanged their produce and wares. At these markets very little or no money was employed. At the great fairs, which were held once a year—for example, at Novgorod Veleki—traders came from the most distant regions, from China, India, Mikliardi (Constantinople), Lumbardi, Gaulland, Angleland, Frakkland, Saxland, Gotland, Heligoland, Vinet, and Iestland. "Lodin, a Norwegian trader, was once at a market in Eistland."[2] At these fairs money was the necessary medium of exchange; and the most important question to be settled in respect of money was the ratio of value between gold and silver coins, for this is where the utmost diversity existed among the various people who brought their goods to the merk. During the four centuries which preceded the Gothic revolt against Rome, that is to say from Sylla to Carausius—the orientals

---

[1] The term merk is still used by the Scots. In their ancient scale of moneys there were 2 doits (fingers) to a boodle, 2 boodles to a plack, 3 placks to a bawbee, and 13⅓ bawbees, or 160 doits, to the merk.

[2] "Olaf Trygvaeson " p. 58. The Flateyarbok contains an animated description of the Great Fair at Novgorod ("Anc. Brit.," c. xix., n^{ote} 26).

valued gold at about 6½ times its weight in silver, the Persians at 13 times, the Greeks at 10 times, and the Romans (from the time of Julius Cæsar) at 12 times. Possibly for the reason that it was a convenient mean between these various ratios the Goths of the third century adopted the ratio of eight for one; in other words, gold coins were to pass current for eight times their weight of silver ones. The Roman libra of this period consisted of five gold aureii, each of 90 English grains. Hence, it contained 450 English grains of gold, and the libra of silver 12×450=5,400 English grains of silver. At the Gothic ratio of 8 for 1, it only required 3,600 grains weight of silver in merk money to pay off a Roman libra of account, and hence it was that this quantity of silver coins came to be known as a merk, or mark.

If we have correctly indicated the origin and significance of this interesting term, the equivalents employed at the great fairs of the Baltic cities during the dark ages were as follows, the integer being the mark of silver coins, weighing about 3,600 grains, the origin of the Saxon mark weight of a subsequent age, but as yet only a sum of money. In this system there were eight silver saigas to the ortugar; 4 ortugars to the ora; 2 oras to the eyrir; and 4 eyrirs to the mark.[1]

At a subsequent period there were 6 bronze penningen to the silver penningar, and 10 silver penningar to the ortugar; but with these and other variations we have at present no concern. As for the relation of the mark and eyrir there is some uncertainty.[2] There was also a coin called a thveit, but its value has not been ascertained.[3]

[1] "German Law," vi , 13; "Bavarian Law," ix., 3, 4; De Vienne, "Livre d'Argent;" Du Chaillu "Viking Age," ii., p. 216
[2] "The eyrir of gold" is mentioned in the Egil saga, c. 7. Compare Du Chaillu, ii., pp. 13, 58 n, 216.
[3] Du Chaillu, ii., p. 238.

A few words here to those numismatists who still linger in the exploded belief that the names of moneys are derived from weights. The mark of moneys was traced by Agricola (A. D. 1550) to the earliest annals of the Cimbrian peninsular; the Roman libra of five solidi is defined in the Theodosian Code, and is mentioned by authors of a much earlier period. It was Elagabalus who ordered all the tributes to be collected in aureii, or else in silver coins of equal value, which, as the law then stood, meant twelve times their weight. The ratio of 14.40 for 1 in the reign of Theodosian, deduced by Rome de Lisle, Boeckh, and other metrologists, is a blunder, based on a wrong reading of the Code, and the modern delusion that a libra always meant a pound weight, which was no more true in the days of Theodosius than it is now. The gold sicilicus, or little solidus, which, toward the end of its career, contained about sixteen grains, and was indicated by the middle of term of £. s. d., was struck by Justinian, and specimens are now in the Madrid collection. Indeed, we are assured by Father Mariana that it was struck at a much earlier date, when, of course, it weighed something more. He speaks of some of these earlier sicilici in his own collection.

Returning to the mark of the Baltic, if we include the whole period of the dark and middle ages, its weight varied in different places from about 3,800 to 3,200 grains, according to the date when the mark was adopted; in other words, according to the fineness of the baugs or coins employed to make up the sum of a mark. As this was to consist of 3,600 grains of silver in baugs or coins equal in fineness to gold standard, and as the Roman gold standard of the third century was $\frac{37}{40}$ fine, it followed that whenever coins fell below this standard they had to be increased in number to make up the Gothic mark of money. This circumstance accounts for the variation in the mark weights of England, Cologne, Holland, Scandinavia, Iestland and Novgorod. The mark weights which are of less than 3,600 grains—as are those of Castile, Stockholm, Riga, Königsberg, etc.—are the progeny, not of early debased coins, but of subsequently degraded weights.

The coins found at Aarleslen and Mallgard are not the only examples of Gothic or Saxon imitations. Molds for making false Roman coins, and the coins with them, have been found beneath King William Street, London; at Lingwell Gate, in Yorkshire; at Edington, in Somersetshire; at Ruyton and Wroxeter, in Shropshire; at Castor, in Northamptonshire; at Epernay, in France; and at other places. Some of these may have been of Roman fabrication, while others were Gothic. The earliest ones mentioned imitated the coins of Claudius; the latest, those of Constantius. Gothic imitations of the coins of Louis Debonnaire have been found in the Netherlands.

The monkish chronicles represent the Goths as being always pirates and destroyers, but the security and prosperity of Vinet, Julin, Bardewic, Luneburg, and other Gothic cities; the great fairs of Holmgard, Gardariki, Eistland, Saxony and Denmark; the organization of the pagan Hansa, which—centuries before the establishment of the Christian Hansa—monopolized the maritime commerce of northern and western Europe; and many other circumstances, prove the contrary. The following incident, which relates to the terrible invasion of Attila (A. D. 450), indicates that the Goths, at all events at this period, were anything but savage people, for it alludes with horror to the cruel ties of the Huns. It is from the Volsunga saga, one of the oldest Norse scriptures still extant.

"King Atli (Attila) tortured his prisoners at the stake. . . . He cut out the thrall's heart, because he would not tell where the gold was. . . . Then he cut out the heart of Hogni, who smiled as he underwent the torture. . . . They showed the heart to King Gunnar (Gondicar I, the Gothic king of Burgundy), who said: 'I know where the gold is, but the Rhine shall keep it sooner than the Huns shall wear it on their arms. . . . Atli, mayst thou fare as ill as thou did'st keep faith with me!'" How strangely this reads like the dying curse of Montezuma's brother, whom Cortez coldly put to death at Shrovetide in 1525, for precisely the same offense! This was because he would not, or could not, disclose the gold hoards or mines for which the Spanish adventurer thirsted. "Oh, Malinché (Cortez), it is long that I have known the falseness of your words, and have foreseen that you would award me that death which, alas! I did not give myself when I surrendered to you in my city of Mexico. Wherefore do you slay me without justice? May God demand it of you!"

Whatever development of civilization was attained by the Goths and other Saxon tribes of the Baltic, it was cut down, root and branch, by the mighty arm of Rome wielding the zealous sword of Charlemagne. Between A. D. 768 and 800 this bigot destroyed hundreds of thousands of the Saxon race, transported vast numbers of the survivors to Upper Germany, filled their places with Germans, leveled their cities—including Vinet, Julin, Bardewic, and Luneburg—almost to the dust, and drove their commerce to Norway, Sweden, Finland, Russia, Britain, Ireland, and even to Iceland.

The exterminating wars which the Western Empire waged against Gothic Saxony explain an otherwise insoluble problem of history. Why are there no Norwegian or Swedish regal coins before the epoch of Charlemagne? Because these countries had no kings. The seat of Ivan Vidfami's power was Eistland or Austriki. It was from this center that, in the fifth century, the Norse fleets ravaged the coasts and began or extended their conquests in Saxony, Denmark, Sweden, Norway, Britain, France, and Spain; and it is with the saigas of Eistland that we must begin our researches into Scandinavian monetary history. The list of Norse kings from Odin to the Skol-konungs of the eighth century are purely fanciful. Jarls and fylki-konungs and vikings of Sweden and Norway there were in plenty, but we are persuaded that no sovereign existed on the northern peninsula, clothed with independent regal attributes, until the Saxon kings were defeated by Charlemagne, and the seat of Gothic power was removed from the southern to the northern, western and eastern shores of the Baltic. In the eighth and ninth centuries, Gothic kings, exercising sovereign powers, disappear from Saxony, whilst others spring up all of a sudden in Denmark, Norway, and Sweden; the germs of Gothic republics are established in Russia and Iceland; Gothic refugees reinforce the populations of Normandy and Britain; and in all of these countries Gothic coins make their appearance. In Scandinavia this period yields us the earliest coins of local mintage; in Novgorod we have an issue of Gothic leather money; in England, where the Goths had often before struck money, they now exhibit us—and that, too, in gold— the pagan coins and Moslem legends of Offa; while in Iceland the Norse colonists went back to the primeval vadmal and fish-money ("sild") of the Saxon coasts. From this period the Saxons disappear from history, and the Scandinavians take their place. Is it not quite evident that these are only two names for the same Gothic people?

We must now make a short digression in order to trace the origin of the pagan Hanseatic League. Under the hierarchical government of Rome, which began with the semi-mythical Romulus and ended with the overthrow of the Tarquins, all corporations *(collegii)* were chartered by the chief-pontiff. These included both sacerdotal and commercial bodies, such as the Fratres Ambarvales, the Luperci, and the trade guilds of Numa. In B. C. 306, the Senate, which had now become republican, forbade the formation of any new sacerdotal communities, and abolished all commercial corporations, new or old. In B. C. 59, when the republic was about to expire, and upon the motion of P. Clodius, provisions were made for the re-establishment and increase of corporations by the Senate— a power, of which, under the hierarchy erected by Julius Cæsar, that ambitious body was afterwards entirely deprived. This power was now again, as in the ancient times, vested in the sovereign-pontiff, and it continued to be exercised by that functionary from B. C. 47 to A. D. 1204, when the long line of Roman hierarchs was broken by the fall of Constantinople. Among the numerous commercial corporations whose remains attest the exercise of this power by the sovereign-pontiff of Rome are the Navicularii of Alexandria and the Nautæ of Paris, both of them companies of maritime adventure. But far more important than these, or any other corporations of ancient or mediæval times, was the Hansa established at a very early epoch by the pagan

Goths, chartered—or more properly licensed—by the Basileus in the fifth or sixth century; greatly damaged by Charlemagne and his successors during the ninth, tenth, and eleventh centuries, and finally destroyed by the papal forces and superseded by the Christian Hanseatic League in the twelfth or thirteenth century. As the Christian Hansa was the earliest trade corporation chartered by or under the authority of the Latin Christian pontiffs, and as all the so-called ancient trade-guilds of the present time came into existence soon afterwards and by virtue of the same sacerdotal authority, it is worth while to rescue from the oblivion into which they have fallen the scant chronicles and remains of the once powerful pagan Hansa, upon whose ashes were planted this crop of Christian companies, the progenitors, in turn, of an entire forest of modern commercial corporations. The word "han" is Mongolian, and means a corporation, guild, company, or association; "hansa" is the Latin form of it. Concerning the origin of the Hansa we have no explicit information, but it may have existed when Cæsar broke up the commercial emporium of the Veneti, which he discovered at the mouth of the Loire, and who sent to their colleagues in Britain and the Netherlands for assistance against his attacks.[1] Two centuries later than this there was a trading station at Scandea, in the island of Cythera, south of the Morea. From its Gothic name, the quarrel its people had with the king of Pontus, where the Veneti formerly dwelt, the fact that it was inhabited by a community of foreigners as well as Delians—and of foreigners, too, who were famous sailors and merchants—as well as from other circumstances, Scandea appears to have been an emporium of the Veneti.[2]

[1] Cæsar, "De Bell. Gall.," iii., c. 9.   [2] Pausanias, "Laconics," 23.

The earliest positive information concerning the pagan Hansa is furnished by Werdenhagen, who informs us that, ages before the establishment of the Christian Hansa, there existed a number of confederated commercial cities on the shores of the Baltic and North Seas, and upon the lower banks of the rivers that empty into them, including the Volkof, Dwina, Memel, Vistula, Oder, Elbe, Aller, Ems, Iessel, Rhine, and Weser: that among these cities were Dantzic (Danes-wic) Julin, Vinet, Bardewic (Bhadrwic), Munster, Dortmund, Nimeguen, Tiel and Deventer, and that the confederacy included such distant places as Novgorod and Cologne; that all these cities practiced freedom of trade; and that they were all destroyed or conquered, and their inhabitants put to the sword, or banished, to make room for a Christian Hansa that was substituted in its place. Julin is described by Adam of Bremen, writing about 1080, as the richest city in Europe. Helmoldus says the same. Meursius calls it the capital of the Vandals, and Gibbon says that the Vandals were Goths. Vinet is described by Helmoldus. Bardewic stood about a mile north of Luneburg. Both of these cities were captured and sacked by Charlemagne, and their inhabitants slaughtered or driven away. In the twelfth century these cities were finally destroyed—Vinet in 1127, Bardewic and Luneburg in 1137, Julin in 1140. Within half a century of this time the Christian Hansa, chartered by the pope, slipped into the place of its pagan predecessor, absorbed its trade, and divided its profits.[1]

Let us now visit the great annual fair or merk of Novgorod, shortly after Ruric made that city his seat of government. Let us rehabilitate the moneys of the pagan Hansa, and read the tablet upon which was in-

[1] "Ancient Britain," ch. xiii.

scribed, in Gothic runes, the value of the various moneys then current in the Baltic. The weights are in English grains. The standard at this period was that of the Arabian coins.[1] The scale of equivalents was 4 ortugar=1 ora; and 8 oras=1 mark. There were probably 3 saigas to the ortugar.

Conjectural Moneys of Novgorod: ninth century.

	Mark: Gold, 240 grs.	Ora: Gold, 30, or Silver, 240 grs.	Ortugar: Silver, 60 grs.	Saiga: Silver, 22½ grs.
Gold Moneys.				
Chinese slug, weight 8⅓ taels.......	20	—	—	—
Indian dharana, 130 to 120 grs.......	—	4	—	—
Old Roman solidus, 90 grs...........	—	3	—	—
Later Roman solidus, 72 grs.........	—	2	1	2
Triente, 24 grs.....................	—	—	3	—
Sicilicus, 18 grs...................	—	—	2	1
Sicilicus, 16 grs...................	—	—	2	—
Moslem dinar, 65 grs...............	—	2	0	1½
Quarter dinar, 16 grs...............	—	—	2	—
Gothic baug (Du Chaillu)...........	1½	—	—	—
Silver Moneys.				
Indian siccals, 84½ grs.............	—	—	1	1
Dirhem: Tahir-bin-Al Husain[2].....	—	—	—	1½
Roman denarius (old)..............	—	—	1	—
Roman denarius, Elagabalus.......	—	—	—	2
Dirhem, 43 grs.[3]..................	—	—	—	2
Half-dirhem, or Iesterling.........	—	—	—	1
Silver baug	—	1½	—	—
Ortugar (Law of Upland, 1296).....	—	—	1	—
Christian pening, 22½ grs. standard.	—	—	—	1
Christian pening, 14 grs., fine	—	—	—	⅔
Christian pening, 7½ grs., fine.....	—	—	—	⅓

Besides these moneys the paper notes of Heentsung, A. D. 807, the leather notes of Edgar, king of Wessex, and of Ruric of Novgorod, also porcelain coins of

[1] For details of which see "Money and Civilization," p. 20.
[2] Phayre's "Coins of Burmah," Num. Orient., Bengal.
[3] The Moslems reckoned 10 dirhems to one dinar, a ratio of 6½. The Goths reckoned 12 dirhems to the dinar, a ratio of 8.

Thibet and Siam, were probably seen at this fair; but we have no accounts of them. There was also probably employed at this fair, as we know there was at the fairs of Baldwin III., in Flanders, a system of clearings called "permutation," by which purchases and sales were offset by debits and credits, only the balances of which were settled in money.[1]

Specimens of nearly all the coins mentioned in the above table have been found in Saxony or Scandinavia. The finds of Moslem coins number tens of thousands, the earliest being those of Abd-el-Melik (A. D. 684-705), and the latest of Al Kader (1010). At this period the Moslems had mastered India. Coins of Abd-el-Melik, Hachem (724-43), Walid II. (743-4), Merwan II. (744-50), Abbas (750-4), Al Mansur (754-75), and Al Mahdi (775-85), together with others, have been found near Christiania, and one coin of the last-named caliph, together with several other Moslem coins, at Eker, between Königsberg and Drammen. A gold coin of Haroun al-Raschid (786-809), besides several other gold and silver Moslem coins, were found at Teisen Tundet, near Christiania, and are now in the museum at that place, where I personally inspected them in 1892. More than twenty thousand Moslem coins have been found in Gotland and elsewhere in Sweden, some of them struck by the caliphs of Spain.[2] The choicest of these, together with some specimens of the porcelain coins of Thibet and Siam, are in the Christiania collection. None of the leather or paper moneys alluded to in the table are known to exist at the present day.

From the period of Ruric (A. D. 862), whom the Moslems called a Frank or a Feringhese, and the

[1] Annales Flandriæ," Anno 958; "Middle Ages Revisited," ch. xviii.
[2] L. B. Stenerson.

Greeks a Varangian, a new era began for Scandinavia. In Norway Harold Härfager (865-933) united the jarldoms and established the kingdom; although, in consequence of the conversion of Olaf Trygvaeson (995-8), a civil war afterwards ensued, and Norway was divided (A. D. 1000) between Denmark, whose king had accepted Christianity, and Sweden, which had not. Under Canute (1014-35) Norway formed part of his united realms of Denmark, England, and Norway, and under Magnus it again became a sole kingdom.

After the death of Gotfried by poison in 819, Denmark was awarded by the pope to Harold, who had been baptized at the Court of Louis le Debonnaire; but the Danes do not seem to have been disposed to accept a Christian king until nearly two centuries later.

Like Norway, Sweden was ruled by petty fylkings, until Biorn united them under one crown and Eric Arsell (993-1001) acquired part of Norway. Thus, in the three Scandinavian kingdoms there existed a peculiar interval, which began in Denmark with Gotfried, in Sweden with Biorn, and in Norway with Harold Härfager, and ended in all of them with the plunder of the temple at Upsala by Hakon Jarl and the definitive establishment of Christianity in the eleventh century.[1] During this interval all the Scandinavian states united their petty rulers, and became sole kingdoms; they were freed from the evils of divided government, though as yet they were strangers to the trammels of Rome. They were devoted to traffic, and possessed an emporium in the powerful republic of Novgorod, through which passed a lucrative commerce with the Orient. "Who can resist the gods and Novgorod?" ran an exultant proverb of the period. But with the

[1] Hakon Jarl (who had been baptized in Denmark) plundered the great temple in Gotland and got much property. Jomsviking saga, cap. l.

termination of this interval, the Hansa, which before the Carlovingian era possessed emporia or staples at every port of northern and western Europe, was restricted to those only which adhered to the pagan religion; for the Christians refused it all accommodation. Thus, in the tenth century the Hanseatic commerce was confined, first, to the Scandinavian states, which being comparatively poor and sparsely populated could take but little of it; second, to some of the French, English, and Irish ports; and third, to Moslem Spain. This last was its chief dependence. In the eleventh century, as Christianity was introduced into the northern Courts (the first Christian pennies known to have been struck in Norway were those of Harold Härdrade, 1047-66), the trade of the pagan Hansa was almost exclusively with Spain. The civil wars in which that country was involved during the minority of Hachem II. greatly injured the trade of the Hansa. Mahomet ben Hachem and other usurpers mounted the throne of Cordova; the city was taken and retaken several times; the aid of Christian princes was invoked by both parties, and always with loss of territory. By the middle of the eleventh century the sun of the Omeiads went down, and the prosperous epoch of the Spanish Arabs came to an end.[1] This was the death-blow to the Gothic Hansa. It lost its remaining emporia in the west. It might buy, but it could no longer sell. Except as to the now distracted kingdoms of Cordova and Granada, Christianity had built a commercial wall around the whole of Europe, within which no pagan was permitted to trade. So the great ships of the Norsemen folded their wings and retired to the Baltic, while the pagan league of the Hansa underwent the

[1] Calcott's "History of Spain," ch. vii.

process of christianization, and fitted itself for a new career. The profits of the Hansa offered to the mediæval church a powerful lever of evangelization. During the interval following the civil wars in Spain, and before the earliest mention of the Christian Hansa (A. D. 1140), occurred the definitive conversion of all the Gothic sovereigns to Christianity; in Sweden Ingo I., in Norway Harold Härdrade, and in Denmark Waldemar I.; though judging from the tone of some of their letters to the pope, the Norsemen accepted the new dispensation with no little distrust of Rome.[1] Christianity is said to have been introduced into the whole "empire," including Novgorod, by Vladimir (him of the 800 wives and 12 sons) in the year 989; but the fratricidal wars between the sons of Yaroslov render it all but certain that, at least so far as Novgorod and Kief are concerned, those great trading centers did not accept it until about the period of the fall of Constantinople. By the middle of the thirteenth century the process of christianization was completed. Kings, people, shipping, wore a new crown, a new dress, a new flag. One more reform remained to be accomplished. The Jews, who had officiated as go-betweens in the commerce of the old Hansa and the earlier commerce of the new Hansa with Spain, were no longer needed. Accordingly some few thousands of them were slaughtered in the streets of London and Paris, and the rest banished to Moslem Spain—or to Hades. When these middlemen were quite disposed of, prices advanced and trade became far more profitable.

[1] Waldemar. King of Denmark, to the Bishop of Rome, greeting (this was Gregory XI., who had threatened him with excommunication):" We hold our life from God, our kingdom from our subjects, our riches from our parents, and our faith from thee, the which if thou wilt not grant it to us any longer we do by these presents resign. Farewell." Boulainvilliers, "Life of Mahomet," p. 3.

The earliest coins imputed to the kings of Sweden are the silver pieces of Biorn, A. D. 818, which imitated those of Charlemagne even to the cross stamped upon them, although Biorn was not a Christian.[1] The next earliest moneys of the North appear to have been the leather notes of Ruric, 862-79.[2] Between this date and the reign of Olaf Trygvaeson of Norway we continue to read of fairs. There, money must have been employed,[3] but no native coins ascribed to this period appear in the public collections, at all events, not in those of Christiania, Paris or London. About the date of the battle of Brunanburgh, Ethelstan, or Ethelred, is said to have offered Olaf a skilling for every plough in his kingdom, if he would make peace.[4] This skilling I take to have been the quarter-dinar of about 16 grains.

There are no Christian coins of Norway until Hakon Jarl, who appears to have conveyed the plunder of Upsala to England, for the "pennies" which he struck from it, and of which Rome received its share as Peter's pence, bear the names of Anglo-Saxon moneyers.[5] Nor, as before stated, are there any native Christian coins until Harold Härdrade. These circumstances offer an emphatic contradiction to the monkish story of the conversion of Norway by Olaf Trygvaeson, for the Roman religion and monetary system always went

[1] Humphreys' "Coin Manual," p. 529.
[2] "Money and Civilization," p. 294.
[3] See the Flateyarbok and the Faerynga and Olaf Trygvaeson sagas (ch. v.).
[4] Egil saga. This same Ethelred paid more than 167,000 "pounds of silver" as danegeld (Du Chaillu, ii., p. 222). Some commentators regard this to mean 167,000 pounds weight of silver bullion. Dr. Henry (Notes, 18), with more reason, makes it £167,000 money. But it is useless to conjecture what it means until we know the date when (assuming the statement to be true) the phrase "pounds of silver" was translated from its original terms.
[5] Greijer. The Ynlinga saga informs us that for a time the tax of Rome scat was collected from the people "for Odin" Very likely. But it is pretty safe to conclude that, unless he lived in Rome, Odin never got any of it.

hand in hand. It is not denied that Olaf himself may have been converted, nor that he committed the cruelties with which he is said to have punished those who refused to accept his new religion; but it is held that the evidence of the coins and the nomenclature of moneys both go to prove that paganism was still the religion of the people. This numismatic evidence is supported by other circumstances. Olaf's son, Olaf II., was expelled from the kingdom by Canute in 1028 and killed in 1030. After Olaf's expulsion Canute reigned until 1029, and after him reigned his son Sveyn, 1030-53, both of them Christian but anti-papal kings. In 1036 Magnus I., the natural son of Olaf II., and a *protégé* of Rome, was awarded the kingdom of Denmark and Norway by the Papal See. In 1046 Harold Härdrade took the kingdom, invaded England, and entered York. After Harold's defeat at Stanford Bridge in 1066 his son, Olaf III., with Magnus II., became joint kings of Norway, and in the following year Hakon became king of Sweden. In 1069 Olaf III. became sole king of Norway, and it was not until the reign of his contemporary, Ingo I., of Sweden, that the great pagan temple at Upsala was destroyed, about 1075, and Christianity definitively though not yet universally established in that country.[1] Nor was it until 1152 that, taking advantage of the dissensions between Magnus IV. and Harold, the Papal See succeeded in establishing an arch-bishopric at Trondheim in Norway. Nor again was it until after two centuries of civil wars, during which the history of that country is written only with the sword, the bludgeon, and the torch, that Christianity was universally established under Magnus

---

[1] "Ancient Britain," xiv., p. 5. Adam of Bremen described the temple of Upsala as being roofed with gold and filled with the greatest riches (Du Chaillu).

VI., the Legislator. The intimate racial, religious, political, and dynastic connection between the states of the Gothic peninsular, render it highly improbable that either of them adopted the new religion much before the other. Sweden could not have been entirely evangelized, whilst Norway was shedding its blood in the played-out cause of Odin; nor Norway have been a Christian state, so long as pagan sacrifices smoked upon the polluted altars of Upsala.[1]

In the ninth century the Scandinavian mark of money contained 240 grains of gold, or 1,920 grains of silver; in the thirteenth century, reign of Magnus VI., there were no gold marks, whilst the silver mark only contained about 1,200 grains. At the ratio which prevailed on the Continent these were worth 100 grains, whilst in Scandinavia they were valued at 150 grains, of gold. In the reign of Magnus VII. (Smek), 1319-43, a mark weight of silver was coined into five marks of money, and half a mark was deducted for seigniorage. If this was fine silver, each mark contained 720 grains, or about the quantity in two American or Mexican dollars of the present day; but I am inclined to believe that all these quantities were of standard metal. During this reign copper coins were first employed in Norway, and toward the close of it even leather money was introduced, each piece studded with a silver rivet. The device of leather money had been carried from Novgorod to England, where Edgar of Wessex, 959-75, made use of it; from England to Norway, where it was employed in 988 by Olaf I; from Norway to France, where it was used by Philip I., 1060-1108; and from France to Sicily, where similar money was issued by William the Bad, 1154-66. It now again served

[1] During the pagan era Upsala was the name for all Sweden. It sounds curiously like the Ober-saala or Ober-icssel of the Low Countries.

to sustain for a time the feeble resources of Norway: "Coriaria pecunia certis argenteis punctis quibis valor in pondere et numero pensavetur variata."[1] But the state was exhausted and nothing could at present revive it. In 1379 Norway struck her last coin.[2] Then she lost her national autonomy and dropped into the lap of Margaret, queen of Denmark. From this time forward until the epoch of Gustavus Vasa, Norway ceased to be an independent state.

The early history of the coinage of Sweden differs but little from that of Norway. Both of these states were erected by "Saxons," who sought a refuge from the exterminating wars of Charlemagne; both of them had thriven upon the profits of the Hansa, and both of them declined when the Hansa fell under the control of Rome. As if to render this decline the more rapid, both countries were overrun with a horde of Roman priests, who fastened themselves like vampires upon every source of revenue, including the silver mines. They reduced the bondr to slavery,[3] worked them in the mines,[4] incited the leudrmen to civil war, usurped their estates, and amused themselves by destroying or defacing the runic monuments, altering the sagas, and inventing a fabulous history for the country which had so generously filled their stomachs and wallets. For venturing to question the right of the Roman priesthood to the estates which they had stolen from the lords, their elected king, Charles VIII. (Canutson), was solemnly excommunicated at high mass by John, Archbishop of Upsala, assisted by six Swedish bishops and the rest of the clergy. "Then they went out of the church to commence a civil war, which lasted seven

[1] Olaus Magnus, cited in Greijer's "History of Sweden," p. 103.
[2] Humphreys.   [3] Voltaire.   [4] Greijer.

years," and which ended with the defeat of Charles and the triumph of their champion, John of Denmark.[1]

In 1396, during the reign of Margaret, the mark of money was equal in value to 45 Lubeck skillings,[2] each of which contained about 9.43 grains fine silver, a proof that the mark weight of Denmark was coined during this reign into 8½ marks of money. As to the Christian talent of Scandinavia which seems to have originated at this period, it was identical with the money mark, and like that coin it contained about 424½ grains of fine silver. It was divided into 48 skillings each of 12 pennies. Each skilling therefore contained about 8.843 grains of fine silver. Under Eric VII. (the Pomeranian), king of Denmark, also known as Eric XIII. of Sweden (A. D. 1434), the mark weight continued to be coined into 8½ marks of money. In 1470 what Humphreys regards as half-pennies of silver were first coined, but it is not safe to accept the denomination of these coins from an author so unfamiliar with Scandinavian monetary law. During the reign of John II. (Hans), of Denmark, Norway, and Sweden (1481-1513), were struck the first gold coins since the pagan era. These were of 240, 120, 60, and 30 grains, and were apparently intended to pass for 8, 4, 2, and 1 marks each respectively. They were of the same type (an armed man standing in the waist of a ship) as the gold coins of Edward III. of England. The writer found several specimens of them in the Christiania collection, one in Paris, but none in the London collection.

As in 1509, according to Greijer, a mark weight of silver was coined into 12½ marks of money, there were

[1] Voltaire.   [2] Greiger, p. 61, . n

about 288½ grains to the mark. If this conclusion be well founded, and the gold coins were pure, the ratio was 9.6 for one, thus 288½ ÷ 30 = 9.6; but, as coinage metal was used in both cases, and as the gold and silver standards differed, the ratio was intended to be 10 for 1. This agrees with the prevailing ratio of the period in northern Europe generally. I have met with a statement elsewhere that the mark weight of silver in 1509 was coined into 5 marks of money, but I can neither reconcile this with Greijer's statement nor with probability.

We now enter upon a period of great interest in the monetary history of Scandinavia—the period of Gustavus Vasa, the liberator of his country, and the political founder of the Protestant religion. The reign of Christian II. had been signalized by the greatest atrocities. Denmark and Sweden were the earliest to accept the religion of Luther (1517), which at that period consisted of little more than a protest against the avidity, the tyranny, and the impious sacraments (so they were regarded) of Rome; and in 1517 the senate of Sweden, wearied with the exactions and tyranny of Troll, the Roman archbishop of Upsala and the primate of the kingdom, passed a resolution recommending his retirement to a monastery. Whereupon Troll obtained a bull from the Pope forbidding the execution of their recommendation and annulling their decrees. Not content with this, the vindictive primate prepared for them a fearful vengeance. At his instigation, King Christian, in 1520, invited two bishops, the whole senate of Stockholm, and ninety-four lords, to sup with him at his palace. There, with the Pope's bull in his hand, Troll caused the whole company to be butchered, and the grand prior of St. John of Jerusalem to be ripped open and his heart plucked out. The two monsters (Christian and Troll) concluded their entertainment by ordering a general massacre of the Lutherans without distinction of rank, age, or sex.[1] This abominable act summoned the entire nation to arms, and for a leader and king they elected Gustavus Vasa, the nephew of Charles VIII. (Canutson).

At that period the Pope's legate in Denmark was an Italian named Arcemboldi. Such was his avidity that, by the sale of indulgences and other artifices, he managed to squeeze out of the poorest country in Europe nearly "two millions of florins," and was on the point of remitting his plunder to Rome when Christian seized it upon the pretext of needing it to subdue his excommunicated subjects.[2] A further measure of this exemplary monarch was the emission of certain base silver pieces, composed chiefly of copper, and cut with a shears, from which they derived the vulgar name of "Christian's klippings." On the one side was the impress of an armed man, on the other three crowns.[3]

It was at this juncture that Gustavus Vasa appeared upon the scene. The people were impoverished; they were unorganized; they had no firearms;[4] but Christian (who was a tyrant as well as a zealot) and his minister (who was little better than a wild beast) had combined to offer them the grossest indignities and inflict upon them the greatest injuries. These had fired the Gothic blood. It was not merely Norway and Sweden that rose up to throw off the shackles of Rome, it was all Scandinavia. Lubeck supplied troops and firearms, and the Chersonesus Cimbrica—that is to say, Jutland, or, as it was now called, the Duchy of Schleswick—transmitted to the tyrant of Denmark a demand

---

[1] Voltaire, iv., p. 65.
[2] Voltaire, iii., p. 185.
[3] Greijer, p. 103.
[4] Voltaire, iii., p. 186.

of deposition which was read to him by a single unarmed man, the chief magistrate of the Jutes, whose act should never be permitted to fall into oblivion. This hero's name was Mons, and it deserves to be written over the gateway of every oppressor. The unlooked-for result of Mon's brave act was the abdication and flight of the cowardly Christian. His uncle Frederick was chosen in his place, and became king of Denmark and Norway; but the real sovereign was Gustavus Vasa. Him the Swedish senate had elected king; and thenceforth Sweden became an independent kingdom and the center of Scandinavian political activity.

In conducting the revolution, which was crowned with the liberation of Scandinavia and the establishment of the Protestant religion, Gustavus made avail of the monetary device instituted by Christian. The latter had introduced the klippings for the sake of personal profit; Gustavus issued them for the benefit of his country. Christian issued his klippings in the place of the silver coins of the kingdom, which he obtained by taxation, melted down, and sold to foreigners for his own emolument; Gustavus issued his klippings to sustain the cause of liberty.

And let it be remarked that I am not here advocating a policy, but chronicling a historical fact; all the great enfranchisements of society have been accomplished with the aid of fiduciary money. The Spartans won their liberties with the iron discs of Lycurgus; the Athenians, before the Alexandrian period, rehabilitated the republic with "nomisma," a highly overvalued copper issue; the Romans overthrew their kings with the aid of overvalued "nummi," whose emissions were controlled and regulated by the State, *ex senatus consulto*. The earliest republic in Europe which had the courage to defy the moribund hierarchy of Cæsar was that of Novgorod whose money was impressed upon leather and, doubtless, issued by the State; the money of the Scandinavian revolution was the "klippings" of Gustavus Vasa, which were issued by the State; the money by the aid of which Gustavus Adolphus saved the Protestant religion from being stamped out by Ferdinand the Catholic was overvalued copper "rundstyks," issued by the State; the money of the Dutch revolution was the pasteboard "dollars" issued by the city of Leyden; of the American revolution, the paper notes issued by the colonial governments; of the French revolution, the "assignats" and "mandats" issued by the National Assembly; and of the anti-slavery war in the United States, "greenbacks." All these moneys were issued and the emissions were controlled by the State. They were not individual notes, nor private bank-notes, but essentially State notes. Indeed, the issuance of fiduciary moneys by the State has so commonly attended all social enfranchisements, that the occurrence of one of these events is almost a certain indication of the other. There is a reason for this, a reason that lies upon the surface. When the people take the government of a country into their own hands wealth naturally hides itself, and the first form of wealth to disappear is the precious metals. The moment a revolution or a civil war is declared gold and silver disappear. Thereupon the emission of fiduciary money by the State becomes imperative, or else the revolution runs the risk of immediate failure, for money is needed to purchase subsistence and arms, to pay troops, and generally to carry on the new government.

Such were the klippings of Gustavus Vasa. Greijer says that they were valued in the laws at four times their metallic worth. They were fabricated at Hedemora in 1520, and after having served the objects of the revolution were decried or repudiated in 1524 without any complaint from the people. Indeed, with these klippings, as with the pasteboard dollars of Leyden, the people preserved them in grateful memory of their liberation.

Before going any further, it becomes necessary for a clear understanding of what follows to trace the mark weight, the mark of money, and the riksdaler, reichthaler, or imperial dollar, from the period of the conjectural Novgorod table to the latest times. In a table printed below, the mark of Ruric is given at 3600 grains. This is adopted because it is an even figure, and agrees with the Anglo-Saxon mark brought to England; but it is more than probable that the mark of this period was, in fact, made to agree with the weights of the Arabian coins, which at that time formed the principal currency of the Baltic, and, therefore, that it weighed some multiple of the dirhem. The Danish and Norwegian common mark is given at 3631.139 grains, and the Danish and Norwegian mint mark at 3607.77455 grains, both by Schmidt's (Tate's) Cambist. The mark of Stockholm is given by Kelly at 4384 Swedish iesen, or 3252 English grains. In the former case I have adopted $3607\frac{3}{4}$ grains, and in the latter 3250 grains, as sufficiently exact for the mint mark. In the numerous changes of government which have occurred to the Scandinavian States, it is not always easy to determine what weights were used by the mints. In selecting the mark believed to have been used for coinage I have sometimes been guided by the nationality of the issuing sovereign, sometimes by the place of mintage, and sometimes by the actual weights of extant coins; but as these were often of irregular alliage, I am not confident of having been always successful. However, for the purposes of the table referred to, the difference is not important.

The silver talent, or thaler, as shown in the chapter of this work on the Moneys of Germany, was the Roman equivalent in value of a gold solidus, afterwards known as a ducat. Hence, during the Renaissance, when the ducat contained about $56\frac{1}{2}$ grains, and in the Ecclesiastical States, where the ratio was 12 for 1, the talent contained about 678 grains, whilst in the Italian Republics (ratio 10 for 1) it contained $565\frac{1}{2}$ grains fine. Such was originally the contents of the croisat, the scudo, the ducatone, etc., these names and others meaning the same broad piece as the talent. In the Scandinavian States during the fourteenth century, where the ratio was still 8 for 1, the mark of money contained about 450 grains. After the firm establishment of Christianity every effort was made by the church to eradicate pagan customs and reminiscences. The use of runic letters was forbidden, the names of pagan kings were suppressed, the pagan sagas were revised, and even the popular use of pagan names for moneys discouraged. Hence sild, saicca, styca, thveit, thrimsa, scat, ortugar, and mark successively fell into disuse, or were changed to Christian denominations. It was in this way that the saicca became the penny, the ora was changed into the shilling, and the mark was metamorphosed into the talent. Notwithstanding these measures, it proved so difficult to change the popular names that the word "mark" continued to be stamped on coins so late as the reign of Adolphus Frederick. However, the plan succeeded far enough to destroy the ancient value of all pagan contracts, rentals revenues, etc., and this indeed may have been the more practical object in view.

Assuming that the substitution of the name "talent" for the "mark" of money was attempted at least as early as the reign of Margaret, it follows that the former contained at that period $452\frac{3}{4}$ grains gross or $424\frac{1}{2}$ grains fine; for, as already shown, such were the contents of the money mark. From that period, until it acquired the name of "riksdaler," the talent can be traced with great precision. Nearly all the weights in the following table were obtained from coins in the Paris collection, kindly weighed in my presence by M. Casanova. With few exceptions they were all very base, many of them showing a heavy alloy of copper. Where net weights are given they are mostly from Greijer and from the appearance of the coins. Greijer's weights seem too high. I fancy that the standard was often much lower than the historian assumed. It will be observed that in the reign of Eric XIV. the talent suddenly rises from about 450 to 560 grains. This was occasioned by changing the ratio from 8 to 10 for 1. After having thus strangely but unmistakably asserted its identity with the ancient mark of money, the (heavy) talent disappeared altogether, and in the succeeding years of the same reign it was replaced by the lighter and more serviceable riksdaler of about 400 grains, divided (now) into 8 degraded marks. Henceforth, excepting during the reign of Charles XI. and Charles XII., and again, during the Napoleonic wars, the riksdaler kept its weight pretty well; whilst the mark of money, which had anciently contained 1920 grains of silver, was so often degraded, that in the seventeenth century it contained less than 30 grains. It was then raised a little and finally destroyed altogether. It is

THE MARK WEIGHT AND THE SILVER MARK OF MONEY.

The following table shows the number of marks of money struck from the mark weight of standard silver and the number of English grains of standard silver in each mark of money. The mark weight of Ruric has been reckoned at 3600, of Denmark and Norway at 3607¾ and of Sweden at 3250 grains.

Year.	Reign.	Marks in ma'k wgt	Mark. Grains.
9 cent.	Ruric............................	0⅝	1920.00
1290	Magnus VI	3	1202.59
1319	Magnus VII.....................	5	721.55
1348	Hakon V.........................	5	721 55
-396	Margaret	8½	424.50
1434	Eric VII.........................	8½	424.50
1509	John.............................	12½	†288 33
1523	Gustavus Vasa..................	22½	*144.44
1527	"	19½	166.67
1543	"	28⅞	112.63
1557	"	26½	122.40
1559	"	26½	*122.40
1546	Christian III....................	27⅛	132.90
1568	Eric XIV........................	65	50.00
1571	John III.........................	32½	*100 00
1575	"	30	*108.33
1579	"	30	*108.33
1590	"	34½	*94.20
1591	"	34¼	*94.20
1603	Sigismund.......................	45	*72.22
1604	Charles IX.......................	36¾	*88 50
1606	"	33½	*97.00
1613	Gustavus Adolphus..............	30	*108.33
1628	"	53	*61.33
1629	"	81½	*39 85
1630	"	114	*28.50
1632	"	48⅞	*66.50
1671	Charles XI	45	*72.22
1690	"	40	*81.25
1694	"	230	*14.00
1699	Charles XII......................	40	*81.25
1711	"	40	*81.25
1719	Ulrica.	43	*77.40
1750	Frederick........................	29	*112.00
1755	Adolphus Frederick.............	28⅞	*112.63
1762	"	32⅞	99 00

NOTES TO THE TABLE. *Deduced from the gross weight of coins in the Paris collection. As these coins are greatly and variously debased, the deductions, so far as net contents are concerned, are only approximative.

†Gross weight.

The Roman imperial (silver) talent or Scandinavian riksdaler.

Year	Reign		Talent. Gr's grs	Talent. Fie grs	Value. Marks.	Notes
1396	Margaret	D	452.80	424.5	1	Union of the Three Kingdoms, 1397.
1434	Eric VII.(VIII.)	D	452.80	424.5	1	1 mark = 32 ortugars.
1509	John	D	432.50	—	1½	Greijer, p. 77.
1523	Gus. Vasa	S	—	—	3	Silver disappears. Issue of klippings.
1527	"	S	—	400.0	3	About this time 24 ortugars to the mark.
1542	"	S	414.85	—	3	The value in marks is conjectural.
1543	"	S	430.50	337.9	3	" "
1544	"	S	447.50	—	3	
1557	"	S	447.50	367.2	3	
1559	"	S	447.50	—	3	/
1546	Christian III.	D	—	398.7	3	Mintage of Guiness, Norway
1561	Eric XIV.	S	537.00	—	—	From 20 or (?) piece, weight 447.50 grs.
1563	"	S	547.38	—	—	From square coin stamped "16 or," 364.92 grs.
1563	"	S	556.41	—	—	" " " 370.94 grs.
1566	"	S	553.20	—	—	" " " 368.80 grs.
1568	"	S	399.63	—	8	" " "8 M."
1571	John III.	S	398.50	—	4	" " "4 M." wgt. doubtful
1575	"	S	447.50	—	4	About this time 8 ore, or 32 ort = 1 mark.
1576	"	S	447.50	398.5	4½	Value in marks conjectural.
1579	"	S	424.00	—	—	From "1 mark" coin, weight 106 grs. gross.
1587	"	S	455.18	398.5	4½	
1590	"	S	448.80	—	4¾	From "3 mark" coin, weight 283.45 grs. gross.
1591	"	S	439.60	—	—	From square "8 or" coin, wgt. 109.9 grs. gross.
1591	"	S	395.20	—	—	" "4 or" " 49.4 "
1594	Sigismund	S	447.50	—	—	
1598	?	S	447.50	—	—	Stamped "Nova Moneta."
1599	?	S	447.50	—	—	" " "
1602	Sigismund	S	368.00	—	—	From "Jehovah" coin, weight 46 grs. gross.
1603	?	S	447.50	—	6	From "4 M" coin, weight 287.77 "
1603	Charles IX.	S	447.50	—	—	"Jehovah" and circle of fire.
1604	"	S	—	398.5	4½	Decree of so-called "Free Coinage."
1606	"	S	451.80	—	6	From "1 M" coin (worn), wgt. 73¾ grs. gross.
1607	"	S	451.80	—	6	From "2 M" coin, weight 150.6 grs. gross.
1608	"	S	447.50	—	—	Jesus Christ; legend "Salvator Mundi."
1609	"	S	438.20	—	—	Jehovah and circle of fire.
1610	"	S	447.50	—	—	Jesus Christ; legend "Salvator Mundi."
1613	Gus. Adolf	S	—	398.5	4	Greijer.
1618	"	S	481.42	—	—	Jesus Christ; legend "Salvator Mundi."
1627	"	S	—	—	—	Round silver-washed copper coin, daler size, stamped "Nova Moneta Cupræ."
1627	"	S	—	—	—	Round copper coin (not washed), same size, stamped "Nova Moneta Cupræ" and "1 or."
1628	"	S	—	398.5	6½	Greijer, p. 295 n.
1629	"	S	—	398.5	10	Greijer.
1630	"	S	—	398.5	14	Greijer.
1632	"	S	454.41	398.5	6	Gross weight from coin; net weight and value from Greijer.
1632	Christina	S	—	—	—	Assignats and transport notes.
1654	Chas. Gust.	S	—	—	—	Copper money and transport notes.
1661	Charles XI.	S	—	—	4	Rundstyks, "1 or," size of present Eng. penny.
1671	"	S	308.60	—	4	From "2 M" coin, weight 154.3 grs.
1686	"	S	—	—	—	Great degradation of silver coins. Greijer.
1690	"	S	317.24	—	4	From "2 M" coin, weight 158.62 grs. gross.
1694	"	S	56.01	—	4	Stamped "In Jehovah we trust" and "1 Reichsthal."
1699	Charles XII.	S	327.12	—	4	From "2 M" coin, weight 163.56 grs. gross.
1711	Charles XII.	S	316.32	—	4	From "2 M" coin, weight 158.16 grs. gross.
1716	"	S	—	333.0	6	Newton.
1719	Ulrica	S	300.88	—	4	From "2 M" coin, weight 150.44 grs. gross.
1720	"	S	469.00	—	4	Partington's "Encyc.," art. "Money."
1750	Frederick	S	441.60	—	4	From "2 M" coin, weight 220.8 grs. gross.
1755	Adolphus Fred.	S	449.92	—	4	" " " 224.96 "
1762	"	S	—	395.5	4	Kelly's "Cambist."
1783	Gustavus	S	452.92	—	—	From a "2⅔ Riksdaler,"
1820	Charles XIV.	S	—	396.8	—	Kelly's "Cambist."
1830	"	S	525.00	394.3	—	U. S. Mint assays.
1837	"	S	525.00	394.3	—	" "
1838	"	S	525.00	394.3	—	" "
1844	Oscar I.	S	—	—	—	
1868	Charles XV.	S	—	—	—	
1872	Oscar II.	S	524.16	393.1	—	"Specie daler," valued at 4 riks gold dalers. Mint closed to full legal-tender silver coins.

noticeable that both the talent and riksdaler, like the later solidi of the Byzantine empire, commonly bore the effigy of Jesus Christ. This was afterwards changed to Jehovah, in Hebrew letters, הוה,, surrounded by a circle of flames. A later form of this type was the legend, "Got heppel," on a very much degraded daler of 1694.

It will be observed that in the ninth century the mark of money contained $\frac{8}{15}$ of a mark weight of silver; in the thirteenth century the mark weight was coined into 3 marks of money; toward the middle of the fourteenth century into 5 marks; toward the end of the same century into $8\frac{1}{2}$ marks; in the sixteenth century from $12\frac{1}{2}$ to 65 marks; and in the seventeenth century from 30 to 230 marks. Although a restoration of the coinage appears to have taken place in 1762 it is probable that the silver mark of money, except as hereinafter mentioned, disappeared at that period altogether.

If we turn from the silver to the gold moneys of Scandinavia, the information supplied to us by historical works and coin collections, though scant enough as to one, becomes still more scant with respect of the other; and the following table is submitted to the reader not without some misgiving as to its entire correctness. However, it is the best that can now be made of the subject. The scale of equivalents down to the sixteenth

was also a two-thirds piece or currency daler of this period, containing about 266 grains fine silver, of which 1½ went to the riksdaler (Greijer, p. 221). A century later, according to Newton's table of 1717, this coin weighed only 222 grains fine; value 4 marks. Overvalued copper coins also formed part of the circulation of Gustavus Adolphus. Some of them were washed with silver, and were evidently intended to circulate as dalers. The legend on them, whether plated or not, was "Nova Moneta Cupræ." The specimens in the Paris collection are dated 1627. Year 1606, reign of Charles IX. Round base silver coins with name of Jehovah in Hebrew letters surrounded by a circle of flames, legend "1 Mark Svenska," gross weight 73¾ grains: Paris collection. This coin is worn, and has probably lost 1¼ grains, so that its gross weight was about 75 grains. Hence there must have been 6 marks to the daler of this date.

Gold Moneys of Saxony and Scandinavia.

Period.	Denomination.	Contents. Grs. fine.	Silver value.	Ratio to silver.	Remarks.
6th cent.	Native baug	360.0	1½ marks	8.0	Du Chaillu, i., p. 549.
7th "	Moslem dinar	63.7	¼ mark	8.0	Value deduced.
9th "	"	63.7	¼ mark	8.0	" "
10th "	"	63.7	¼ mark	8.0	" "
11th "	"	61.5	¼ mark	8.0	" "
12th "	Besant (about)	60.0	¼ mark	8.0	
1481	Mark of John	28.8	1 mark	10.0	Jutland Code.†
1481	Large coin of John	230.4	8 marks	10.0	See text. 32 örtugas = 1 mark. Paris collection. Gross wt. 234.54.
1604–11	Half ducat: Chas. IX	27.3	2 marks	13.3	Mark only contains 13,6 grs. gross.
1634	Ducat: Gus. Adolph	48.6*	marks	—	Posthumous issue (Humphreys).
1632–54	" Christina	52.6*	marks	—	Paris collection.
1660–97	Quarter ducat: Chas. XI	13.0*	marks	—	" "
1720	" Ulrica	52.5*	marks	—	" "
1746	" Frederick	53.2*	marks	—	" "
1758	" Adolph. Fred.	53.4*	marks	—	" "
1777	" Gustavus III	52.4*	—	14.8	Greijer values at 94 Lub. "skil."
1779	" "	53.7*	—	14.8	Paris collection.
1820	" Charles XIV	51.9	—	—	Kelly, ii., p. 160.
1830	" "	51.9	—	—	McCulloch.
1837	" Chas. XIV	48.6*	—	—	Paris collection.
1838	" "	52.6	—	—	App. "Encyc."
1850	" Oscar I	—	Variable	—	
1868	Carolin, Charles XV	44.9	—	—	Pollock values at 10 "francs."
1872	" Oscar II	44.9	—	—	" "
1872	Ducat: Oscar II	46.2	—	—	

NOTES TO THE TABLE. *Gross weight. The standard was (apparently) nearly fine. †During the period of Marco Polo's residence in China, about 1290, the ratio in the Province of Karam was 8 for 1, and in the City of Yunnan 5 for 1. Wright's "Marco Polo," 1854, pp. 263-7.

century was 32 ortugars (afterwards called skillings) to the money mark; for example, in the reign of John, 1481-1512, there appear to have been always 32 ortugars to the money mark, but in the reign of Gustavus Vasa, the money mark was divided into 24 ortugars. At this point the gold money mark disappeared, and marks were henceforth made of debased silver. In 1604, according to Greijer, there were but 24 ortugars to the mark; thus, 16 Gotland or 8 Swedish pennies$=1$ ortugar; 3 ortugars$=1$ öre; 8 öre$=1$ mark. As both the value of silver to gold, and the number of silver coins to the mark, were continually lowered by legislation, it follows that the contents of the gold mark diminished with great rapidity, a fact which accounts for its disappearance. The ratio of silver to gold from the earliest period to the Renaissance was 8 for 1; during the Renaissance 10 for 1; after the Dutch revolution about 13 for 1; in the eighteenth century (1777) 14.82 for 1; and since that time, more or less, the same as in the Netherlands.

We are now prepared to trace the copper system of Scandinavia, which, as with Russia before the present century, was of more importance than either the gold or silver coins.

The copper klippings of Christian and Gustavus Vasa were followed in 1569 by a third issue of the same character. These were the klippings of John III. In 1575 this issue was retired, and the country was relieved from klippings until 1589, when John introduced another issue of them. (Greijer, p. 178.) Meanwhile the revolution had broken out in the Netherlands, and the burghers had taken the monetary system into their own hands by establishing private or individual coinage. It was now no longer Charles V.

nor the counts of Holland who determined how many gold-ducats, or silver dollars, or florins, should be coined and added to the circulation, but the burghers of Leyden, Deventer and Amsterdam. This legislation had been followed by an extraordinary influx of the precious metals into the Dutch ports. The example and good fortune of Holland was not lost upon the Swedes, who perhaps fancied that by copying the legislation of the United Provinces they would promote a like influx of silver into Stockholm. But they were mistaken. It was not individual coinage which had filled the Dutch ports with gold and silver, but the Dutch fleets and buccaneers of the East and West Indies, and the Dutch traders in Japan. However, the Swedes, as yet unconscious or heedless of these circumstances, went on with their second-hand legislation. In 1604, by the statute of Nordcheping, it was enacted that half an ounce (say 203 grains) of standard silver should pass for 16 öre, also that a rixdaler (398½ grains standard) should pass for 36 öre. This decree gave an advantage to coins over metal of about 15 per cent, a pretty heavy seigniorage, the whole of which it was practical to evade by sending the silver to Amsterdam and there having it coined into florins and exchanged for Dutch wares and products for shipment to Stockholm. As for the monetary function, which this decree conferred upon bullion, it was wholly ineffective. Nobody wanted bullion. Even although he got 15 per cent more metal in the same sum, he preferred dalers.

In 1607, the king (Charles IX.) tried a new experiment in money. He decreed that whosoever brought to the mint 4 riksdalers (1594 English grains of silver), or who brought 4½ ounces of silver (1828⅛ grains), should receive 4½ currency dalers.[1] I have not the text

[1] Patent of January 7th, 1607.

of this act before me, and cannot give either the contents or value of these new dalers. They should contain about 350 grains each, but I have found no such coin of this date in the Paris collection. As no limits were placed upon the deposits of silver, and as the right of the depositor to demand coined dalers for his metal was not restricted, this decree was called a "Patent of Free Coinage." It should have been termed "An act enabling the king to grant to the burghers one of the chief prerogatives of State." That prerogative was the right and the power to increase the currency by employing the mint to turn metal into coins, and the right to diminish the currency by melting these coins down to metal. With such a see-saw as this in hand the burghers were armed with a terrible power over the fortunes of their fellow-subjects. Fortunately for the prosperity of Sweden, the Dutch system did not work successfully in that country. Sweden was poor; no vikings now entered its ports laden with the plunder of other lands, and very little silver was in circulation. In 1613, after the peace with Denmark, a degraded currency daler was in circulation which could not have contained more than about 266 grains, for it required one and a half of them to equal in value one riksdaler.[1] In the same year the ransom of Elfsborg was agreed to be paid in four years, whereas, in fact, it was not paid until the end of six years. It was collected by a tax on the people, levied according to class, and made payable in coins, silver bullion, copper, iron, rye or malt, the merchandise at fixed prices. (Greijer, p. 221 n.) Perhaps the best proof of the scarcity of money consists in the fact that in 1613 the inevitable over-valued coppers, now no longer called klippings but "rundstyks," again made their appearance in the cir-

[1] Greijer, p. 221.

culation. This was followed by another emission in 1625, and the following paraphrase from Mr. Bryce's "Holy Roman Empire" informs us to what a memorable use this issue was put by the king:

"In 1619 Ferdinand II. ascended the imperial throne of Germany. The arrangements of Augsburg, like most treaties on the basis of *uti possidetis*, were no better than a hollow truce, satisfying no one, and conscientiously made to be broken. The Church lands which the Protestants had seized and Jesuit confessors had urged the Catholic princes to reclaim, furnished unceasing ground of quarrel, and the smoldering hate of both parties was kindled by the troubles of Bohemia in the Thirty Years' War. Jealous, bigoted, implacable, skillful in forming and masking his plans, and resolute in carrying them to completion, this champion of Rome had as nearly destroyed the Protestant religion of Europe as Charlemagne had destroyed the Arrian Christianity of the Lombards and the ancient worship of the Gothic races. Leagued with Spain, backed by the Catholics of Germany, and served by such a leader as Wallenstein, Ferdinand proposed nothing less than the extension of the empire to its ancient limits, and the recovery of its suzerainty over all the Christian states. Denmark and Holland were to be attacked by sea and land; Italy to be re-conquered by the help of Spain; and Maximilian of Bavaria and Wallenstein were to be rewarded with principalities in the ancient Gothic provinces of Mecklenburgh and Pomerania. The last-named general was all but master of the northern lands, when the successful resistance of Stralsund and an unexpected event of still greater importance turned the wavering balance of the war. In 1630 the Goths once more crossed the Baltic, and turned their arms against Rome. Ferdinand had required the restitution of all Church property occupied since 1555. The Protestants were helpless, and Europe was on the point of being again subjected to the murderous vengeance of Rome, when it was saved by the Gothic king. In four campaigns he destroyed the arms and prestige of the Catholic emperor, ravaged his lands, emptied his treasury, and left him at last so enfeebled, that no subsequent success could make him or his cause again formidable."

The rundstyks of Gustavus are noteworthy for another reason; they gave rise to one of the most interesting monetary experiments known to the history of the north. The modern sciolists of money are never tired of chanting the sing-song of the dialecticians that money is a commodity—that it is subject to the economic laws pertaining to commodities, among which is "supply and demand," and that its value must necessarily conform to the cost of the production of this commodity. If this be true it can make no essential difference of what commodity money is made, provided that it is valuable, imperishable, susceptible of being readily coined, etc., nor how much or little of it is coined. We are now about to see a monetary system based on this delusion. The overvalued copper money of Sweden, issued by the Crown, reached such vast proportions that by the middle of the century it had fallen to or near its value as metal. Thus, at a period when the Dutch and English ports were enriched with the plundered treasures of India and America, the Gothic defenders of a faith, which enabled the nobles and burghers of those lands to enjoy this wealth in peace, were enduring the bitterness of poverty and putting up with the inconvenience of a copper currency.

A remarkable document, of which a copy exists in the Norden collections, delivered by Axel Oxenstiern to Gustavus Adolphus, bears this title: "According to his majesty's gracious command this is my humble opinion touching the copper trade and copper coinage."
. . . "So long as copper was at a good value, and the coinage was limited in amount, so that it only supplied the wants of the community, and answered to their requirements, and was so kept within bounds that he who wished to have silver could obtain it, one coinage was as good as another; but after the value of copper fell it drew down the coinage with it and diminished its value, so that we may indeed suffer and be silent on account of the prince's edict, but that does not alter the opinion and common sense of men." He then advises that the copper mines should be thrown open to individual enterprise—the sooner the better—with other advice concerning the old copper mines and the old Copper Company.[1]

After the death of Gustavus the embarrassments of the treasury compelled his daughter Christina to issue, in 1644, a sort of exchequer-bill, known by the name of "assignats" or "assignations," which appear to have circulated as money. Turning, in this extremity, to Holland for a suitable financial expedient, Sweden found one in the Wissel Bank of Amsterdam, and in 1656 a private institution, on much the same plan, was established in Stockholm by a man named Palmstruck. This bank received deposits of coin, bullion, and rundstyks, for which it granted credits, and in 1658 issued receipts known as "transport-notes," which,

[1] Greijer, p. 295 n. The Copper Company was, in 1629, obliged to restore the copper trade to the Crown, having made vain attempts to keep up the price. The copper coinage, first introduced into Sweden in 1625, formed part of this system (Ibid., p. 222). Compare the treatise on the old Copper Company and copper coinage in the time of Gustavus Adolphus, by Master Wingquist, "Scandia," vol iv. (Ibid., p. 227 n.)

from their superior convenience, soon drove the copper rundstyks into the vaults of the bank and usurped their place in the circulation. This plan worked so well that in 1668 the government took over Palmstruck's bank, which it chartered in that year as the Riks-Bank, or Royal, or National Bank of Sweden, and embarked, without further reserve, in a monetary system based upon copper metal. It cut large plates of hammered copper into squares and oblongs, some of them weighing thirteen or fourteen pounds,[1] and, stamping them with an appropriate device and their value (that of the metal) in each corner, issued them as money.

Upon the theory of the schools there could be no practical objection to this money nor to the "free coinage" of it, except its bulk and weight, and as to bulk and weight, there was the bank ready to receive it on deposit, and issue in its place transport-notes payable in copper-plates. But soon a difficulty arose, for which no provision had been made, and which the schoolmen had not foreseen: the value of copper continued to fall, and with it fell the purchasing-power of the copper-plates, and of the notes that represented them. It was then perceived that gold and silver made a superior metallic money, not because they cost more than copper to produce, but because they possess an attribute which is possessed neither by copper nor any other commodity. There is a vast accumulation of gold and silver in the world saved up from distant ages. Hence their value—which is not that of their cost of production, but (with open mints) that of their numbers and function as coins—is slow to obey any change, however great, in the cost of producing new metal. As there was no

[1] One of these plates, formerly in my possession, was 10 inches square, three-eighths of an inch thick, and weighed 6 lbs. 13 oz. avoirdupois. But I have seen them of double this size and weight in the Paris collection.

like accumulation of copper, every shipload that came in from Amsterdam further and further lowered its value, and every withdrawal for the arts enhanced it. At length, on account of the fluctuations which occurred in its value, it became entirely useless for money.

During the Regency of Christina (1633-45) it was resolved that, "Instead of the copper coinage which his late Majesty had determined to let fall of itself, as it had already mostly disappeared, a good and sterling coinage, yet somewhat under the standard, should be issued." There is no sterling coinage of this period in the public collections.

"The copper cross-pieces, struck and issued by order of Gustavus, seem to have had no currency. The Swedish agent in Holland, Eric Laurencson, offers to send them back again (Letter of the Council to the Chancellor, January 14, 1633). The government was constrained to order that debts which had been contracted in copper money should be paid according to the value which the riksdaler bore at the time, namely, until 1628, 6½ marks to the riksdaler; 1629, 10 marks, and afterward 14 marks, as ascertained by the Crown receipts. Thenceforth the riksdaler was to be worth 6 marks, or 48 öre, but the copper öre, or rundstyks, in circulation were at the same time depreciated to half their value, and the government undertook to cause silver coins to be struck."[2]

The failure of the copper ingot system gave rise to another monetary experiment, this time with a tragic ending. After the defeat of Charles XII. at Pultowa and his return from captivity money was scarce and credit low in Sweden, but the genius of his financial adviser, Baron Goertz, saw a way to remove every

[1] Greijer, p. 295 n.   [2] Ibid.

difficulty. George Heinrich de Goertz, Baron von Schlitz, was born of a noble family in Holstein. He joined Charles XII. at Stralsund on his return from Turkey, and through his activity and intelligence was soon placed at the head of affairs. His scheme for establishing the currency was to issue not copper ingots but copper dollars, which, as they bore the king's stamp, were made full legal tenders, and were light and adapted for the pocket, he imagined would circulate at their nominal value without difficulty. This they would have done but for several circumstances, none of which appear to have been sufficiently considered by this otherwise excellent and conscientious minister. First, the government was too prostrate and weak to sustain a fiduciary money. Second, Goertz did not place any limitation upon the coinage. This (limitation) is the main principle and essence of money, without which—no matter of what substance the symbols are made, whether of gold, silver, copper or paper—it must fail to discharge its function equitably. Third, the copper dollars which he struck, unlike the exquisitely finished sesterces of the Roman Republic, were rudely made and therefore easily counterfeited. Fourth, he seemed indifferent to the rights or prejudices of the ecclesiastical, noble and burgher classes, whose rents and other sources of income were grossly and inequitably reduced through his neglect to secure the overvalued dollars from depreciation. He caused to be struck upon these dollars, not the images of the ancient Gothic gods, as some authors allege, but of Jupiter, Mars, Phœbus, Saturn, etc., and this, too, was deemed an offense to those who were injured by the depreciation which occurred. The pieces were of about the same size as a silver shilling of to-day, and were stamped "4 daler silf. mynt," being overvalued nearly a hundred times. Finally, as if to render these coins as odious as possible, it was asserted and believed that after an interval the tax officers would be instructed to refuse them in payment of taxes from the peasants,[1] but such inequity and rashness seems incredible. This system, coupled with issues of base silver coins, heavy copper plates, and paper notes, to neither of which were any limits prescribed or observed, continued in force during the life of the king; but the moment his death occurred, in 1718, and his sister Ulrica Elenora mounted the throne, a declaration was promulgated whereby the paper notes were wholly abolished, and the copper dalers were reduced by several successive steps to something near their metallic value. The next measures taken by the princess royal and her council are thus described.[2]

"A charge was drawn up against Goertz, who was accused of peculation, of having ruined public credit by imaginary money, of having formed a design to destroy the king and army by advising him to a ruinous campaign in the inhospitable kingdom of Norway, and so on. . . . Goertz, to whom the assistance of counsel was refused, defended himself with great ability, and clearly invalidated almost every article of the impeachment. His straightened circumstances were a proof that he had applied none of the public money to his own use; the necessity of the times apologized for his substituting overvalued money to satisfy the wants of the treasury, and possibly such a measure might have proved of national advantage had it been pursued with more discretion. Notwithstanding Goertz's defense was clear and irrefragable, the case went on without regard to formality or perhaps to equity. The court and the citizens seemed equally determined to hound

[1] Greijer, p. 295 n.   [2] "Modern Univers. Hist.," xxx., pp. 284 85.

him to death. . . . He was condemned to lose his head, and at a place appointed for the execution of thieves and felons.'"¹ This cruel sentence was enforced March 3, 1719.

The insertion of a design to "ruin public credit with imaginary money" in the indictment against Goertz reads very much like the apology of the regicides for their murder of the Mongol ruler of Persia in 1294, that he had criminally substituted paper for metallic money. Indeed, one indictment may have been borrowed from the other.² Voltaire, citing the memoirs of Bassevitz, gives an entirely different version of the Goertz affair. He does not say that the primate was executed either for circulating copper dollars in Sweden or advising a campaign in Norway, but for the abortive plots and intrigues which he set afoot for the recovery of the Baltic provinces.³ This seems very much more likely.

Besides the Goertz dollars, the base silver coins, and the paper currency of Charles XII., there were in circulation some of the old copper plates and the transport-notes of the Riksbank; indeed, this continued down to 1763, so that from first to last the copper plates enjoyed a circulation of more than a century. In addition to these strange elements of money in Sweden, there was a copper plate system in Wismar. By the treaty of Westphalia, 1648, the city of Wismar, in Mecklenburg-Schwerin, had been ceded to Sweden, which established there a court of appeals for its possessions in Germany. In 1715, during the prevalence of the copper plate bank notes and copper dollar system of Sweden, copper

---

1 "Modern Univers. Hist.," xxx., p. 288.
2 Wright's "Marco Polo," p. 217.
3 Voltaire, "L'Empire de Russie," ii., 8. It is a curious fact that the Goertz dalers were called Mynt-saicen, a retention of the ancient denomination of the saicca, saiga, sicca, or shekel, for the meaning of which so many metrologists and numismatists have searched in vain (De Vienne, "Livre d'Argent;" Brucker, in Hildebrand's "Jahrbok," 1864, i., p. 161).

ingots or plates were issued in Wismar of the denominations 4, 8, and 16 skillings, and the sizes 2, 2⅛, and 3¾ inches square. Facsimiles of these pieces, which are now very rare, are published in Maillet's "Monnais Obsidionales et de Necessité," Bruxelles, 1868. They are all dated 1715, and soon after this date they disappeared from circulation, and found their way to the Riksbank of Stockholm.[1]

During the last half of the eighteenth and first quarter of the nineteenth century the currency of Sweden was nominally based on silver dalers, but, owing to the wars in which the State was involved, it really consisted of somewhat depreciated government notes, both of which, it is perhaps needless to say, were inconvertible. This depreciation, and the desire to resume coin payments, gave rise to the coinage of new silver dalers, designed to exactly equal the value of the depreciated notes, for which, it was expected, they would become interchangeable. It will be remembered that the old specie riksdaler (in which these notes were payable) contained about 390 English grains fine silver. The new coins were the riksdaler-banco, containing about 146¼ grains fine, or three-eighths of the specie daler, and the riksgald (royal debts) daler, containing about 97½ grains fine, or one-fourth of the specie daler. The former represented the value of the bank-note, the latter that of the government note. Each of these dalers was subdivided into 48 skillings, each of 12 rundstyks.[2]

As, by the Royal Ordinance of October 26th, 1829, the government notes were made legal-tender for riksgald dalers, and no adequate provision was made for their retirement, the new coins, when not exported,

[1] Consult my "History of Money, Ancient," p. 199.
[2] Consult table of the Talent or Riksdaler in the text.

were added to the circulation, and they still further lowered the value of all dalers, including themselves. Upon observing this, the government hastened its arrangements for the retirement of its notes, and the operation was eventually concluded satisfactorily, not, however, until the confusion caused by the presence of three different classes of metallic dalers, skillings and rundstyks had led to great annoyance.[1]

By the legislation of 1854, the old specie riksdaler and the new riksdaler-banco were abolished, leaving the riksgald daler the sole "unit of circulation" (a much better term than the misleading "unit of value" of the American statutes). The riksgald daler was now termed the riksmynt daler, its subdivisions of skillings and rundstycks were abrogated, and it was subdivided anew into 100 öre.[2] This legislation went into effect January 1st, 1858.

The religious fanaticism of Christian II., which had arrayed against him both the nobles and the commons of Sweden, also occasioned the secession of Norway from the Scandinavian union. The election of Frederick I. by the Danes, though it failed to conciliate the multitude who supported the standard of Gustavus Vasa, appears to have satisfied both the peoples of Norway and Denmark, whereupon, in 1523, these two States were joined under one government, and they so remained until 1813-14, when Norway again united with Sweden.

The monetary history of Denmark and Norway du-

[1] Lieut.-Colonel F. S. Terry, in two pamphlets, "The Great Currency Problem" and "Independent Standards," London, 1893, proposed to "restore silver" by introducing into other states a like system of two metallic moneys, the one silver, the other gold, both open to "free coinage," and both without limit, in either of which moneys people would be free to make their bargains. The Dutch authors of the Act of Charles II. gave us one illimitable and ever-varying measure of value; Colonel Terry's plan would give us two.
[2] Appleton's "Encyc,," xv., p. 217.

ring most of this interval has been already sufficiently illustrated. Previous to 1813 the Danish monetary valuations were 1 specie riksdaler equaled 1½ sletdalers, 4 orts, 6 marks, 96 skillings, 192 fyrkes, 288 witten, or 1152 pfennings Danish; or one half of the like denominations in Hamburg, or Lubeck, or Schleswig-Holstein money. Thus the Danish specie riksdaler equaled 3 marks, or 48 skillings "Lubs," etc. In other words, the mark or skilling of Lubeck, etc., was worth twice as much as the mark or skilling Danish.

There were at this period no less than five different kinds of money used in Denmark. These were as follows:—

1. "Specie." The basis of this money was the "specie" or "effective" riksdaler of 390 down to 375 English grains fine, valued in law at 6 marks, or 96 skillings, etc., as above stated.

2. "Currency." This money consisted of suspended bank or government notes, and, according to Dr. Kelly, was $22\frac{11}{12}$ per cent worse than "specie." This is presumed to mean in the year 1821, when the author wrote, but of course the relation was variable. The books of merchants, tradesmen, and others (except those of the bank of Altona, which adhered to "specie") were kept in "currency." "Specie" and "currency" were the two principal moneys. Besides these, there were:

3. "Sundish specie," in which Sound dues were levied on foreigners. This was $2\frac{5}{8}$ per cent worse than "specie."

4. "Crown money," in which Sound dues were levied on native vessels. This was $15\frac{35}{64}$ per cent worse than "specie."

To enhance this confusion of moneys, the silver

"specie" coins were struck by the Danish mint mark of about 3607¾ grains, while the gold coins and the "currency" and "Crown" silver coins were struck by the Cologne mark of 3608 grains. The difference was small, yet it was sufficient to occasion annoyance in the computation and value of large sums. This dissonance of mint-weights arose out of the fact that the king of Denmark was also the duke of Holstein, and, as such, his coins had to agree in some sort with those of the empire. The "specie" ducat of Denmark contained 52.6, and the "current" ducat 42.2, grains fine gold. The "Christian" contained 93.6, and the "Frederick" of 1813-39 contained 91¼, grains fine gold. The gold coins were not legal-tender, and they fluctuated in value, from day to day, in silver coins. Bargains (special contracts) could be made in gold coins, but as silver coins formed the basis of the monetary system, such bargains were rarely made, and the gold coinage constituted an expense to the government, for which the charge of ¼ of 1 per cent seigniorage was deemed an inadequate compensation. The gold coins were commonly exported to Germany, where they were hoarded by the peasants.[1] A further source of confusion in the monetary system of Denmark arose from the circumstance that, whilst in Bergen the system of money was based on the Danish riksdaler of 6 marks, or 96 skillings, in Christiania, Drontheim, Larwigen, Kopperwic, and other places in Norway, a riksdaler was employed of 4 orts, or 24 skillings Danish.[2] A final confusion was occasioned by the fluctuations of the Danish paper

---

[1] All these details will be found in the communication of G. Strachey, Esq., to the British Foreign Office, printed in the "Report of the Royal Commission on Coinage," 1868, p. 234.

[2] Schmidt's (Tate's) "Cambist," p. 86, also mentions a Norwegian daler of 120 skillings; but I have not been able to identify it.

currency, which, being continually increased in amount, varied in Danish "specie" or silver riksdalers, a subject which will be explained after disposing of the specie system introduced in 1813.

In this new system one of the old riksdalers was coined into two; in other words, 18½ new riksbank dalers—as they were called—were struck from a Cologne mark of silver, so that each one contained 195 English grains fine. This daler was divided into 6 marks or 96 skillings, like the old riksdaler "specie," therefore both the dalers, marks, and skillings, since there was no limit to their coinage, were worth only half as much as the former ones.

"The bank of Copenhagen has undergone many essential changes since its first establishment, and in order to understand its present state, it may be necessary to take a general view of those alterations. It was originally founded, in 1736, as a bank both of deposit and of circulation. In 1745 it was released from the obligation of discharging its notes in coin, and it continued still to make advances to the State and to individuals in paper, by which shares became greatly enhanced in their value.

"This bank had issued paper to the amount of eleven millions of riksdalers, when the king returned their deposits to the shareholders and became himself the sole proprietor. The paper issued was twenty times the amount of capital, in consequence of which specie disappeared, and notes were fixed as low as 1 riks dollar.

"To remedy this inconvenience, in 1791, all further emission of notes was forbidden, and a progressive liquidation of the paper was ordered. A new bank, called the Specie Bank, was created, which was to be independent of the government. The money deposited might be drawn out at pleasure, or transferred by assignment, and its issue of paper was limited to a certain extent. In 1804 the new notes lost 25 per cent in exchange with the currency in which they were payable, and the depreciation continued to increase until 1812, when it became excessive.

"In 1813 a new bank was established under the direction of the king, and, therefore, entitled the Royal Bank of Denmark. Its chief object was to reduce the paper then in circulation, which was depreciated to one-sixth of its nominal value; and in a new issue the dollar was equivalent to five-eighths of the old paper dollar, which reduced the composition to $\frac{5}{48}$. In 1817 this bank was converted into a National Bank, by making a certain proportion of the property of the kingdom a guarantee for the liquidation of its paper.

"For this purpose all property was to pay 6 per cent to the bank, and until the capital is paid the interest charged for each deficiency is $6\frac{1}{2}$ per cent per annum. Valuation of property in this case is regulated by the public taxes, and all the payments are to be made in silver or in paper of the full value of silver, according to a certain rate of exchange, which is fixed quarterly; but as this institution engages to pay off seven millions of riksbank dalers annually, persons paying in their quota at the bank are allowed a drawback of five-sixths of the taxes.

"This bank issues its own notes, which are gradually paid off; and it is intended, when the new paper is entirely reduced, to issue notes payable to bearer on demand. All revenues and great transactions are paid in this paper, according to the rate of exchange. This rate is called riksbank silver value, which may be sometimes more and sometimes less than the riksbank daler. All private contracts and current transactions are understood to be settled in such paper, unless real silver is stipulated for; likewise all payments of public actuaries and to the army; but custom-house duties are settled in real silver.

"In January, 1821, the debts of the bank were computed as follows:—1. Seven millions of riksbank dalers of public stock, which it has undertaken to pay. 2. Seven millions of bonds for the redemption of the former paper money of Holstein, etc. 3. A debt of seven millions, lately contracted for the diminution of the bank-notes in circulation. 4. The bank-notes in circulation, which are computed at twenty-two millions.

"The capital is estimated at thirty-three millions of riksbank dalers, and the bank is besides computed to possess about three millions in silver and in buildings. The surplus of its annual revenue, the principal part of which arises from the interest of its security on real estates, is employed in the reduction of the bank-notes in circulation. The contributors of 6 per cent from estates, as well as voluntary contributors, are shareholders, and are equally entitled to interest, etc."[1]

This system was modified in 1839, by further provisions for the retirement of the paper money, similar to those of Sweden, already described, except that in the case of Denmark, the riksbank silver daler of 195 grains fine remained the "unit of circulation." It was, therefore, worth a trifle more than two Swedish riksgald, or riksmynt, dalers.

On September 20, 1872, a convention of the three Scandinavian States was concluded at Copenhagen, which was ratified at Stockholm on December 18, 1872.[2]

---

[1] Kelly's "Cambist," ed. 1821, i., p. 79.
[2] The text of this convention will be found in the "Report of the U. S. Monetary Commission" of 1876, part I., p. 71.

It provided for a common system of coinage, based on the gold kroner (crown) of 6.22 English grains fine, divided into 10 öre. This coin, or rather its multiples (four kroner being the smallest piece), was made full legal-tender in all the States, and was opened to "individual coinage;" in other words, the State is obliged to coin anybody's gold bullion substantially free of expense, the seigniorage only amounting to from ¼ to ⅓ of 1 per cent *ad valorem*. The silver coins were limited in legal-tender function to five specie riksdalers, equal (nominally) to twenty kroner, and their coinage was reserved to the State. In a word, the Scandinavian States practically demonetized silver, and adopted gold coins and "open mintage" as the basis of their monetary systems. Each State retained its own paper money system. The notes, so long as they continue to be redeemed in gold coins, are full legal tender within the State of issue—an attribute of which they are to become divested whenever redemption fails. "In the transcription of obligations contracted in the earlier money, the basis of conversion adopted was the proportion of silver to gold of 15.08 for 1." This simply means that obligations contracted in specie riksdalers of practically 375½ grains silver are now payable with four kroner, containing 24.9 grains of gold. "The ratio of transcription" in Denmark was 15.675 for 1. Both the gold and silver coins of each State are accorded legal course in the others, subject, as to silver coins, to certain internal arrangements.

These provisions were adopted in the Danish, Swedish, and Norwegian laws of May 23, 1873, May 30, 1873, and June 4, 1873, and by the treaties of May 27, 1873, and October 16, 1875, which went into effect April 1, 1876, and were rendered obligatory from January 1, 1877.

CHAPTER XIII.

THE NETHERLANDS.

Ancient Saxony—Origin of the Dutch—Their maritime character—Early moneys—The pagan Iesterling, Engel, and Guilder—Trade with Saracenic Spain—Moslem and Esterling ratios—Pepin, the Short—The Christian ratio—Compromise ratio of the Baltic—The Säiga—Fall of the Eastern Empire—Coinages of the Renaissance—The Ducat, or Florin—Proposed Anglo-Flemish Convention—Florins and Nobles of Edward III.—Disagreement respecting the ratio—Burgundian ratios—The Ducaton, or Thaler—The Stiver—Causes of the Dutch revolution—Religion and Money—The right of coinage—Corruptions of money during the Renaissance—Sudden enhancement of gold by Charles V.—Revolt of the Netherlands—Demonetization of gold—Paper money of Leyden—The Wissel Bank—The Bank of Amsterdam—Sols banco—Burgher coinage—It destroys money and substitutes metal—Selfish policy of Spain—The Buccaneers—Plunder of the Spanish galleons—Opening of the sea route to the Orient—The Dutch colony of New Amsterdam (New York)—The English follow the Dutch in all these measures—Sir Thomas Gresham—Dutch coinage ratios from the earliest times to the present—The Mark—Hanseatic money—Successive monetary systems of the Burghers from the sixteenth to the nineteenth century—Gold and silver alternately demonetized—Bank issues and insolvency—Recent demonetization of silver—Present currency of the Netherlands—Importance of the ratio as a guide to history—Urgent necessity for reform of the Dutch monetary system—The Future.

The early history of money in the Netherlands is included in that of ancient Saxony, of which an outline appears in my "Ancient Britain." The present treatise begins substantially with the Carlovingian or Mediæval or German empire, under which the various lordships, which afterwards constituted the provinces of the Netherlands, were held in vassalage. These were Holland, Zeeland, Utrecht, Guelderland, Groningen, Over-iesel or Overyssel, and Friesland; afterward called the Seven United Provinces. These, with three other provinces, carved out of the Generality governed by the States-General, make the present kingdom of Holland. The eight remaining provinces of the Netherlands now make the kingdom of Belgium.

It will conduce to a better understanding of the Dutch monetary systems to explain, at the outset, that the ancient Batavians were not descended from the people of the highlands, or Germany, and shared neither their customs nor religion. The Batavians were a portion of that martial and amphibious race who carried the worship of the Sun and the art of navigaion from the Gulf of Finland to the British Channel; and were so mingled with the Iesthonians, Veneti and Norsemen, that no ethnological nor philological theory has ever satisfactorily traced their genealogy, or accounted for their early history. Their rivers, provinces, and towns, as Iessel, Ober-Iessel and Ies-la-Chapelle, afterwards Aix-la-Chapelle, were named after the sun-god; they were fishermen, traders and pirates; and so were their neighbors and kinsmen, the Veneti and Norsemen; and that is about all we know of them, until Charlemagne, including them among the pagans of Saxony, drove his pious sword through some of their obdurate hearts, and obliterated their genealogy by introducing German blood into the remainder. The conquest of the Veneti and Batavians by Cæsar, the allusion to them in the "Germany" of Tacitus, the revolt of the Frisians against the exacting rule of Tiberius, the rise of Carausius the Menapian, the subjection of the Low Countries to the Western and Carlovingian empires, and the history of the Pagan Hansa, all of which subjects are treated either in the work above alluded to, or else in my "Middle Ages Revisited," may interest the student of a larger history; but cannot, in the present state of historical knowledge, lead to any more satisfactory information concerning the origin of the Dutch people.

The oldest Dutch coins are attributed to Arnold II.,

count of Flanders, 964-89. The oldest Dutch coins in the British Museum are some small thin silver pieces of Bruno III., count of Frisia, A. D. 1038-57, a vassal of the emperors Henry III. and Henry IV. These pieces, which are in fairly good condition, weigh from 10.2 to 10.4 English grains each. I shall revert to them further on; meanwhile it is necessary to observe that, although they are among the oldest Dutch coins, they are not among the oldest Dutch moneys. These were ieschen (corrupted to eschen), iesterlings or engels, and gulden. The first and second of these names, like those attached to the sacred coins of China, India, Greece and Rome, are evidently derived from that of the sun-god. Engel is probably derived from an effigy on the iesterling. The last belongs also to a pagan era, for although now it is that of a silver coin, the name evidently belongs to a time when it was a gold one, and therefore to a pagan period; because under the Christian empire no gold coins were permitted to be struck except by the sovereign-pontiff in Byzantium. The gulden was probably the maravedi of about 40 grains weight.

From near the beginning of the eighth to the close of the tenth centuries—when, as attested by the numerous finds of Moslem coins in Esthonia, Julin, Gotland, Frisia, etc., an active trade was conducted in the Baltic and North Seas and coastwise down to Saracenic Spain, by the Norsemen, Dutchmen and Moslem—Moslem coins and valuations must have been familiar to the maritime provinces of northern and western Europe. The influence of the Moslem ratio of value between gold and silver is especially noticeable. The ratio in the Roman and Christian systems was, until the thirteenth century, always 12 for 1; that in the Indian and

Moslem systems, 6½ for 1. This radical difference in the relative coinage value of the precious metals, maintained on both sides for centuries with little attempt at compromise or reconcilement, enables us to detect with ease the predominating influence, whether Christian or pagan, in any given system of coinage. It is the infallible numisometer of religious opinion during the mediæval era. Measured by this criterion, the Dutch coinage was decidedly pagan; for the earliest known coins of the Low Countries were the silver säigas mentioned in the barbarian codes, containing about 18¼ grains of fine silver, and exchanging for the gull skillingar, gold shilling, ora, quarter-dinar, quarter-mancus or quarter-solidus, the worn or degraded triente, or the guilder or gulden—for the same coin, at one time or another, was known by all of these names—at the rate of 8 for 1. As the weights of the säiga and gold shilling were the same, this made a like ratio (of 8 for 1) between the coinage value of silver and gold. The Jutland code of the thirteenth century, which mentions this ratio of 8 for 1, is probably altered from a pagan code of an earlier period.

The first attempts to introduce Christian coins into the Netherlands must be credited to Pepin. Before his time—if we may rely upon the Chronicle of Aquitaine, wherein 40 deniers (of 17½ grains each) are valued against a besant or solidus of about 70 grains fine—a compromise ratio was introduced into the coinages and valuations of the provinces subject to the fainéant proconsuls of the Byzantine Empire. This was 10 for 1—a mean between the pagan 8 and the Christian 12. Pepin struck 264 deniers from the Roman pound weight of silver, and valued 40 of these at one gold besant of 66¼ grains—a ratio of 12. For himself, he totally abstained from the coinage of gold, which he left entirely to the Basileus.[1]

The Saxon and Frisian codes and capitularies of the Carlovingian era, which might have thrown great light upon this subject, are hopelessly corrupted and muddled. All that we can discern with certainty is that the conqueror was as resolute to follow his father in changing the pagan ratio, as he was merciless in exterminating the pagan religion of the Netherlands. "Ubi contentio contra Saxones te Frisones extorta fuit, ibi volumus ut 40 dinariorum quantitatem solidus habeat quem vel Saxo vel Frisio ad partem Salici Franci cum eo litigantis solvere debet."[2] When this passage is compared with the Frisian code, tit. xvii., art. 76: "Tres denarii novae monetae solidum faciunt," their utter irreconcilability only leaves us room to perceive that Charlemagne was striking new silver coins and changing the ratio to the sacred 12 for 1; but it does not inform us from what other ratio the change was being made. However, not only the weight of the säiga, as deduced from the codes and extant coins, but also the analogies offered by the Moslem, the Norse, and the Anglo-Saxon coinages of the same period, including the first coinage of Alfred, enable us to determine this with confidence. The Dutch pagan ratio was evidently 8, the ratio of the rois fainéants was 10, and the fundamental one of Pepin and Charlemagne was 12. In subsequent ages the ratio fluctuated in the coinage laws between $6\frac{1}{2}$ or 8 on the one hand and 12 on the other, as pagan or Christian influences alternately governed the vassal, but often heretical, counts of the Netherlands provinces. Pepin's absten-

[1] Guerard, "Polyptique d Irminon."
[2] "Saxon Capitulary" (after A. D. 801), cap. xi.

tion from the coinage of gold was respected and imitated by Charlemagne.[1]

The Dutch monetary equivalents of the earliest period known to us were 32 eschen = 1 silver iesterling or engel; and 8 engels = 1 gulden or gold shilling.[2] With the decline of the Roman solidus, so declined the shilling, or little solidus, and with the latter declined the sterling or engel. During the seventh and eighth centuries, when Moslem coins and valuations were current in the Baltic, the gold shilling ceased to be coined, and was superseded by parts of the gold dinar of 63¾ grains fine. The silver dirhem of 41½ grains fine, of which ten went to the dinar (a ratio of 6½ for 1), was also in circulation among the Dutch; a fact attested by the immense numbers of them found in recent years on the coasts of the Baltic and North Seas. From these circumstances I regard the silver pieces of Friesland, mentioned above, as typically quarter-dirhems. It is of no practical consequence whether they are regarded as quarter-dirhems or half-deniers; only, if as half-deniers, they should bear a ratio of 12 to the gold shilling of the empire, which they do not; whereas, if as quarter-dirhems, they should bear a ratio of 6½ to the quarter-dinars of Saracenic Spain, which they do.

There is no evidence that the ratio of 12 was employed in Holland, except at sporadic intervals, that is to say, under Pepin, and possibly for a brief period under Charlemagne; for the latter struck few or no gold coins, probably none. It may have been again employed in the earlier Hapsburgh coinages of the fifteenth

[1] Guerard, "Polyptique d'Irminon."
[2] The eis was also a weight, of which 32 went to the weight engel, 640 to the ounce, and 5120 to the weight mark of 3798 English grains. The name gulden was, in the thirteenth or fourteenth century, conferred upon a degraded "ducat" of about the same contents as the Moorish maravedi. By the imperial edict of 1524, the gulden was to contain 37 1-6 English grains fine gold.

century. At all other periods, as is shown in a table further on, the ratio in Dutch coinage and mint valuations, from the Carlovingian period down to the year 1524, varied from 8 to 10 for 1.

From the date of their earliest coinages, down to the fifteenth century, the coins of the Netherlands which have fallen under my observation present no features of especial interest. The collection in the British Museum is not only wanting as to several provinces and numerous reigns of the Dutch princes, but many of the coins are in bad condition—clipped, bent, perforated with holes, or otherwise mutilated. Among the best specimens are a small silver coin of the count of Nassau, 1229-71, and another of Reynaud II., 1326-43—both of the quarter-dirhem type. Another of Philip le Beau, dux Geldria, weighs $41\frac{1}{2}$ grains gross, and is evidently intended for a dirhem. The earliest gold coin in this collection is one of Charles Egmont, duke of Gueldria, 1492-1538. It is stamped with the figure of a saint, who is styled the "patron of Gueldria," weighs 50.6 grains gross, and is apparently of about 22 carats fine. An earlier one, struck by Charles of Flanders, 1467-77, also stamped with the effigy of a saint, and weighing 51 grains gross, is in the possession of Mr. Lincoln, the London numismatist. These coins are ducats. There are no ducats of the fourteenth century in the Museum collection, yet that is the period when they possess the highest interest; for they were then connected with the history of England. In 1343, after Edward III. had been authorized by the emperor to coin gold, and whilst he was making preparations to exercise this prerogative, it was intimated that the Flemings sold their wares only for Flemish gold florins (ducats), which were valued so highly in English silver coins as to render payment in the latter unprofitable to English merchants. In other words, by paying gold ducats with silver coins, the islanders are represented to have suffered a disadvantage; whereupon the crown resolved that they should be enabled to pay with gold ones. Hence the issue of English double ducats of the year 1344. But as these were valued at six shillings, or 12 times their weight of silver, whilst the Flemish ratio was probably 10 for 1, the Flemings declined to accept them; whereupon they were decried and withdrawn from circulation within the year. Still bent upon issuing a gold coin that should not only retain its place in the home circulation, but also obtain some currency abroad, Edward next (within the same year) issued the noble at six shillings and eight pence, a ratio of 11.06 for 1; the seigniorage being 9 per cent. But this coin the Flemings also objected to unless they were to be struck (under Edward's letter of authority) in Flanders, and also unless an amicable division could be made of the profits arising from their coinage. For this purpose commissioners were sent to Ghent, Bruges, and Ipre; but nothing came of the negotiations. The ratio which ruled in the Netherlands must have compelled the Flemings to demand either a re-valuation of the noble, or an entire abandonment of the seigniorage; conditions to which the English envoys were not authorized to assent. Froissart and Grafton both assert that a gold coin with the name of Edward was struck in Antwerp at this period; but no such coin has ever been found.[1]

In 1436 Holland was annexed to Gothic Burgundy,

[1] Del Mar's "Middle Ages Revisited," chap. xix. The "dubble-ies" was in use during the present century ("Tour in Holland," by Wm. Chambers, 1842).

and in 1477 to Austria,[1] which governed it until 1506, when it was inherited by Charles V. of Germany, or Charles I. of Spain, himself a native of Ghent. During the Burgundian period, some of the Dutch ducats now called double ducats weighed 67 grains (British Museum ducat of Utrecht), and were 23 carats $3\frac{1}{2}$ grains fine (Budelius, p. 249, "Old Double Ducat"). Hence they contained $56\frac{1}{8}$ grains fine—substantially the same as the Venetian sequin of the thirteenth century. The halves were called gulden. The coinage ratio was 9 for 1, an inference derived from the silver ducat or ducaton, whose weight at this period varied from 513 to $507\frac{1}{2}$ grains gross. It was valued equally with the heavier ducat or double gulden. None of these broad ducaton pieces are in the collection of the British Museum, but they are frequently mentioned by Budelius, where their weights and finenesses are given with great minuteness. They varied from 0.936 to $0.916\frac{2}{3}$ fine, and were variously called ducatons, riders, talents, king's-thalers, and Netherlands pennies. They were commonly struck down to the reign of Philip II., and occasionally down to the present century; but their value, as related to the gold coins, was seriously impaired, as will be presently related, by the arbitrary legislation of Charles V. There was also a silver dollar of about two-thirds the same contents, which was valued at a gulden—a ratio of 9 for 1. This piece was the prototype of the existing German thaler, the old Turkish grouch, and many other coins.

If it seems difficult to believe that gold stood at so low a ratio to silver in the fifteenth century, perhaps

[1] The Austrian mint ordinance relating to the Netherlands was issued by Maximillian at Breda, December 14th, 1489. It provided for a gold florin 39¾ English grains fine, valued at 12 times its weight in fine silver, a provision that practically nullified the ordinance and discredited the florins.

the following ratios, taken from the coinages of France during that century, will render our deduction more credible:—Year 1403—ratios, 7.31, 7.84 and 7.87; 1411—6.64 and 6.85; 1417—9.60 and 6.40; 1418—6.67; 1419—7.30; 1421—9.49; 1423 (2nd Charles VII.)—10.22; 1425—10.94; 1428—7 45; 1435—12.59; 1437—7.97; 1447—10.93; 1456—10.79; 1473 (13th Louis XI.)—10.94; and 1475—10.98.[1]

It was during the thirteenth or fourteenth century that the stiver was added to the Dutch denominations of money. The ancient Roman libra of account had consisted of five solidi, or twenty quarter-solidi, or gold shillings. In like manner the Arabian maravedi (the Dutch gulden) was divided in Holland into twenty stivers. At a later period the Dutch talent, or silver ducaton, was divided into twenty stivers, each of about 25 grains of silver; the talent and gulden were therefore of the same value. When, in still later times, the ducaton, talent, thaler, or dollar, was lowered in weight, the stiver became a bronze or copper coin.[2]

The printing-press, the discovery of America, and the teachings of Erasmus—the Dutch leader of the Reformation—all of which influences made themselves felt at about the same time, have been variously put forward by historians as the motive for the Revolt of the Netherlands. No doubt that all of these influences contributed to bring about the end; no doubt that religion was the most powerful of them all, and that the proceedings of the Councils of Trent, Ratisbon and Worms, and the sudden and sinister alliance be-

---

1 Del Mar's "Money and Civilization," p. 202.
2 In Locke's essay on "Money" it is stated that the Dutch ducaton bore a premium in Holland of 1½ per cent over the newer and less valuable silver coins of the same denominational value, and that the ducaton passed for 3 guilders and 3 stivers. Locke was in Holland in 1682, and must have been thoroughly familiar with this subject; yet I cannot make these statements agree.

tween the pope and the emperor, who down to this time had made numerous concessions to the Protestants, which now the emperor revoked, were among the immediate provocations to rebellion. But there was still another motive behind this revolution. The learned Abbé Raynal disclosed this motive, in alluding to the disgust of the Netherlands with that edict of Ferdinand which had forbidden them to take part in the gainful commerce of the East and West Indies, by restricting it to "subjects of Castile."¹ Religion may have swayed the noble and even the common people; it was commerce that swayed the burghers.² This is proved by the revolt of Ghent in 1539, the ground for which was that the emperor's quarrels with Francis debarred the citizens of the town from the rich trade with France, and loaded them with taxes which they protested they could not afford to pay. It is also proved by the relative importance of the demands which were made by Prince Maurice, upon the conclusion of his campaign against Charles. After providing for the liberation of the imprisoned Elector, these demands were, first, that the grievances in the civil government should be redressed; and, last, that the Protestants should be allowed the free exercise of their religion.³

Among these civil grievances none could have been more heavily felt in Holland than the monetary decrees of Charles V. In 1524 this monarch had raised the value of his gold coins in the Netherlands from 9 or 10 to $11\frac{7}{8}$ times their weight in silver coins. This occasioned so much dissatisfaction that in 1542 he returned to a ratio of 10 for 1 by degrading his silver dollars—a

---

1 Raynal, 12mo. ed , i., p. 138.
2 "The parliament and the people, in their addresses to Queen Elizabeth, always mentioned the reformation of the coin, after that of religion, as one of the principal events of the reign" (Lord Liverpool's "Letter to the King," ed 1880, p. 111.
3 Robertson's "Life of Charles V.," iii., p. 252.

mode of reparation hardly more satisfactory than had been the original offense. But the worst was to come. In 1546 Charles suddenly enhanced the value of his gold coins to 13⅓ times their weight in silver ones. In effect, this edict reduced the circulating medium of the Netherlands, which consisted substantially of silver coins, to scarcely more than two-thirds of its value previous to the year 1524. It was a blow that everybody felt and felt at once; and it probably exercised no little influence to support both the operations of Maurice against Charles and the subsequent and more important operations which William of Orange directed against Philip.

To justly estimate the onerous character of this last monetary ordinance of Charles, it should be explained, for example, that it reduced the silver ducaton to two-thirds of its former value, or, which is the same thing, it raised the value of gold nearly 50 per cent, by substituting a debased ducat, first of about 37 grains, and next of about 35 grains fine, in place of the old ones of about 54 grains fine. Budelius (p. 249) mentions a ducat of Deventer on the Iessel, of 67 eschen, or 49.7 grains, which was only 17½ carats fine, and therefore contained but 36¼ grains fine, and a "kaiser's ducat," evidently of Charles V., only 14 carats fine, and containing (if of the same gross weight as the former) only 29 grains fine; whilst the ducats of Philip, of the same gross weight, were only 16 carats fine, and therefore contained but 33⅛ grains of gold. Such a violent and sudden alteration of the value of money amongst a commercial people produced the greatest distress and commotion; and in view of the insurrections which have followed close upon the heels of arbitrary monetary decrees in other States, it cannot be doubted that this measure was at least one of the causes that contributed to the revolution of 1572.

From this date, indeed, commenced a new era, not only in the monetary system of the Netherlands, but also in all the other states of the Western world. To understand its significance we must make a brief retrospect concerning the right of coinage.

In the imperial monetary system, which was planned by Julius Cæsar, matured by Augustus, and retained with more or less constancy down to the fall of Byzantium in 1204, the only full legal-tender money having a forced circulation in all parts of the Empire consisted of the gold coins struck by the emperor at Rome or Byzantium. The Emperor (in another capacity) also struck silver coins; so also did the proconsuls, the subject kings, and the municipalities,[1] but as these coins had only a local course, and in some cases were entirely destitute of legal-tender function, and as the imperial taxes and tributes were payable only in imperial gold coins, or else in exactly twelve times their weight in silver ones (purity for purity), it mattered but little to the Imperial fisc what variations took place in the coinages of the latter. The senate, which after the Augustan period was the mere creature of the sovereign, enjoyed the monopoly of the bronze coinage. The lost Treaty of Seltz, which was made between Charlemagne and Nicephorus, not only necessarily defined the boundaries of the Eastern and Western empires, it must have contained a provision securing the monopoly of the gold coinage to the Basileus; for, as a matter of fact, no gold coins were ever struck by any other Christian prince until after the fall of Byzantium. For the Netherlands, this covers the

[1] Adam Smith (i., p. 320, Hartford ed., 1804) talks of the "allodial" right of coinage. This is sheer nonsense, and bespeaks a fundamental misconception as to the nature and function of money.

entire period from Charlemagne to Frederick II.

The Imperial system, therefore, consisted of something like what is now being proposed by currency doctors—a universal money for the whole European world, but with this essential difference: the Basileus alone struck such universal money, and therefore possessed the power to regulate its volume; whereas, according to the plan which is now being matured, each State—and especially if it permits unlimited coinage, subject to the demands of private individuals—will strike such money for itself, and there will be no united control of the volume. Whether such money be made of one metal or two metals will be of no consequence; it can never become an equitable or stable measure of value.

From the fall of the Greek capital to the revolt of the Spanish Netherlands, a totally different system of money prevailed in the states of Europe. Every king hastened to strike his own gold coins: Frederick of Germany, Alfonso of Leon, and Sancho of Portugal, in 1225; Louis of France, in 1250; the Republic of Florence, in 1252; and Henry III., of England, in 1257. Silver coins were also struck by these powers, and also by the barons and prelates subject to their authority; and both gold and silver coins were commonly made full legal-tenders, at the ratio of value fixed by each State. The supreme right of coinage, which previously was always wielded and but rarely abused by the Basileus, was now both exercised and abused by every petty prince in Europe.

During the Empire the gold coins had been stamped with sacred images and devices, a plan which, in a superstitious age, sufficed to preserve them from abuse. After the fall of Byzantium this restraint was relaxed;

the sacred images disappeared from the gold coins, and both these and the silver coins were altered so often and so suddenly that it is difficult to follow either their composition or value. Edward II., of England, Philip le Bel, of France, and Charles I., of Spain, were only types of the mediæval adulterer of coins. The practice was continued down to the beginning of the seventeenth century; and notwithstanding the apologetic theories or protestations of patriotic writers, no sovereign of this period was guiltless of it. Some of the alterations were no doubt rendered necessary by the dwindling stock and uncertain supplies of the precious metals, or were made for other good reasons; for, as Mr. Hallam has remarked, no ill results appear to have followed them. But others, as attested by their evil consequences, were evidently made for private profit to the king, or else resorted to as a ready means to fill an exhausted treasury.[1]

In 1524 and 1546 Charles V. suddenly raised by proclamation the legal value of his gold coins in Holland from 9 or 10 to 13¼ times their weight in silver coins; and by this imprudent device managed to temporarily replenish his barren coffers. This was the straw that broke the patience of his long-suffering subjects. The Netherlands showed signs of revolt; even Spanish America remonstrated, and eventually (in 1608) the latter secured a notable concession of the regalian prerogative of money. Meanwhile, and during the reign of Charles, the revolutionary tendency in Holland was checked; but with the accession of Philip the Bigot it burst into fierce flames. The "Confederation of Beggars" was formed in 1566; the revolution was proclaimed in 1572; paper money was issued in 1574; the Jews of Amsterdam organized a sort of Wissel

[1] Of this character were the coinages of Edward VI., of England.

bank in 1607; and the bank of Amsterdam, which, under the authority of the city, imitated and then destroyed the Wissel bank and forbade the Jews from dealing in exchange, was established in 1609. "Free," or properly speaking, "individual" coinage, as it is still called by the Dutch, had long been permitted by the degenerate Moslem governments of India, where Albuquerque found and Mascarenhas copied it (1555). From the Portuguese the evil institute was inherited by the Dutch East Indians, and by them it was brought to Holland. It was among the first measures resorted to by the revolutionary government, who, however, limited their legal-tender coins to silver, which was coined into "guilders," or florins, of $160\frac{1}{2}$ grains fine. The operation of this system was promoted by the exchange transactions of the Jews, and the guarantee which their individual credit afforded to importations and deposits of bullion. It was further stimulated by the extension of Dutch commerce and by the superior credit of the bank of Amsterdam, with whose transactions substantially commenced the present system of individual money.

In this connection it will be interesting to observe that two years after the first edict of Charles V., to wit, in 1526, Henry VIII. of England felt obliged (in consequence of that edict, "forasmuch as coins of . . . . . gold. . . be of late days raised . . . in the emperor's low countries," and because there was an active trade with Flanders) to raise the value of the angel-noble of 80 grains gross, from 6s. 8d. to 7s. 4., and two months later to 7s. 6d., in silver coins. Following is the text of the ordinance:

"Henry the Eighth, by the grace of God, King of England and France, defender of the Faith, lord of

Ireland, to the most reverend Father in God, our most trusty and most entirely beloved councillor the lord Thomas, cardinal of York, archbishop, legat de Leicestre of the See Apostolic, primate of England, and our chancellor of the same, greeting. Forasmuch as coins of money, as well of gold as of silver, be of late days raised and enhanced both in the realm of France, as also in the emperor's Low Countries, and in other parts, unto higher prices than the very poise weight and fineness and valuation of the same, and otherwise, than they were accustomed to be current; by means whereof, the money of this our realm is daily, and of long season hath been, by sundry persons (as well our subjects as strangers, for their particular gain and lucre) conveyed out of this realm into the parts beyond the seas, and so is likely to continue more and more, to the great hindrance of the generality of our subjects and people and to the no little impoverishing of our said realm, if the same be not speedily remedied and foreseen: We, after long debating of the matter with you and sundry other of our council, and after remission made unto outward princes for reformation thereof, finding finally no manner of remedy to be had at their hands, have, by mature deliberation, determined that our coins and moneys (as well of gold as of silver) shall be, by our officer of our mint, from henceforth made of such fineness, lay (alloy), standard, and value, as may be equivalent, correspondent, and agreeable to the rates of the valuations enhanced and raised in outward parts, as is afore specified."

It will be recollected that during the Empire the supreme right of coinage was vested in the Augustus, or Basileus, who, in fact, never permitted the gold, or full legal-tender, coinage to go out of his hands;

and that during the mediæval period (after A. D. 1204) it fell to the various princes and prelates who had inherited the prerogatives of the dead Empire. We shall next see it fall under the control of the Dutch and English merchants.

Under the private coinage law of the republic, the bank of Amsterdam, a private institution, received deposits of any kind of silver coins, giving credit only for the fine metal contained in them, and measuring its value in sols banco of twenty to the Dutch florin. Its payments were made upon the same basis. The bank also received gold coins on deposit, valuing them (in sols banco) at what they actually fetched in the mart of Amsterdam. This custom deprived the gold and silver coins of Holland of such part of their value as they had previously derived from royal seal, proclamation and seigniorage. It swept away alike the sacred effigies of Rome and Byzantium, the heretical inscriptions of Julin and Bardewic, the unjust valuations of Madrid and Sevilla, and the temptation everywhere to tamper with any money destined for use in Holland. Indeed, it destroyed money altogether; it made a market value for the precious metals, a thing hitherto unknown; it practically established unlimited coinage, and thus substituted metal, in place of money, as the measure of value.

These revolutionary acts met with such immediate and marked success that they soon afterwards influenced the legislation of other States. Hitherto the precious metals obtained in America had vainly sought to evade the coinage exactions of the European princes; now the door of escape was open; they had only to be sent to Holland, turned into guilders and ducats, and credited as silver metal under the name of sols banco. But as the Spaniards and Portuguese still controlled the American mines and jealously conveyed their precious products to the mints of the mother country, how were they to be practically diverted to Holland? The Dutch fleets and their allies, the buccaneers of the West Indies, at once answered this question, and the early settlers of New Amsterdam could have told many a tale as to how the plunder was safely transported to Holland. At a later period, when the English took New York, this class of bullion was quietly removed into Massachusetts, and there converted into honest "pine-tree" shillings.

Under the stimulus of "free" coinage, an immense quantity of the precious metals now found their way to Holland, and a local rise of prices ensued, which found one form of expression in the curious mania of buying tulips at prices often exceeding that of the ground on which they were grown. So rapidly did the influence of Dutch "free" coinage extend, that it induced the king of Spain to concede to his American colonies a right which had descended from the pagan gods to the pagan emperors, and from the pagan and Christian emperors to the independent princes who had seized the fragments of the Empire, but which had, never yet been conferred upon a Christian vassal or vassal state.[1] This was the right to coin gold, a right which was conceded to the American viceroys by the royal ordinance of 1608. But we have not yet done with the tulip mania. In 1648, when the Peace of Westphalia acknowledged the independence of the Dutch republic, the latter stopped the "free" coinage of silver

[1] The emperor Charles IV., of Germany, 1347-78, "gave to all the members of the empire the privilege of issuing gold coins with any stamp they choose" (Partington, on the ducat). This was quite superfluous, for in fact most of the members of the empire had usurped this privilege a century previously.

florins and only permitted it for gold ducats, which in Holland had no legal value. This legislation discouraged the imports of silver bullion, checked the rise of prices, and put an end to the tulip mania.[1] However, it had other and far more important results. During the wars which ensued between Holland and England, the latter found so many reasons for admiring the government and administration of its rival, that it commenced to copy them in every detail, in some cases where the advantages of imitation were doubtful, or had passed away. The English deposed their king and established a republic in 1653; they planted colonies in America to rival those of the Dutch; they chartered their East India company on the same lines as the Dutch; they encouraged Morgan and other buccaneers to pillage the Spanish plate-ships and settlements; and they adopted "free" coinage. The English commercial literature of this period—for example, the works of Sir Josiah Child, Andrew Yarranton, and others—is filled with suggestions to follow the policy of the Dutch, whether as to colonies, navigation, banking, interest laws, coinage, warehouses, or land registries; and all of these measures were soon afterwards enacted in England, except the last one, which still hangs fire. Holland had dropped "free" mintage for legal-tender coins in 1648; even France afterwards tried it in 1679, only to drop it in 1689. England, under the influence of its favored classes, adopted it in 1666, and held on to it until, through other means, she had gained the commercial supremacy of the world, and was enabled (chiefly during the last and present centuries) to urge it upon other states. Then she dropped silver.

The monetary system of the Netherlands, which be-

---

[1] This mania had already been discouraged by a resolution of the States-General, dated April 27th, 1637, which threw some difficulties in the way of enforcing time-bargains in tulips.

gan with the Republic, consisted, first, of demonetizing gold—an act in which can be perceived more of resentment against the arbitrary decrees of the Spanish monarch than wisdom in laying the foundations of a state. Second, it consisted of pasteboard dollars, which were issued in 1574, during the siege of Leyden, and of which some half-a-dozen specimens are now in the British Museum collection. These "greenbacks" of the revolution the Hollanders preferred to keep rather than exchange for coins—*ad perpetuam liberationis divinæ memoriam*—in perpetual memory of their divine liberation from tyranny.[1] That they circulated beyond the precincts of Leyden, and effected an important augmentation of the currency and a rise of prices, is attested by the following quotations from Budelius (p. 269): The gold real, 1579, 45 stivers; 1580, 46; 1583, 47½; 1586, 52; and 1590, 53 stivers. The Philips silver thaler, 1579, 43 stivers; 1580, 45; 1583, 47; and 1586, 50 stivers. Here we see a gradual rise in the value of both gold and silver coins. In what? Certainly not in either gold or silver stivers, but in currency, and that currency necessarily of something else. Under the circumstances that something else could only have been wholly or partly of paper.

Thirdly, the Dutch system consisted of silver coins struck by the State, both on its own account, and for the account of individuals ("free" coinage), and there-

[1] Borniti, de Nummis, ed. 1605, i., p. 15. The revolutionary moneys of Leyden were of white pasteboard, round, about 1½ inches in diameter and stamped or embossed to resemble a coin. They took their origin in the first, but were perfected during the second, siege—that of 1574. Their denominations were 24 and 40 stivers. The former bore on one side, "Haec libertatis ergo," on the other "Godt behoede Leyden," or God protect Leyden. The latter had the city arms on one side, and "Pugno propatria" (Davies' "Hist. Holland," London, 1842, ii., pp. 9, 10). Silver pieces of the same stamp as the pasteboard ones were also issued ("Catalogue Schulthess-Rechberg," 7048).

fore without limit as to numbers. These coins—guilders and their multiples, namely, the ducaton, the reichsthaler etc.—were legal-tenders to any amount. There was also "free" or individual coinage of gold; but as coins of this metal were no longer legal-tender in Holland, they were struck for circulation in other States, who, in using them, escaped the seigniorage and other coinage exactions of their sovereigns. Fourthly, subsidiary coins of silver and copper, which the Dutch State struck only for itself. Fifthly, the banking system, already described.

At the period when the decrees of Charles V. so greatly and suddenly raised the value of gold coins, Thomas Gresham, an English mercer and financier, was applied to by the ministers of Edward VI. of England for a loan of money. In the third year of his reign this boy king had arbitrarily raised the value of his silver coins to a ratio of 5.15 for 1 of gold; in his fourth year to 4.82 for 1; and in his fifth year to 2.41 for 1.[1] The profit made by the king in these transactions was, in the first instance, 113½ per cent; in the second, 128 per cent; and in the third, 356 per cent.[2] Gresham was unable to comply with the ministers' request, but said he thought he could raise the money in Antwerp. Accordingly, he was commissioned to proceed thither and effect the loan. He remained in Antwerp until after the death of the king and fall of the ministry, meanwhile advising them, what he had not ventured to set forth in London, namely, that a bad money will drive away good; and that before he could procure the needful loan in Holland, it was necessary for Edward to reform his monetary system. This correspondence has been lauded by Mr. Henry Dunning MacLeod with fulsome praise, and the first portion of

[1] Lord Liverpool, p. 101.   [2] Ibid., pp. 101, 102.

it formulated into what he has called "the Gresham law." That bad money, when made lawful, will drive away good, by causing the latter to be hoarded, is a law or principle of money which will be found in the "Frogs" of Aristophanes and the "Maxims" of Theognis, written some eighteen or twenty centuries before Gresham's time; a principle that every tradesman in the interval had learnt by heart.[1]

For example, in 1341, after the emission of black money by Edward III., a great mass of sterlings and silver plate was collected in London and Boston, for private conveyance to the Continent; in other words, the bad money drove out the good; and everybody knew it.[2] This law applies equally to cabbages. It is not a law of money, but a truism that applies to all things. However, Gresham's remarks, perhaps, had the effect to bring about that permanence of the English monetary system, for which Elizabeth afterwards received so much credit; that princess having merely "completed the plan of reform which Edward had projected (or assented to) and had begun to carry into execution."[3]

Gresham successively served Mary and Elizabeth; and by the latter was honored with knighthood. But did he serve the English people; did he serve the interests of the State? Not at all. He was faithful only to his own class, the money-lenders of London. Not a word appears in his correspondence of the tremendous monetary revolution that was then brewing in Holland; not a word of the imperial edicts that had raised the value of imperial gold from 9 or 10 to $11\frac{3}{8}$, and from

---

[1] "Maxims of Theognis," line 21: "Nor will any one take in exchange worse when better is to be had."
[2] "Middle Ages Revisited," chap. xix.
[3] Lord Liverpool, p. 104.

11¾ to 13¼; not a word of the resistance to these unjust decrees, or of the fact that the regalian prerogative, which jurisconsults and statesmen in all ages had shown to be indispensable to the exercise of independent sovereignty, was in jeopardy of falling into the hands of Dutch monopolists, and might afterwards fall, as it did fall, into the hands of English ones. This was the prerogative of coinage. Gresham was silent on this subject, and his silence on such a subject far outweighs the merits of that "discovery" for which his admirers have claimed him so much credit.[1]

But, indeed, who has properly written the history of Gresham's times; who has dived into this supernal but obscure subject of money, except men of the very same class who profited in pocket by the Dutch Revolution, its institution of private coinage and the subsequent private control of bank issues? Nobody. Is it yet clearly understood that whatever degradation of money was committed by the emperors, whatever debasement was afterwards committed by the kings, these have since been vastly exceeded by the dishonest use made of "individual" coinage and the control of bank issues? Not at all. The Emperors of Rome controlled the emissions of European money for thirteen centuries, and the kings and dukes for nearly four centuries afterwards; whilst the usurers have held it, to the present time, for about two centuries. It is not too much to say that during these two centuries greater monetary changes have been made and more losses have been occasioned to the industrial classes of the European world than were made by all the degradations and de-

---

[1] Gresham remained in Antwerp until 1553. In 1553 Mary, and in 1558 Elizabeth, ascended the throne. In the last-named year Gresham was sent as ambassador to Parma, and in 1559 he was knighted (T. F. Burgon, "Life and times of Sir Thomas Gresham," London, 1839, 2 vols. 8vo; Ward's "Lives of the Gresham Professors," p. 8).

basements of the Imperial and regal periods put together. Monetary systems have been changed from gold to silver, from silver to gold, and from both silver and gold to paper; tens of thousands of worthless banks have been erected, thousands of millions of worthless notes have been issued, and the entire products of industry have been seized and perverted to the enrichment of a class, who know only how to scheme, to undermine and to appropriate the earnings of mankind. The right to issue money needs a radical reform; and the State which reforms it first will secure for its citizens far greater advantages than can be derived from Zollvereins, tariff bills, or any other kind of commercial legislation. "The control of money," says an eloquent writer on the subject, "is the ground upon which an international or cosmopolitan combination 'finances' the world and 'farms' humanity."[1]

Writing in 1776, Adam Smith was at great pains to inform us what a strong institution was the "burghers'" Bank of Amsterdam, how "for every guilder in gold or silver to circulate as bank money, there is a correspondent guilder in gold or silver to be found in the bank. The City is guarantee that it should be so. The bank is under the direction of the four reigning burgomasters, who are changed every year. Each new set of burgomasters visits the treasure, compares it with the books, receives it upon oath and delivers it over with the same awful solemnity to the set which succeeds; and in that sober and religious country oaths are not yet disregarded. A rotation of this kind seems alone a sufficient security against any practices which

[1] Reginald Fenton, Esq., formerly of Kimberly, South Africa, now of San Diego, California. "The distribution of wealth and the exploitation of some men by others are dependent upon money." Count Leo Tolstoi in his Essay on Money in Kitson's "Scientific Solution of the Money Question" *pref.* and p. 168.

cannot be avowed. Amidst all the revolutions which faction has ever occasioned in the government of Amsterdam, the prevailing party has at no time accused their predecessors of infidelity in the administration of the bank. No accusation could have affected more deeply the reputation and fortune of the disgraced party; and if such accusation could have been supported, we may be assured that it would have been brought. In 1672, when the French king was at Utrecht, the Bank of Amsterdam paid so readily, as left no doubt of the fidelity with which it had observed its engagements. Public utility and not revenue was the original object of this institution." Alas, for Dutch burgher patriotism, and the credulity of our great Scotch sophist! When, fourteen years later, that is to say, in 1790, the French again invaded Holland, they found the bank empty and insolvent. Even whilst Adam Smith was penning his panegyrics, it was secretly loaning away bullion which belonged to its depositors and noteholders. Its pious burgomasters were forsworn, the City was dishonored, and the world received its hundredth useless lesson on the folly of trusting to the stability of a monetary system which is not absolutely under the thumb of the State.

Coinage Ratios in the Low Countries (after 1579 in Holland only).

Period, A. D.	Ratio.	Remarks.
30	8	Revolt of the Frisians against fiscal exactions of the Romans. The Roman imperial ratio was always 12 silver . 1 gold; but silver bore a higher value in the Eastern trade of the Baltic, and the Frisians (possibly from choice) paid their tributes in ox-hides ("Tac. Ann.," iv., c. 72). The prevalent ratio of the Baltic was 8 for 1 ("Anc. Brit.," chap. xvii).

Period, A. D.	Ratio.	Remarks.
286	8	Revolt of Carausius the Menapian. The mark of silver coins was in use as early, at least, as this date (vide Agricola, writing about 1550). Its substitution of the Roman libra of account, which now consisted of 5 gold solidi, each of about 90 grains fine, or else 12 times their weight in silver, implies a local ratio of 8 for 1.
Saxon	8	In the pagan coinages of Friesland, Jutland, etc., there were 8 silver siccals säigas[1] or iesterlings, each of about 18¼ grains fine, to the gull siccal, or skillingar, of the same weight: a ratio of 8 for 1.
752	10	Forty silver deniers, each of 17½ grains fine (300 to the livre weight) equal 1 imperial solidus (now) of about 70 grains fine: a ratio of 10 for 1. "Anon. Chron. Aquitaine," written in 843 and alluding to the period previous to Pepin's monetary reform of A. D. 754-68. Same authority, for same period, gives 25, instead of the ancient 20, quarter-solidi to the livre of account; leading to an inference that the Basileus struck light gold shillings to compensate for the heretical ratios of the North.
753	11	De Vienne, "Livre d'Argent," p. 23.
754	12	Pepin struck 264 deniers from the Roman pound weight and valued them at 40 to the solidus (now) of 66⅔ grains fine: a ratio of 12. The gold shillings were valued at 22 to the livre of account, of which the mint master took one for himself, a proof that they were still light (De Vienne, pp. 20, 21).
779	12	Decretale precum. Charlemagne, in this decree, re-established the value of the gold shilling at 20 to the libra; he afterwards attempted to raise the value of these pieces by valuing them at 16 to the libra; but judging from the equivalents given in the Saxon and Frisian Codes, which he altered at this period, the attempt failed (De Vienne, p. 42).

[1] According to the German law, vi., 3, "the säiga (or säica) is the fourth part of the tremissis; it is one denarius, and two säigas are two denarii. A tremissis is the third part of a solidus and equals four denarii." The manuscript which gives this valuation is of rather a low date. The Bavarian law of a much earlier period accords to the säica the value of three denarii: "Si una säica, id est tres denarios furaverit .... Si duas id est sex denarios" (Tit. ix., Art. 3, 4). There can be little doubt that, still more anciently, the säica was the sicca of the Orient which found its way through Tartary to the Baltic and there became degraded.

Period, A. D.	Ratio.	Remarks.
813	12	Last year of Charlemagne. Petition of Council of Rheims against light solidi, which would not pass for 40 deniers (De Vienne, p. 36). Imaginary scheme of international money (Ibid.)
814	12	Unique solidus of Louis Debonnaire of suspiciously fine execution, in Paris collection. Were this genuine it would be the last gold coin struck by any Christian prince, except the Basileus, until A. D. 1225.
864	10	Charles the Bald: Edict of Pistes.
922	8	Inferential valuations of the besant in the ducal silver coins of Holland, Flanders, Brabant, etc.
1090	—	Poid de marc, a weight derived from marks (coins) introduced into France under Philip I. Down to this time it was only used in the Netherlands and England. Du Cange; Saigey; De Vienne, 58.
12th Cent	8	Hanseatic money. The ratio under the pagan Hansa was probably 8 for 1; under the Christian Hansa, at first, probably 10 for 1 ("Anc. Britain").
1204	—	Fall of Constantinople: end of the pontifico-imperial monopoly of coining gold for the Roman world.
1220	8	Jutland Code of 13th century.
13th Cent.	10	Numerous changes of the ducal mint-laws during this and the two following centuries, the prevailing ratios being 8 to 10 silver for 1 gold. In 1284 the earl of Holland and Zealand purchased silver in England (Anderson's "Hist. of Commerce," sub. anno).
	10	From valuation of the gold noble of Edward III. of England, in the ports of Flanders ("Middle Ages Revisited").
	9	Burgundian period of Flanders, 1384 to 1477. The prevailing ratio was, however, 10 silver for 1 gold.
1477	9@10	Earlier coinages under the German imperial house of Hapsburg. The ratio in England (4 Edward IV.), year 1464, was 10½ for 1.
1489	12	Later Hapsburg coinages. Edict of Breda by Maximillian, Dec. 14th. Abortive attempt to re-establish the Cæsarian ratio.
1511	9@10	Gold nobles (half-marks) and silver groots of Flanders, Lorrain, Bar, etc., ratio 10; ducaton, ratio 9 for 1.
1519	9@10	Charles V.: earlier coinages.
1524	11⅜	Charles V. Edict of Esslingen, June 19th, raising the value of his gold coins.

Period, A.D.	Ratio.	Remarks.
1529	11⅜	Charles V. The Holland mark-weight of 3797.2 English grains was this year officially compared with the Paris mark of 3777.5 English grains; and the former found to be 19.7 grains heavier (Boissard, p. 259). If the mark-weight developed from the mark of coins ("Anc. Brit.," ch. xvii), the superior weight of the Holland over the Saxony mark-weight probably arose when Pepin compelled 12 instead of 11 esterlings to be paid for a gull skillingar. The Amsterdam mark-weight was 3798 English grains.
1542	10	Edict of Esslingen by Charles V. Degraded Carolus dollars 354½ grains gross, or 302½ grains fine silver, valued at 20 stivers or one gulden of about 30 grains fine gold.
1546	13⅓	Edict of Charles V., again raising the value of his gold coins.
1552	13⅓	Thomas Gresham at Antwerp (Spanish government begins, 1555).
1556	13⅓	Abdication of Charles V.
1566	13⅓	Confederation of Dutch leaders against Spanish government.
1572	—	Revolution. Mercantile system of individual or "free" coinage. Gold demonetized.
1574	—	Pasteboard revolutionary money of Leyden.
1579	—	Union of Utrecht: separation of Belgium.
1581	—	The right of coinage, previously conferred by imperial authority upon the counts of Holland, transferred to the Spanish crown by Philip II., king of Spain and hereditary count of Holland; an act that further incensed the Hollanders.
1589	—	"Market" or conflict ratio of 11 3-5 (Desrotours).
1598	—	Philip III, of Spain, cedes the Netherlands to Albert of Austria and the Infanta Isabella.
1607	—	Wissel Bank of Amsterdam.
1609	—	After the Edict of Esslingen the coins were greatly clipped, and both the Wissel Bank and the Bank of Amsterdam, which this year superseded it, were established, among other objects, to remedy this evil.
1609 to 1624	—	Rise of the Buccaneers; numerous captures of plate; and opening of Dutch oriental trade by sea. Immense sums of gold and silver obtained from Japan.
1628	—	Spanish plate-galleons captured near Matanzas with several million livres in gold and silver (Van Loon).

Period, A. D.	Ratio.	Remarks.
1640	14.45	"Market" or conflict ratio 12½ for 1 (Desrotours, 1785; Gaudin, 1803).
1648	14.45	Independence of Holland recognized by Spain. Individual coinage limited to gold, which, however, at the mint ratio of 14.45, is undervalued as compared with foreign mints. (The Spanish mint ratio of 1650 was 15 for 1.)
1672	14.45	Most of the gold ducats of the German states now struck in Holland for individual account.
1717	14.45	Newton's report gives the ducat or 5-florin gold piece, stamped "Legem Imperii," at 52.39 grains fine, and the silver florin at 148.9 grains fine; a ratio of 14.31 (Kelly, ii., p. 153, hints at Inexact Assays: this might account for the discrepancy). Newton also says the ducats were current in Holland for 5¼ guilders. This is evidently correct, and indicates a "mint-conflict" ratio, or so-called "market" ratio of 14.92. The imports of gold noticed by him were due in some measure to the large foreign coinage of ducats in Holland.
1734	14.45	Desrotours says 14.45; Dutot says 15.67, which last is incorrect.
1785	14.45	Desrotours.
1791	14.45	Hamilton's Report of this year says 14.90; evidently the "conflict," not the "coinage," ratio. Gold coins being now greatly undervalued, as compared with foreign mints, they cease to circulate in Holland.
1806	15.20	Law of December 15th. "Double standard" under Louis, king of Holland. Gold 400-stiver piece 193.4 grains fine. Silver 50-stiver should contain 403 2-3 grains fine; actual contents (Kelly) 367.9 grains fine: ratio 15.2 for 1.
1816	15.87	Union with Belgium. Mint Act, September 28th, 1816. The "William" of 10 florins was to contain 93.465 grains fine gold; the florin 148.39 grains fine silver: legal ratio 15.8765. The assays of Eckfeldt and Du Bois gave but 46.52 grains fine to the ducat, and 148.74 grains fine to the florin: actual coinage ratio 15.98. Gold coinage for individuals stopped. Silver coinage for individuals (one and three-florin pieces) again permitted. Chevalier, p. 155, says that there was no gold in circulation until 1839. Foundations of New (present) Bank of the Netherlands, 1814.

Period, A. D.	Ratio.	Remarks.
1830	15.87	Separation of Belgium.
1839	15.60	Gold coins again circulate in Holland (Chevalier; Vrolik).
1847	15.60	Russian gold "scare." Mint Act, September 26th, 1848. Gold demonetized. The silver florin lowered to 145.85 grains fine (Schmidt's "Tate's Cambist;" Del Mar's "Money and Civilization," p. 17).
1850	15 60	Gold coins melted and sold at a loss of ten million florins (Vrolik).
1857	15.60	Gold coins again cease to circulate in Holland (Chevalier, pp. 78, 149).
1873	15.60	Nevada silver "scare." In accordance with an Act of the previous year the individual coinage of silver was this year suspended.
1875	15⅝	Mint Act. June 6th. Ten-florin gold coins to contain 94.334 grains fine, and open to individual coinage. Mint still closed to individual coinage of silver. Old silver coins not demonetized ("Etalon boiteux," Greven).
1877	15⅝	Same provisions extended to Colonial coinage (Greven).
1884	15⅝	A portion of the circulating silver authorized to be melted and sold, in order to buy gold for bank payments.
1893	15⅝	The money of Holland now consists chiefly of paper notes, about £16,000,000, secured by a "reserve" in gold and supplemented by a subsidiary silver circulation. Population about 4½ millions, exclusive of Colonies. The home circulation fluctuates between £3 and £4 per capita, coins and paper combined.

From this table it will be observed that the ratio in the Netherlands, from the earliest times nearly to the reign of Pepin, was 8 for 1; in the early part of the Carlovingian era, about 12 for 1; between that period and the fall of Constantinople, from 8 to 10 for 1; during the ducal period about 10 for 1; and that it was fixed by Charles V. at 13¼, whereupon gold was demonetized through the influence of the East Indian traders and the burghers. Since that time the ratio in Holland has followed that of Spain and France.[1]

[1] The ratios in Holland which appear in Dr. Adolf Soetbeer's works are purely hypothetical, and were probably not intended to be regarded as the results of any examination of the coinage laws or coinages of that country.

In Holland the history of the ratio is almost the whole history of money. It was the ratio that distinguished its earlier monetary systems from that of Rome; it was the ratio that, until the Carlovingian era, marked it a pagan State, allied, by commerce, with the pagan cities of the Baltic and the great pagan Hansa, whose fleets transacted the maritime commerce of all northern and western Europe; it was the ratio that proclaimed the monetary systems of its ducal masters a cross between that of a struggling nationality and Imperial Rome; it was the ratio that fanned into a flame the embers of that resistance to Imperial authority which had been crushed under foot, but had never wholly lost their fire; it was the ratio by means of which the traders and money-lenders first asserted their undue importance in the State; and it was the ratio, snatched by their strong hands from the prerogatives of the Crown, that has enabled them to rule the State and make Holland "a nation of usurers." When they wrested from the Empire what is virtually the prerogative of coinage, they demonetized gold and declared silver coins alone fit for the high function of legal-tender; when the monarchy of 1816 was erected, they submitted to a system of gold and silver coins; but no sooner did the lapse of time strengthen their hands, and the great yield of the Russian gold mines afford them a pretext, than they agitated and brought about that reliance upon a single metal (at a time) which constitutes the fulcrum of the mercantile system. Here the real character of the burgher class discloses itself. Their patriotism was not for Holland, but for the burghers. Dr. Vrolik has in vain endeavored to defend them from this imputation, by alleging that the "silver standard" was not adopted after the discovery of gold in California, but before it.[1] But he has adroitly omitted to mention that it occurred upon the heels of the great discoveries of gold in the Ural, and that it is distinctly traceable to that event. Leon Faucher very correctly attributed to this unpatriotic class an "insurrection of fear." It was fear for their beloved securities that superinduced this measure, which cost the State ten millions of florins and the Dutch people ten thousand millions; and it was the same craven fear that in 1873 induced this class to clamor for that "gold standard" which now sustains their investments, but which lowers their claims of patriotism to the sordid level of their breeches pockets.

The existing Bank of the Netherlands was established at Amsterdam in 1814, nearly on the plan of the Bank of England. Its original capital, of which the king was always to hold one-tenth, was five million florins. This capital was doubled in 1819, and has since increased to twenty million florins. The bank has the right to strike coins for the State, to issue circulating notes, discount bills, lend money, and deal in bullion and foreign coins. It was this institution which, in opposition to Lord Liverpool, furnished the reasons for monetizing gold, and for establishing the "double standard" in 1816; which showed in 1847 (the Russian gold mines were then very productive) that gold was unfit for legal-tender money; which in 1873 (zenith of the Comstock Lode) proved, with equal facility, that silver was useless, and gold the only proper metal for money; and which doubtless stands ready, whenever the relative production of silver shall decline, to furnish equally pliant arguments against more plentiful gold and in favor of scarce silver. In a paper read by Pro-

[1] Speech of Dr. Vrolik in "Rep. Inter. Monetary Conference, 1881."

fessor H. B. Greven, of Leyden, before the British Association at Manchester, September 7th, 1887, it is stated that in 1881-82 the Bank's stock of gold fell to £600,000, and that, to provide against a recurrence of such a calamity, an Act was passed in April, 1884, which empowered it "to sell at market prices a quantity of twenty-five millions silver florins, when the state of the currency required it." According to this authority, the regulation of the currency of Holland lies between the Bank and the bullion-brokers. It is a healthy national constitution that can survive such a combination.

CHAPTER XIV.

GERMANY.

Until A. D. 1204 the right to coin gold in Germany was a pontifico-imperial prerogative—It then practically became a regalian right, which in great measure was absorbed by the two principal German states—Legalized as a regalian right by the Golden Bull—Exercised as such by numerous princes and by the burghers, until 1871, when it was acquired for North Germany by the New Empire—Thereupon it was almost immediately abandoned to the burghers—Monetary systems of Germany during the regal period—French forgers of the sixteenth century—Earliest monetary conventions—Sudden enhancement of gold by Charles V.—The German states and burghers demonetize gold—Silver becomes the sole material of legal-tender money—Monetary systems of North Germany—Conventions of sixteenth, seventeenth, and eighteenth centuries—The ratio—The banks—Paper money—Plunder of Napoleon—His downfall—Confederation of the Rhine—New system—Weights—Origin of the ducat, skilling, and thaler—Constitution, convention, and currency thalers—Later monetary conventions—Quantity of money circulating in Germany—History of the ratio—Burgher or "free" coinage—The California scare—Treaty of 1857 tabooing gold coins—The Nevada scare—Legislation of 1871-73, demonetizing silver coins—French War Indemnity—Great increase of paper money—Efflux of gold in 1873-74—Operation of the new mint laws—Gold and silver production of Germany—Dr. Soetbeer, the evil genius of German monetary policy—The future.

THE history of money and monetary systems in Germany springs from the monetary laws of the Roman Empire, a subject which has been treated at length elsewhere. Briefly, the right to strike gold coins was vested exclusively in the Sovereign-pontiff, who usually resided, and exercised this function, in Rome or Byzantium. Such coins were unlimited legal-tender in all parts of the Empire. The principal gold coin was the solidus, or besant, of 72 down to 60 grains fine.[1]

[1] The solidus descended from the aureus of 131¼ grains, and in the thirteenth century was lost in the ducat of 56 grains. This again was in the sixteenth century degraded to the gulden of 37 -1-6 grains. There it expired, and became a silver coin. The weights of the solidus given in the text are those which prevailed during the Roman Imperial monetary system.

Five of these made the libra of account.[1] The striking of silver coins was shared between the Emperors and the subject princes, prelates and municipalities of the empire. The Imperial silver coins were legal-tender in the "Imperial," not in the "Senatorial" provinces; the other silver coins had only a local course. The striking of bronze coins was reserved to the Senate. The Imperial tributes were collected in gold coins, or else in silver coins containing exactly twelve times as much fine metal as the gold ones. Hence, for a solidus of gold, was demanded a talent of silver.

Substantially, this system continued unchanged until after the fall of Constantinople, in 1204, when all the princes of Europe commenced to strike gold coins for themselves; and the Roman Imperial system fell, to rise no more. With the exception of a certain unique and very doubtful gold piece attributed to Louis de Debonnaire, no Christian prince of Germany ever struck a gold coin until Frederick II., in 1225, issued his magnificent augustals. Instead of making their weight conform to the besant of his day, Frederick put in these coins nearly 82 grains fine gold, the weight of a double maravedi or dobla of the Saracens:—a fact, which, when added to other circumstances, sufficed in brief time to consign them to the melting-pot. Although the right to strike gold coins was not legally acquired by the German princes until it was conferred, together with the working of mines, by the Golden Bull of Charles IV., December 25th, 1356, yet practically these princes were governed by the example of Frederick, and as a matter of fact many of them had issued gold coins before the date of the imperial ordinance.[2] This

---

[1] Theodsian Code, lib. xiii., tit. ii., 11; "Ita ut pro singulis libris argenti quinos solidos inferat." Argenti here means money, not silver.

[2] Edward III. of England was authorized to coin gold in 1337, but Henry III. in 1257 had coined gold without authority ("Middle Ages Revisited," ch. xxx.) See other English gold coins on a previous page of the present work.

closes the first period of German monetary systems. The palsied hand of Rome had reluctantly dropped the prerogative of gold, and a host of independent cities and princes had purchased or picked it up. We shall presently see what they did with it.

From the fall of Constantinople to the discovery of America is a period of great confusion in the monetary history of Germany. Although the Roman empire had lost its control of money, it had still enough vitality to split Germany into two great parties, whose perpetual antagonism and undying hatred served to keep the country always embroiled in civil wars. The ensuing political chaos is faithfully reflected in the coinages. They exhibit every kind of corruption, deceit, degradation, debasement and even forgery. To crown all, the ratio of gold to silver, which the Roman and Byzantine monarchs, throughout all their vicissitudes, had kept constant for nearly thirteen centuries, was now changed almost every day, by some one or other of the numerous princes who divided, distracted and misruled the splendid empire of Charlemagne. Whether their motives were governed by the interests of their principalities or by the desire of private gain, is hardly worth discussing. Their monetary experiments were too trivial to furnish the basis of monetary principles, and they yield scarcely more than a single lesson of any value to posterity. It is this: that the right of coinage, which during this period fell from the Basileus into the hands of kings, princes, prelates and burghers, was abused by the latter, not because they were rulers, but because they were petty ones, so petty that their private interests were scarcely less important than those of the State, and, indeed, cannot always be distinguished from them. In other words, it was not the

States, but the petty rulers of the Renaissant period who tampered with money.

These corruptions of money, the pet theme of politico-economical pedantry, were in many cases a necessity of the times. It was the period of the First Renaissance. Europe, enthralled for thirteen centuries by the pontiffs of Rome, had recently thrown off its shackles and begun its march of progress. On Midsummer Day in 1237, the emperor Frederick assembled at Vaucouvers the first secular council of nations ever held in Europe; in 1241 he wrote to Henry III. that the affairs of the world were no longer to be monopolized by the priesthood; whilst the magnificent eagles which he stamped upon the imperial coins in place of the agonized saints of a previous period, were no less significant than his resolute defiance of pontifical tyranny. With the inauguration of this progressive era commenced a great increase of industry, of wealth and of population. Mines of gold and silver can neither be discovered nor rendered productive at pleasure. They are not amenable to man's control, but are the subjects of adventitious discovery and fortunate development. Hence in progressive eras supplies of the precious metals fail to keep pace with the demands of society. During the Renaissance felted paper was a novelty and printing was unknown. How was a measure of value to be supplied sufficiently ample to sustain prices? The people answered this question by clipping the coins, and the princes of Germany tacitly supported the action of the people by degrading and debasing their subsequent issues. It is scarcely to be expected that these multiplications of money should have kept even pace with the demand for its use. The clippings probably failed to supply the additional requirement for money; the legal degradations and debasements probably exceeded it. Because princes sometimes took advantage of the public necessity for increased money to make some profit for the State by debasing it, is no just warrant for condemning either their honesty or wisdom, especially at this late day, when the circumstances of the times are unknown or forgotten. They probably did the best they could do under the circumstances. As the stock of gold and silver relatively diminished, these metals increased in value. Rents and other fixed payments running through long terms became unjustly and oppressively augmented. To have refrained from debasing the coins would have been to increase the burdens of the people until they found relief in revolt and the overthrow of the State.

Debasement of the coinage during the period of the Renaissance, was in fact commonly inaugurated not by the prince, but the people. It was done by clipping, sweating, or otherwise diminishing the quantity of fine metal in the coins; so that, when under a subsequent edict of debasement and re-coinage they came to the mints, the princes really gained little or nothing by the transaction, and merely gave the force of law to what was already an accomplished fact.

In vain were the most terrible penalties enacted against those who tampered with money—as torture, hanging, drawing and quartering. These penalties were boldly risked every day by people who had never committed any other offense, and would probably never have committed this one but for the pressure of that law of legal-tender from which the mines of this period afforded an insufficient relief.

I repeat, that the monetary experiments of the Renaissant period, whether in Germany or any other of the

Western Christian states, are of little use as guides to modern legislation. A portion of them were not the experiments of States, but the financial shifts of individuals; another portion were dictated by the hampered and stationary condition of mining as compared with a growing population and commerce; while still another portion (changes in the ratio) were due to the loss of that central control which the Roman imperial government, at Constantinople, had exercised over the coinage and the silver valuation of gold. Hence it is that among the few writers on money who have condescended to consult history on this subject, and who have a case to make against this or that kind of money, they invariably select this period of chaos for the foundation of their special pleadings. Leave out of view the Roman control of money and its loss with the fall of Constantinople, ignore the influence of the Moslem and Gothic monetary systems, avoid all mention of the usurpation of the coining prerogative by the trading companies, adventurers and monopolists of the sixteenth and seventeenth centuries, and you can prove anything you like about money,—you can even prove that money is not money at all, but merely bits of metal whose value is governed by the present economic cost of their production in the mines!

Although the right of coinage continued to be exercised by numerous rulers in Germany, down to the period (1817) when it fell to the new empire, yet it was practically absorbed for several centuries by the Austrian and Prussian monarchies, whose extensive territories, numerous population, diversified industries, or great military resources, enabled their coinages to substantially fill the channels of circulation.[1] The strangest

[1] For history of money in Austria, see "Money and Civilization," ch. xviii.

circumstance is that the new empire had no sooner acquired this most important of all imperial or regalian rights, than, under the advice of Dr. Soetbeer and his Metallic School, it was immediately abandoned to the burghers. Fortunately, it is within the power of the imperial government to resume this prerogative whenever it chooses. This is a subject to which we shall revert further on.

On June 8th, 1386, that is to say, shortly after the ordinance of Charles IV., the four electors of the Rhine entered into a coinage union which had for its object the uniformity of the coins and their preservation from abuse. This was distinctly a national act, the happy precursor of that Bund which five centuries later drew all the North German states from under the moldy and rotten canopy of Rome to that of a common Fatherland. In the sixteenth century the importance of the new supplies of gold and silver from America led to a rise of prices, which, beginning in Spain, soon spread to France and the commercial cities of Europe, but not yet to Germany. In that country the comparative scarcity of money was to some extent supplied by the spurious mintages of an organized band of forgers, who resided in France. The marquis of Tavannes, a representative noble, rendered his class odious and his name ridiculous by recommending the coinage of iron commodity money in place of gold and silver coins, with the selfish view to arrest the rise of prices. He assures us that many French nobles of this period retained professed forgers in their castles, dignified them with the title of "philosophers," and fraternized with them by admitting them to their tables. Because they refrained, or professed to refrain, from counterfeiting French coins and confined their operations to German ducats, thalers and florins, they complacently deemed themselves free from all reproach. The example set by the barons was followed by the monarch. Charles IX. (1560-74) was himself an expert forger of coins, and devoted much of his leisure time to this elevating pursuit. The practice reached its climax in the reign of his successor, Henry III., when, owing perhaps to the precautions taken in Germany, the art of baronial forgery fell into inferior hands and suffered a rapid decline. Salcede, who was executed for treason in 1582, had purchased a large estate from the profits of forging German coins.[1]

In the same century a Correspondenz was formed between several of the German states, providing mainly for uniform coinages and a general circulation. The texts of several monetary ordinances of this period are given by Budelius.

This century witnessed an extraordinary event in Germany. During the regal period—from the thirteenth to the sixteenth century—the common ratio of silver to gold in the coinages of Germany was about 10 for 1. By an imperial edict dated at Esslingen, November 10th, 1524, Charles V. ordered the mark of gold to be coined into 89 gold guilders, $\frac{11}{12}$ fine, and the mark of silver into 8 talents, or thalers, $\frac{15}{16}$ fine. As this talent and guilder had the same value, this was a ratio of 11.38 for 1. In 1546 the emperor, who,

[1] Tavannes, pp 132-33; Brantome, iv., cap. Fran., p. 29, in Wraxall's "Hist. France," ed. 1795, ii., p. 334; Busbeg, Letter viii., in Wraxall, ii., p. 438.

[1] The legislators who met at Nuremburg in 1437 even went so far as to hint at private mintage as a remedy for the corruption of coins, a suggestion that was actually realized some two centuries later. Such a device, as it afterwards proved, was indeed a remedy for corrupt coins, but not for an unstable and fluctuating measure of value; a proof, if any were needed, that coins separately and coins collectively, or a monetary system (like separate individuals and the body politic) conform to very different natural laws.

although he struck no gold coins in Spain, monopolized the coinage of gold in Holland, Germany, Italy and America, suddenly raised by proclamation the value of his gold coins to $13\frac{1}{3}$ times their weight in silver of the same standard. These arbitrary acts lie at the base of the Dutch revolt, and had much to do with the subsequent history of Germany. That vast country was not yet sufficiently united for revolt, but it expressed its reprobation of this measure by boycotting gold. One after another the German rulers forbade or discouraged the tendering of gold coins in payment of debts. From this time forward the gulden was commonly paid in silver coins; the ample ducaton, or talent, of silver, supplanting the unpopular and discredited ducat of gold.

The arrest of commercial development, which followed these conflicting acts, was one of several causes which led to the disturbed state of Germany during the seventeenth century. Religion has commonly been assigned as the pretext both for the revolt of the Netherlands and the Thirty Years' War. Upon a closer inspection of the circumstances which gave birth to these great events, the decrees of Charles V., the demonetization of gold, the fall of prices, and the industrial depression that followed, will all be found lurking behind.

But the fierce passions evoked by these wars, and the horrible scenes which characterized the last one, swept away all recollection of the causes that led to them.[1] Though many valuable treaties on money had been written in the interval—notably those republished by Budelius—which ought to have directed public attention to the subject, they were consigned to obscurity. The Peace of Westphalia should have been accompanied

[1] Bayard Taylor's "Hist. Germany," pp. 409-10.

by the rehabilitation of gold; but no statesman of the period appears to have perceived the plain truth, that Germany could not share the commercial prosperity of the maritime states of Europe so long as she excluded from her legal-tender circulation one-half of the world's accumulations of the precious metals.

The German monetary systems of this era were almost universally based upon silver coins. In Prussia, for example, the circulation (not to mention base silver coins and coppers) was filled chiefly by the currency-thaler, legally of $257\frac{3}{4}$ English grains fine silver, actually 252.6 grains fine, and the gold ducat, of legally 53.14, actually 52.6 grains fine, each ducat being nominally valued at $2\frac{3}{4}$ currency-thalers. This was a nominal ratio of $13\frac{1}{4}$, and a coinage one of $13\frac{1}{6}$ for 1; thus—$2\frac{3}{4} \times 257.75 = 708.8125 \div 53.14 = 13\frac{1}{3}$; or, $2\frac{3}{4} \times 252.6 = 694.25 \div 52.6 = 13\frac{1}{5}$. But gold coins were not legal-tender; people accepted or refused them at pleasure, and virtually their coinage was relinquished to individuals who deposited their bullion in the mints of Holland or England, where it was coined into ducats or nobles that had no permanent legal value in Germany. In short, the Prussian system of money stood essentially in the same attitude that it did when Germany refused the gold coins of Charles V.

Beyond the so-called empire, the effects of the ill-timed ordinance of 1546, though of an entirely different character, were fully as eventful. That command of the ratio which Rome had so long maintained by the force of pontifical law, Spain had acquired through her practical monopoly of the supplies of the coinage-metals from America. The edict of Charles V. flung this advantage away. It taught the kings of Spain (for Charles was king of Spain as well as emperor of Germany) a new device whereby to replenish their treasuries. In 1641 they raised the value of their gold coins to 14 times that of silver; in 1650, to 15; and in 1690 to 16 times. Here this strained device broke down and Spain lost the hegemony of the ratio. The abandonment of the coinage of both the precious metals in Holland and England to individuals, and the virtual demonetization of gold in Germany, had erected, for the first time in the history of the European world, a conflict price, or international mint ratio of value, between the precious metals, which at the last-named period stood at about $14\frac{1}{2}$ for 1. Measured by the conflict-ratio, that in Spain was too high; in Prussia too low. In deference to the new arbiter of mint ratios, the crown of Spain hastened, in 1760, to lower the value of its gold to $14\frac{1}{4}$, and in 1775 to raise it to $15\frac{1}{4}$. The imperturbable Prussians simply varied the premium on gold ducats. (Kelly.)

Returning from this digression to an account of German monetary conventions; in 1667 was effected the coinage agreement (Recess) of Zinna, to which the Electors of Saxony and Brandenburg and the house of Brunswick-Luneburg were substantially parties. Passing over some minor ordinances of 1669 and 1680, in 1690 a coinage union, based on the Lubeck system, and establishing a common coinage rate, was effected at Leipsig between the same parties. This rate was made common throughout the now shadowy empire by the decree of September 10th, 1738. (Kelly). On September 21st, 1753, a coinage treaty was effected between Austria and the electorate of Bavaria, to which in the following year several other German States acceded. The table on page 358 shows that under this treaty was struck a convention-thaler of $353\frac{3}{4}$ grains fine silver. In 1763 an imperial decree—which, however, excepted Prussia, Hanover, Liege, Swedish Pomerania, Hamburg, Lubeck and Holstein; that is to say, the kernel of the future North German Bund—established a convention coinage rate of 20 florins, or 13½ riks thalers currency, or 10 riks thalers effective, to the mark of fine silver. This gives 180.4 grains fine silver to the florin, 270.6 grains fine silver to the riks thaler currency, and 360.8 grains fine silver to the riks thaler effective. The table on page 358 shows that the Austrian "effectives" struck under this convention actually contained but 353.7 grains, and that Saltzburg alone struck them of full weight. On February 22nd, 1765, and January 19th, 1766, coinage unions were effected at Frankfort and Worms between the Electors of Mainz and Treves, the palatinate Landgrave of Hesse-Darmstadt and the free city of Frankfort; and in 1772 these conventions were modified.

Meanwhile the fluctuations of gold and the unsatisfactory condition of all monetary institutes, occasioned by the arbitrary mint laws of Spain and the surrender of the coinage in Holland and England to individuals (called "free coinage"), promoted the foundation of the banks of Berlin and Breslau in 1765, and suggested the Prussian royal ordinance of 1766. This ordinance extended to the banks and their branches throughout the king's dominions. Following an ancient Roman precedent, the king authorized and ordered their accounts to be kept in "pounds," or "thalers banco," each divided into 24 banco groschen, and these into 12 banco pfennigs; hence there were 288 pfennigs to the "pound." Although Prussia did not see fit to join with Austria in the Convention of 1753, she nevertheless coined a silver thaler, not indeed of precisely the weight provided by that Convention, but very close to it, and fully or more than equal in weight to the Convention thalers of the other German states. This was the so-called Prussian Convention thaler of (actually) 359 grains fine. It was also the "pound" or "banco thaler" of Frederick the Great. We shall revert to its historical origin later on. The currency thaler of 252.6 grains fine was $29\frac{5}{8}$ per cent lighter than the banco thaler. These the banks gave credit for at the rate of $31\frac{1}{4}$ per cent worse than banco, and thus made a profit of $1\frac{5}{8}$ per cent on all deposits of silver "currency." (Kelly.) The gold ducats, of (nominally) $2\frac{3}{4}$ currency thalers each, fluctuated, in silver money price, with the conflict-ratio. During the third quarter of the eighteenth century the ducats and "Fredericks," or pistoles, the latter (nominally) of 5 currency thalers each, were taken by the Prussian banks at a price in silver which closely agreed with the Dutch mint ratio of $14\frac{1}{2}$; whereas towards the close of the century, and for a long time afterwards, it was distinctly influenced by the combined Spanish and French ratios of $15\frac{1}{2}$. (Kelly.) The banks of Prussia were authorized by the decree of 1766 to issue notes of 10, 20, 50, 500 and 1000 "pounds" each, but these were not legal-tenders until a later period.

The political storm which ravaged Europe towards the beginning of the present century was not without its effects on the monetary history of North Germany. The Confederation of the Rhine was established in 1806, and expired in 1813; the paper notes of Prussia were nationalized in 1806 and are in circulation to-day. By a decree published in 1807 they were to be taken for coined money, at a rate of exchange to be officially promulgated from time to time. Between

December 1st, 1807, and February 28th, 1809, the premium on silver money fluctuated between 7 and 27 per cent; in June, 1809, the notes stood at 36 per cent of their nominal value; June, 1810, at 84½ per cent; January, 1812, 13½: December, 1812, when, of eight million thalers issued, there were believed to be only three quarters of a million in circulation,[1] the notes stood at only 44½ per cent; June, 1813, 26½ per cent; July, 1813, 24½ per cent; December, 1813, 49½ per cent; January, 1815, 88 per cent; January 5th, 1816, 99 per cent; afterwards at par.[2] The Saxony treasury notes never fell below 98, and the government retired them in 1804 at an agio, which began at 9 pfennigs and ended at 1 pfennig, per thaler.[3] But Prussia was in the center of the hurricane, and was obliged to increase her emissions of paper, and to enforce its circulation. In January, 1815, refusal to accept the notes at par, except in certain cases, was made punishable by a fine of 500 to 1000 thalers, or by six to twelve months' imprisonment. In April, 1815, it was ordered that the moiety of all taxes should be paid in paper money, or that, if not, 8½ per cent should be added as a penalty. In 1827 this penalty was reduced to one silver groschen; and although long fallen into desuetude, it was not abolished until 1870. In 1830, 1841 and 1848 the banks sustained runs for the redemption of the paper money. In the run of 1848 the demand did not exceed 40,000 thalers per day, nor altogether 100,000 thalers.[4] Previous to this (1846) the amount annually presented for redemption did not exceed four-fifths of 1 per cent.[5]

In the early part of the century the stock of the precious metals in Germany was greatly reduced by the depre-

[1] Decree of January 19th, 1813, sec 9. [2] Roscher, i., p. 454; ii., p. 14. [3] Ibid., i., p. 448; ii., p. 5. [4] Bergius, "Tubinger Zeitschrift," 1870, p. 226. [5] Rau, 'Archiv,' v., pp. 125, 207.

dations of Napoleon, who sent the spoil to France, and thus conferred upon its mints that hegemony of the ratio (the Spanish 15½) which it held for nearly a century, but to which it was entitled neither by prescription, nor through its mines, nor its commercial advantages.[1]

With the downfall of Napoleon, Germany resumed her wonted calm and industrial progression.

On June 8th, 1815, the Confederation of the Rhine was supplanted by the Germanic Confederation, which for a time united not only North Germany, but also Austria, Bavaria and Wurtemburg.

The monetary system of North Germany at this period is described by Dr. Kelly. It was based on the currency thaler, which he gives at 257.78 grains fine silver. The gold ducat of 53.14 grains fine, was valued nominally at 2¾ currency thalers—a nominal ratio of 13⅓ for 1. The gold Frederick, or pistole, of 93.45 grains fine, was nominally valued at 5 currency thalers —a nominal ratio of 13.8 for 1. The first is the old Charles V. ratio; the second a modification of it. But neither of these ratios was effective, for gold coins were not legal-tender and the ducat commanded a premium of 20 per cent and the pistole 15 per cent; making the effective ratio about 16 for 1, the same as in Spain. However, during the first quarter of the century the premium on gold fluctuated within limits that varied the effective ratio between the Spanish mint ratios of 15½ and 16; a proof, if one were needed, that the hegemony of the ratio was not in Germany.[2]

The system of weights for the precious metals in Cologne during the sixteenth century is thus given by Budelius:—32 ieschen or eisen, or moments=1 esterling, engel, or pennyweight; 19 engels=1 ounce; 8

[1] This subject is treated in "Money and Civilization."
[2] Kelly, i., p. 34.

ounces=1 mark. The ies contained 0.74177625, say ¾ of 1 English grain; the esterling, 23.737 grains; the ounce, 451; and the mark, 3608 grains.[1] The Cologne weights of the eighteenth century are thus given by Dr. Kelly:—17 ieschen, or eschen=1 pfennig 4 pfennigs=1 quintlin; 4 quintlins=1 loth; 2 loths 1 ounce; 8 ounces=1 mark. The ies contained 0.829045, say 0.83 of 1 English grain; the pfennig, 14.09375 grains; the quintlin, 56¾ grains; the loth, 225¼ grains; and the ounce and mark, the same as before. To the experienced metrologist it is evident that both of these are hybrid systems, originating remotely in the octonary numbers and relations of the sun-worship practiced in the countries of the Baltic. In the first system it takes 4864 ieschen to make a mark; in the second, it takes but 4352. The odd numbers of 19 engels to the ounce and 17 ieschen to the pfennig—taken in connection with the common use of coins in ancient times, both for weights, measures and other numerical relations—suggest that the basis of the system was not the mark, but the ies; a suspicion that, could it be safely established, would upset a good many current theories, both metrological and numismatic.[2]

The weight system of Troy (Troyes) was as follows: —1⅓ ieschen, or moments=1 grain; 24 grains=1 esterling, or pennyweight; 20 esterlings=1 ounce; 8 ounces=1 mark of 3840 English grains. Here the ies contains exactly ¾ of a grain.[3]

The system of Nuremburg (Noribergensis) was as follows:—1 pfennig=14.336 English grains; 4 pfennigs =1 quintlin; 4 quintlins=1 loth; 2 loths=1 ounce; 8 ounces=1 mark of 3670 grains.[4]

1 In this system 2 ieschen were called a duisch; 3 a trii; 4 a quart, etc.
2 Some features of this subject are discussed in "Money and Civilization," chap. i., and "Ancient Britain," chap. xvii.
3 Budelius, p. 30.   4 The subdivisions are from Budelius, whilst the equivalents in English grains are from Kelly.

It is well known that the name of the ducat is derived from dux or duke, but the significance of the name is lost in failing to observe that the coin itself is a degraded solidus, and that it was called a ducat only after the right to coin it was lost by the Basileus and usurped by the dukes, prelates or vassal princes of his moribund empire. The last gold coins struck by the Basileus were the solidi of the Comnenus family, toward the close of the twelfth century, containing each a trifle under 60 grains fine gold; the first ducat was struck by Alfonso IX., of Leon, in 1225, and contained 54½ grains fine gold.[1]

The name of the skilling is evidently derived from the oriental "sical," or cut money, whence we have also "sicca," "shekel," "scissors," "chisel," and many other names for cutting-instruments and their products. Cut-money and knife-money were both common in the Orient, and doubtless made their way, at a very remote period, across the steppes of Tartary to the Baltic.[2]

In a former work I followed the voice of numismatic authority and assigned the origin of the name "thaler," or "dollar," to "thal," or "dol," a vale or valley, and repeated the idle tale of Budelius about the Joachimsthals and Count Schlick. I am now convinced that the thaler has a far more significant origin. The ancient Greek and Roman systems both include coins or sums of money called talents, neither resembling nor immediately connected with the weights called talents. In the regal and ducal systems of the Renaissance, when the prevailing ratio was 10 silver for 1 gold,[3]

[1] "Middle Ages Revisited," ch. xx.   [2] Ibid., ch. xxxvi.
[3] "Della Decima, della Moneta e della Mercatura," Florence, 1765, shows that from 1262 to 1495 the mint ratio in Florence was always close to 10 for 1, sometimes a fraction over and sometimes under.

broad silver coins were struck, each containing 10 (in the Gothic States 8) times as much fine metal as a gold ducat, and known variously as a talent, ducatone, cross, scudo, ecu, or silver ducat, and valued as one gold ducat. From the thirteenth century, when it contained 565½ grains fine silver, the talent, or thaler, gradually dwindled down to about 400 grains, when it was known in Germany (this was in the sixteenth century) as a Constitution thaler. During the following century the thaler lost some 30 or 40 grains more, and was called a Convention thaler. When another hundred grains were lost it was called a currency thaler. The following tables exhibit the gradual degradation of this famous coin.

Talent or silver thaler of the Renaissance and afterwards.

Eng. grs. fine.
Croisat of Genoa (Newton).......................565½
Same piece, called scudo (Kelly)..................565½
Scudo, Piedmont, 1770 (K).......................490
"   "   1755 (K)........................489
Ducaton, Holland, old (K)........................474¾
"   new (K)..........................471¾
"   Liege, 1671............................465⅓
"   Tuscany, 1676..........................460
Scudo della Croce, Venice (K)...................458¼
"   of Genoa, 8 lire, 1796 (K)..................457½
"   Ligurian Republic, 1805 (K)................454⅓
Ecu of Lorraine, 1710 (K).......................427

German Constitution thalers.

Austria, Sigismund, silver gulden................452
Esslingen, Charles V., 1524, silver gulden.......423¾
Augsburg,   "   1551,   " 425
"   "   1559,   "   60 kreutzers.353½
Cologne, reichs or riksthaler, 18th century......404
Nuremburg.......................................402¼
Hanover...400⅓
Austria, before 1753............................390

German Convention thalers—mostly eighteenth century.

Hamburg reichs-thaler, 1687 to 1850, average weight.385¾
Frankfort-on-Maine, 1772........................365½
Saxony..360¼
Brunswick, 1753.................................359 1-5
Prussia, Nuremburg and Manheim.................359
Bavaria, 1753...................................358¾
Saltzburg.......................................358 1-5
Austria 1753 (nominally 361 gr.) actually.......353¾
Cologne...353¾
Hesse Cassel....................................353

Germany Currency thalers—eighteenth century (*Kelly*).

```
South Germ., riks thal.  Treaty Sept. 21st, 1753, legal....270.6
Hesse Cassel, riks thaler, 1778, actual..................270.3
     "           "     1789..............................250.9
Poland, 1794, new riks thaler...  .......................254.3
Prussia, riks thaler.....................................252.6
Auspack (Prussia) old riks...............................250.6
Saxe-Gotha, riks.........................................248.1
Bareuth (Prussia) old riks...............................223.3
```

These tables show the gradual degradation of the thaler in Germany. In Spain and America during the eighteenth century it never fell below $371\frac{1}{4}$ grains fine, and there it stands to-day in the coinages of the United States. In Spain it has since fallen to 349.17 grains fine, whilst in North Germany, where it is still an unlimited legal-tender, it contains but $257\frac{1}{6}$ grains fine and is legally valued at three imperial marks.

On the 25th of August, 1837, a monetary convention was concluded at Munich between several States of the German empire.[1]

On the 30th July, 1838, a monetary convention was concluded at Dresden between the States of the Zollverein, in which the old weight of the Cologne mark (3608 English grains) was recognized as equal to 233.855 metric grammes. The mark of fine silver was agreed to be coined into 14 thalers, or $24\frac{1}{2}$ florins. From 1st January, 1841, the thaler above defined was to be the sole full legal-tender money of the Prussian States, Saxe-Royal, Electoral Hesse, Saxony, Saxe-Altenburg, Duchy of Saxe-Coburg and Gotha, Schwartzburg-Rudolstadt, Schwartzburg-Sonderhausen and the Reuss States. The florin was to be the sole full legal-tender money of Bavaria, Wurtemburg, Baden, Ducal Hesse, Saxe-Meiningen, Ducal Saxe-Coburg and Gotha, Nassau, Principality of Schwartzburg-Rudolstadt, and Frankfort. Besides this, a new coin of 2 thalers, or $3\frac{1}{2}$ florins, was to be struck, 7 to

[1] MacGregor's "Statistics," i., p. 543.

the mark fine, which should be legal in all the States of the Zollverein.¹

The coinage laws above established were ratified by the Treaty of Berlin, March 8th, 1841. Coins fabricated agreeably to these provisions were declared the legal-tenders of the Union.²

On March 27th, 1845, a coinage treaty was effected at Munich.

On October 21st, 1845, a monetary cartel was effected at Carlsruhe, to provide for the punishment of all offenses against the prerogative of coining and of issuing paper money. To this cartel, and to another one effected February 19th, 1853, all the States of the Zollverein were parties.

The total circulation of a given State is the most important feature of its monetary system, since it is that which influences prices, and can be made to exercise a most powerful influence in stimulating or retarding industrial progress. Yet it is precisely that feature concerning which we commonly possess the least reliable information. The usual method of estimating the circulation is to add together the coinages, the paper emissions, and the imports of coins, and to subtract the exports and an allowance for re-coinages, wear, tear and loss. But this method is so defective that it can only furnish a remote approximation to the truth.³ The table below embraces most of the estimates which have fallen beneath the author's observation. Such estimates as were originally made in other denominations of money than German currency thalers are reduced to that denomination upon the following rough scale of equivalents:—3 imperial marks (of 1871)=1 currency thaler; 1½ currency thalers=1 convention thaler, or 1

---

1 MacGregor's "Statistics," i., p. 544.   2 Ibid., i., p. 507.
3 For a more ample discussion of the subject consult "Science of Money," chap. iii.

Spanish or American dollar; 6⅔ currency thalers=1 English pound sterling. Sums of money in millions of currency thalers.

Estimated Circulation of Prussia (Millions of Thalers).

Year.	Silver.	Gold.	Total Coin.	Paper.	Grand Total.	Pop.	Per Capita.
1790	—	—	33⅓	6⅔	40	5	8
1804	—	—	—	—	60	10	6
1805	—	—	—	—	57⅓	7	8¼

Estimated Circulation of New German Empire.

Year.	Silver.	Gold.	Total Coin.	Paper.	Grand Total.	Pop.	Per Capita.
1837	—	—	—	—	240	30	8
1850	—	—	—	—	400	34	12
1867	400	20	420	60	480	38½	12½
1867	403	15	418	62	480	38½	12½
1870	581	34	615	253	868	39	22¼
1870	554	30	584	253	837	39	21½
1870	490	30	520	253	773	39	19¾
1871	554	30	584	260	844	40	21
1872	420	45	465	356	821	41	20
1873	426½	106½	533	459	992	42	23½
1874	—	—	557	453	1010	42	24½
1876	466½	266½	533	402	935	43	21¾
1876	—	—	346	335	681	43	15¾
1876	233	343	676	323	999	43	23¼
1877	220	230	550	317	867	43	20
1878	400	133	533	300	833	43	19½
1879	298⅔	516⅔	815⅓	273⅓	1088⅔	44	24½
1879	266⅔	266⅔	533⅓	273⅓	806⅔	44	18⅓
1885	297	581	878	300	1178	46¾	25¼
1892	300	467	767	458	1225	48	24½
1893	315	900	1215	470	1685	49½	34
1894	300	387	687	480	1167	50	23⅓
1895	317	616	933	480	1413	50	28¼

The authorities for the above table are as follows: 1790, Arthur Young.[1] 1804, Krug.[2] 1805, U. S. Finance Report 1834.[3] 1837,[4] 1850, 1867,[5] Del Mar;

1 Rau, ii., p. 191, says that in 1780 Berlin bank-notes commanded a premium, but he fails to say in what. Probably in Convention thalers. 2 Krug, i., p. 244; Roscher, i., p. 374, n. 1. The discrepancy in the population is probably due to the inclusion of Prussian Poland, for which, however, Krug makes no allowance in his estimate of the circulation. 3 This estimate (1805) was made by the authorities of Prussia, forwarded to the government of the United States, and published by the latter in their annual Finance Report. 4 Memminger credits Wurtemburg in 1840 with a total money of about 12 currency thalers per capita (36 million gulden), whilst B. Hildebrand credits the Electorate of Hesse in 1853 with about 8 currency thalers per capita, of which nearly one-half were paper notes (Roscher, i., p. 374 n. 2). 5 In August, 1869, the various states of the Confederation (exclusive of Bavaria, Wurtemburg, and Baden) had in circulation paper money to the amount of 40,652,742 thalers ("Rep. U. S. Bu. Stat.," Sept., 1873)

1867, 1870, 1870, 1870,⁶ 1871,⁷ Soetbeer in 1881, revised in 1885; 1872, Rep. U. S. Bu. Statistics Sept., 1873; in 1873 there was a crisis;⁸ and in 1874 an efflux of gold;⁹ the first two estimates for 1876 are anonymous;[10] the third one is from Wagner in Rep. U. S. Mon. Com., 1876, i., pp. 195-6; the estimates for 1877 and 1878 are anonymous; 1879, Soetbeer;[11] 1879, London "Statist" May 17, 1879; 1885, Soetbeer; 1892, Indian Curr. Com., 1893, p. 211; 1893, Leech;[12] 1894, Del Mar; 1895, a German banker.

It is evident that some of these estimates are little more than conjectures, based upon currency theories. Soetbeer's later estimates are too high in gold. A tolerably safe and approximately correct estimate of the circulation of all Germany would probably be £1 per capita at the beginning of the cenutry; something less than £2 in 1850; and about £3 10s. at the present time. The average circulation of all Europe and America in 1893 was about £3 per capita, including paper money. At the rate of £1 10s. per capita Germany has in circulation more than an average share of the money of the Western world.

Besides her circulating money Germany possesses a

6 This is a revised estimate made by Soetbeer, and is probably nearer the fact than his previous statements relating to this period. On January 21st, 1870, the Bank of Prussia and its branches had in circulation 142¼ million thalers, the other banks of the Confederation 70¼ millions, and South Germany say 40 millions; total, 252½ millions ("U. S. Bu. Stat.," Sept. 1873). The coin estimate (after Soetbeer) is given in Roscher, i., p. 374, n. 2   7 Year 1871. In this estimate the paper money is evidently understated.   8 Year 1873. Paper money 106 millions more than previous year.   9 In 1873-4 a portion of the French War Indemnity gold was drawn away from Germany. In 1875 the issues of paper money were 1,205 million marks ("U. S. Com. Rel.," 1875, p. 534).   10 In 1876 the paper money was wrongly stated at 1,038 million marks ("U. S. Com. Rel.," 1876, p. 304). Of this amount 402 millions were "uncovered" "(U. S. Con. Rep.," 1875).
11 Year 1879. In Soetbeer's estimate the gold is greatly exaggerated.
12 Mint Director of the United States (Report, 1893, p. 52). The Director says: "Uncovered notes, 59,680,000 American dollars," equal to 89,520,000 German thalers. As "uncovered notes" involves an assumption and a theory which as applied to currency statistics may not be sound, I have included the whole issue of notes. However, its extravagant amount of gold renders the estimate worthless.

war-chest of the precious metals, which, according to Arthur Young, amounted in 1790 to £15,000,000 sterling in silver, and which at the present time is said to consist of 40,000,000 thalers in gold.[1]

Before taking leave of the statistics of the circulation it may be proper to observe that German monetary statistics are not exceptionally inflated; that exaggeration characterizes such statistics in most countries; and that the world's commerce is in fact conducted upon a much smaller metallic basis than is commonly supposed.

In a footnote to the table given above it is held that to include in the circulation of a State only that portion of its paper money which is "uncovered" by a reserve or guarantee of coins or securities involves an assumption and a theory which may not be sound, and that for this reason all the paper money issued was included in the table. It is now in order to briefly examine this subject. The assumption referred to is that when coins or bullion are deposited as a reserve to secure the payment of notes, it is erroneous to count both the coins or bullion and the notes as portions of the circulation. The answer to this is that so far as regards bullion, it is not money, that it is not counted in the circulation at all, and that to omit to count the notes issued upon its guarantee, or assumed guarantee, would be to omit an important element of the circulation. The same answer applies to government bonds—indeed, to any other form of reserve except full legal-tender coins. With regard to the latter, could it always be positively ascertained what proportion of the reserve consisted of such coins, it is admitted that to count them, together with

---

[1] Arthur Young, "Travels in France," i., p. 519; "Rep. U. S. Bu. Stat.," Sept. 1873, p 137; "Rep. Indian Curr. Com.," 1893, p. 211. The German war-fund (Act, Nov. 11th, 1871) is at Spandau entirely withdrawn from circulation.

the notes issued upon their guarantee, as portions of the circulation, would be erroneous; but such is not the case. Banking establishments do not, as a rule, specify what proportions of their reserves consist of full legal-tender coins. For example, the Bank of England has the right under the Act of 1844 to hold one-fifth of its reserve in silver, which, whether coined or uncoined, is not full legal-tender. But it is not required to, and in fact does not, inform the public how much of its reserves consists of such silver. I am privately informed that at the present time no portion of its reserve consists of silver. According to Professor Greven the Bank of the Netherlands enjoys a similar privilege, the proportion of silver being not merely one-fifth, but whatever the Bank deems proper. Says that authority: "Every banker knows that when he needs gold for export, and the Bank (of the Netherlands) cannot pay in gold, it will give him so much silver as will enable him to buy a quantity of gold equal in value to so many gold coins as the notes offered for payment represent." In the United States the same bag of coins often masquerades now as the reserve of one bank, and now of another. How far similar subterfuges are employed in the various private banking establishments of Germany is not known, and in the absence of such knowledge it is deemed safer to include the entire paper issues in the circulation. This at least is a known quantity; the "reserves," as experience has too often and too sadly proved, may only exist in the playful imagination of that fortunate class who have secured the prerogative to issue bank money. So much for the assumption that the value of bank reserves should be deducted from the sum of coins and notes. Now for the theory of "uncovered paper."

According to this theory the privilege to issue paper money is justified if the issuer retains a reserve, let us say, in full legal-tender coins, sufficient, under ordinary circumstances, to meet the demands for the payment of his issues. This is a very disingenuous presentation of the case; and the economists, never suspecting its artfulness, have been content to discuss the amplitude of reserves and other details of a like character, wholly neglecting to inquire whether there is not another aspect of the reserve theory which is of superior importance to the State, than security for payment of the notes. That superior aspect is the absence of any guarantee that the notes shall remain in the circulation—a guarantee that has never been demanded by governments and never offered by private banks of issue, from the fatal day when they were first chartered to the present. And yet it needs but little reflection to perceive that the interests of the State, of society, of industry, of commerce and the arts, are jeopardized a thousand times more by a contraction of the currency than by the losses which A, B, or C may sustain in failing to receive payment for the notes they may hold of the banks. Such losses are the misfortunes of individuals, and are soon repaired; but contraction of the currency is a wound inflicted upon the State—or in other words, upon the active forces which constitute its strength—and against such a wound, bank reserves offer no defense whatever.

Some particulars of the history of the ratio in Germany have already been given. The following remarks and table will render this account more complete and continuous. Down to the thirteenth century the ratio in the coinages of the northern states of Germany, including Lubeck and Hamburg, varied but slightly from the Roman pontifico-imperial ratio of 12 for 1. During the thirteenth century the influence of the Roman ratio for the first time exhibited signs of decline. Less silver and more gold was now put into the coins of the various Christian states or provinces, and still less into those which, like Pomerania and the Baltic provinces, had been but recently converted to Christianity, and had previously coined at the Gothic pagan ratio of 8 for 1. For example, the talent of 1484 only contained 451 grains, a ratio of 8 for 1; while in the coinage of the Teutonic monk-knights during the last thirty years of the fifteenth century the ratio was 9 for 1.

The enhanced value accorded to silver in the German states during the Renaissant period is shown in the following valuations derived from the average of purchase (not the issues) of the Lubeck mint:—A. D. 1411, average for eight years past 12 for 1; 1451, average for forty years past 11.7 for 1; 1463, average for twelve years past 11.6 for 1; 1475, average of several North German coinages for one year 11 for 1. Speaking generally, the coinages of the Renaissance exhibit a ratio of about 10 for 1; but the exceptions were numerous. However, the ratio never exceeded 12 for 1; and silver was sometimes raised to a fourth, a third and even to half the value of gold, weight for weight.

With the discovery of America commenced a new order of affairs. The control of the ratio, which Rome had lost and the Christian princes of Europe had acquired, was now monopolized by Spain, through its command of the new supplies and its comparatively vast coinages of the precious metals. We have seen how these advantages were abused by Charles V., and our table will therefore commence with the ratios estabished by that monarch.

The ratio between silver and gold in Germany.

Year.	Prussian legal ratio.	German conflict ratio.	Remarks.
1524	11⅜	10.00	Edict Chas. V. at Esslingen.
1546	13⅓	10.00	Edict Chas. V. Gold boycotted by the Germans.
1551	13⅓	11.17	Deduced from coinages of Upper Germany.
1559	13⅓	11 44	Deduced from coinages of Ferdinand I.
1623	13⅓	11.74	Deduced from coinages of Ferdinand II.
1641	13⅓	12.00	Desrotours; the empire generally.
1667	13⅓	14.15	Deduced from coinages of Upper Germany. Leopold I.
1669	13⅓	15.11	Deduced from coinages of Upper Germany. Leopold I.
1690	13⅓	14.50	Deduced from quotations in Berlin "banco."
1753	13⅓	14.50	Coinage Convention of Vienna, September 21st.
1766	13⅓	14.50	Deduced from quotations in Berlin "banco."
1780	13⅓	15.00	Deduced from quotations in Berlin "banco."
1790	13⅓	15.50	Deduced from quotations in Berlin "banco."
1821	14.0	15.50	Law, September 30th. Frederick d'or 103.1 grains = 5 thalers of (nominally) 257¾ grains each.
1687 to 1850	14.8	14.50 to 15.50	Hamburg (only). The gold ducat varied from 51½ to 52¾, average 52⅛ grains fine, but was not legal-tender. Average Convention thaler 385¾ grains fine; legal value, half a ducat; ratio 14.8; thus, 385.75 × 2 = 771.50 ÷ 52.125 = 14.8 (Newton; Kelly).
1851	—	15.50	Various conflict ratios, 15.21 to 15.59.[1]
1866	15½	15.50	North German Bund.
1871	15½	15 50	New Empire. Gold coin system adopted [2]

NOTES TO TABLE.—[1] During the years 1851-65 gold was highest in 1851, and lowest in 1854. In other years the ratio fell between these extremes ("Rep. U. S. Mon. Com.," 1876, i., p. 192). [2] One hundred and fifty million currency thalers retained in the circulation; but the legal-tender of all other silver coins limited to 20 marks, or 6⅔ thalers, in any one payment.

It must be remembered that for a great portion of the period embraced in this table we are dealing not with one government and one law, but with many governments and many laws, and it should be read with allowances. The legal or mint ratios shown in the first column are mainly those of Prussia and the North German Bund; the first ones (11⅜ and 13¼ for 1) were fixed by Charles V., and the second (15½ for 1) by the mint laws of the Bund in 1866. During the interval, 1790 to 1866, there appears to have been no legal ratio in Prussia, and the value of gold followed the conflict ratio, which, however, was mainly governed by the Spanish and French mint ratios of 15½, established in 1775, 1785 and 1803. The Hamburg (and approximately the Lubeck) mint ratio during most of this period was 14.8 for 1; but as gold coins were not legal-tender, they followed the conflict which resulted from the mint ratios adopted by the principal coining states of the period, namely, Spain, England and France. The conflict ratios shown in the table are approximate quotations intended to cover all North Germany; but as, during the period it embraces, Germany held no control of the ratio, these quotations are little more than reflections of the prices paid for gold (in silver) at the mints of the principal foreign coining states.

We are now prepared to continue our account of those monetary conventions which have done so much to bring the German states under a united and powerful rule. On January 24th, 1857, was effected the important coinage treaty of Vienna. At this period the commercial world was agitated by a strange disease; the fear that so much gold would be produced from the mines and pass into the form of money, that a disastrous rise of prices—that is, disastrous to millionaires—

would ensue sufficient to shake the foundation of society. In vain had Von Humboldt, whose familiarity with history and whose acquaintance with mining should have entitled him to speak with some authority on the subject—in vain had this most illustrious of Germans and of savants assured the world that the vast disparity between the world's stock of coins of the precious metals, compared with any additions that might be made to it, rendered the latter a very trifling factor in the account; in vain had he shown that but a small proportion of the mining product of gold and silver was fabricated into money; in vain did he advert to the increasing needs of an augmenting population.[1] In vain had Hume and other able writers shown that rises of prices occasioned by an increase of metallic money had benefited not only the poor, but the rich as well. The individuals who had controlled the coinage of money, and augmented or restricted its volume at pleasure, the money-lenders and usurers of Frankfort and Amsterdam, knew better. Von Humboldt's book, "The Fluctuations of Gold," was consigned to oblivion, and the essays of the Metallic School were hailed with applause, translated into all languages, and published in every country of Europe and America. This school taught the luminous doctrines that value is both a noun and an adverb; it is both a thing, an attribute and a relation; it is and it is not the same as price: "price is value in relation to a substance;" money is both a noun and an adverb; it is a thing and an attribute of a thing; it is a commodity; it is a measurer of commodities; it is also an attribute conferred upon a commodity; stand-

---

[1] "Any increase in the production which our imagination could call into existence would appear infinitely trifling compared with the accumulation of thousands of years now in circulation, especially when we consider the small proportion coined into money and the large proportion absorbed in the arts" (Von Humboldt's "Fluctuations of Gold," Berlin, 1838).

ard is the material of which legal-tender coins are made; it is a certain weight of a certain metal; and it is a certain degree of fineness of any metal; the unit of money is both the whole volume of money and each indivisible fraction of it; money is metal, and metal is money; finally, the national honor is subject to the comparative output of the gold and silver mines! All these and many other sophistries will be found in the essays of Harris, Chevalier and Lord Liverpool.[1] It is easy to perceive that they may be made to lead to any conclusion. Accordingly, in England, they led Mr. Maclaren to advocate life assurance on a silver basis, and Mr. Cobden to recommend corn rents and payments in kind. In Germany this school of muddled logic and easy principles loudly demanded the retention of silver coins for the sole money of the Fatherland; and it was in the midst of this patriotic vociferation that the Treaty of Vienna was drafted and signed.

It was declared to be enacted in pursuance of article ix. of the Treaty of Carlsruhe, July 19th, 1853, between Austria, the principality of Lichtenstein and the States which were parties to the Treaty of Dresden, July 30th, 1838. Thus the Coinage Treaty of 1857 embraced Austria, Prussia, Bavaria, Saxony, Hanover, Wurtemburg, Baden, Electoral Hesse, Ducal Hesse, Ducal Saxony, Oldenburg, Saxe-Meiningen, Saxe-Coburg, Gotha, Saxe-Altenburg, Brunswick, Nassau, Anhalt-Dessau, Cothen, Anhalt-Bemburg, Schwarzburg-Sondenhausen, Schwarzburg-Rudolstadt, Lichtenstein, Waldeck, Pyrmont, the Reusses, the Lippes, Landgraviate Hesse and the City of Frankfort.

[1] Chevalier's essays were published in the "Revue des Deux Mondes" shortly after the opening of California. Most of the sophistries enumerated in the text will be found in the first chapter of his subsequent work, "The Fall in the Value of Gold," translated by Cobden.

The right of coinage as to full legal-tender silver (vereinsmunze), and as to gold coins, was conferred upon private individuals. The drudgery of striking the coins was to be done by the States. No limits were assigned to the coinage of silver thalers or gold pieces, and only temporary ones to that of florins. Gold coins were forbidden to be made legal-tender in any of the States. The full legal-tender coins were: first, currency thalers, of which thirty were to be struck from 500 metrical grammes, or one zollpfund of 7716 1745 English grains, hence each of 257.2 grains fine; second, Austrian florins, of 45 to the zollpfund, or each of 171.47 grains fine; and third, South German florins, of 52½ to the zollpfund, or each of about 147 grains fine. The thalers were to pass for 1½ Austrian, or 1¾ South German florins; and all of these coins were to be full legal-tender in all the States. The alloy to be added was such as to make them all of the metrical standard, or nine-tenths fine. The gold coins were to be crowns of 50 to the zollpfund of fine gold, hence each of 154⅓ grains fine. Austria alone might continue to strike ducats until the end of 1865. The right of coining the subsidiary silver coins, scheidemunze, was reserved to the States. The smallest pieces were to be one-sixth of a thaler, or one-fourth of an Austrian florin. The zwanzeiger, or twenty-creutzer, or one-third florin piece, was abolished. The entire emission of subsidiary silver coins (this was reserved to the States) was limited to five-sixths of a thaler per capita; and offices were to be assigned for their redemption in full legal-tender coins. Gold coins might be received at the State treasuries at a price in silver coins to be fixed for a period not exceeding six months at a time. The position of the gold coins was that of mere bullion;

and as such they ceased to circulate, and soon found their way to the melting pot.

The paper-money and bank-notes of each State were permitted to circulate in the other States so long as "adequate" provision was made for their redemption in full legal-tender silver coins. In the case of the Bank of Prussia, which in 1872 issued two-thirds of all the paper money circulating in Germany, and in that of the other most important banks, this was legally one-third and (for a time) actually two-thirds, in thalers or florins. An exception was made with respect to Austria, whose circulation was almost entirely of paper; but such exception did not extend beyond January 1st, 1859. However, Austria soon afterwards seceded from the convention altogether.[2] No provision was made against a contraction of the currency by the melting or export of coins, or by the retirement of bank issues.

In this convention we perceive the mediate germs of the Latin Union of 1865, and the Scandinavian Union of 1872; but of far more significance is the fact, which can scarcely be doubted, that it helped to pave the way to the North German Bund of 1866 and the Empire of 1871. Nevertheless much remained yet to be done in unifying the monetary systems of Germany. At the conclusion of the war of 1866 there still remained no less than ten different systems of German moneys:

[1] We have no data of the gold coinage from 1857; but of 175 million thalers, net, of gold coined during the years below there were estimated to have remained in existence down to 1867 not more than 15 or 20 millions. Gold coinage in millions of thalers: Old Prussia, 1764 to 1867, 85.7; New Prussia (Hanover, Electoral Hesse and Frankfort), 1834 to 1867, 37.3; Brunswick, 1764 to 1867, 50.0; Hamburg and Lubeck, 1790 to 1867, 1.9; Saxony, 1839 to 1867, and Ducal Hesse, 1819 to 1855 (together), 0.9; Bavaria, Wurtemburg, and Baden, 1837 to 1867, 1.6; total, 177.4; less re-coinages, 2.5 net issues, 174.9 ("Rep. Bu. Stat.," Sept., 1873, p. 143). See also Prof. Wagner in "Rep. U. S. Mon. Com.," 1876, i., p. 191.

[2] Some other provisions of this treaty will be found in "Money and Civilization," p. 339.

First, the Prussian system of the currency thaler, divided into 30 groschen of 12 pfennigs each.

Second, the system of Royal Saxony, Ducal Saxe-Gotha, Saxe-Altenburg and Brunswick, which divided the currency thaler into 30 groschen of 10 pfennigs each.

Third, the duchies of Mecklenburg-Schwerin, Mecklenburg-Strelitz and Lauenburg, which divided the currency thaler into 48 skillings of 12 pfennigs each.

Fourth, the free cities of Hamburg and Bremen, which divided the currency thaler into two-and-a-half marks current, or into 40 skillings of 12 pfennigs each.

Fifth, the system of marks banco of the free cities of Hamburg and Altona and the vicinity.

Sixth, the gold coin system of the free city of Altona. This was based on the louis d'or, or pistole, of 1-84th of a pfund, say 92 grains of fine gold, valued at 5 currency thalers—a ratio of about 14 for 1. Here the thalers were divided into 72 groschen.

Seventh, the talent ("specie-thaler") of Schleswig-Holstein, of 9¼ talents to the Cologne mark of fine silver, say 390 grains each, subdivided into 60 skillings current.

Eighth, the subdivisions of the South German florin system, which not only prevailed in Bavaria, Wurtemburg, Baden and Hesse-Darmstadt, but also in Frankfort-on-the-Main, Nassau, Schwarzburg-Rudolstadt, Saxe-Meiningen and Saxe-Coburg.

Ninth, the gold coinage system of the free city of Bremen.

Tenth, the "banco" system of Prussia.

In recounting the steps by which these diverse systems of money—the remains of the chaotic monetary period, 1204 to 1524—were brought into harmony, I am compelled to copy the word "standard" in a perverted sense. Standard properly means alliage, or fineness; as when we say sterling standard, which means for silver 0.925 fine, or metrical standard, 0.900 fine. A new and wholly unwarranted meaning was conferred upon this word by Harris (1757); and this has since passed into all the literature on the subject of money. Standard was by him and is now used to mean the material of which the full legal-tender coins of a state are made. Thus England is said to employ the gold standard, India the silver standard, etc. But in this sense it is misleading, because it assumes that the money of England consists of gold, the money of India of silver, etc.; whereas in fact the money of England consists of gold coins and bank notes, both of which (except the bank notes as from the bank) are full legal tender; whilst the money of India consists not of silver, but of silver coins. In like manner has the phrase "unit of money" been perverted. The unit of money properly means all the money in a given state; and, as shown in my "Science of Money," chap. i., it cannot properly or distinctively have any other meaning. But unit of money, or monetary unit, or unit coin, has acquired the meaning of the principal denomination of money, as the sovereign in England, the franc in France, the imperial mark in Germany, etc. This is misleading, because it assumes that the value of money is determined by the quantity of metal contained in the so-called unit; whereas it is in point of fact determined by the arithmetical denominations and aggregate volume of all the "units," including paper notes, no matter how much or how little metal the former may contain. This principle is admitted, but often forgotten, by all the leading economists and writers on money. With these explanations we are ready to proceed with our history.

The various steps taken or proposed by the German government of 1866 toward further unifying the coinage are recounted at length in the "United States Commercial Relations," 1867, p. 447. The most important of the proposed steps was an entire re-coinage for the whole of Germany, and the substitution of gold for silver as the material of the full legal-tender coins. These great measures relating to the monetary system of Germany have since been actually realized; and, as usual with all great events, they have been ascribed to a wrong origin. They are attributed to the Franco-Prussian war and the Indemnity provided by the treaty of Frankfort; whereas in point of fact they constituted, together with the right of individual coinage and the privilege of issuing bank notes, a political move, intended to allay any opposition which the aristocratic and moneyed classes of Germany might be disposed to evince toward that Unification in which their importance was otherwise sooner or later destined to be obliterated. In a word, the "gold standard" was part of the price of German liberty. Its origin, though not its motive, is very distinctly set forth in the following official communication from Consul-General Murphy to the State Department of the United States, dated Frankfort, August 13th, 1867, and printed in the volume of Commercial Relations above cited:—"As there have been made already several proposals in regard to the establishment of a unit coin for the whole of Germany, which will be discussed as soon as the North German parliament will have appointed a committee to deliberate on the subject of a joint measure, weight and coin, I beg to furnish a few remarks taken from a treatise of a privy councillor of the Prussian government. . . . It is also proposed that the German states should change the silver standard into the gold standard."

To trace the origin of this movement it is necessary to observe that the claim of individuals to have their bullion coined into money at their own pleasure was no sooner asserted in Holland, Germany and England, than it led to another claim in behalf of the class to which such individuals belonged. This was that the money so coined should pass current, not merely in the State of which they were subjects, but in all States—a claim that took form in the organization of societies for the promotion of so-called International Coinage. An organization of this character was formed so early as the beginning of the seventeenth century, since which time numerous others have emerged into existence, all of them supported by men of the highest respectability, intelligence and wealth. Several of these organizations, still in existence, date back to the middle of the present century; and it is to their efforts, more than to any other agency, that is to be ascribed, first, that demonetization of gold which was so distinctly ratified and confirmed by the treaty of 1857, and that subsequent demonetization of silver which was planned before 1867 and effected in 1871-3.

Thus, in the International Monetary Conference held in Paris in 1866, Privy Councillor Meinecke, the Prussian commissioner, declared that in the interest of international circulation (a sophistical phrase that disclosed the motive power behind him) his government might be willing to abandon its "silver standard" in favor of a "gold standard;" but first they had to come to an understanding on the matter with the other states of the North German Confederation as well as with those of South Germany, who had signed with them the mint treaty of 1857.¹ That the motive power behind Meinecke was not the interests of the Prussian government is evinced by the arguments advanced in John G. Fichte's well-known work in favor of a distinctive national money, and from the declaration of Von Schultz, that to sign away the independence of the State in reference to money would constitute an act of treason.²

The Franco-Prussian war of 1870 furnished an opportunity for furthering the interests of individual coinage. The world's production of gold, which in 1852 amounted to £38,740,000, had gradually fallen in 1868 to £21,940,000, and in 1869 to £21,240,000; and it was foreseen that, at least for some years, it would fall, as it did fall, still lower On the other hand, the world's production of silver, which in 1852, and for many years before and afterward, stood at about £8,000,000 per annum, suddenly jumped during the years 1864-9 to £10,000,000 per annum, and with the practical opening of the great Comstock lode bade fair to reach, as it did reach, a much higher total.³ We have seen that the Treaty of Vienna was dominated by the California scare of cheap gold. It is quite evident that the monetary provisions of the Treaty of Frankfort were equally dominated by the Nevada scare of cheap silver. These provisions are set forth in another work.⁴ In effect, they stipulated that the five milliards (£200,000,000) war indemnity to be paid by France should be paid in gold coins or their equivalent. The indemnity, together

---

1 "Commercial Relations," 1867, pp. 448-9.
2 "Science of Money," p. 47, note 1; "Money and Civilization," p. 288, note 1; "Int. Conf.," 1878; "Int. Conf.," 1881, p. 9; London "Times," Feb., 1886. Sir Wm. Harcourt said he was "not willing to place the currency of England at the mercy of foreign States." London "Times," April 4, 1895. Almost precisely the same thing was said by Alexander Hamilton a century previously.
3 "Hist. Prec. Met.," ch. xxii.   4 "Mon. and Civ.," ch. xvi.

with interest and other charges, amounted in fact to about £234,512,292. It was paid during the interval between May 10th, 1871 and December 4th, 1874, and, according to M. Léon Say, with only £20,491,797 in coins, of which nearly one-half were silver, the balance being liquidated by bills of exchange for French credits in foreign countries. According to another account, France lost £40,000,000 in gold and gained £2,600,000 in silver, while Germany gained £33,540,000 in gold, and lost £2,600,000 in silver, the difference between the forty millions of gold lost by France and the thirty-three and a half millions of gold gained by Germany having gone to other countries. ("Mon. and Civ.," ch. xvi.)

It was with this promised accession of gold that Germany adopted the Mint laws of 1871-3, and authorized those increased emissions of paper money which brought upon her a panic in the midst of a plethora. So long as a State resigns its prerogative of coinage and the issuance of circulating notes into the hands of individuals, so long is it exposed to monetary crises. These phenomena were unknown previous to 1572 in Holland, and 1666 in England; they will never cease until the fatal legislation of those years is repealed—in short, not until the State assumes the control of its own mints and paper emissions. The laws of 1871-3 had for their object, First, the creation of a new and uniform coin for the whole German empire. This was the imperial mark, of which 1395 went to the zollpfund weight of fine gold. Each mark would therefore contain 0.35842 metrical gramme, or 5.532 English grains fine gold. This money (in pieces of 5, 10 and 20 marks) was to be full legal-tender. Second, except as to the old currency thaler, of which there were supposed to be from

135 to 150 millions still in circulation, and whose full legal-tender function was retained for the present, no silver coins were thenceforth to be legal-tender for more than 20 marks. These provisions entirely reversed the policy of 1857; then gold was demonetized, now it was silver. Third, new subsidiary silver coins were provided for (called silver marks), of which 100 were to be struck from a zollpfund of fine silver; hence each mark contained 5 grammes, or 77.15 grains, fine. The emission, until further notice, was limited to 10 marks per head of population. These coins were made redeemable at the imperial and state treasuries with full legal-tender coins. Fourth, "whenever the mints should not be engaged in coining for the government they were free to coin (only) twenty-mark gold pieces on private account, on payment of a seigniorage not to exceed 7 marks per pfund of pure gold." This substantially surrendered the gold coinage to individuals, yet wisely left the mint gates in keeping of the Crown. Fifth, provision was made for calling in all the old silver coins except the thalers above mentioned, recoining them into imperial silver marks, and selling the surplus silver if any. This surplus, as the event proved, amounted nominally to about 200,000,000 thalers, and it was the German demonetization of silver and the sale of this vast amount of bullion in the London and other markets that precipitated the fall in silver which occurred soon after. Sixth, all paper money issued by the states was to be withdrawn by January 1st, 1876, and replaced by imperial paper money. This excellent provision was not extended to the issues of private banks.

The legal equivalents between the old and new money were—1 currency thaler = 3 marks, and the other pieces in proportion. The ratio of silver in the thalers to gold in the marks is 15½ for 1; and as at present (there is now a "market price" of silver) there is a profit of about 100 per cent in coining the thalers, it is natural to expect that a good many surreptitious silver coins of full weight and fineness will find their way into the circulation. This is a danger which invites the solicitude of the German imperial government.

The table relating to the circulation, however faulty may of its details, furnishes the best guide as to the manner in which these various provisions were actually carried into execution. In 1870 the silver circulating in Germany probably did not exceed 500,000,000 thalers; it has since been reduced to about 300,000,000, of which probably one-half consists of thaler pieces. The gold scarcely exceeded 30,000,000; it has been successively increased and diminished, until now (excluding the war-chest) it amounts to about 367,000,000 to 400,000,000 thalers. The paper circulation, which before the war did not exceed 150,000,000 thalers, has since amounted to over 450,000,000; it was then curtailed and is now increased to 480,000,000. The present circulation therefore consists of about 300,000,000 thalers silver, 367,000,000 gold and 480,000,000 paper; total 1,167,000,000 to 1,200,000,000 thalers, or about 24 thalers or 72 marks per capita of population. An eminent German authority who was consulted on the subject estimated it one-sixth higher.

The statistics of the reduction of gold and silver ores in Germany have been ingeniously employed to swell the estimated production of silver throughout the world. It may be stated at the outset that nearly all of the gold and most of the silver produced in Germany is from foreign refractory ores, whose metalliferous contents have already been credited to the countries of their production. These are chiefly America, Australia and Spain. The product of gold in Germany for the year 1830 was about 10 pounds troy, chiefly in Saxony and Hanover; in 1850, 20 pounds; 1860, 70 pounds (average of three years); 1870, 167 pounds (average of three years); 1880, 800 pounds; 1890, 3,600 pounds; at the present time it is about 6,000 pounds, and valued at about £300,000 sterling. This gold is extracted in minute proportions from lead and copper ores. The peroxide of iron obtained in roasting arsenical ores is impregnated with chlorine gas, washed with water, and the gold precipitated with sulphureted hydrogen. The resulting sulphide is roasted, washed with hydrochloric acid, and smelted with borax and niter. The production of silver in 1830 was about 72,000 pounds troy; 1850, 100,000 pounds; 1860, 150,000 pounds;[1] 1870, 240,000 pounds; 1880, 360,000 pounds; 1890, 800,000 pounds, and at the present time about 900,000 pounds, of which about two-thirds are from foreign ores. The production of native silver, therefore, does not exceed 300,000 pounds, or in value about £450,000 sterling. In Dr. Soetbeer's work, translated and printed by the American government in 1887 for the guidance of statesmen (U. S. Cons. Rep., No. 87, p. 477), the production of silver in Germany is stated at more than twice this sum; and in that sciological monument, the "Report of the Director of the Mint upon the Production of the Precious Metals in 1892," it is stated at more than thrice. Both of these works were printed on the government press in vast numbers, and distributed gratis to the public. They were soon followed by the legislative cessation of full legal-tender silver

[1] For 1865 the product of the Hartz was given at 28,000 pounds troy; Prussia, 68,000; Saxony, 80,000; and other German states 2,500: total 178,500 pounds (Phillips on "Gold and Silver," p. 320).

coinage (repeal of the Bland and Sherman Acts), a tremendous fall in the price of securities, the insolvency of numerous credit institutions, and a general paralysis of trade.

These disastrous consequences are not confined to the United States, but are common to the commercial world to-day. They are directly attributable to the selfish and unpatriotic clamor of a class of whom Cobden in England, Chevalier in France and Soetbeer in Germany were the gifted exponents and dupes. The result is, they have killed the goose that laid the golden eggs. Their views, unhappily carried into practice, have ended in an almost total paralysis of trade; and this will lose to their masters ten times more money than the latter can possibly gain by the demonetization of one of the precious metals and the contraction of the basis of credit. Like Storch, like Bungé, like every zealot who has been permitted to influence the monetary policy of an empire, they have been the evil geniuses of their Fatherland. Soetbeer knew but little of the numerous monetary experiments which had been made in Germany. He was totally ignorant of those which had been made in other countries. His works evince no knowledge of the conditions under which the precious metals have been won from nature, nor obtained by one nation from another. He fancied that the value of coins was due to the economical cost of producing, by the aid of free labor, the material of which they were composed; and he had the effrontery to reduce them all to kilogrammes of gold and silver. Such was his great talent and persistency that he infected a numerous and intelligent school with the same mad notions. The thousands of millions which the Spaniards extorted from the tears and blood of the Indians, the plunder which Bonaparte carried out of Germany, nay, even the vast Indemnity which the Germans recently exacted from France, and which was paid under his very nose, he weighed with the scales of a bullion dealer and he reduced to a fanciful "cost of production." With the experience of ages treasured up in the laws of the empire in which he dwelt, with the Roman Institutes and Codes at his elbow, he totally failed to comprehend the meaning of value or the function of money; and by reducing the latter to metal he converted the complicated transactions of modern societary life to the savage level of barter, in which that which is offered with the right hand is valued by something held in the left. The idea that numisma, nummus, money, is a Measure, a measure whose limits can only be equitably adjusted by the State, never entered his mind. Yet he might have readily found it in Plato and Aristotle, and Paulus and Humboldt; nor could he have failed to find it in the laws of his own country, had he ever deemed it worth his while to read them with care. His pernicious advice was followed so blindly as to extort from the suffering farmers and peasants a cry of distress expressed in no less than two hundred petitions to the Imperial Chancellor and the Reichstag (December 10th, 1886), which piteously begged for relief from the evils of hoarded money and the clutches of the usurer.

Germany has a brilliant future before her. Her people are hardy, industrious and intelligent; her religion comes from the free air of the Baltic; her laws are based upon the garnered wisdom of ages; her mechanical aptitude is the legacy of Rome; her domain is spacious, her soil exuberant, her climate genial, and her ruler enterprising, progressive, and impatient to develop the vast resources of the State to whose guidance he has been called. But he may rest assured that in these times such development depends in no slight degree upon the adoption of a stable and equitable system of money; and that such a system is not the one demanded by the class of individuals who practically monopolize the issues of the imperial mints, and by means of this all-powerful engine usurp for themselves functions that rightfully belong to the German people and the German state.

CHAPTER XV.

PRIVATE COINAGE.

Five great eras in the history of money—Pontifico-royal period—Republican period—Pontifico-imperial period—Royal period—Private Coinage period—Moslem origin of private coinage—Omission of the coinage prerogative from the Koran—Its assumption by the Moslem conquerors of India—Private coinage practiced by their permission—Consequent degradation of the Indian monetary systems—Arrival of the Portuguese in India—Private coinages of Albuquerque at Goa—Private coinages of the Dutch in India—Private coinages of the British East India Company—Idolatrous effigies on their coins—Private coinage enunciated in the Star Chamber of England—Private coinage sanctioned by Charles II., who concedes or bargains away the royal prerogative—Disastrous consequences to the commercial world—Frequent failures of banks of issue—Incompetency of the banking class to regulate either national or international Measures of Value—Demand for the resumption of the State prerogative—Progress of this movement to the present time.

IF we survey the entire history of money (not merely as in Chap. V., with reference to the Ratio), it divides itself into five distinct periods. First, the Pontifico-royal period, which lasted from the earliest times to the epoch of the Greek republics. In the pontifico-royal period money was coined exclusively in the temples, and stamped with the sacred emblems of religion. Second, the Republican period, when money was controlled by the senates of Sparta, Clazomenæ, Byzantium, Athens and Rome. Third, the Pontifico-imperial period, when the coinage was assumed by the Cæsars, and so regulated by them that for thirteen centuries its essential features remained substantially unaltered. Fourth, the Kingly period, when the princes of the West, having freed themselves from the dominion of

Rome, seized the coinage prerogative and exercised it independently. Fifth, the period of Private Coinage, when the goldsmiths and merchant adventurers chartered to trade with and despoil or conquer the Orient, obtained control of the royal prerogative of coinage, and thus opened the door to that last of degradations, Private Coinage. This period has not yet ended.

But although the East India companies introduced private coinage for the first time into the states of Christendom, this was not the beginning of it. Like many other modern institutions of money, Private Coinage is of Moslem origin. In the Empires of antiquity the minting of money was a sacerdotal function, and as such it was exercised as to gold and controlled as to silver by the sovereign-pontiffs of Rome and Sassanian Persia, when Mahomet and his undaunted followers issued from Arabia to overthrow these great powers. Whether in scorn of what he regarded as their idolatrous religions, or from a neglect due to his own illiteracy, Mahomet omitted from the Koran those sacred injunctions which at that period were necessary to preserve the coinage prerogative from violation. It was in consequence of this neglect that the brave but rapacious adventurers who conquered India deemed themselves at liberty to abuse the coinage, until their issues ceased to command public respect. This is where private coinage crept in to supply that indispensable public Measure of Value which the State had failed to preserve from degradation and instability.[1]

Such, in fact, was the position of affairs in many of the Moslem states of India when Albuquerque, after

[1] The public, societary, or communal nature of the Measure of Value is recognized in the Mint Code 33 Vict., ch. 10: "The Treasury may from time to time issue to the master of the Mint, out of the growing produce of the Consolidated Fund, such sums as may enable him to purchase bullion in order to provide *supplies of coin for the public service.*"

subduing the petty principality of Ormuz, raised the flag of Portugal upon the battlements of Goa. Among the conqueror's earliest acts was the issuance of an unauthorized and debased coinage of gold, silver and copper. His professed object was to relieve a local dearth of coins, and to gain credit and renown for his lord the king; his real one to buy the gold which he might fail to plunder, and sell it (in Portugal) at cent per cent profit. Among the native coins of Goa and of Southern India generally was the gold hun, stamped with the boar emblem (the varaya), one of Vishnu's incarnations. This coin corresponded in weight and fineness with the Arabian dinar, whilst the dirhem had its exact counterpart in the bargan of silver, of which ten went in value to the hun, or varaya. The ratio between the silver and gold in these coins was therefore 6 or 7 for 1, whilst at the same time that in the coinages of Portugal was 11 or 12 for 1. When the Dutch gained a footing in the Indies they found there a similar state of affairs, and they fell into similar practices of private coinage and monetary chicane. The example became infectious. The British East India Company followed suit. It struck idolatrous coins, under native permission, in 1620; and, with the door thus ajar to private coinage, it was easily pushed wide open. An intrigue with this object was introduced into the Star Chamber during the reign of Charles I., which blossomed during that of his son, in the Act 18 Charles II., c. 5, an Act that bargained away the Measure of Value, upon which must depend, for countless generations, the share of all public burdens and the distribution of all wealth. Under this legislation the royal prerogative was placed in abeyance; and, beyond its power to determine the ratio, the State practically lost its control of money. In 1816 the Crown was persuaded to suspend the exercise of its power over the ratio. In this manner was silver demonetized. By the operation of an obscure and unnoticed clause in the Mint Act of 1870, so much of the power as the Crown retained to terminate such suspension and demonetization was removed, and the last remnant of a prerogative whose exercise is essential to the autonomy of the State was innocently surrendered to private hands. Practically, since 1816 the Measure of Value for the vast transactions of the British Empire has not been Money, which may be limited by law and counted by tale, but Metal, which cannot thus be regulated, and which therefore has been resigned practically to the control of a class whose chief interest in the State has been to render it subservient to their own private advantage.

What has been the result? From the day when the royal voluptuary resigned a prerogative which, more than any other one, pleads for the continuance of kingly rule, to the present time, the commercial community has been subjected to alternate epochs of monetary contraction and expansion, in which much of what it accumulates at one period is insidiously filched from it at another. The reader has but to glance at Chapter 17 of this volume to be convinced of the entire truth of this observation. The suspensions of banks of issue therein shown involved losses to the note-holders and others amounting to more than all the gold and silver money in the world several times over. Not only this; the surrender of the prerogative of coinage has tended to estrange the Crown from the People, whose disappointment has manifested itself in many painful symptoms. No man who takes pride in the glorious past of this Mother of States, and who would preserve that past from obliteration, should refrain from referring to these dangers, or pointing the way to avoid them in future. More than this; such dangers menace not the peace of England alone, they affect the entire commercial world.

The plain facts are these: two centuries ago the king of England plundered the goldsmiths of London of all their ready money. Partly for the reasons already mentioned herein, and partly, perhaps, to make amends for this act, his son substantially sold and surrendered to the goldsmiths the State prerogative of coinage. Owing to England's commercial supremacy (due to the energy of her people, not to the plans of goldsmiths) this made the latter the sole arbiters of the Measure of Value, not merely of England, but of the Western world. These tremendous powers have been wielded with such inadequate perception of the equities and consequences they involved, with such lack of scientific or financial skill, and in so narrow and selfish a spirit, that its arbiters have repeatedly plunged the commercial world into bankruptcy and confiscated or inequitably redistributed its accumulated earnings, either for their own benefit or else to save themselves from the effects of their own blundering.

From this selfishness, ill-management, blundering and recklessness, from the evidence which they have given before government commissions on this subject, both in this country and in others, from the countless books and pamphlets in which they have contradicted each other, both as to fact and opinion, on the subject of money, as well as from many other evidences, it has become quite obvious that the goldsmith class, which includes the managers of banks of issue, are less competent to understand and regulate the Measure of Value than are the representatives of the People, whose patriotism, conservatism, and societary instinct furnish a far more reliable basis for the stability of Money than the doctrines, the prejudices, or the selfishness of a limited class.[1]

Even amongst themselves this class has been unable to agree with regard to the diagnosis of monetary troubles, or the proper remedies to apply. Chaos in legislation had bred chaos in doctrine. All that has been perceived clearly, either by them or anybody else, is that since the era of Private Coinage and Private banks of issue the industrial and commercial world has suffered repeated reverses, for which no indemnity has been offered and no practical remedy discovered. But the synchronism of these events has itself disclosed the source of the trouble and indicated the correct treatment. That treatment is the resumption by the State of its ancient prerogative of money. Upon referring to Chapter 18, which gives an account of the present monetary systems of various States, the reader will observe that Private Coinage has been forbidden as to silver in all the Western States (except Mexico), and that as to gold it is a dead letter, because all the available supplies of this metal have become concentrated in four or five principal States, chiefly as war-funds. The Movement to couch the world's indebtedness in only one of the two metals which had previously answered for the bases of its monetary systems, has served its purpose; but it has had other results than those anticipated by its promoters. It has already terminated the private coinage of silver; it now threatens to put an end also to the private coinage of gold.

[1] Consult the writer's examination of Mr Albert Gansl, banker and agent of the Rothschilds before the U. S. Monetary Commission, printed in their Report at Washington, 1876, i., app., p. 49. Also Mr. Chaplin's examination of Lord Farrer, "Rep. Royal Com. on Agricultural Distress," 1895, part ii.

The States which in 1873 were duped into doubling their indebtedness have outlived their resentment, and become reconciled to a loss which has enabled them to dispense for the future with that mischief of Private Coinage, which alone rendered such loss possible. Most of them now exercise, for the first time in centuries, a more or less complete control over their own monetary systems; and the sense of relief and security which has followed the change has communicated itself to other States, and stimulated a popular demand for the entire interdict of Private Coinage. Such is the gist of the Resolution passed at the recent Convention of St. Louis, and such will also doubtless be the outcome of many future monetary and political conventions. In effect, the demand is that the State or Crown should resume its ancient prerogative; the State now is identical with the Crown, for the State alone can stop the alternate melting down, shipping to and fro and re-coinages of metal which lie at the base of monetary disturbances. The contention henceforth may be not whether the symbols of money shall be made of one metal or of two metals, but that the State and not the money-changers shall control its issues.

CHAPTER XVI.

STATISTICS OF THE RATIO.

Different ratios at some periods in Orient and Occident—Coinage controlled by priesthood—Ratios in India from earliest times to 1893—Ratio in Roman Republic and Empire—Ratio in Spain from 1475 to 1895—Ratio in Portugal from 1510 to 1891—Stable ratio under Roman Empire—Evil effects of private coinage—Results of closing mints to silver.

THE coinage ratios of silver to gold in the Gothic and Saxon States, the Moslem States, England, Scandinavia, the Netherlands and Germany have been shown in their appropriate chapters. To complete the subject it only remains to adduce the ratios in India, Rome, Spain and Portugal.[1]

At the earliest period of which we have any positive knowledge the coinage ratio in the Orient was 6 or $6\frac{1}{2}$ for 1, whilst at the same time it was 13 for 1 in Persia. Down to the epoch of Mahomet it seems to have been the policy of every state in the West, which secured any important share of the Eastern trade, to value its gold coins at twice the quantity of silver for which they exchanged in the Orient. Such was the case with Assyria, Babylonia, Persia, Macedon, Egypt under the Ptolemies, and Imperial Rome. It is evident that no such enormous disparity of value as this could have been maintained if private coinage had been permitted, either in the Orient or Occident. Neither could any small or weak state have upheld such a condition of affairs. The control of money and trade must have been in very powerful hands to maintain gold in the West at twice its value in the East, or silver in the East at twice its value in the West. Whose hands were these? The answer is, the priesthood; the priests of

---

[1] The coinage ratios in China, Japan, Persia, Assyria, Judea, Egypt, Greece, the Italian States, France, Austro-Hungary, Russia, and some of the American States are given in my former works.

Brama or Budha in the East, the priests of Cyrus, Darius, Tiglath-pil-Esar, Nebu-Nazaru, Osiris, Alexander, Ptolemy and the Cæsars in the West. With the advent of Mahomet all this changed, the priests of the West lost their power, and the same ratio prevailed at Delhi, Bagdad and Cordova. When Rome resumed her sway over the long-lost province of Spain the Eastern ratio entirely disappeared from the coinages of Europe; when her emissaries reached India it began to fade from the Orient. To-day the ratio of Cæsar, as modified by the legislation of Charles V., Philip V. and Louis XVI., dominates the monetary system of every state in the world.

Ratio of Silver to Gold in India.

Year.	Ratio.	Remarks.
B. C. —	1	Archaic epoch. Inference deduced from the use of electrum coins composed of gold and silver. Gibbon ("Misc. Works," vol. iii., p. 420) says the commonest ratio in remote times was 1 = 1. Agatharchides; Strabo, lib. xvi., c. 18; and Del Mar, "Hist. P. M.," p. 239. Chabas ("Researches on the Papyrus of Boulak")says 1¼ = 1 in Egypt.
—	4	Vedic epoch. Inference deduced from quaternary tale relations in the Vedas, noticed by Thomas ("P. K. D.," p. 4).
1650	5	Braminical epoch. Pococke. Inference deduced from quinquennial tale relations of moneys in Braminical scriptures.
1367	6	First Budhic epoch. Prinsep. From weights of coins, Leon Faucher deduces ratios of 2½ and 6@8 for 1.
521	6½	Second Budhic epoch. India (valley of the Indus) plundered by Darius Hystaspes. Persian ratio 13 for 1. Herodotus. Sir A. Cunningham, p. 5, says 8 for 1 in India, but I think he is mistaken.
332	6¼	India (valley of the Indus) plundered by Alexander. Alexandrine (Egyptian) ratio 12½ for 1.
312	6¼	India (valley of the Indus) plundered by Seleucus Nicanor, Epiphanes.
A. D. 400	—	Fahian mentions gold, silver, and copper coins and cowries in India.
629	—	Hiuen Tsiang mentions gold, silver, and copper coins in India (Beal, i., 54).

STATISTICS OF THE RATIO 395

Year.	Ratio.	Remarks.
A. D. 700	6½	India plundered by the Moslem, whose raids extended A. D. 698-1001. This is the period when the latest alterations are believed to have been made in the Code of Manu. Its tale relations of coins are chiefly octonary.
1150	8	Delhi. "Middle Ages Revisited," ch. xi., note 39A.
1290	4@10	Marco Polo. Ratios prevailing in places on his route, the highest being at the seaports of China ("Middle Ages Revisited," ch. xi., note 39A).
1295	7(?)	Jul-al-ad-din mohurs, 163.8 grains fine; later ones, 154.84 grains fine (Harrison).
1324	7@8	Mahomet-bin-Tuglak. Thomas ("P. K. D.," pp. 232-7).
1351	6½	Firoz-Shah. Tale relations octonary. Eight silver adalis 140 grains fine = one gold mohur 175 grains fine; a ratio of 6½ for 1.
1398	7	India plundered by Timur or Tamerlane the Tartar.
1450	7	Bahlol-Lodi. Reduction of the silver tanka to 56 grains (Cunningham, 24).
1498	6@8	Voyage of Vasco de Gama ("Hist. Money Anc.," p. 106).
1510	6½	Native ratio at Goa between gold huns and silver bargans.
1520	6@8	Coasts of India plundered by Portuguese, Dutch, and French ("Hist. Mon. Anc.," p. 106).
1542	9	Sher Shah. Earliest arrivals of silver from America. Rupee 174-4 grains nearly fine. (Harrison; Thomas, "P. K. D.," p. 5, says 178 grains; elsewhere 175 grains).
1545	9	Regular silver shipments from Acapulco, about £200,000 a year.
1555	9½	Akbar the Great, Grand Mogul. Rupees 170½ grains fine (Harrison). Private coinage interdicted. Seigniorage 5½ per cent. For ratio and seigniorage, "P. K. D.," 424-6.
1587	—	East India Companies formed. Portuguese, 1587; Dutch, 1595; English, 1599; the last incorporated, 1613.
1599	—	Queen Elizabeth refuses permission to the East India Company to circulate Spanish coins in India, and requires them to use coins with the royal effigy. Hence the "portcullis" coins.
1601	9.0	"Portcullis" silver coins, viz. dollars, halves, quarters, and eighths, struck in London by the Crown for the East India Company for use in India. A few years later, similar coins were struck of gold (Humphreys, "Coin Manual," pp. 461, 524; Harrison; Thurston).
1620	10.0	East India Company mint erected at Madras, which strikes "three-swamy" or Laksmi pagodas, by permission of the native Rajah (Harrison: Thurston).

Year.	Ratio.	Remarks.
A. D. 1639	—	Private coinage suggested in the Star Chamber of England.
1655	—	Cromwell destroys the East India Company's charter, but is compelled to renew it.
1666	—	Private coinage authorized in England, 18 Chas. II., ch. 5.
1671	10.0	East India Company's mint erected at Bombay (Poole; Harrison says 1678).
1677	—	East India Company authorized by the British Crown to coin gold, silver, copper, or lead, with its own devices
1697	10.0	Auranzib, Grand Mogul. Ratio deduced from materials in Gibbon. Gold coins of this emperor competed in the circulation with the native gold huns of Southern India. Both were of the same contents.
1739	10@11	India plundered by Nadir Shah, of Persia.
1749	10.0	India plundered by the East India Company (Taylor's "Hist. India;" Partington's Encycl., art. "East India Company").
1759	10.0	Wm. Winfred Webb, "Currencies of Rajputana," 1893.
1766	16.4	New monetary system of East India Company. Mohur, 149.72 grains fine, valued at 14 sicca rupees, 175.0 to 175.8 grains fine, both full legal-tenders.
1769	14.8	Mohurs, 190.086 grains fine, valued at 16 sicca rupees, 175 to 175.8 grains fine; both full legal-tenders.
1774	15.0	Bombay mohurs and rupees of same weight, the former 0.9926 fine (same as Venetian sequin), making the ratio (nearly) 15 for 1 (Kelly's "Cambist," i., p. 94).
1793	14.8	Silver coins sole legal-tenders. Mohurs 189.4 grains fine, valued at 16 rupees, 175.9 grains fine. Ratio 14.86 for 1. Harrison says 14.81.
1800	15.0	Bombay mohur of 164.68 grains fine, valued at 15 Lucknow rupees of same weight and fineness; both coins fell legal-tenders.
1818	15.0	Mohurs, 187.65 grains fine, valued at 16 sicca rupees, 175.9 grains fine, both coins full legal-tenders (Harrison). Mohurs, 165 grains fine, valued at 15 Company rupees of same contents (Kelly, i., p. 91; ii., p. 147).
1821	14.8	Bengal. Mohur and sicca rupee, mint regulation, 14.857 for 1; assay ratio, 14.827 for 1 (Kelly, ii., p. 147).
1821	13.9	Madras. Star pagoda and current rupee, mint regulation, 13.872 for 1; assay ratio, 13.857 for 1 (Kelly, ii., p. 147).
1821	15.0	Bombay. Gold rupee and silver rupee, mint regulation and assay ratio give like results. (Kelly, ii., p. 147).
1835	15.0	September 1st. Silver coins sole legal-tenders

Year.	Ratio.	Remarks.
A. D.		throughout all British India. Mohurs, 165 grains fine, valued at 15 rupees, same contents.
1838	15.0	January 1st. Demonetization and withdrawal of sicca rupees.
1841	15.0	Gold and silver coins both full legal-tenders.
1852	15.0	Silver coins sole legal-tenders.
1858	15.0	The British Crown resumes its prerogative of the government of India. End of the East India Company.
1863	15.0	First systematic issues of paper money.
1893	15.0	June 23rd. Individual coinage of silver suspended, the outstanding silver rupees remaining full legal-tenders.

Some of the "portcullis" coins mentioned under the year 1601 were testoons and other base issues of Edward VI., countermarked with a portcullis. (Proc. London Num. Soc., April 25, 1895.)

The Roman Ratio.

Year.	Ratio.	Remarks.
B. C.		
316	9	Scrupulum coinage.
268	10	Ogulnius and Fabius, Consuls.
218	10	Second Punic War.
206	10	Claudius and Livius, Consuls.
78	9	Sylla. Social Wars.
45	12	Julius Cæsar, sovereign-pontiff.
13	12	Augustus Cæsar, sovereign-pontiff. From the Julian era no change was made in the ratio to the Fall of the Empire in 1204, during the whole of which time it remained fixed at 12 silver for 1 gold.
A. D.		
1204	12	Alexis IV., sovereign-pontiff. Fall of the Empire.

Turning from the ratio within the Empire, which was always 12 for 1, to the ratio without, we have seen that down to the eleventh or twelfth century the ratio in the Orient and in the Moslem kingdoms of the Levant and Spain was 6½ for 1; in the Gothic or semi-Gothic States—e. g. the Netherlands, Denmark and Scandinavia—it was 8 for 1; and in Britain (with certain exceptions), Germany (before and after the Carlovingian rule), and France, 8 to 10 for 1.

The following tables of the ratio in Spain and Portugal are recensions of my former essays on this subject. They are given in this place in order to embrace all the information which the author has been enabled to collect down to the present time.

The ratio in Roman Spain was 12 for 1; in Gothic Spain, 8 for 1; in Moslem Spain, down to the reign of Abd-el-Raman III., 6½ for 1. After that period it began to again yield to the influence of the Roman ratio, which by this time was re-established in the neighboring State of France (Edict of Charles the Bald). Meanwhile the petty Gothic kingdoms of Northern Spain had adopted the Moslem ratio. For a time the greatest confusion prevailed, but this finally ended with the general adoption of the Roman ratio by the Christian princes of Spain. In the twelfth century Pope Innocent III. ordered the king of Aragon (Pedro II.) to restore his (silver) coins, a fact that evinces the papal desire to exercise the prerogative of money. In the reign of James I. of Aragon the ratio was 12. After the Fall of Constantinople the ratio again fell into confusion, the Moslem princes usually coining at 7 or 8, and the Christians at 9 or 10 for 1; but there was no uniformity in each class by itself. In the fifteenth century Henry IV. coined at 7½ for 1.[1] By this time the Moslem power was near its end, and its influence upon the ratio almost lost. The following table shows the Spanish ratio from 1475 downward:

[1] "Mon. and Civ.," p. 101; from Saez.

The Ratio in Spain.

Year.	Ratio.	Remarks.
A. D.		
1475	10.985	Castile and Leon.
1480	11.555	All Christian Spain.
1483	11.675	Ferdinand and Isabella.
1497	10.755	Edict of Medina.
1502	10.755	Expulsion of vast numbers of the Moors.
1537	10.755	Silver permitted to be coined in America, subject to the Quinto tax.
1545	10.755	Oriental ratios raised generally from 6½ to 10.
1546	13.333	American bullion now chiefly silver.
1565	13.333	One-fifth of American product sent direct to Asia.
1580	13.333	Gold coinage forbidden in America.
1608	13.333	Gold coinage permitted in America.
1611	13.833	A million of Moors expelled from Spain.
1641	14.0	Locke, on "Money."
1650	15.0	White's "Report to the U. S. Congress."
1675 to 1734	16.0	Harris (ii., 122) notices change of ratio. Spain loses control of ratio and adopts the Portuguese ratio. In 1734 silver coins 6 per cent premium.
1760	14.25	French ratio 1726 to 1785 was 14.46 for 1.
1765	14.875	Calonne.
1775	15.536	—
1779	15.875	Calonne says 14.875; a blunder.
1786	16.380	—
1821	16.0	Some coinages show ratio of 15.85.
1864	15.476	First change since 1821.
1868	15.5	Figuerola Law, October 19, following the Latin Monetary Union.
1876	15.5	Decree of August 20th, suspending "free" coinage of silver, and announcing the intention to limit silver legal-tender to 150 pesetas. Actual currency, inconvertible bank paper, 1½ per cent under silver and 3 per cent under gold.
1890	15.5	The ratio merely nominal; bank paper filling the circulation.
1895	15.5	Same.

The Ratio in Portugal.

Year.	Ratio.	Remarks.
A. D.		
1510	11.0	Bullion trade opened at Goa. Indian ratio 6½.
1545	13.3	Trade opened with Japan, where the ratio was 8 4-10.
1580	13.3	From 1580 to 1640 Portugal belonged to Spain.
1641	14.0	Spanish ratio.
1668	16.0	War with Spain ended in 1665.
1688	16.0	Edict of August 4th.
1722	15.9	Standard lowered from 0.916⅔ to 0.908.
1747	13.3	Weight of silver coins lowered.

Year.	Ratio.	Remarks.
A.D.		
1797	12.0	Suspension of coin payments 1797.
1798	13.3	Restoration of the coin weights of 1747.
1802	13.2	Slight variations of standard in coin assays.
1808	13.2	Do. do.
1811	13.3	Do. do.
1822	15.9	Lowering of gold coins in weight.
1834	15.9	—
1835	15.9	—
1838	15.3	Lowering of the silver coins in weight.
1847	16.4	Further lowering of the gold coins.
1854	14.2	Silver limited to 5 milreis legal-tender.
1880	14.1	No further change of legal-tender law.
1891	14.1	Suspension of coin payments Ratio merely nominal.

It will be remarked that as, one after another, the Western states fell under the sway of Rome, whether the lord of that Empire was pagan or Christian, their coining or valuing ratios obeyed the Roman rule of 12 for 1, and never stirred from it until the Empire fell. With that event order and regularity disappeared. Every prince coined for himself, and often with little regard for his neighbor. The consequence was the wildest dissonance of the ratio. It is abundantly evident from the events of the period that this evil would soon have cured itself. The German princes entered into numerous conventions to harmonize their diverse systems. At quite an early period in the history of England as an independent state her sovereigns also made several attempts of this character, until in an evil moment Charles II. threw all these efforts away by flinging his great prerogative to the money-changers.

However, their control of money in its larger, its political sense, is drawing to an end. They have employed the lever of private coinage to enhance gold and depress silver, until now the former stands at double and the latter at half its former value. But something else has also happened; the doors of the world's silver mints have been shut in their faces; and in the limited silver coinages of the various states, the customary ratio of 15 or 16 to 1 has been maintained without alteration ("Etalon boiteux"). If the common belief of mining men throughout the world is well founded, namely, that owing to the attraction of open mints, silver has hitherto been produced from the mines at a loss,[1] then it follows that the closure of the mints to silver and the relinquishment of unprofitable mining will sooner or later not merely restore silver to its former value, but enhance it to a point where, as was the case thirty years ago, gold at the customary ratio fell to a discount in the twin metal.

[1] Ample testimony supporting this opinion will be found in the author's "History of the Precious Metals," chap. xxix.

CHAPTER XVII.

BANK SUSPENSIONS SINCE THE ERA OF PRIVATE COINAGE

Suspensions of Bank of England—Samuel Bernard—Bank of France—Bank of Venice—Bank of Stockholm—Bank of Copenhagen—Bank of Austria—Bank of Russia—United States Banks—Caisse d'Escompte—Bank of Amsterdam—Bank of Ireland—Bank of Portugal—Bank of Genoa—Banks of Prussia—Specie Banks of Copenhagen—Pontifical Banks—Banks of Brazil—Country Banks in England—Argentine Confederation Banks—Banks of Issue in Ireland—Bank of San Carlo—English Private Banks—Banks in Papal States—Banks of Brazil—Planters' Bank—Bank of the United States—Turkey—Russia—Peru—Argentine—State Banks of United States—Sonta & Co., of Brazil—Overend, Gurney & Co.—Banca Romana—Austrian Banks—Bank of Spain—Bank of France—Baring Brothers—Bank of Portugal.

SUSPENSIONS of banks of issue under the system of private coinage and of private issues of circulating notes:

1696. Bank of England stopped payment of its notes two years after it started (McCulloch, "Dict. Com.," ed. 1844). Resumed 1698.

1714. Philip V. stopped payment of his treasury bills and caused the failure of Samuel Bernard, the principal banker in Europe.

1717. Bank of France stopped payment and scaled its prodigious issues down to a mere fraction of their face value ("Mon. and Civ.," p. 238).

1717. Bank of Venice failed before it became a bank of issue; it stopped payment again this year when it was a bank of issue.

1718. Bank of Stockholm stopped payment of its issues.

1745. Run on the Bank of England thwarted by the device of paying in shillings and sixpence (McCulloch, 78).

1745. Bank of Copenhagen stopped payment of its issues.

1762. Bank of Austria stopped payment of its issues.

1766. Money of India changed from copper and bullon to silver, causing a great withdrawal of silver money from Russia, Scandinavia, the Netherlands, England, etc., and many bank failures in those countries.

1768. Bank of Russia (originally Bank of Assignats) stopped payment of its issues; 1796, stopped again; resumed in 1843 at the rate of one silver rouble for $3\frac{1}{2}$ paper; stopped payment again in 1854 and has not since resumed. The circulating money of Russia at the present time consists entirely of inconvertible paper notes and base silver and copper coins.

1775. Bank failures in the United States.

1783. France. The Caisse d'Escompte stopped payment ot its issues; in 1787 it stopped again; in 1793 the National Convention swept it out of existence, and supplanted its dishonored notes with assignats ("Mon. and Civ.," p. 243).

1789. Bank failures in France.

1790. The Bank of Amsterdam, which was popularly supposed to have a coin behind every one of its issues, a belief in which Adam Smith concurred, was discovered to be destitute of any coin reserve whatever, and hopelessly insolvent.

1793. One-third of all the English banks of issues stopped payment (McCulloch).

1796. Bank of Russia stopped (see 1768.)

1797. Scarcity of silver coins in England relieved by the issue of Spanish dollars and other silver coins countermarked or minted by the Bank.

1797. February 26th. The Bank of England stopped payment of its issues for twenty-four years, when it commenced to redeem its own notes at a discount. During the process of redemption, England, being a creditor State, drew so heavily upon the stocks of coins in other States as to compel their banks also to stop payment. This occurred in almost every State in Europe and America. In short, the perturbation caused by the change from copper to silver money in India lasted until the opening of California, a period of nearly ninety years.

1797. Bank of Ireland stopped payment of its issues (McCulloch).

1797. Bank of Portugal stopped payment of its issues ("Mon. and Civ.," p. 138).

1797. Bank of Venice stopped payment of its issues. This was its third failure (see above). The bank was finally wound up in 1808 ("Mon. and Civ.," p. 36).

1798. The euphemistic character of the term "free coinage," when applied to the coinage of England under the Act of 1666 (this being virtually a monopoly of the Bank), is thus exemplified by Mr. Hawkins:— "In the year 1798, in consequence of the extreme scarcity of silver money, Messrs. Dorrien and Magens sent a quantity of bullion to the Mint to be coined, according to the law, which had never been repealed, by which it was enacted that any one sending bullion to the Mint might have it coined into money upon the payment of certain dues. The whole was actually coined into shillings, . . . but the very day on which the bankers were by appointment to have received the coin, an Order of Council was received commanding it all to be melted, upon the ground that the proceeding had been irregular, and that no coinage was lawful without the sanction of royal proclamation. Very few indeed of these pieces escaped the crucible. Specimens, however, exist in the collection of the British Museum."

1800. Bank of Austria, originally Bank of Vienna, stopped payment of its issues. In 1810 an abortive attempt was made to "resume" in "redemption notes" at 3 for 1; 1810, abortive resumption in "anticipation notes" at 5 for 1; 86, the newly established Bank of Austria bought up the now demonetized "anticipation notes" at their market value. In the midst of this operation the new bank suspended coin payments ("Money and Civilization," p. 333). Resumed in 1824, when the remaining "anticipation notes" were retired at 2½ for 1. 1848. Suspension of coin payments, which still continues, the currency of Austria consisting entirely of paper notes and minor silver and copper coins. Preparations are now (1895) being made to "resume" with gold coins. With this professed object a loan of £40,000,000 gold is announced to have been negotiated with the Rothschilds.

1800. Bank of Genoa (or House of St. George) stopped payment of its issues. It had been a bank of issue since 1673 ("Money and Civilization," p 40).

1801. Germany. The Banks of Prussia and many other states stopped payment of their issues in consequence of the losses and apprehensions occasioned by the Napoleonic wars. This monetary disturbance on the Continent was soon after reflected in England and America.

1804. Judging from the issuance of Spanish dollars

countermarked "Bank of England, 1804," and "Five-shilling dollar," the royal prerogative of coinage appears to have been again exercised by the Bank.

1804. Specie-Bank of Copenhagen stopped payment of its issues.

1810. Hundreds of banks stopped payment of their issues in England, the United States and other commercial states; the consequence of monetary disturbance on the Continent.

1811. July 11th. The Bank of England again exercised the royal prerogative by striking 3s. and 1s. 6d. silver coins. Legend, "Georgius III., Dei Gratiâ Rex. . . . Bank token, 3s., 1811" (to 1816). Gross weight 227 English grains (Keary's Henfrey, p. 264).

1816. British mints closed to the private coinage of silver, unless reopened by royal proclamation. No such proclamation was issued down to 1870.

1814—1819—1825. During this period nearly all the private banks of issue in the United States stopped payment, owing to the drain of coins to supply the Bank of England. Reports of Gallatin and Crawford, Secretaries of the Treasury.

1820. Ecclesiastical States. The pontifical banks, Dello Spirito Santo and Monte di Pietá, stopped payment of their issues, owing to the drain of metal to England. All payments above 5 scudi were made in the inconvertible (legal-tender) notes of these institutions, which were at a discount in coins.

1821. Bank of Brazil stopped payment of its issues ("Money and Civilization," p. 155).

1825. To save itself from the discredit of having to again "suspend," the Bank of England issued as money a million of £1 and £2 notes accidentally found in a box (McCulloch, "Dict. Com.," p. 81).

1825. Seventy country banks in England stopped payment of their issues.

1826. Above a hundred country banks in England stopped payment. The Duke of Wellington, who was in the Cabinet this year, said that but for the strenuous exertions of the Rothschilds the Bank must have stopped payment ("Notes of Conversations with the Duke of Wellington," by Philip, fifth earl of Stanhope, p. 211).

1826. Argentine Confederation (La Plata). All the banks stopped payment of their issues. In 1866 "resumption" takes place at 25 for 1; 1876, suspension of resumption; 1881, resumption of "resumption;" 1891, suspension of resumption. At the present time (1895) the currency of the Argentine consists entirely of inconvertible paper notes, with minor coins for small change.

1828. Between 1804 and this year all but eight of the banks of issue in Ireland (about fifty in number) stopped payment (Sir H. Parnell, "Observations on Paper Money").

1829. Spain, July 9th. Bank of San Carlo stopped payment of its issues ("Money and Civilization," p. 117).

1830. Between 1809 and 1830, 311 English private and provincial banks stopped payment (McCulloch, p. 95). The report of the Secret Committee appointed by the House of Commons in 1836 showed a most disgraceful state of affairs (McCulloch, p. 96).

1834. Bank of England notes made legal-tender (except from the Bank) for all sums above £5 (McCulloch).

1835. Banks in the Papal States suspended (Kelly, p. 293).

1835. Brazil. All the banks stopped payment of their issues, and have never since resumed. The currency of Brazil consists entirely of paper notes, with nickel and copper coins for small change.

1837. About May 1st. Louisiana. Planters' Bank stopped payment of its issues, and caused the failure of J. L. and S. I. Joseph, agents for the Rothschilds in New York. The stoppage of this great house, with assets aggregating over seven million dollars, precipitated the fall of all the banks in the United States.

1837. May 10-16. United States. The removal of the government deposits from the banks, the enforcement of the law requiring collectors of the revenue to refuse all except government money, and the failure of the Josephs precipitated a crisis, in which fell the (second) Bank of the United States (a private bank with governmental patronage), together with about eight hundred branches and country banks, all of which stopped payment of their issues.

1839. After a temporary resumption, the Bank of the United States, and with it all the country banks, stopped again. General resumption took place about 1845; but the effects of this wide-spread disaster were observable for more than twenty years.

1841. United States. Out of the convulsion of 1837 the Bank of the United States was the first to raise its head (1839), but it failed again, and finally, in 1841, when the government withdrew its patronage.

1842. United States. Between 1830 and 1842 no fewer than 311 banks of issue succumbed in the United States, precisely the same number as failed in England between 1809 and 1830 (see above) (McCulloch, p. 114).

1847. England. Run on Bank of England. October 25th, Bank Act suspended.

1848. Bank of France stopped payment of its issues (Tooke, "Hist. Prices," vi., p. 48; "Mon. Civ.," p. 264).

1848. Bank of Austria stopped payment of its issues (see above).

1848. England. Numerous English provincial banks stopped coin payments (Morier Evans).

1850. Buenos Ayres. All the banks stopped payment.

1853. Russia stopped payment (see above, sub anno 1768).

1854. Turkey stopped payment.

1857. England. Commercial panic and run on the Bank of England. November 12th the Bank Act again suspended.

1857. United States. In consequence of the panic in London, and the withdrawal of metal to support the Bank of England, nearly every private bank of issue in the United States was compelled to "suspend." However, in the course of a few months they all resumed again.

1857. Peru and Argentine stopped payment.

1861. United States. In April, 1861, the Civil War broke out; in August the Federal government borrowed from the private banks chartered under state laws $50,000,000—coin; on December 28, 1861 (so little coin was there left in the country), the most important of these banks stopped coin payment of their issues, whereupon all the rest (some 1800 in number) followed suit. The combined circulation of these banks, of which not one-fifth was ever redeemed, amounted to over $400,000,000. The existing private banks of issue, called "National" banks, were chartered by the Federal government under the Act of 1864, and their issues are secured by a deposit of government stock with the Treasurer of the United States.

1864. Failure of Souta & Co., of Rio Janeiro. This precipitated the failure of the Bank of Brazil and several other Brazilian (private) banks of issue. Whereupon the government took the note issues into its own hands. There have since been no failures ("Mon. and Civ.," p. 159).

1866. May 10th. England. Failure of Overend, Gurney & Co., Limited. A commercial panic occurred in London on the following day.

1866. Italy. During the war with Austria the Italian treasury and banks stopped payment in coin, the former issuing corso forzali, in which the latter redeemed their issues. In 1876 Italy borrowed £16,000,000 in gold, with which to resume coin payments. By the year 1893 this money found its way out of the country; a number of banks, including the Banca Romana, failed; and to-day there is but little money to be seen in circulation besides inconvertible paper and minor silver and copper coins.

1866. Austrian banks suspended payment.

1868. Spain. The Republic adopted the Figuerola law, similar to that of the Latin Union, although it was opposed by the Bank of Spain. So far as the coinage of gold is concerned, it was never carried out. The monarchy was restored under Amadeo in 1870; it fell in 1873, and a new Republic was set up in 1874, whereupon the Bank of Spain stopped coin payment of its issues. Since resumed in silver.

1870. Bank of France suspended coin payment of its issues ("Mon. and Civ.," p. 264). Resumed in gold, 1880.

1873. September 18th. Panic in New York, owing

to greenback contraction. Temporary suspension of coin or other legal-tender payments by over two thousand banks throughout the United States. The Treasury issued twenty million dollars of additional greenbacks, the panic was allayed, and the banks "resumed" (in greenbacks) soon afterward.

1874. Suspension of the Bank of Spain (see above).

1875. August 3rd. The banks of Peru suspended coin payment of their issues.

1875. Turkey suspended.

1876. May 6th. Argentina. General suspension of all the banks. Gold coins 30 per cent premium in "redemption" notes; since increased to 250 per cent premium.

1878. City of Glasgow and West of England banks stopped coin payments.

1885. Greece suspended

1890. November. Baring Brothers, one of the principal bankers and the largest bill-drawers in the world, stopped payment. This caused a wide-spread panic, in which numerous banking institutions fell both in England and other countries.

1890. December. The demands on the Bank of England caused the public discussion of a "Restriction Order," or suspension of the Bank Act. The crisis was allayed by the timely loan of £3,000,000 gold from the Bank of France, influenced by the Rothschilds.

1891. Bank of Portugal stopped coin payments of its issues.

CHAPTER XVIII.

EXISTING MONETARY SYSTEMS.

France and the Latin Union—Germany—Great Britain—Portugal and Brazil—Scandinavia—Japan—History of Financial Legislation in the United States—Holland—Italy—Spain—Russia—Austro-Hungary—Turkey—British India—China—Argentine Republic—Chili

France and the Latin Union.—A conference between "the four states whose monetary system rests on a numeration by francs," viz., France, Belgium, Switzerland and Italy, resulted in the Latin Monetary Union of December 23rd, 1865, taking effect August 1st, 1866. It provided for uniform coins; the unlimited private coinage of gold coins and of silver 5-franc pieces, both 0.900 fine, both to be full legal-tenders; and for a restricted coinage of subsidiary silver pieces 0.835 fine with a legal-tender limit of 50 francs. "Unlimited private coinage for nothing, or at brassage, logically means one metal, and that one metal means the dearer one, on account of the higher *ad valorem* cost of (not the charge for) coining the cheaper one. Accordingly, when the international delegates met again (June 17th, 1867), although the convention was called ostensibly only to unify the coinages, it discussed the entire monetary question, and, as the natural result of a discussion which omitted all reference to the origin, history and operation of the British Act of 1666, carried a resolution in favor of what is called gold monometallism."[1] This resolution was soon afterwards engrafted upon the legislation of the States which agreed to the Latin

[1] "Money and Civilization," p 275, where a full account appears of the origin and progress of this movement.

Union, in the shape of a *New Mint Code*, which now (1867) included the States of the Church, Greece and Roumania; whilst efforts were made to popularize it in Great Britain, Germany and the United States.[1] In 1873, after the Franco-Prussian war (and, as it was pretended, in reply to the previous gold monometallic legislation of Germany in 1871, for which see below), France and the Latin Union limited the (State) coinage of silver five-franc pieces, without, however, limiting the legal-tender of the pieces already coined. The net result of these measures is that at the present time (1895) nearly all the gold of the various Latin Union states is accumulated in France. There is but little in Belgium or Roumania, and none in Switzerland, Italy or Greece; the currency of these States consisting chiefly of paper notes and silver or subsidiary coins. On the other hand, the currency of France consists of gold and silver coins and Bank of France notes, backed by a reserve consisting of £70,000,000 gold and £50,000,000 silver, coined at $15\frac{1}{2}$ to 1 gold. The gold reserves of the Bank are substantially a war-fund.

Germany.—The gold movement of 1866 is described on p. 377. On October 20th, 1868, a commercial convention (Handels-tag) was held in Berlin, at which were represented 119 German cities. The subject of money was discussed at length; and although not the slightest reference was made to the origin, history, or operation of Private Coinage, a resolution in favor of that measure was adopted in the following words: "Res. 3. Monetary unity, and at the same time such a general monetary reform as befits the age, can be brought about by the simultaneous adoption by all the German States of the single standard with full application of the decimal system, in pursuance of the principles recommended by

[1] "Money and Civilization," pp. 276-7.

the International Monetary Conference at Paris in its Report of July 6th, 1867." (Mon. and Civ.," p. 276.) Private Coinage is involved in the term "single standard," which, like "double standard," "bimetallism," etc., implies that metal is money; whereas this can only even seemingly be the case when Private Coinage is permitted. The military events of 1870 led to the imperial federation of the German States, April 16th, 1871. On December 4th, 1871, an Act was passed which provisionally established the "double standard" at 15½; stopped the further Private Coinage of full legal-tender silver, without demonetizing or retiring such of these coins (thalers) as had already been coined; ordered a new coinage of gold pieces of full legal-tender; and made provision, without setting a time, for the retirement of the thalers whenever the Chancellor of the Empire *should see fit*. By the Act of July 9th, 1873, definite provision was made for the establishment of the "gold standard," not without leaving the door open to the renewal of the "double standard," should such a policy be deemed expedient. This was done by permitting the thaler silver coins to remain in circulation as full legal-tenders, at three marks each. A similar prudential measure, that of trusting the Executive with the power to alter these enactments, was incorporated in the British Monetary Law of 1816. The power granted by Congress to the American Executive—that of exercising the option to make payments out of the Treasury in either gold or silver coins—is of quite a different character. The German Act of 1873 suspended the Private Coinage of silver. All new silver coins were limited in tender to 20 marks. All old silver coins were called in, melted down and sold as bullion. At the present time the currency consists of gold and silver coins and bank notes, in the proportions shown on a previous page. The gold at Spandau and a portion of the reserve held by the Bank, is substantially a war-fund.

Great Britain.—In 1774 (14 George III., c. 42), in consequence of the prevalence of light or underweight silver coins, they were limited in tender to £25. This was continued by various Acts down to 1797, in which year (38 George III., c. 59) the private coinage of silver was suspended. The Act of 1816 (56 George III., c. 68) was passed during a suspension of coin payments (except of such minor coins as were issued or countermarked by the Bank of England, for an account of which see *ante*). By this Act the mints were closed to the private coinage of silver, and all silver coins, whether light or heavy, were limited in tender to 40s. In section 9 it was provided that "from and after such day as shall be named and appointed in and by any proclamation which shall be made and issued for that purpose by or on behalf of his Majesty, by and with the advice of his Majesty's Privy Council," such legislation might be revoked. Down to 1870 no such proclamation was ever issued. In that year a *New Mint Code* was enacted, section 11 of which provided that her Majesty, "with the advice of her Privy Council from time to time by proclamation (may) do all or any of the following things, namely, to regulate any matters relative to the coinage and the mint *within the present prerogative of the Crown*, which are not provided for by this Act." The present prerogative of the Crown does not empower it to revoke the silver demonetization of 1816. There is no mistaking the identity of that golden thread which runs through the Latin Union Mint Codes of 1867, the British Mint Code of 1870, the German Mint code of 1871, and, as will presently be seen, the new Mint Code of the United States, of 1873, and the Codes of numerous other countries enacted soon afterwards. It is of precisely the *same tissue* in all of them. The present currency of Great Britain consists of gold (full tender) and silver coins (limited tender) and Bank of England notes of £5 and upwards. These last are full legal-tenders, except from the Bank itself.

Portugal and Brazil.—It was largely through the working of the Methuen Treaty (1703) that Portugal in 1854 copied the British system of 1816, suspended the Private Coinage of silver, limited the legal-tender of silver coins to five milreis, and ostentatiously declared the British sovereign a full legal-tender in Portugal. These regulations should never have been made. Neither before nor since their enactment have gold payments been customary in Portugal. This is proved by the course of exchange between Lisbon and London. The actual legal-tender was called "lei," and it consisted of a fixed proportion of coins, chiefly silver and copper, and of paper notes.[1] Such few gold coins as were formerly included in "lei" have since disappeared from the country. At present legal-tender is made altogether in the inconvertible paper notes issued by the Bank of Portugal. These, together with subsidiary coins, form the actual currency of the State. The monetary situation in Brazil is somewhat similar; nor has the commerce of either country suffered any harm in consequence. The foreign merchants of Lisbon and Rio Janeiro keep their accounts in £. s. d., quote the local paper money at a discount, and wear tall black hats in midsummer. Certain of these circumstances are gravely set forth in the Report of the Director of the United States Mints for 1894, as though they had to do with the monetary systems of Portugal and Brazil.

[1] "Mon. and Civ." p. 136.

In like manner the Chinese merchants of San Francisco keep their accounts in taels, mace and candareen, in which they mark the fluctuations of American gold, and wear plaited pigtails all the year round. Such is their pleasure; but as yet it has not been observed to have had any marked effect upon the monetary system of the United States of America.

Scandinavia.—On September 20th, 1872, a monetary union was adopted by Sweden, Norway and Denmark, which was followed by a *New Mint Code*, whose provisions took effect in 1873 and 1875. Under this code the private coinage of silver was suspended, and the legal-tender of silver coins limited to five "specie riksdalers." At the present time the currency consists chiefly of silver coins and bank notes.

Japan.—In 1872 this state adopted a *New Mint Code*, forbade the Private Coinage of silver, limited the legal-tender of silver yens or dollars and of all minor coins, and adopted what is known as "the gold standard." In 1878 (May 27), after "the gold standard" had duly departed from the country, the full legal-tender of silver coins was restored and Private Coinage again permitted. In 1883 a public loan issued in Japan, originally payable in gold or silver coins, was made specifically payable in silver coins.[1] In 1894 the Private Coinage of silver was again suspended.[2] The currency is entirely of silver coins and government and bank notes.

United States of America.—The Act of 1792 provided for the coinage of a silver dollar to contain $371\frac{1}{4}$ grains of fine silver and of multiples of a dollar to contain 24.745 grains fine gold. These coins were to be struck substantially free of expense for and on account of such persons as might choose to employ the mint for that

[1] From 1872 to 1893 nine-thirteenths of all the gold struck since the first named date left the country. "British For. Office Report," 1893, No. 315, p. 9. [2] London "Times," January 28th, 1895.

purpose; thus establishing private coinage at a ratio of value between the precious metals, in the coins, of 15 for 1. In addition to these coins the silver dollars of Spain and her American vice-royalties, besides several other less important foreign coins were made full legal-tenders in the United States at rates regulated by their contents of metal as compared with the American dollar. As a matter of fact the principal coins in circulation down to 1853 were the Spanish and Spanish-American silver dollars and their fractional parts. In 1834, when the gold mines of the Alleghany Range had become productive (they were worked by slaves), and had given rise to something more than the nominal coinage of gold which had preceded that event, it was observed that the ratio of 15 for 1 was out of harmony with the prices paid for the precious metals at the mints of Spain, France and other European states. As Spanish coins were the principal ones in circulation in the United States, the ratio was changed to (approximately) 16 for 1, by lowering the American gold dollar to 23.22 grains fine metal; the American silver dollar (same contents as the Spanish silver dollar) remaining unchanged. In 1853 the American fractional coins (parts of the silver dollar) were debased in fineness and limited in tender to five dollars. In 1857 the foreign coins were lowered in legal-tender value; whereupon they soon after ceased to circulate. In April, 1861, the Southern States seceded from the Union and civil war ensued. On December 28, 1861, the "State banks" of issue (private corporations organized under the laws of the various States) stopped payment, and then notes, which at that time formed almost the only circulating money of the country, fell into discredit, and were either accepted at a discount or refused altogether. On February 25, 1862, the Federal government passed an act authorizing the issue of Treasury notes ("greenbacks"), which were payable in themselves and therefore irredeemable. In 1864 the Federal government passed the "National Banking Act," which was designed to change the private banks, incorporated by the States into private banks incorporated by the general government. To promote this object they were offered several advantages, among them, their notes (to be issued upon the security of Federal bonds) were to be made legal-tenders to and from the government. This plan was successfully and rapidly carried out. Until the close of the war and for several years afterwards, the notes of these "national" banks and those of the United States Treasury (greenbacks), of which latter there were several issues and several kinds, formed the only money in circulation. The customs duties were levied in coins and these were used in payment of the interest on the Federal bonds. The surplus coins (if any) were sold by the government for greenbacks. Beside the greenbacks, which amounted to about four hundred million dollars and which may be regarded as a debt, or not, according to the construction placed upon the legislation of the period, the Federal government had contracted debts, funded and unfunded, chiefly the former, to the amount of nearly three thousand million dollars, according to the Report of the Revenue Commissioner, S. S. Hayes. In 1865-6, the funded portion of this debt had been contracted in and all of it sold for greenbacks, at an average of less than forty cents to the coined dollar. About one-half of this debt (chiefly in six per cent and five per cent bonds, with interest payable optionally in gold or silver coins) was held in Europe, chiefly in France, England or the Netherlands, or else on European account.

Under Code Napoleon, articles 1895 and 1897, all debts of money in France were payable in such money as was current on the day of payment. Under the Civil and Common laws, as laid down by Sir Matthew Hale (State Trials, the Case of the Mixed Moneys), the same rule was maintained in England. Indeed a similar principle will be found in the legislation or jurisprudence of all Christian States. But this did not satisfy the foreign holders of the American war bonds, who, fearing that the debt might be paid in greenbacks, had never ceased to clamor for the retirement of that money. Failing in this object, they employed every means to secure payment of the bonds in a better money than that in which they had paid for them; and in this endeavor they eventually succeeded. The steps will now be described by which the debt, in accordance with their demands, was practically made payable in gold coins only and of a fixed weight and fineness. For this valuable concession no consideration was ever paid to the government.

In 1868, one of the two great national parties having declared itself favorable to the retention of the greenback in the circulation, it was suddenly deserted by its leaders on the eve of the Presidential election and, as a consequence, defeated at the polls. The Chairman of the National Committee of this party was August Belmont, who was also the agent in New York of the great European house of Rothschild. The signal of desertion, known as "The Betrayal," was given by Manton Marble, editor of *The New York World*, the trusted organ of the party.

In March, 1869, Mr. Robert Schenck, better known in connection with the Emma mine and the author of a handbook on the game of "poker," secured the passage of a bill which made the debt of the United States, at that time nominally about $3,000,000,000, payable in "coins" of a fixed weight and fineness. The *New Mint Code* of February 12th, 1873, c. 131, destroyed the Private Coinage of silver by indirection, in omitting the word "dollar" from the empowering clause relating to silver coins. After this, in codifying the Statutes generally, December 1st, 1873, sec. 3586, the Code Commissioners made an unauthorized and unwarranted alteration of the law by limiting the legal-tender of "all" silver coins, including the outstanding silver dollars, which, together with Spanish silver dollars, had been full legal-tenders since the foundation of the Republic. Both of these Acts (of 1873) were passed during a suspension of coin payments, and without eliciting public attention. The Monetary Commission of 1876 reported that the Mint Code of February 12th, 1873, was "not read except by title;" that President Grant, who signed it, "had no knowledge of what it really accomplished in relation to the demonetization of silver," as was evinced by his public letter of October 3rd, 1873; and that the design of demonetization was (afterwards) completed by an obscure provision of law upon an erroneous assurance from the Committee on Revision of the Statutes. (Report, pp. 89-90.) This surreptitious legislation was not discovered, nor did it attract public attention until 1875-6. In 1878 (Bland Act) the full legal-tender of silver dollars was restored, but not Private Coinage. Under the rulings of the Secretary of the Treasury the legal-tender of silver dollars has been so far rendered nugatory that all demands upon the Treasury have been met in gold coins. With regard to the demonetization of silver which was accomplished by the two Acts of 1873, Mr. Carlisle, since Secretary of the

Treasury, said in the House of Representatives, February 21st, 1878: "The conspiracy which seems to have been formed here and in Europe to destroy by legislation and otherwise from three-sevenths to one-half of the metallic money of the world, is the most gigantic crime of this or any other age. The consummation of such a scheme would ultimately entail more misery upon the human race than all the wars, pestilences and famines that ever occurred in the history of the world." It will be observed that in every monetary convention which followed that of 1865 the professed object was the unification of money, whilst the one actually accomplished was the demonetization of silver; that in every case the means employed was indirection and secrecy; and that the vehicle used was always a *New Mint Code*. Mr. John Jay Knox, one of the officials who in 1869-70 lent his assistance to the preparation of the American Mint Code, when the matter was brought home to him acknowledged his part in it, and boasted that he was "proud of his work."[1] No one will begrudge him the distinction it confers. The net result of this measure upon the American currency is that it now consists chiefly of paper notes. The silver dollars are chiefly held in the Treasury, in place of "silver notes" in circulation. Gold coins, except in the mining States of the Far West, are not in circulation. The Treasury continues to pay gold money by borrowing it from time to time upon new issues of Government bonds. This is the same policy laid down in the British Mint Code of April 4th, 1870, section 9. Owing to the limitations placed upon the silver and paper issues of the United States, and to the readiness of the American Treasury to pay gold money on demand, gold coins command no premium.

[1] London "Economist," December 26th, 1885.

Holland.—The laws of May 21st, 1873, and June 6th, 1875, suspended the Private Coinage of silver, and limited the legal-tender of silver coins to ten florins. The currency is now chiefly of silver coins and paper notes.

Italy.—Under a renewal of the Latin Monetary Union dated January 31st, 1874, and the law of July 17th, 1875, the Crown suspended the Private Coinage of silver, and limited the legal-tender of silver coins to 50 lira. To maintain those payments in gold coins to which it had committed itself, the State afterwards (1882) borrowed £16,000,000 in gold, all of which, together with what gold was previously in the kingdom, has since disappeared, leaving the State pledged to pay in gold, without any gold with which to pay. The circulating money of Italy now consists entirely of subsidiary silver and copper coins and of paper issues, gold commanding a premium of 5 to 10 per cent in paper.

Spain.—The Republic of 1868 (Figuerola Law, October 19th) was induced to copy the provisions of the Latin Monetary Union so far as to adopt gold coins for unlimited money, and to limit the legal-tender of silver coins. These regulations survived the Republic, the monarchy of Amadeo, 1870, the restoration of the Republic in 1874, and the restoration of the monarchy (Alfonso) in 1875. The law of August 20th, 1876, suspended the Private Coinage of silver, except as to metal produced by the mines of Spain. This last-named provision has since been abrogated, whilst the suspension of Private Coinage continues. But its gold having left the country, the State was obliged to reinvest the silver pesos (five-peseta or five-franc pieces) with full legal-tender power, which attribute they now enjoy. The minor silver coins are limited in legal-tender to ten pesos. The currency consists entirely of silver coins and Bank of Spain notes, in which gold coins command a premium of about 20 per cent.

Russia.—The law of November 13-25, 1876, adopted gold coins as sole full legal-tenders, and reduced the legal-tender of silver coins to 5 roubles 15 copeks, no Private Coinage of silver being permitted.[1] The result of these measures has been that gold coins are at a premium of 50 per cent, while the currency consists entirely of subsidiary silver coins and Bank of Russia notes. The gold held by the bank does not enter the circulation, and is substantially a war-fund.

Austro-Hungary.—The decree of March, 1879, suspended the Private Coinage of silver, but did not limit the legal-tender of silver coins.[2] The law of 1892 ordered the discontinuance of the coinage of four and eight gulden (gold) pieces, and substituted the gold kroner of 0.304878 grammes, or 4.7 English grains fine, equal in legal value to half a florin—a nominal step toward uniformity with the franc system, because the real money of the country consists, and has consisted for a long period, only of subsidiary silver coins and paper notes. The Private Coinage of kroners is not permitted, so that the State has largely resumed the prerogative of coinage. The ratio between the kroners and the silver coins is 13.69 for 1. Provision has also been made for a foreign gold loan of £40,000,000, with which *it is stated* to be the intention of the government to make gold payments in kroners, as sole full legal-tenders.

Turkey.—No Private Coinage is permitted in this State. In 1882 full legal-tender was limited to gold coins, but, except as to Constantinople and some other large cities, and except as to customs duties, the "be-

[1] "Money and Civilization," pp. 314, 320.   [2] Ibid., p. 340.

shlik" system of silver coins (0.830 fine) has since been substantially restored. A full account of "beshlik" money will be found in "Money and Civilization," chap. xix. The present currency consists of "beshlik" silver, together with paper notes.

British India.—An order in Council, dated 23rd June, 1893, suspended the Private Coinage of silver, but otherwise made no important change in the monetary system. Silver rupees therefore remain full legal-tenders for all purposes and any amount. These and the note issues of the Currency Department constitute the currency of the country.

China.—The currency of this State consists of bronze coins. In 1834 silver was surreptitiously coined at Fukien, and a few years later in Canton, as well as in the district of Shunlik, south of Canton. These issues, however, have since disappeared. The only lawful moneys of the Empire are the familiar bronze "tchen" or "chuen." These, the sixteenth century Portuguese called sapecas, and the English now call cash. One thousand of these make, in value, a tael of (bronze) money. In a mediæval Chinese scale of equivalents a tael of money meant a tael (coin) of silver, which coin contained something like what is now known as a tael weight of silver. But the tael of 1,000 chuen has no longer any relation to silver. The present cash system would resemble that of the Roman nummulary system of B. C. 369, mentioned in Chap. I., but for the fact that the Roman nummi were limited and overvalued, whilst cash, at all events at present, do not command more than their value as metal. There is another and still more important difference; the Chinese cash are open to Private Coinage, but the Roman nummi were not. The fall in value of the Chinese cash is due either to over issues or to counterfeiting. The cash of to-day should each weigh 54.7 English grains (8 to the avoirdupois ounce), and contain 54 per cent of copper, 42¾ per cent zinc, and 3¼ per cent lead, but they vary in composition according to the mineral or metallic resources of the various provinces in which they are cast. In the early part of the present century the annual authorized or reported issues of chuen seem to have been about 1,200,000,000, worth 1,200,000 money taels.[1] In 1865 the authorized or reported issues were 2,460,-000,000 chuen, worth 2,460,000 money taels,[2] but this may have been an exceptional year. In certain provinces, and for periods of ten, fifteen, or twenty years, the authorized issues of chuen have been entirely suspended.[3] The unauthorized coinage and the counterfeiting of cash are made capital offenses;[4] but none of these regulations are believed to be strictly observed.

Several efforts have been made by the Imperial government to supersede the chuen system, which, since the decline of the symbols to their metallic value, has ceased to possess any "economical" merit beyond that of non-exportability. These efforts have hitherto been without success, the chief obstacle in the way being Private Coinage and the profit and power which it confers. The question of safety to the State is, however, of great importance in this connection.

In 1845 (Opium war) the Emperor Taoukwang caused silver dollars to be cast at Hangchow and Formosa. They were called Soldiers' Pay, a name that indicates their use. These were afterward so cleverly imitated in base metal by the private coiners that they lost credit and disappeared from circulation. In 1853 (Taiping Rebellion), owing to the scarcity of copper, large issues

[1] "H. M. A.," p. 41; "Chinese Repository," ii., p. 279.
[2] Dr. S. W. Bushell in "Jour. N. C. Branch of Royal Asiatic Soc.," 1880, N. S., No. xv.   [3] "H. M. A.," p. 40.   [4] Ibid., p. 37.

of iron chuen were made, but these were soon rendered useless by the abundance of counterfeits, an industry in which, odd to relate, the so-called Budhist (really Taoist) monks made themselves prominent. Popular dissatisfaction with these coins gave rise to some disturbance at Pekin in 1857. With poetic justice they are now only used for pious offerings at Taoist shrines. During the Taiping rebellion the rebel Emperor (Hun-seu-tseun) issued silver coins, with the legend "Sacred money of the Tai'ping."[1] These, of course, have disappeared. At the same time the imperial government (1852, or third year of Hieng-fung) issued two classes of paper notes: first, to represent the bronze chuen; second, to represent Shanghai taels of silver bullion; in other words, two money taels of coined chuen for one tael weight of uncoined silver. For some unexplained reason (probably foreign counterfeiting) the chuen notes fell in 1861 (first year of Toung-che) to 3 per cent of their face value, or 97 per cent discount. In 1880 they were only worth 10 per cent of their face value, or 90 per cent discount. Being receivable, as recited on their face, "for the purchase of titles of rank," they retained some value on account of this ignoble function. The fate of the silver notes has not been related, but they probably fell from the same cause—forgery by foreigners. After these unsuccessful experiments the monetary system relapsed into its previous condition, namely, that of bronze coins, reduced by excessive issues, or else successful counterfeiting, to their commodity value; and such is the system to-day. In 1887 certain Chinese officials ordered a number of

[1] This pretender was born at Quang-si about 1815, died by suicide at Nanking, June 30th, 1864. "He announced himself as the restorer of the worship of the true god, Shang-ti, . . . the brother of Jesus and the second Son of God." Besides the name of Hun-seu-tseun, he assumed that of Tien-teh, or Celestial Virtue, besides many others (Haydn).

coin presses from Birmingham. These are employed at the present time (1895) by the viceroys of Kwang-tung (Canton) and other provinces in striking silver coins for soldiers' pay; but as yet the introduction of silver money into China has been comparatively limited. It is, however, going on at an accelerated rate.

Large sums of money—and at the Treaty ports, and with or amongst foreigners, all sums—are stipulated to be paid in foreign silver coins, or in silver bullion measured by the tael weight, of which there are several local varieties, the most popular being the Shanghai "currency tael." This consists of a Shanghai or Chauping tael weight (565.7 English grains) of ingot silver, $\frac{11}{12}$ fine, equal to 518.56 grains fine silver, or 1.39$\frac{2}{3}$ American silver dollars, mint value. This tael is identical in weight with the European silver talent, thaler, or ducaton of the mediæval ages, and may have had the same origin. It is in this silver bullion (called shoo, from the shape of the ingots, and sycee, from their standard of fineness) that the recent Chinese 7 per cent customs mortgage silver loan was effected in London and Berlin, the exchange rate paid by the subscribers being 3s. English gold coin per Shanghai tael. Besides the proceeds of this loan and a few million taels deposited in banking-houses or private hoards, there is no silver money or bullion available for money in the Chinese empire. The seven hundred and fifty million dollars' worth of silver in China reported by the Director of the United States Mints (Report, 1894, p. 45) evinces the prodigious fertility of this gentleman's imagination, but has not the remotest relation to fact, the metallic currency of China consisting substantially of copper symbols.

Argentine Republic.—The law of September 29th, 1875, authorized the Private Coinage of gold, admitted certain foreign gold coins to full legal-tendership, limited the legal-tender of silver coins to twenty dollars, and forbade the Private Coinage of silver. Eight months afterward (May 16th, 1876) the government bank suspended coin payments, and gold coins rose to a premium of 30 per cent, since increased to about 250 per cent. The currency of the country is entirely of inconvertible paper and minor coins.

Chili.—Under the law of January 9th, 1851, the gold peso contained 21.1845 English grains fine, and the silver peso 347.22 grains fine metal, a ratio of about 16.4 for 1. The contents of these coins were repeated in the law of November 26th, 1892, which stopped the Private Coinage of silver, limited the legal-tender of silver pesos to 10 pesos, and (the actual money of the country consisting entirely of inconvertible notes and small change coins) provided for "resumption" on July 1st, 1896, in gold coins, at double their previous value in silver coins—a ratio of 32.8 for 1. On January 29th, 1895, the Senate passed an Act for the redemption of the paper currency on June 1st, 1895, at the rate of about 18d. English gold to the paper peso; but this Act yet awaits the approval of the Chamber of Deputies and the purchase of gold wherewith to make such payments, there being no gold coins in the country. The British sovereign, formerly legal-tender for five pesos, is now legal-tender for ten pesos; but this and all other enactments encouraging the currency of gold coins are as yet little more than dead letter.

From the foregoing recital it will be observed that the practical political outcome of the Gold Movement of 1865-73 has been to concentrate the gold coins of the world in the banks of four or five of the principal States, and that the currency of the remainder consists entirely, or chiefly, of silver coins and paper notes.

INDEX.

INDEX.

Aarlesden, 119, 255.
Abd-el-Melik, 56, 92, 126, 137, 147, 268.
Abd-el-Raman I., 126.
Abd-el-Raman II., 177.
Abd-el-Raman III., 126, 234.
Abstention from coining gold, 311.
Ace, 81, 99, 214.
Act of 1666 (see also Private Coinage), 320, 388.
Coinage), 320, 388.
Adam Smith (see Smith).
Adrian (see Hadrian).
Adulteration of Coins (see Tamperings and Forgeries), 194, 200, 211, 227, 321.
Aelfric, grammarian, 177, 183.
Africa, 130.
Agricola cited, 122, 153, 260.
Albata Coins, 205, 209, 211, 213.
Albuquerque, 322, 387.
Alchemist, 240.
Alexandria, 130.
Alfred, King of Wessex, 157, 174, 175, 311.
Alfred-Guthrum Treaty, 155, 160, 175.
Al-Hachem (see Hachem).
Alloys of Money (see Standard).
Al-Monstain-Billah, n., 177.
Alterations of Money, 179, 225, 228, 331, 338, 343.
Amber, 139.
America (see Spanish America, etc.), 128, 146, 245, 349, 350.
American Revolution (See Revolutions), 349.
Amsterdam, 292, 295.
Anachronical Moneys, 114, 117.
Anglo-Normans, 187.
Anglo-Saxons, 110, 151, 187, 311.
Antwerp, 314, 328.
Apotheoses, 388, 427.
Arabia (see Moslem), 105 n., 128, 161.

Arcadius and Honorius, Sov.-Ponts., 96, 98, 108, 111.
Archaeology, 161.
Argent, Argenti, Argento, Argentum, etc., 97, 202.
Argentina, 428.
Aristotle, pref., 384.
Arrian cited, 40.
Arsacidae, 118.
Arsura, 160.
Aryandes, 81.
Assays (see Pix), 216.
Assignats, 280, 292.
Athelred II., King of Wessex, 181.
Athelstan III., King of Wessex, 158, 179.
Attila, 262, 272.
Augustus (Octavius), Sov-Pont., 35, 100, 101, 125, 147, 148, 319, 424.
Aurar (see Ora), 111, 256.
Aureus, 154.
Austria, 315, 351, 370, 371, 424.
Austriki (see Iestia).

Bacchus, 131, 213.
Bahdr and Bahdrwick, 262, 266.
Baldwin III., 194.
Bangle (see Baug, Baugle, Rings, etc.).
Bank of Amsterdam, 331, 403.
Bank of England, 402, 415.
Bank of Stockholm, 292, 402.
Bank Suspensions, 402.
Banks and Bankers, 107, 292, 293, 303, 304, 322, 328, 330, 339, 352, 354, 400.
Bardewic, 262, 266.
Bargain, Silver Coin, 388.
Barter, 195, 384.
Base Coins (See Tamperings, &c.), 203, 207, 212, 216, 217, 219, 230.
Basileus, 71, 125, 199, 250, 253, 311, 319, 320, 357.

434 INDEX

Baugles (see Baugs), 115.
Baugs, or Ring-Money, 115, 116, 165, 255.
Bawbee, 258 n.
Beaumaris Castle, 216.
Benefices, 41.
Beornwulf, King of Mercia, 170.
Berbers of Africa, 131.
Berthulf, King of Mercia, 170.
Besant, Bezant, of Byzantine Solidus, 104, 185, 189, 194, 209, 212, 216, 235, 247, 250, 310, 342.
Bills of Exchange, 195, 228, 322.
Black Money, 233, 235, 329.
Blanc Silver and Blanc Money, 206.
Boodle, 258.
Boycott of Gold, 349; of Silver, 421.
Bramins, Laws of the, 80.
Brass Coins (see Copper).
Brazil, 416.
Bread, Measured by £. s. d., 98.
Britain, 120; Arabian remains in, 140; Coinages of, 120; Moneys of, 149, 139; productions of, 139; Roman Conquest of, 120.
British East India Company, 388.
Bronze Coins (see Copper).
Brunanburg, Battle, 179, 276.
Buccaneers, 289, 325, 326, 335.
Budhism, 427.
Bullet Money of Cochin, 116.
Bullion, Domestic and Foreign, 321.
"Bullion Money," 218, 288.
Bunge, 383.
Burgred, King of Mercia, 158, 170, 173.
Burgundy, 111, 314, 334.
Byzant (see Besant).
Byzantium, 91, 131, 189.

Caernarvon Castle, 216.
Caesar, Caius Julius, 34, 63, 70, 89, 90, 101, 119, 120, 145, 247, 256, 264, 265, 308, 319, 394, 397.
Calcott's "History of Spain," cited, 270.
California, Gold Scare, 338.
Canute, King of Mercia, Northumbria and Denmark, 183, 269.

Canute II., King of "England," 158, 273.
Caracalla, Sovereign-Pontiff, 37, 154, 257.
Carat, or Karat, 141-2.
Carausius, Joint Emperor of "the West," 100, 308, 333.
Carlovingian System, 63.
Cash, 425.
Castles, 216.
Caursina, 229.
Celts, 119.
Charlemagne, Emperor of Germany, 60, 105, 114, 153, 160, 170, 254, 263; 265, 266, 275, 308, 311, 312, 320, 334.
Charles Martel, 140.
Charles the Bald, 172, 334.
Charles I., King of England, 216.
Charles II., King of England (see Act of 1666), 388.
Charles V., Emperor of Germany, 315, 334-5, 349.
Charles IX., King of Sweden, 289.
Chevalier, Michel, cited, 370.
Child, Sir Josiah, cited, 326.
Childeric, 109.
Chili, 429.
China, 139, 195, 425.
Christ, Jesus, 56, 74, 135, 284, 427.
Christian Moneys, 104, 272, 310.
Christian II., King of Sweden, 277, 300.
Christiania, 255.
Christianity, 104, 130, 140, 173.
Christina, Queen of Sweden, 295.
Christnalas, 88.
Chronology, 116.
Cicero, cited, 85, 108, 195.
Circulation, 123, 207, 222, 305, 318, 337, 361, 381.
Civil Law (see Codex).
Civilization, Affected by Money, 107.
Claudius I., Sovereign-Pontiff, 112.
Clearing-house (see Permutation of Merchandise).
Clippers of Coins, 188, 201-2, 205-8, 212, 215, 229, 231, 235, 313, 344.

INDEX

Cloth Money (see Vadmal).
Clothaire, 108.
Clovis, 104, 108.
Cnut (see Canute).
Codes, Barbarian, 310, 311, 333-5.
Codex Justinianus, 97 n, 252, 384.
Codex Theodosianus, 94, 96, 108, 154, 260, 342, 384.
Coelwlf I., King of Mercia, 170.
Coelwlf II., King of Mercia, 170.
Coenwlf, King of Mercia, 170.
Coinage, a Mark of Sovereignty, 147, 179, 248, 249, 319, 339.
Coinage of Gold, a Pontifical Right, 247, 249, 320.
Coinage Systems (see Monetary).
Coins, 89, 119, 179, 317, 339; Counterfeit (see Forgeries); Finds of, 309; Light (see Light Coins); Proclamatory, 90; Restoration of, 90; Sacred, 90, 319; Statistics of, 372 n; Used as Weights, 153, 214.
Combustion, 191, 196.
Commerce, 317, 322, 338, 349, 363, 383.
"Commodity Moneys," 291.
Commons, House of, 246.
Companies (see Corporations).
Comstock Lode (see Nevada).
Conflict Ratio (see Ratio), 335-6.
Constans II., Sovereign-Pontiff, 134.
Constantine I., Sovereign-Pontiff, 250.
Constantinople, fall of, A. D., 1204-82, 264, 271, 334, 342-3.
"Continental" Notes of the British American Colonies, 217, 240.
Contraction and Expansion, 372, 389.
Control of Money (see Prerogative, Regalian, &c.), 331, 379, 389, 392.
Convention Coins, 236, 240.
Conway Castle, 216.
Copenhagen, 255.
Copper, Monetary Systems, Coins, Mines, Mining, &c., 21, 22, 33, 35, 45, 49, 55, 83, 118, 190, 217, 221, 288-89, 292, 295, 328, 342, 388.

Copper-plate Money, 294, 296.
Corn Rents, 196, 370 n.
Cornwall, 205-6, 209, 211-12, 216.
Corporations, 264.
Corruptions of Coins (see Tampering); of ancient texts (see Mutilations).
Cortez, Hernando, 133, 262.
Cost of the Precious Metals (q. v.), 240, 207, 401.
Counterfeit (see Forgeries), 229, 261, 296.
Crimen Majestatis, 192.
Crockards, 216, 220, 228.
Crown (see Royal).
Crusades, 252.
Currencies, 327.
Currency Contraction, 389.

Daler (see Dollar).
Danegeld, 181, 185.
Danes of Denmark, 171; of England, 171, 174.
Dantzic, 266.
Dealbandum (see Albata).
Debased Coins, 199, 227, 228, 252, 318, 330, 343, 345.
Degraded Coins, 199, 227, 228, 235, 252, 330, 343.
Dei Gratia, 241.
"Demonetization" of Gold, 371; of Silver, 306.
Denmark, 301.
Demonetization of Money, 99.
De Vienne cited, n, 57, 111, 153, 214, 333.
Deventer, City, 266, 318.
Diffusion of Wealth Effected by Money, 107.
Dinar, 56, 135, 156, 188, 312.
Dinara, 115.
Dirhem, 115, 135, 312, 388.
Dobla, 162, 238, 342.
Doit, 258.
Dollar, 381-3, 357-58.
Domesday Book, 123 n, 129, 160, 180, 188, 197.
Doom-Rings, n, 121.
Doomsday (see Domesday).
Druids, 109.
Ducat, 183, 282, 313-14, 318, 357.
Ducaton, 282, 314-15, 318, 328, 357.
Dutch, East India Companies, 387.

Eadgar, King of England, 267.
East India Companies (see British and Dutch), 396.
Easterling, Iesterling (q. v.), 207.
Eastern Empire (see Roman Empire).
Ecclesiastical Forgers and Adulterers of Coin, 192, 200, 206, 210, 215, 233.
Ecclesiastical Laws, 192.
Ecclesiastical Mints and Coins, 193, 199, 200, 204-5, 210, 226, 247, 251.
Edgar, King of Wessex, 181.
Edgitha, Mother of Edward the Confessor, 184.
Edmund I., King of Wessex, 180.
Edward Confessor, King of Wessex, 149 n, 158, 184, 249.
Edward I., King of England, 156, 182, 203, 215, 219-20, 223, 234, 250.
Edward II., King of England, 219-20, 321.
Edward III., King of England, 134, 198, 216, 221, 234, 235, 253, 313, 329, 342.
Edward VI., King of England, 321 n, 328.
Edward-Guthrum Treaty, 176 n.
Egbert, King of Wessex, 158, 169.
Egbert (son of Offa), 170.
Egypt, 116, 127, 148.
Eissel, River (see Iessel).
Eistland, Province (see Iestia).
Elagabalus, Sov.-Pont., 69, 260.
Electrum Coins, 121.
Elizabeth, Queen of England, 329, 395.
Emirs, Coins of the, 126, 146.
Emperor-Worship, 109.
Empires, Eastern and Western, 246.
Endorsement, 196.
Engels, 309.
England (see Britain), 71, 149, 313-14, 328; ratio in (see England's Independence (q. v.). Ratio), 157, 328.
Equities of Money, 107, 320.
Eric I., Pagan King of Denmark, 175.

Eric II., Pagan King of Denmark, 175.
Eric XIV., King of Sweden, 311-12, 283-4.
Esthonia (see Iestia), 255, 104.
Ethelbert I., King of Kent, 111.
Ethelbert II., King of Kent, 104, 105, 151, 158, 167.
Ethelbert, King of East Anglia, 158, 167.
Ethelred II., King of Wessex, &c., 158.
Ethelwulf, King of Wessex, 171.
Etruscans, 109.
Exchequer, 190, 193, 196, 220-21.
Exchequer Bills, 292.
Exports of Coin and Bullion, 85, 101, 219, 228, 230, 233, 235-36, 240, 250, 329.

Fabulous History (q. v.), 20.
Fairs, 182, 194, 252, 258-9, 261, 266.
Family Coins, myth of, 38.
Fatimites, 127, 144.
Fayoum, 130.
Ferdinand II., Emperor of Germany, 320.
Feria (see Fairs), 258.
Feudal System, 103, 105, 166.
Fiduciary Money, 100, 279.
Finds of Coin (see Treasure Trove)
Fisc, 79.
Fish Money, 115, 254, 264.
Flemings, 240.
Florins, 240.
Follis, or Purse of Coins, 53.
Foreign Coins, 107, 210, 219, 231, 250, 255.
Forgeries (see Counterfeits), 73, 84, 114, 119, 141, 192, 218, 231, 261, 343, 347.
Frakki (see France).
Frakkland (see France), 258.
Franco Prussian War, 378.
France, 107, 110, 111, 117, 140, 150, 160, 200, 268, 412.
Fratres Ambarvales, 264.
Frederick II., Emperor of Germany, 184, 224.
"Free" Coinage (see Private Coinage), 245, 320, 342.
Free Trade, 194.

INDEX

437

Frisia, n., 111.

Gardariki, 261.
Gaul, 110.
German Empire, 307, 319, 343, 384, 413.
German Monetary System, 380, 413.
Germany, 22, 262, 290, 308, 341, 342, 355, 370, 372.
Getae (see Goths).
Gibraltar, 132.
Goa, 388, 395.
Godwin, Earl of Kent, 184.
Goertz's Copper Dollars, 295.
Gold Coin, 62, 68, 75, 78, 122, 190, 211, 230, 238, 287, 302, 320, 328, 337, 350, 357, 371; Earliest in Europe, 320, 325, 342.
Gold, Domestic and Foreign, 231.
Gold Mining, 70, 72, 306.
Gold, not Coined by Vassals, 34, 75, 81, 134, 148, 190, 196-97, 224, 239, 309-10, 325.
Gold Plate, 219.
Gold Standard, 376.
Golden Bull, 342.
Goldsmiths, 216, 219, 390.
Gotfried, King of Denmark, 171, 269.
Goths, 108, 133, 151, 254, 263, 309.
Goths, Moneys of, 105, 113, 124, 263.
Governments and Moneys, 107.
Great Fairs (q. v.).
Greek Empire (see Roman Empire).
Greenbacks, 280.
Gresham, Sir Thomas, 328, 335.
Groats, 221.
Grouch, or Turkish Dollar, 315.
Guerard cited, 57, 111, 311.
Guilds (see Corporations), 50.
Gulden, 312, 315, 348.
Gunnar, King of Burgundy, 262.
Gunnvaldsborg, 164, 257.
Gustavus Adolphus, 291-92.
Gustavus Vasa, 275, 277, 286, 300.
Guthrum, 70, 174, 175.

Hachem I., 238, 268.
Hachem II., 238, 270.
Haco, King of Norway, 181.

Hadrian, Pope, 158, 169.
Hadrian, Sovereign-Pontiff, 248.
Hakon, Jarl, 269, 272.
Hale, Sir Matthew, cited, 38, 196, 208, 220, 237.
Halfdane, the Black, 175.
Hall, Marked Plate, 219.
Halting, Standard (Etalon Boiteux), 401.
Hamburg, City, 196.
Hanseatic League, 160, 195, 261, 264, 270, 275, 308, 334.
Hapsburg Coinagers, 312, 334.
Harmonies of Money, 107, 141.
Harold, King of Denmark, 171, 174, 269.
Harold, Harfager, 269.
Harold Hardrade, 271-72, 273.
Harold II., King of England, 182, 184.
Haroun-al-Raschid, 153, 268.
Harris, Joseph (1757), cited, 214.
Hastings, the Viking, 175.
Haulds, or Hauldermen, a Gothic caste, 117.
Heen Tsung, Emperor of China, 182, 267.
Hegemony of the Ratio, 351.
Heligoland, 258.
Henry II., England, 190, 193, 199.
Henry III., England, 92, 98, 188, 190, 195, 198, 210, 212, 215, 224, 238, 248, 342, 344.
Henry VIII., England, 322.
Heptarchy, systems of the, 107, 121, 165.
Heraclius, Sov.-Pont., 130, 141.
Herring Money (see Sil).
Hierarchies, 127, 146, 147.
History, 21, 101, 105.
Hoards of Money, 207, 216, 302, 384.
Hokeday, 184.
Holland (see Netherlands).
Honorius (see Arcadius).
Hucsos, or Hyksos, Kings of Egypt, 116.
Hun, Oriental Gold Coin, 388, 396.

Iaku, Gold Coin, 213.
Iceland, 114.
Ideal Moneys, pref., 101.

Idolatrous Coins (see Christian), 388.
Ies, 18, 123, 308, 314.
Ieschen, 309.
Ies-sel, River, 162, 266, 274, 318.
Iesterling (see Sterling).
Iestia, Province, 139, 159, 258, 261, 263, 309.
Image Worship, 109.
"Imperium" Theory of Coinage, 23, 147.
Ina, King of Wessex, 111, 169.
Indemnity, Franco-Prussian, 378, 384.
Indentures of the Mint, q. v.
Independence of England, 197, 199, 210, 217, 223-24, 228, 235, 241, 243, 245, 248, 251.
India, 136, 195, 388, 425.
Indians, American, 383.
Indulgences, sale of, 278.
Ingot Money, 40, 292, 295.
Institutes of Justinian (see Codex).
Interest Bearing Paper Money, 107.
International Conventions, 344.
International Moneys, 377, 412, 429.
Internments, Monastic, 170, 173.
Interregnum, the Great, 245.
Ireland, 158, 200, 208.
Iron Coins, 119, 347.
Isabella, Wife of Edward II., 232.
Italiote Coins, 32.
Italy, 423.
Ivan Vidfami, 263.

Jaku of Gold (see Iaku).
Japan, Japanese, 89, 122, 289.
Jehovah, Name of, on Coins, 285, 286.
Jews, 85, 92, 97, 128, 207-8, 212, 216, 218, 229, 271, 321.
John, King of England, 182, 193, 207-8.
John II., King of France, 154, 182.
John II., King of Denmark, Sweden, and Norway, 276.
John of Nikios cited, 130.
Jornandes cited, 96, n.
Judith, Daughter of Charles the Bald, 172, 175.

Julin, City, 254, 261-62, 309, 324.
Julius Caesar (see Caesar).
Justinian Code (see Codex).
Justinian I., Sovereign-Pontiff, 92, 97, 260.
Justinian II., Sovereign-Pontiff, 92, 134.

Kahinah, Queen of the Berbers, 132.
Kent, Kingdom, 152.
Khuen, Khuen-Aten, 116.
Klippings, 278-79, 288.
Knife-Money, 357.
Koran, 144, 146, 192 n, 387.
Kremnitz, 73.
Kroner (Sweden), 306.

Land Measured by £. s. d., 98, 214.
Lands Granted to the Church, 171.
Latin Monetary Union, 372, 383.
Law, the Basis of Money, 36.
Leather Money, 18, 181-2, 200, 208, 215, 221, 263, 267, 272, 274.
Legal Tender, 107, 205.
Liber Pater (see Bacchus), 42.
£. s. d. System, 29, 49, 94, 95 n, 98, 104 n, 105-6, 115, 149, 178, 180, 181, 213, 222.
Libra of Money (see Livre).
Libra of Weight (see Livre).
Light Coins, 217, 233, 235, 415.
Limitation, the Essence of Money, Preface, 292, 296.
Livius Drusus, 83.
Livre of Money and Accounts, 39, 49, 54, 60, 98, 256, 259, 316, 342.
Livre of Weight, 50, 51, 59, 97.
Livy, cited, 57, 97.
Lombards, 216.
London, 170, 175, 238, 239.
Louis IX., 182, 248-49.
Louis, le Debonnaire, 170-71, 261, 334, 392.
Lowndes cited, 159 n, 191, 217, 221, 227.
Ludica, King of Mercia, 170.

MacLeod, H. D., cited, 60 n, 328.
Magna Charta, 209-10, 224.
Mahomet, 105, 128.

INDEX 439

Mallgard, 255.
Mancus, 72, 124, 150, 155, 162, 174 n, 211.
Mania, 128.
Manillas, 117.
Maravedi, 115, 123, 188, 205, 216, 236-37, 316, 342.
Marc Antony, 29.
Marco Polo, 395.
Mark, Banco, 324, 373.
Mark, German Imperial, 379.
Mark, Money, 121, 123, 153, 162, 177 n, 180, 189, 204 n, 259-60, 274, 276, 281, 284.
Mark, Weight, 121, 153, 260-61, 281, 284, 302, 334.
Markets, 154, 194, 258.
Martel (see Charles Martel).
Massachusetts Mint, 325.
Massacre of St. Bride's, 181.
Massacre of Stockholm, 277.
Massacre of Jews (q. v.), 212, 212 n, 271.
Matthew Paris cited, 211, 227, 248.
Maundy Money, 49.
Measure of Value, pref., 215, 388, 390.
Menapia, 308, 333.
Mercantile System (see Exports, &c.), 251, 338.
Mercia, a Kingdom of Britain, 152, 170.
Merk (see Fairs), 258 n.
Merovingians, 70, 109-10, 157.
Metallic Limitation to Money, 103.
Metallurgy, 158.
Metals, 77, 102, 324, 389; for Money, 324.
Michieli, Doge of Venice, 182.
Mexico, 262.
Mikliardi, 258.
Miliaresion, 150.
Mine Slavery (see Slavery), 102.
Mines, Mining, 91, 100, 102, 108, 222, 248, 292, 368.
Mines, Royal, 100, 247.
Mint Act of 1666, 214, 388.
Mint Indentures, Acts and Codes (see Act of 1666), 108, 220, 223, 232, 243, 336-37, 347, 352, 378, 389, 403-29.
Mints, 91, 100, 162, 203, 208, 216, 231, 235, 242, 406.

Minuta, 123.
Mir, or Commune of the Russians, 152, 258.
Mithcal, 141, 237.
Moawijah, Caliph, 134.
Monasteries (see Internments), 208.
Monetary Commission and Conventions, 236, 242, 251, 305, 347, 351-52, 359-60, 368, 377.
Monetary History, Divisions of, 386.
Monetary Policy, 383.
Monetary Systems, 21, 28, 58, 143, 162, 174, 191, 199, 200, 203, 212, 253, 267, 326, 331, 336, 341, 343, 380.
Money a National Institution, 224, 247, 378, 387; Principles and Nature of, pref., 24, 36, 99, 103 n, 107, 119, 121-22, 253, 255, 291, 294, 343, 370, 378, 384, 389; Right to Create, 122, 253, 319, 386.
Moneyers, or Minters, 91, 100, 156, 158, 193, 201, 203, 272.
Moneys, Alterations of, 191, 252, 318.
Monograms, Sacred, on Coins, 53.
Mons, the Gothic Hero, 279.
Moors, 399.
Moslems, 115, 125, 188, 207, 312.
Mourdanish, 237.
Mousa-ben-Nosier, 132, 159.
Municipal Money, 107.
Murcia, 152 n.
Mutilation of Ancient Texts, 117, 117 n.
Mythology, 101.

Napoleon, 355, 384.
National Attributes or Marks, 224, 247, 387.
National Money, 225, 247, 378, 388.
Nautae Parisiaci, 264.
Navicularii, 264.
Navigation, 308.
Nero, Sov.- Pont., 97.
Netherlands, 255, 307, 423.
Nevahend, Battle of, 131.
Nevada Silver Scare, 337, 339, 378.
New Amsterdam, 325.

440 INDEX

New York, 325.
Nimeguen, 266.
Noble, or Half Mark, 198, 241, 314, 322, 334.
Nomisma, vii., 384.
Normans, 123.
Norsemen (see Goths).
Northumbria, 152, 160, 170, 175, 200.
Norway, Norwegians, 272, 300.
Novgorod, Province, 152, 159, 263, 269, 271; City, 152, 159, 182, 195; Veleki, 258, 262.
Numerical Character of Money, pref., 293, 375.
Numero, ad, 196.
Numismatics, 236, 260, 273.
Nummulary Grammar, 225.
Nummulary Systems, pref., 22.
Nummus, 20.

Ober-Iessel, 274 n, 307.
Obole, 152, 213, 239.
Octavius Augustus (see Augustus).
Odericus Vitalis, 160.
Odin, 263 n, 272.
Offa, King of Mercia, 105, 151 n, 152, 158, 169, 180, 190, 263.
Olaf I., Trygvaeson, King of Norway, 182, 258, 269, 272, 273.
Olaf II., King of Norway, 164, 257.
Ommiades, or Omeiads, 126, 270.
Ora, Coin, 111, 118-19, 124, 162, 176 n, 178 n, 259.
Ora, Weight, 121, 188.
Oriental Trade and Ratio, 86, 91, 102, 269, 317.
Osbrecht (see Osbright).
Osbright, King of Northumbria, 155, 160.
Overvalued Silver Pennies, 167, 181, 187-88, 212, 220-21, 236.

Pagan and Christian Moneys, 310, 388.
Pagan Effigies on Coins, 296.
Pagodas, 388, 395.
Papal Indulgences (q. v.).
Paper Moneys (see Leather, Pasteboard and Banks), 107, 292, 298-99, 304-5, 321, 327, 353, 361-62, 372, 375, 397.

Parliament, 246.
Pasteboard Dollars, 280, 281, 327.
Paulus cited, 21, 253, 384.
Pax Sterlings, 187.
Payment in Kind, 197.
Pegge, Dr. Samuel, cited, 212.
Pennies (see Sterlings), 150, 166, 180, 224, 232.
Pensum, ad, 191, 106.
Pepin, le Bref., 62, 109, 150, 157, 312, 333.
Permutation of Merchandise, 194, 268,
Persia, 128, 135.
Peso, 428.
Peter's Pense (see Rome-Scat), 169, 200, 253, 272.
Philip I., King of France, 182.
Philip IV., le Bel., King of France, 219, 226, 247, 251.
Philip II., the Bigot, King of Spain, 92, 321, 335.
Phocas, Sovereign-Pontiff, 109.
"Pinetree" Shillings, 217, 245, 325.
Pix, Trial of the, 84, 203, 217, 247, 251.
Plack, Scotch Coin, 258 n.
Plantagenets, 198-99, 218, 223, 250.
Plate and Plated Coins, 217, 219.
Plato cited, 21, 384.
Pliny cited, 17, 30, 31, 36, 82, 86, 97, 117 n, 250.
Pollards, 216, 219, 228.
Poltowa, Battle, 295.
Pontificate, 125, 253, 344, 350.
Population, 207.
Porcelain Coins, 267.
Portcullis Coins, 395.
Portugal, 416.
Pound, or Pondo, 29, 30, 59, 95, 353.
Pound of Account (see £. s. d.).
Pounds, Shillings and Pence (see £. s. d.).
Precious Metals, Production and Consumption, 324, 337, 378, 382; Cost of production, 291, 346, 383, 401; Movements, 288, 326, 402; Stock on Hand, 207, 294, 345, 363, 369, 413.
Prerogatives of Money, 23, 24, 27, 35, 37, 44, 46, 48, 60, 67, 73,

93, 101, 146, 166, 180, 224, 231, 232, 252, 319, 330, 337, 343, 387.
Private Coinage, 37, 64, 147, 231, 248, 288, 289, 294, 306, 322, 325-28, 336-37, 346-47 n, 351, 371, 376, 377, 379-80, 386-87-88-89-91-92, 400; Its Origin, 387, 395.
Proconsuls, Roman, 100, 249.
Provincial Moneys, 107.
Prussia, 350, 353.
Puritans, 326.

Quantitative Theory, pref., 294.
Queipo cited, 143, 153.
Quindecemvirs, 140, 224.
Quinto, 146.

Ragnar Lodbrok, 171.
Ramtenkis (Rama-tankas), 88.
Ratio (Gold to Silver): Chilian, 429; Chinese, 287 n, 393; Christian, 310, 311; Dutch, 310-11-12, 317, 321-22, 329, 332, 337; Egyptian, 395; English, 158, 169, 184, 193, 238, 241, 314, 328, 397; Etruscan, 109; Florentine, 60; Frankish, 109, 312, 317; French, 168, 193, 225, 316, 393, 397; Germany, 317, 343, 348, 350, 355, 365, 367, 381, 397; Gothic, 79, 105, 121-22, 140, 165, 259, 274, 277, 283, 288, 313-14, 398; Greek, 259; Indian, 79, 89, 104, 158, 388, 394; Italian, 357; Japanese, 122, 399; Moslem, 79, 105, 109, 129, 139, 140-41, 156-57, 165, 170, 188, 236, 266, 309-10, 394-95-98; Oriental, 87, 168, 259, 397, 398; Pagan, 310; Persian, 259, 393; Portuguese, 388, 398-99, Prussian, 351, 367-68; Roman, 37, 38, 59, 63, 79, 87, 91, 96, 105, 109, 123, 139, 140, 157, 158, 166, 172, 178, 180, 189, 194, 223, 238-39, 256, 259, 275, 309, 311, 319,332, 343, 393, 397, 400; Sacred, 311; Spanish, 168, 318, 351, 355, 397-98; Special, 306; Hegemony, of the, 351, 355; Conflict, 335-36, 351, 367-68; International Mint, 351; Exceptional, 366.
Rations Used as Money, 163.
Rayed Effigies on Coins, 50.

Raymond Lully, 240.
Redeemable Coins, 107.
Redemption Notes, 405, 429.
Regalian Rights (see Prerogative, etc.), 236, 242, 247, 251, 330.
Regenfroy, King of Denmark, 171.
Regulation of Money (see Control), 240.
Religion Indicated by Moneys, 104, 272.
Rett, or Indemnity, 179.
French, 319.
Revolutions: Roman Moneyers, 50; Ghent, 317; Netherlands, 316, 319, 321, 329, 349; French, 280; England, 326; British Colonies in America, 245.
Riksbank of Sweden (see Bank of Stockholm).
Riksbank of Sweden, Daler, New, 303.
Riksbank of Sweden, Daler, Old, 393.
Riksbank of Sweden, Silver Notes, 305.
Riksdaler, 300, 303.
Riksdaler, Banco, 300.
Riksdaler, Effective, 301.
Riksdaler, Specie, 301.
Riksgald Daler, 300.
Riksmynt Daler, 300.
Ring Money (see Baugs).
Rise of Prices (see Tulip), 327, 369.
"Robbers' Dens," 194.
Roderic, King of Spain, 105.
Roger II., King of Sicily, 105.
Rolla, 175.
Roman British Towns, 110, 111.
Roman Coins in England, 189.
Roman Empire, 319.
Roman Government Restored, 104, 110, 111.
Roman Monetary Systems, 101, 107, 123, 148.
Roman Pontificate (see Pontificate), 125, 253, 344, 350.
Roman Provinces, 100, 107, 110.
Roman Sacred Constitution, 125, 189, 212.

INDEX

Rome-Scat (see Peter's Pence), 116, 153, 169 n, 272 n.
Rothschilds, The, 391 n, 407.
Rounding (see Clippers).
Royal Mines (see Mines).
Royal Prerogative (see Prerogative).
Royal Proprietors of Banks of Issue, 303, 339.
Rundstycks, 280, 289.
Runes, 114, 121-22, 152, 267, 275, 282.
Rupee, 425.
Rurik, 182, 266, 267, 272.

Saal, or Iessel (q. v.).
Sacae, 254.
Sacred Character of Gold, 25, 35, 66, 74, 79, 80, 89, 104, 105, 118, 127, 148, 189, 212, 320, 324, 386.
Sacred College (see Quindecemvirs).
Sagas, 113-14, 117, 257, 258, 275, 282.
Saiga, 162, 259, 310-11.
Salic, 162.
Saracens (see Moslems).
Sassanian Coins, 142.
Saxons, Saxony, 105, 254, 263, 275, 307, 308.
Scad (see Scat), 115.
Scalam, ad, 190, 196.
Scandinavia, 107, 140, 151, 254, 277.
Scat, 104, 107, 115, 121, 150, 158, 161, 162.
Score, 95 n.
Scot (see Scat), 115.
Scotland, 200, 258.
Scrupulum, 27.
Scyphates, 88, 189.
Scythia, 113, 116.
Seigniorage, 20, 68, 100, 107, 35, 242, 274, 289, 302, 306, 314, 324, 328.
Sesterce, 30, 102.
Shad (see Scat), 161.
Shekel (see Sicca).
Shilling, Gold, 57, 96, 104-5, 111, 123, 156, 168, 199, 209, 224, 257, 260, 310, 312.
Shilling of Account (see £. s. d.), 168, 183, 209.

Shilling, Silver, 104 n, 168, 257.
Sicca, Sical, Shekel, 162, 267, 298, 357.
Sicilian Coins, 104 n.
Sicilicus, Scilling, Shilling (q. v.), 104, 155, 357.
Sil, Sild, 115, 264.
Siliqua, 150, 237.
Silver Plate (q. v.), 71, 219.
Silver Coinage Relegated to Vassal Kings, 197, 204, 319.
Silver, Domestic and Foreign, 231.
Silver Money, 71, 76, 88, 224, 329.
Slavery, Mining, 275.
Smith, Adam, cited, 331.
Social Aspects of Money, 122 n.
Soetbeer, 337 n, 347, 362, 382.
Solidus (see Besant), 257.
Sols Banco, 324.
Sophisms of Money, 291, 319 n, 369, 370 n.
Spain, 129, 140, 200, 350-51.
Spanish America, 321, 326, 347, 350, 383.
Spanish-American Silver Scare, 347.
Spanish-Arabian Empire, 200, 309.
Special Contract Law of Money, 302.
Spoil, 90, 121, 136, 146 200, 207, 289, 291, 335.
St. Albans, 210, 212, 216.
St. Louis Convention, 392.
Stability of Money, 320, 348 n.
Standard, 37, 212, 214, 219, 247, 252, 260, 267, 274, 283, 323, 339, 369, 371, 374.
Staples or Emporia, 195, 269, 270.
Star Chamber, 388, 396.
State Control of Money, 279.
Stephen, King of England, 193, 200.
Sterling, 149, 159, 160, 295.
Sterlings, or Pennies, 149, 151, 159, 187, 192, 208-9, 215, 221, 224, 229, 232, 235, 255, 295, 309.
Stiver, 316.
Storch, Count Henri, 383.
Styca, 121, 162.
Sun-Worship, 308-9, 356.

INDEX 443

Suspension of Coin Payments, 402.
Svastica, 121, 122.
Sveyne, Canutson, King of Norway, 273.
Sveyne, King of Mercia and Northumbria, 258.
Sweated Coins, 345.
Sweden, 276, 417.

Tael (see Talent), 425.
Talent (see Dollar), 95, 276, 282, 285, 315-16, 342, 349, 357-58, 373, 428.
Tampering with Money (see Adulterations, Debasements, Degradations, and Forgeries), 198-99, 211, 321, 344-45.
Tanka, Silver Coin, 144.
Tarik, 132.
Tavannes, 347 n.
Taxes, 103, 142, 297, 304, 317, 319, 354.
Tel-el-Amarna, 116.
Ten Divisions of the Solar Circle, 94.
Ten Silver for One Gold, 95.
Teutonic Monk-Knights, 366.
Thaler (see Dollar), 350, 379.
Theodebert, 109, 109 n.
Theodosian Code, (q. v.).
Thirty Years' War, 290, 349.
Three Necessities, The, 172.
Thrimsa, 162, 178, 183 n.
Tiberius, Sov.-Pont., 308.
Tin and Tin Coins, 121, 200, 204-6, 208-9, 213 n, 216, 221, 230.
Tithes, 142.
Titles of Nobility Sold, 427.
Toledo, 133.
Topes, 86 n.
Tournois, or Turneys, 234.
Tower of London (see Mints), 208-217.
Trade Corporations (q. v.), 346.
Transmutation of Metals, 240.
Transport-Notes, 292, 298.
Treasure-Trove, 185 n, 202, 247-48.
Treasury (see Exchequer).
Treaties (see Monetary Conventions).
Trial of the Pix (q. v.).
Tributes, 133, 134, 260, 319, 332.
Triente, 159, 209, 310.

Tulip-Mania, 325.
Turkey, 110, 113, 424.
Twelve a Sacred Number, 94.
Twelve Divisions of the Solar Circle, 94.
Twelve Silver for One Gold, 91.
Tyke or Turk Dialect, 149.

Uncovered Notes, 363.
Uniform Moneys, 320, 347, 379, 412.
Unit Coins, 376.
Unit of Circulation, 300.
Unit of Money, 99, 375.
Unit of Value, 301.
United States, 359, 383, 404-411, 417-22.
Upsala, 162 n, 263, 272-3.
Ural Gold Scare, 337.
Usurers and Usury, 234.

Vadmal, 115-16, 264.
Valens, Sov.-Pont., 96.
Value, pref., 100, 200, 369, 384.
Vandals, 131, 266.
Varangians, 269.
Varaya, 388.
Veneti (see Vinet), 189, 195, 265, 308.
Vienne, De (see De Vienne).
Vinet, 159, 254, 258, 261-62.
Vishnu, 388.
Von Humboldt, 369, 384.

Waldemar I., Denmark, 224 n, 271.
Wallenstein, 290.
War-Chests, 363, 415.
Watchtowers, City of, 149.
Weight, Coins Used for, 213.
Weights, Systems of, 355.
Werdenhagen cited, 266.
Wessex, Kingdom, 171.
Wiglaf, King of Mercia, 170.
William I., King of England, 123, 154, 184, 190.
William II., King of England, 158, 192.
William the Bad, King of Sicily, 182.
Williamsby, 164, 257.
Winet (see Vinet).
Wismar, 298.
Wissel Bank of Amsterdam, 292, 322, 335.

Woote, Emperor of China, 182.
Worship of Augustus, 41, 131.

Yarranton, Andrew, cited, 326.
Yes-sel, or Yssel (see Ies-sel).

York, 170, 175.

Zecchin, 183.
Zikka (see Sicca), 162, 183 n.
Zodiac, 95 n.

THE END.

www.ingramcontent.com/pod-product-compliance
Lightning Source LLC
Chambersburg PA
CBHW032131010526
44111CB00034B/578